Documents and Images for the Study of Paul

Documents and Images for the Study of Paul

NEIL ELLIOTT

and

MARK REASONER

Editors

Fortress Press
Minneapolis

Documents and Images for the Study of Paul

Copyright © 2011 Fortress Press. All rights reserved. Except for brief quotations in criti-cal articles or reviews, no part of this book may be reproduced in any manner without prior written permission from the publisher. Visit http://www.augsburgfortress.org/copyrights/contact.asp or write to Permissions, Augsburg Fortress, Box 1209, Minneapolis, MN 55440.

Cover design: Laurie Ingram
Cover image: Saint Paul, d. 65, Ivory diptych of life with scenes of his preaching, Italian c. 400 A.D. The Art Archive/Bargollo Museum Florence/Alfredo Dagli Orti (www.picture-desk.com)
Book design: PerfecType, Nashville, TN

Library of Congress Cataloging-in-Publication Data
Documents and images for the study of Paul / Neil Elliott and Mark Reasoner, editors.
    p. cm.
Includes bibliographical references and index.
ISBN 978-0-8006-6375-9 (alk. paper)
1. Bible. N.T. Epistles of Paul—Extra-canonical parallels. 2. Bible. N.T. Epistles of Paul—Criticism, interpretation, etc. 3. Paul, the Apostle, Saint. 4. Rome—Religion. 5. Philosophy, Ancient. I. Elliott, Neil, 1956– II. Reasoner, Mark.
BS2650.52.D63 2010
227'.095—dc22

                        2010027464

Manufactured in the U.S.A.

15 14   13   12   11   1   2   3   4   5   6   7   8   9   10

CONTENTS

PREFACE

This book began with Neil Elliott's proposal to create a resource illuminating the first-century context of the New Testament writings, focused on Paul and his world in much the way David R. Cartlidge and David L. Dungan focused on the Gospels in their volume *Documents for the Study of the Gospels* (revised and enlarged edition; Minneapolis: Fortress Press, 1994). Neil proposed a partnership to Mark Reasoner, who benefited from a sabbatical from Bethel University to write a first draft of the whole manuscript, including his own fresh translations of many of the materials included here. Neil then revised, supplemented, and reorganized the materials in accordance with an agreed outline.

We wish to thank Bethel University for the opportunity accorded by Mark's sabbatical. Thanks are due as well to Fr. Silvio Sassi, Superior General of the Società di San Paolo, for the invitation to Neil to participate in the International Seminar on St. Paul in Ariccia in 2009 and to Br. Walter Rodriguez for his generous hospitality and advice, especially regarding the museums where a number of the photographs in this book were taken.

Warm thanks, also, to Fortress Press Editor-in-Chief Michael West for the confidence he showed in this project from the start and to Marissa Wold, Josh Messner, Esther Diley, Maurya Horgan, Kristin Goble, and Jeff Reimer for their diligent and talented efforts to bring the book into print. In addition to acknowledgments elsewhere in the book, special thanks also to Davina C. Lopez and Laura Nasrallah for advice concerning images.

Finally, our deep gratitude to Mary Ellen and Wendy for their patience and good humor through the process of bringing this book to publication.

A word about style and translation: we have modernized some older translations to avoid "thee" and "thou" language but have often left the masculine "man" or "men," which arguably reflects the male-focused character of one or another ancient text. We use "god" when the term is used generically and "God" when an author speaks of or to his or her own deity.

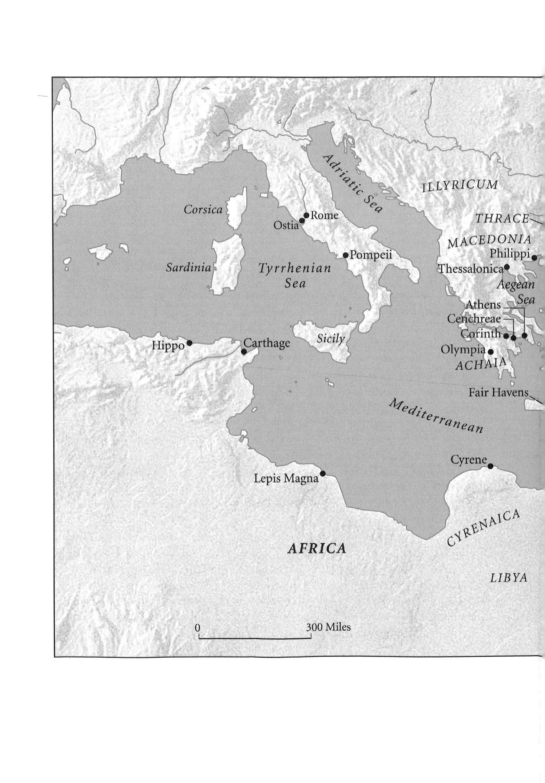

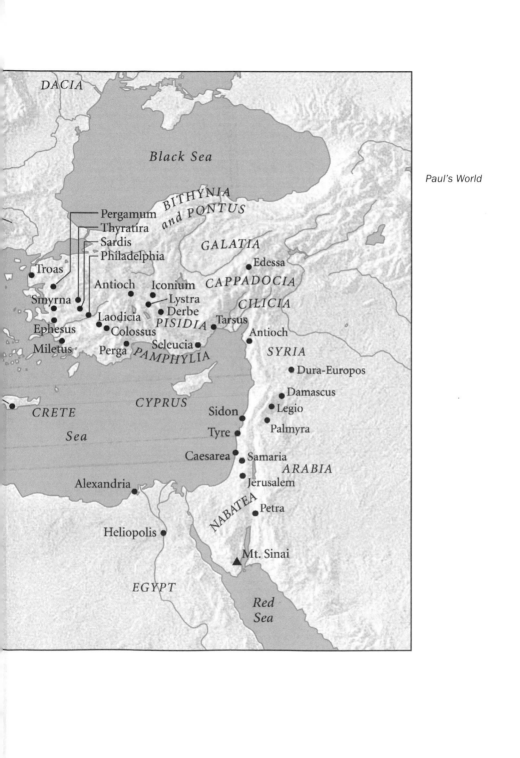

Paul's World

TIMELINE

We include here only a selection of significant dates that may help orient readers to the materials included in this book. The chronology of events in Paul's life is a subject of considerable discussion among scholars: See the brief review and bibliography by L. C. A. Alexander, "Chronology of Paul," Dictionary of Paul and His Letters, 115–23.

63 B.C.E.	Pompey invades Judea, asserts Roman control; *Psalms of Solomon* is probably written soon thereafter. Returning to Rome, Pompey allies himself with Cicero (106–43) and Julius Caesar (100–44).
44	Caesar assassinated; his grandnephew and adopted son Octavian (63 B.C.E.–14 C.E.) vows to avenge him.
31–27	After defeating the armies of Mark Antony and Cleopatra and compelling their suicides, Octavian returns to Rome and is hailed as Augustus by the Senate; he rules with tribunician power until 14 C.E.
10 B.C.E.—10 C.E.	Paul is born some time in this period.
4 B.C.E.	Herod the Great, who had deftly negotiated alliances with Mark Antony and then Augustus, dies; his son Antipas rules Galilee, his son Archelaus rules Judea and Samaria.
6 C.E.	Archelaus proves so unpopular that Augustus deposes him and imposes military rule in Judea.
14	At Augustus's death, his stepson Tiberius comes to power.
30	Jesus is crucified.
31	At Tiberius's death, Gaius (Caligula), whom Tiberius had made his son in his will, comes to power.
34/35	After some time as a persecutor of the *ekklēsiai* in Judea, Paul receives a "revelation" of the risen Christ. He goes away to Arabia then returns to Damascus three years later.
37/38	Paul comes to Jerusalem to meet Peter and other apostles, then travels to Syria and Cilicia. He proclaims the gospel there over the next fourteen years.
38–41	Some Jews in Alexandria sue for citizens' rights; Greek citizens respond with violence in "history's first pogrom." Philo (c. 30 B.C.E.–45 C.E.) leads an embassy of protest to Rome; they hear Gaius's plan to install a statue of himself in the temple.
41	Gaius is assassinated by his own officers; the Praetorian Guard puts Tiberius's nephew Claudius in power. He immediately issues a decree suppressing riots in Alexandria. *Fourth Maccabees* may be written shortly thereafter.

49	Claudius orders the expulsion of some Jews from Rome.
51/52	Paul visits Jerusalem again for a conference with the other apostles; the "Antioch incident" may have happened close in time. Paul then travels to Galatia and Macedonia, then is arraigned before Gallio. He subsequently works in Ephesus, organizing the collection for Jerusalem.
54	Claudius dies, probably poisoned. His adopted son Nero requests that the Senate confer divine honors upon Claudius.
55 or 56	Paul writes Romans in anticipation of his trip to Jerusalem with the collection.
56/57?	That trip ends in disaster as Paul is confronted by a mob in the temple precincts (according to Acts); he is subsequently hauled before a series of Roman magistrates, being imprisoned for two years in Judea according to Acts.
59-62	According to Acts, Paul is tried by Festus; appeals to Rome; spends two years awaiting trial in Rome (according to Acts).
64–68?	According to 1 Clement 6:1, Paul and Peter are put to death under Nero, who targets Christians for persecution in the wake of the great fire in 64.
66–70	Roman provocations spark revolt in Judea. In 68 Nero kills himself to avoid capture in a military coup. The Romans at last conquer Jerusalem and destroy the temple. Yohanan ben Zakkai escapes Jerusalem; he will be a leading figure in the formation of what will later be called "rabbinic Judaism."

Fig. 0.1. *Saint Paul. Byzantine fresco from the monastery in Sopo-cani, Serbia. Photo: Scala/Art Resource, New York.*

Introduction: Exploring Paul's Environment

Paul has been challenging readers for a long time. Already in the late first or early second century, the author of 2 Peter wrote that some things in Paul's letters were "hard to understand, which the ignorant and unstable twist to their own destruction" (2 Pet 3:16). Many a contemporary reader may sympathize! When we read Paul's letters today, we face some of the same challenges that early believers faced as they heard those letters read when they came together, the first being simply to understand them.

We come to an understanding of most things we encounter by comparing them with other ideas or images in our experience. This book is therefore a window onto ideas and images that can be used to help us understand Paul. None of the documents and images presented here is offered as a claim regarding the *source* of Paul's ideas. We cannot prove what Paul had read, seen, or studied, a point we will repeat throughout the book. But we can encounter some of the ideas and images from the worlds in which Paul and his first communities lived and thus form a better picture of Paul's context.

The Appetite for Parallels: A Cautionary Note

Of course, citing relevant documents or images is not sufficient for the careful interpretation of a text ("exegesis"). It is possible to "feed" a passage from Paul's letters with too many parallels. The meaning of the text then becomes bloated in a way that is unhealthy for exegesis, rather as overfeeding a goldfish might risk the goldfish's health.[1] If one feeds Paul's letters with parallels, the given sentence or paragraph one is reading may grow out of all proportion to its context in the letter in which it appears. In everyday conversation, none of us means by what we say all of the possible meanings of the words we use. It is better, then, not to "overfeed"—not to try to "stuff" all possible parallels into our exegesis of a text. But—to stretch the metaphor in the opposite direction—it is just as important not to use too small a fishbowl: not to restrict too narrowly the possible meanings of a text. This caution is all the more important when we are dealing with an environment as distant from us—and as expansive—as Paul's world.

Exegesis is "the process of careful, analytical study of biblical passages undertaken in order to produce useful interpretations of those passages" (*ABD* 2:682).

Why is it that we readers of scripture are often tempted to import into a Pauline text more parallels than are helpful? There is, first of all, the joy of discovery. It is exhilarating to find a text that seems to be a verbal or conceptual parallel with a passage from Paul. Once the discovery is made, there is an often irresistible temptation to argue that the new parallel provides a key—even *the* key!—to understanding Paul.

With the early-twentieth-century discoveries of papyri in Egypt, the Dead Sea Scrolls, and ongoing epigraphic finds, there seems to be a steady flow of parallels as if from a spigot that cannot be turned off. Already in 1961, Samuel Sandmel cautioned biblical scholars against "parallelomania," which he defined as "that extravagance among scholars which first overdoes the supposed similarity in passages and then proceeds to describe source and derivation as if implying literary connection flowing in an inevitable or predetermined direction."[2] We take that caution seriously and understand our task here to be more modest: we seek to offer texts and images that can illuminate aspects of Paul's environment. Our selection of one or another text, or our identification of a comparison that may be relevant to one or another passage in Paul's letters, should hardly be taken as a proposal that we have found the decisive key to a passage's interpretation.

Neither, of course, should the reader assume that Paul's gospel would immediately have been perceived as the *opposite* of one or another text from Paul's environment, as if Paul's context was an unrelenting moral darkness into which he brought an otherwise unavailable light. That is the way he often wrote, of course: see, for example, Rom 13:12; 1 Cor 4:5; or 2 Cor 11:14. But before we can understand what such language would have meant to Paul's hearers, we will need as thorough a familiarity with his environment and as nuanced an appreciation of his rhetoric as we can attain.

Other Available Resources

Our introductory sample of documents and images from Paul's world is far from comprehensive. Students who wish to pursue any of the themes raised in this book may consult a number of helpful reference works, sourcebooks, and monographs identified in the notes (though there, too, we make no claim to comprehensiveness).

The quest to use extrabiblical evidence in order to understand scripture began in the Renaissance. In the eighteenth century, J. J. Wettstein published a New Testament with references to Greco-Roman and Jewish literature in the margins. A modern edition of his book is still available today, and those who read German can find in the volumes of the *Neuer Wettstein* series the actual texts of some of the relevant parallels.[3]

In the twentieth century, the prototype of a book like this one, Adolf Deissmann's *Light from the Ancient East*, appeared in 1908.[4] Paul Fiebig's concise volume *Die Umwelt des neuen Testaments* (The Environment of the New Testament) continued this trend.[5] In 1956, C. K. Barrett published what would become a best-selling English volume, *The New Testament Background*, a book that has been expanded and reprinted for decades and remains popular today.[6] A very different book with a similar title, *New Testament Backgrounds*, is a collection of learned essays on various aspects of the New Testament in light of cultural parallels. It will prove equally useful to some readers.[7] Meanwhile interest in the wider literary, philosophical, and religious Hellenistic environment of early Christian literature, including Paul's letters, has been well served by a growing number of sourcebooks.[8] Some have focused particularly on women's lives and women's religious experience.[9]

Books presenting documents to be read specifically alongside the letters of Paul have also been published since the early twentieth century, when Adolf Deissmann published a book on Paul in his historical context.[10] Beginning even earlier, scholars have established tables of verbal or thematic parallels among Paul's letters and between the letters and other biblical texts, first as supplemental material in an edition of the New Testament.[11] In 1975, Fred O. Francis and J. Paul Sampley published *Pauline Parallels*, a resource for students and scholars alike that offers tables of parallels among Paul's letters and between those letters and other New Testament texts, organized around formal elements and thematic similarities.[12] Subsequently Walter Wilson has published a collection of biblical parallels to Paul's letters that indicates explicit and possibly implicit occurrences of intertextuality between Paul's letters and the scriptures he read—that is, Israel's scriptures in Greek.[13] And as we shall see, these resources are accompanied by a veritable explosion of studies on Paul's social and cultural context.

> **Intertextuality** refers to an author's or speaker's interaction with other texts that readers or hearers are expected to recognize. It can take the form of explicit **citation, quotation,** or **allusion.**[14]

What Difference Do "Parallels" Make in Our Reading?

Anyone embarking today on the study of the apostle Paul will quickly discover a wide and potentially bewildering array of perspectives on Paul and interpretations of his thought. Was he Christianity's first theologian or, even as an apostle of Jesus Christ, did he remain a devout Jew? Was he an enthusiastic "convert" or a renegade "apostate" from Judaism? A teacher? A missionary? A philosopher? A mystic? A socially conservative conformist or an anti-imperial agitator? All these views find defenders today.

Even among scholars who agree on the importance of avoiding anachronism and stereotype in the effort to understanding Paul in his own historical and cultural context, how one or another interpreter appeals to materials from the ancient world can frame a number of different reconstructions of that context. Would Paul have come across to his contemporaries as an educated Pharisee, steeped in Jewish lore, or as a freelance "philosopher" trading on his facility with the conventional topics of Stoic or Cynic teachers? Or would the dominant first impression that Paul made on his hearers have been that he brought a message like nothing they had encountered before?

Different interpretations of Paul arise, are developed and modified, and—depending on their inherent strength and on the theological and cultural climate in which they appear—thrive, endure, or lapse into obscurity over time. Within the discipline of historical criticism, the inherent strength of an interpretation is measured by the interpreter's ability to make convincing comparisons between Paul and aspects of the first-century environment that is being proposed as a relevant context. At the same time, which parallels are seen as convincing can depend, in some part, on how well they corroborate an accepted interpretation.

In his essay "Parallelomania," Samuel Sandmel criticized a particularly dramatic example: Hermann Strack and Paul Billerbeck's *Kommentar zum Neuen Testament aus Talmud und Midrasch* (Commentary on the New Testament from Talmud and Midrash).[15] As Sandmel noted, the sheer number of supposed parallels that this *Kommentar* provided for various New Testament texts from much later rabbinic texts convinced many European and American interpreters in the early and mid-twentieth century that they provided genuine insight into the New Testament. Sandmel identified significant problems of method in Strack and Billerbeck's approach, however.

Especially in the wake of the Shoah,[16] the pervasively negative judgments regarding Judaism that appeared in the *Kommentar* came to be seen as prejudicial. This change in perception, as much as Sandmel's pointed criticisms of the method employed in Strack and Billerbeck's *Kommentar*, led to a significant decline in scholars' estimation of the *Kommentar's* usefulness. The point is that the climate of scholarship around Paul—and, correspondingly, the perception of what is a relevant indication of "context" and what is not—can change over time.

It has become customary in the last decades of the twentieth century and the beginning of the twenty-first for scholars to speak of "paradigm shifts" in our understanding of Paul. Such shifts have been occasioned, in no small part, by the landmark works of Rosemary Radford Ruether, Krister Stendahl, and E. P. Sanders in the 1970s.[17] One result is that the sort of generalization that Günther Bornkamm could make about Paul in the mid-twentieth century—that in all of his letters "Paul's opponent is not this or that section in a particular church, but the Jews and their understanding of salvation"[18]—is rather rare today.

Instead, the so-called New Perspective, announced by James D. G. Dunn more than twenty-five years ago, has now become something of an established view that is itself the object of continuing examination, modification, and critique.[19] Its popularity among scholars who nevertheless present a rather diverse range of interpretations under its aegis has led to questions of definition: just what *is* the "New Perspective"? The points of broadest consensus center on the inadequacy of an earlier reading of Paul, sometimes dubbed the "Protestant" or even the "Lutheran" reading, which construed the apostle's theology as a doctrine of justification by faith fundamentally opposed to a characteristically Jewish doctrine of justification by works of law. Sanders's critique rendered that old opposition (and the prejudicial view of Judaism on which it depended) historically untenable and morally repugnant in the eyes of many. The obvious next question, as Sanders put it, is "what, in Paul's view, was wrong with Judaism?" (see chapter 4).

But if Sanders's critique of older answers has proven widely compelling, his own constructive answer to that question has not been universally accepted. (Nor, to be fair, have the subsequent proposals of any other interpreter!) The result is a complicated and messy landscape that, in the words of Daniel Marguerat, "resembles a city devastated by an earthquake. People scurry about in every direction, some assessing the damage, others verifying what still stands. Everyone takes the measure of the changes to come but no one dares to build again, out of fear of a new shock."[20] No one, Marguerat ventures, can hope to comprehend all of the post-Sanders terrain—though some have ventured to map out distinctive "schools," most recently, Magnus Zetterholm in his survey *Approaches to Paul*.[21]

Recent decades have seen an explosion of studies exploring various aspects of Paul's context in the Hellenistic world, often published in collections of essays.[22] One of the most thorough is *Paul in the Greco-Roman World: A Handbook*, edited by J. Paul Sampley, in which scholars offer essays placing Paul and his rhetorical practices in their wider Hellenistic setting. Each essay provides references to a wealth of comparative material.[23] Owing to the abundance of that material, however, it is still necessarily left up to the reader in most cases to track down the helpful references in order to find the original sources. More recently, John Dominic Crossan and Jonathan L. Reed offer a number of photographs and citations from ancient literature in the course of their anti-imperial portrait of Paul.[24] None of these books provides full citations of all the literature they cite: indeed, to do so would require a small library! That sort of comprehensiveness is not our purpose either. Rather, we intend to provide readers a firsthand encounter with some materials that represent the larger world to which all these earlier studies point.

Crossan and Reed illustrate another recent development: increased attention to Paul's political context, and especially to aspects of the early Roman Empire, represented, for example, by the work of the Paul and Politics Group of the Society of Biblical Literature.[25] Since Paul and his congregations lived simultaneously amid the currents of Jewish tradition, Greek culture, and Roman government, it seems increasingly appropriate today to refer to Paul's "three worlds"—though of course Paul lived in but one world, in which he, like his contemporaries, navigated different claims on his allegiance and identity. Speaking of multiple "worlds" may help us to organize different sets of data but is finally artificial.

We seek to avoid referring to **"Paul's churches"** or **"Pauline Christianity"** for several reasons. First, it is clear from the New Testament that Paul joined a movement already in progress. Even when he helped to found a congregation (as in Corinth: 1 Cor 3:6, 10), he did not work alone. Further, Paul often faced disagreement or opposition within even those congregations he had helped to found. It is therefore not clear in what sense we should call the congregations "his."

Finally, the word *church* can evoke anachronistic assumptions of established congregations, meeting in large, dedicated buildings, led by professional clergy, organized into national denominations, enjoying public recognition (in the United States, First Amendment protection and the property tax exemption as well as employer recognition of the "weekend"), and dedicated to "religious" concerns. **The Greek word ekklēsia** was used in Paul's day especially for a civic assembly of townspeople or citizens and had civic or political connotations that other, more purely "religious" terms (like *thiasos*) did not. We will use "congregation" or "assembly" to translate the word here.

No single aspect of these worlds can be taken as the key to understanding Paul, his congregations, and his letters. Debates over which of these "worlds" is more important for understanding one or another aspect of Paul's thought, or over how these three worlds intersected in the lives of the assemblies, will no doubt continue. These are lively questions, and they continue to command our own attention and to exercise our own imaginations as scholars.[26] Our purpose here, however, is not to argue for a particular view of Paul but to gather for the student documents and images from his world(s) that bear comparison with one or another aspect of his thought and practice.

How to Use This Book

Any selection of materials from the abundance of Paul's world of course involves choice, but we do not wish by our choices to predetermine or preclude possible comparisons. We have deliberately sought to include materials often neglected in an earlier generation of scholarship that was preoccupied with the problematic relationship of Paul to Judaism. Furthermore, our inclusion of images is meant not only to bring to life the rich visual world through which Paul moved but also to highlight the symbolic and iconographic vocabulary that constituted the mass media of the first century and, as such, would have been better known to many of Paul's contemporaries than any of the texts that follow.

Introductions to the texts and questions for reflection at the end of each chapter are presented in order to prompt readers to see possible similarities and differences between Paul's letters and the roughly contemporaneous texts that are cited. These questions might be used before as well as after reading a chapter. Readers might also wish to write imaginative exercises in which they imagine themselves in one or another role illustrated in the texts and, perhaps, respond to an aspect of one or another of Paul's letters.

We have used critical signs in the text as follows:

Missing letters or words restored or reconstructed by a translator or editor: [square brackets]

The completion of words abbreviated in a text: (parentheses)

Omitted letters or words that have been supplied by a translator or editor: <angle brackets>

Gaps in the original text: ellipses within brackets [. . .]

Unnecessary letters in the text: {curly brackets}

In many cases, we expect that scholars and students alike may be able to think of other and better questions than ours when reading the texts and images here alongside Paul; ours are only a starting point. Similarly, we expect that our colleagues who use this book in classrooms may wish to augment our selection with additional materials to develop particular aspects of Paul's context. We invite students to pursue their curiosity by exploring further any of the avenues opened up here. Toward both ends, we have included lists of recommended readings at the end of each chapter to point readers toward additional resources; references in the endnotes address particular questions of interpretation.

The book is arranged thematically in an order that might serve as the outline of a course syllabus. The indexes of biblical and apocryphal writings and other ancient literature let readers quickly identify particular documents or images that bear on one or another of Paul's letters for classes taking either a chronological approach to Paul or one organized according to the order of letters in the New Testament. A map of Paul's world and a timeline are included as well for the reader's convenience (pp. viii–xi).

We hope the result is a useful and inviting resource for the study of Paul. This book will have served its goal if in the end it moves readers to take up and read Paul's letters again.

QUESTIONS FOR REFLECTION

1. What are the potential dangers of seeking "parallels" for themes or concepts in Paul's letters?
2. In what ways do contemporary readers risk reading their own assumptions into the interpretation of Paul and his letters?

FOR FURTHER READING

Brief introductions to Paul and current scholarship:

Roetzel, Calvin J. *Paul: The Man and the Myth.* Paperback ed. Minneapolis: Fortress Press, 1999.

Wright, N. T. *Paul: In Fresh Perspective.* Minneapolis: Fortress Press, 2005.

Zetterholm, Magnus. *Approaches to Paul: A Student's Guide to Recent Scholarship.* Minneapolis: Fortress Press, 2009.

Reference works and tools:

Dunn, James D. G. *The Theology of Paul the Apostle.* Grand Rapids: Eerdmans, 1998.

Francis, Fred O., and J. Paul Sampley. *Pauline Parallels.* 2nd ed. Philadelphia: Fortress Press, 1984.

Freedman, David Noel, ed. *The Anchor Bible Dictionary.* 6 vols. New York: Doubleday, 1992. Cited throughout as *ABD*.

Hawthorne, Gerald F., Ralph P. Martin, and Daniel G. Reid, eds. *Dictionary of Paul and His Letters: A Compendium of Contemporary Biblical Scholarship.* Downers Grove, Ill.: InterVarsity, 1993.

Sourcebooks:

Aune, David E. *The New Testament in Its Literary Environment.* Library of Early Christianity 8. Philadelphia: Westminster, 1987.

Boring, M. Eugene, Klaus Berger, and Carsten Colpe, eds. *Hellenistic Commentary to the New Testament.* Nashville: Abingdon, 1995.

Sampley, J. Paul, ed. *Paul in the Greco-Roman World: A Handbook.* Harrisburg, Pa.: Trinity Press International, 2003.

Fig. 1.1. *The apostle Paul as philosopher, with cloak and basket of scrolls. Third-century-c.e. fresco in the catacomb of St. Domitilla, Rome. Photo courtesy of the Rev. Greg Apparcel, Santa Susanna Church, Rome.*

1 | Paul's Self-Presentation

As the book of Acts tells it, upon his entry into a new city, the apostle Paul routinely made his way to the synagogue, where he encountered Jews as well as non-Jews who had been attracted to some aspects of Jewish life and worship.

Luke calls these non-Jewish sympathizers or adherents of the synagogue people "who fear God" (13:16), "worshipers of God" (16:14; 18:7), and "devout Greeks" (17:4). The example of the centurion Cornelius, "a devout man who feared God with all his household; he gave alms generously to the people [that is, to the Jewish community] and prayed constantly to God" (Acts 10:1-2), and the similar scene in Luke 7, where Jews ask Jesus to act on behalf of a centurion who "loves our people and . . . built our synagogue for us" (7:5), have given rise to the hypothesis that first-century synagogues in the Diaspora included a semiofficial class of non-Jewish adherents called "God-fearers," a hypothesis to which we will return in chapter 5.

Acts also depicts Paul speaking in public, perhaps in the city square (the agora: 14:8-18; 17:17); in Athens, at a gathering place for philosophical debate on the Hill of Mars in Athens (the Areopagus: 17:19-34); in Corinth, in the house of a God-fearer next door to the synagogue (18:7); and in Ephesus, in a lecture hall, apparently sponsored by a patron (19:8-10). His regular practice in Acts, however, was to begin in the synagogue of a city.

We see a different picture from Paul's own letters, where he addresses his hearers as having "turned to God from idols" in response to his preaching (1 Thess 1:10; compare 1 Cor 6:9-11; Rom 6:16-19). He is clearly not addressing Jews. This is only one of several differences between Acts and what Paul says about his work (see chapter 2), but it raises a question. If, during the initial presentation of his message, Paul could not rely on his audience already sharing certain premises with him—belief and reverence for only one god, the god of the Jews; respect for Jewish scriptures; and the abandonment of idol worship—then how did he make his first connection with them? Even if some in his audience had attended a synagogue but had not committed themselves to it, how would they have perceived him?

Because we normally encounter Paul today as we *read* his letters in published English translations of the Bible, it is easy to imagine him as a *writer* addressing readers in his own time. We will return to the topic of Paul as a writer of letters in chapter 2. We know, however, that Paul probably dictated his letters, more or less precisely, to an *amanuensis*—a skilled scribe, such as Tertius (Rom 16:22)—then dispatched the letter with a member of his apostolic team, who would then read the letter aloud to the assembled recipients (many of whom may have been illiterate). Letter carriers were expected not just to read the written words but to "perform" them in order to convey the author's meaning as completely as possible.[1] It is just as appropriate, then, to speak of Paul's *hearers*.

Our concern in this chapter is with the way Paul presented himself to others. How did he introduce himself to his hearers, and what would his hearers—especially his non-Jewish hearers—have made of him?

On "Jews" and "Gentiles": Throughout the book we will refer to "non-Jews." The New Revised Standard Version and other English translations—as well as a majority of scholars—use the word Gentiles to translate the Greek word *ethnē* (sg. *ethnos*). But *ethnos* means a "people," not an individual, and Paul never uses the singular *ethnos* to mean a non-Jewish person (see Rom 10:19, where he uses the word to refer to Israel as a people). The plural is often translated "peoples" or "nations," and Paul seems often to use it to refer to individuals from the peoples other than Israel. The capitalized English word *Gentile* does not correspond to any specific identity in the ancient world.[2]

Slave of Jesus Christ, Called an Apostle

Paul opens his letter to the Romans—a congregation he did not found—by identifying himself this way:

> Paul, slave of Christ Jesus, called an apostle, separated to the gospel of God, which was promised beforehand through his prophets in the holy scriptures concerning his son, who came from the seed of David according to the flesh, who was designated son of God in power by the Spirit of holiness on the basis of the resurrection of the dead, Jesus Christ our Lord, through whom we have received grace and apostleship for the obedience of faith among all the nations

on behalf of his name, among whom you are, even you—those called Jesus Christ's; to all who are in Rome, loved by God, called to be holy: Grace to you and peace from God our Father and the Lord Jesus Christ. (Rom 1:1-7)

Here Paul begins his most carefully constructed self-introduction with his name, the phrase "slave of Christ Jesus," and then an enigmatic two-word phrase, literally, "called apostle." What could he expect his audience to hear in those terms?

He did not mean that he was only "called" an apostle and was not a real one. The question is not an idle one. We know that Paul was not recognized by all Jesus-followers as a legitimate apostle, as the extended, passionate defense of his apostolic status in 2 Cor 10:1—12:13 makes clear, and as shorter claims to this status confirm (1 Cor 9:1; 15:8-10; Gal 2:9; 1 Thess 2:3-12). Some readers think they detect other cracks in the apostolic persona. Note how Paul does not repeat the word *apostle* when paralleling his ministry with Peter's (Gal 2:8) and how he admits that for some people he is *not* an apostle (1 Cor 9:2). Paul is ever aware of how differently he operates in comparison with the rest of the apostles (1 Cor 9:4-18; 2 Cor 11:7-11; 12:13; 1 Thess 2:5-9; 2 Thess 3:6-10). On the other hand, he clearly expects some congregations to recognize the title *apostle* in general (see Rom 16:7; 1 Cor 4:9) and even when he does not use the title itself, he expects hearers to acknowledge his authority—for example, to "command" them to do their "duty" (Phlm 8). With some important exceptions (to which we return in chapter 6), later church tradition has resoundingly affirmed Paul's authority as an apostle—even "the apostle."[3]

"Apostle is Paul's most common self-designation."[4] Related to the Greek verb *apostellein*, "to send," the term, like its Latin equivalent *legatus* (or the Hebrew šāliaḥ), is used for those who are sent by others—in this case, by Jesus Christ—and carry the authority of the one(s) doing the sending.[5] The Hebrew term was later sometimes used for someone sent by a religious authority to exercise that authority in a specific way over others. Acts 9:1-2 seems to portray Saul, before he became known as the apostle Paul, fulfilling such a function for the high priest in Jerusalem. Later, Paul claims not to care how authoritative the leaders of the church in Jerusalem are and insists that *Christ* "sent" him as apostle to the nations (Gal 2:6, 8-9). It is his being "called" as an apostle *by Christ* that alone validates his apostleship; thus at other points in his letters Paul emphasizes that he does not come on his own initiative but that he was "sent" by Jesus.[6] Paul's coming to a congregation is therefore a momentous event: he claims to come with the authority of Jesus, which may involve judgment on the congregation.[7]

Paul is clearly invested in the title and role of apostle. He defends that role against opposition (2 Cor 10:1—12:13). Further, although Paul can claim that the status of the Jerusalem apostles meant nothing to him (Gal 2:6) and that they only "seemed to be pillars" (Gal 2:9), the larger argument makes sense only if Paul and his hearers assume that those apostles carried real authority. Though he was not, like the Jerusalem apostles, called as a follower of Jesus, Paul nevertheless claims and adapts the term *apostle* to fit and to authorize his own ministry. He declares that he not only enjoys the approval of the Jerusalem apostles and collegiality with them but also that he exercises a divinely given independence from them in his dealings with his communities (1 Cor 4:3-5).

The word *apostolos* seems to have played a unique role as a technical term in early Christianity, but the concepts of being "sent" from God and a servant or "slave" of God were not unique to that movement.

1. Israel's prophets as "called" and "sent" (Septuagint)

Although the Greek term *apostolos* appears only rarely in Jewish scripture, Israel's prophets are often depicted as being "called" and "sent" (Greek *apestalmenos*, a cognate of *apostolos*) by God. Note also that Paul's speech about God having "set him apart from birth" (Gal 1:15) echoes the third text below.

> Then [the Lord] sent one of the seraphs to me, and in his hand he held a coal, which he had taken from the altar with a pair of tongs, and he touched my mouth and said: "See, this has touched your lips and your wrongs are forgiven and your sins are cleansed away."
>
> And I heard the voice of the Lord saying, "Whom shall I send, and who will go to this people?"
>
> And I said, "See, here I am; send me [*aposteilon me*]!"
>
> And he said, "Go and say to this people:
>   'Listen intently, and do not comprehend;
>   look intently, but do not see.'
> For the heart of this people has become thick,
>   and they hear poorly with their ears,
>   and they have shut their eyes,
> so that they may no longer see with their eyes
>   and hear with their ears,
> or understand with their heart and turn
>   that I might heal them."
>
> (Isaiah 6:6-10 LXX)
>
>
> The spirit of the Lord is upon me,
>   because he has anointed me:
> he has sent me [*apestalken me*] to bring good news to the oppressed,
>   to heal the broken-hearted,
> to proclaim release to captives
>   and recovery of sight to the blind,
> to announce the favorable time of the Lord
>   and the day of recompense,
> to comfort all who mourn. . . .
>
> (Isaiah 61:1-2 LXX)
>
>
> Now the word of the Lord came to me saying,
>   "Before I formed you in the womb I knew you,

and before you came forth from the womb I made you holy;
I appointed you a prophet to the nations."

Then I said, "Ah, sovereign Lord! See, I do not know how to speak, for I am only a boy." But the Lord said to me,

"Do not say, 'I am only a boy';
for to all to whom I send you [*exaposteilō se*], you will go,
and whatever I command you, you will speak.
Do not be afraid of them,
for I am with you to deliver you," says the Lord.

(Jeremiah 1:4-8 LXX, trans. Elliott)

2. The philosopher as "sent" by God (Epictetus)

The language of being "sent" by a god was used beyond the bounds of Judaism. Asked how one should consider the prospect of entering upon life as a Cynic, the first-century philosopher Epictetus insisted first that one should think of the decision not as one's own initiative but as a response to a divine order: "for in this great city [that is, the world], there is a lord of the household who assigns tasks." He explains that the Cynic must not be distracted by any feelings save those that spring from moral resolve and that the Cynic life is a life lived under public scrutiny. The Cynic must be utterly committed to the "right use of the imagination":

Then, thus prepared, the one who is a Cynic in truth is not satisfied with these things but must know that [he or she] has been sent from God as a messenger [*angelos apo tou Dios apestaltai*], first to convince human beings concerning good and evil—that they have been deceived and rather seek the reality of good and of evil where it is not to be found, and fail to recognize it where it truly is; second, to act as a scout, as did Diogenes when taken away to Philip after the battle of Chaeroneia. For the Cynic is a scout regarding which things are friendly to human beings and which are hostile.

Later in the same discourse, Epictetus describes the message the Cynic must declare to others, holding oneself up as an example:

And how does it happen that one who has nothing—someone naked and homeless, without shelter, possessions, servant, or even a city—do conduct themselves serenely? Behold: God has sent you someone to show you, by deed, how it is done.

(Arrian, *Discourses of Epictetus* 3.22.23-24, 45-46; trans. Reasoner)

"Servant" (or Slave) of Christ

In Israel's scriptures, Moses (Exod 14:31) and the prophets are repeatedly described (as are other leaders including Joshua and David) as God's "servants" whom God sent to Israel. Jeremiah uses the phrase frequently (Hebrew *'ebed*; Greek *pais*, pl. *paides*: Jer 7:25; 25:4; 26:5; 33:5; 42:15; 51:4 LXX). The Second Isaiah apparently refers to himself by the same phrase (Isa 49:5-6; LXX using both *doulos* and *pais*).

The description of the prophets as "servants of God" became stereotyped in later Jewish writings. Paul uses the Greek term *doulos* to describe himself as a "slave" of Christ.

Citizens of ancient Athens or the Roman Empire perceived actual slaves as inferior beings—a necessity in slaveholding societies, as Orlando Patterson observes.[8] The grim reality of the life of most slaves and their recurrence as stock characters in Greek and Roman literature, including the New Testament, has been amply described in recent studies by J. Albert Harrill and Jennifer Glancy.[9] A passage from Aristotle is typical of this attitude.

3. The slave's inferiority (Aristotle)

It is thought that what is just is something that is equal, and also that friendship is based on equality, if there is truth in the saying "Amity is equality." And all constitutions are some form of justice; for they are partnerships, and every partnership is founded on justice, so that there are as many forms of justice and of partnership as there are of friendship, and all these forms border on each other and have their differences closely related. But since the relations of soul and body, craftsman and tool, and master and slave are similar, between the two terms of each of these pairs there is no partnership; for they are not two, but the former is one and the latter a part of that one, not one itself; nor is the good divisible between them, but that of both belongs to the one for whose sake they exist. For the body is the soul's tool born with it, a slave is as it were a member or tool of his master, a tool is a sort of inanimate slave.

(Aristotle, *Eudemian Ethics* 1241b.12-24, trans. Rackham, LCL)

Dale B. Martin reminds us, however, that the slaves of wealthy and powerful citizens could themselves exercise some of the considerable authority of their masters and enjoy far more secure and comfortable circumstances than most of the free poor. He notes that "the enslaved leader" could serve as a theme in a certain sort of populist rhetoric and at last suggests that "within early Christianity, *slave of Christ* signified authority by analogy to the authority of the managerial slave."[10] Paul could have played, he concludes, on that use of the term.

We should also mention here one possible explanation for the claim made in Acts 21:39 that Paul was a citizen of Tarsus, in Cilicia, and the claim in 22:25-29 that he was a Roman citizen as well. Centuries later Jerome passed along the story (though he does not identify its source) that Paul's parents were removed to Cilicia after their home region, Gischala, was conquered by Rome. If his parents were carried off as slaves but then they or Paul were manumitted by a Roman citizen of Tarsus, Paul would have received citizenship. (This might also explain his Roman name, *Paulus*, of which the Greek *Paulos* is the equivalent.)[11] We cannot draw an unequivocal conclusion but note that if Paul were indeed a citizen, it is all the more remarkable that he never refers to his citizenship in his letters but instead repeatedly adopts the title "slave."

The Figure of the Philosopher

One proposal for how we should imagine Paul making his initial contact with an audience is the model of the philosopher or teacher of virtue. The ancients spoke of "schools" of Stoic and Cynic philosophers, traditions in which teachers passed on their doctrines to their students in succession. There were formal schools, like the Stoa in Athens (from which the Stoics, or *stōikoi*, took their name), or the Stoic school in Tarsus; but more often, individuals who had studied with a teacher—and some who had not—presented themselves as itinerant teachers of philosophy for hire. Cynics were notorious for such "freelance" philosophizing.[12]

> The Greek word *kynikoi* (**"Cynics"**) comes from *kynos*, "dog," and refers to a "doglike" life lived in defiance of social convention—for example, doing things in public that "respectable" people do privately.

4. The Virtues of a philosopher (Dio Chrysostom)

Some of the characteristics of the genuine philosopher—on whose services the welfare of a city depends—are listed by Dio Chrysostom (c. 40–120 c.e.), in the course of recommending himself as just such a philosopher to the Alexandrians. Noteworthy are the variety of ways Dio imagines philosophers may present themselves and seek to be supported; Dio's own apparent ambition to be supported by the city itself; and the way he seeks to distinguish himself from others (in part, by claiming to be called by "some deity" to philosophize).

> But you have no such critic, neither chorus nor poet nor anyone else, to reprove you in all friendliness and to reveal the weaknesses of your city. Therefore, whenever the thing does at last appear, you should receive it gladly and make a festival of the occasion instead of being vexed; and even if vexed, you should be ashamed to call out, "When will the fellow stop?" or "When is a juggler coming on?" or "Rubbish!" or some such thing. For, as I have said, that sort of entertainment you always have in stock and there is no fear that it will ever fail you; discourses like this of mine, which make others happier and better and more sober and better able to administer effectively the cities in which they dwell, you have not often heard—for I do not care to say that you would not listen to them.
>
> And perhaps this situation is not of your making, but you will show whether it is or not if you bear with me today; the fault may lie rather at the door of those who wear the name of philosopher. For some among that company do not appear in public at all and prefer not to make the venture, possibly because they despair of being able to improve the masses; others exercise their voices in what we call lecture-halls, having secured as hearers men who are in league with them and tractable. And as for the Cynics, as they are called, it is

Fig. 1.2. *An unnamed Cynic philosopher. Statue, second century* C.E. *Museo Capitolino, Rome. Photo: Yair Haklai.*

true that the city contains no small number of that sect, and that, like any other thing, this too has had its crop—persons whose tenets, to be sure, comprise practically nothing spurious or ignoble, yet who must make a living—still these Cynics, posting themselves at street-corners, in alleyways, and at temple-gates, pass around the hat and play upon the credulity of lads and sailors and crowds of that sort, stringing together rough jokes and much tittle-tattle and that low badinage that smacks of the marketplace. Accordingly they achieve no good at all, but rather the worst possible harm, for they accustom thoughtless people to deride philosophers in general, just as one might accustom lads to scorn their teachers, and, when they ought to knock the insolence out of their hearers, these Cynics merely increase it.

Those, however, who do come before you as men of culture either declaim speeches intended for display, and stupid ones to boot, or else chant verses of their own composition, as if they had detected in you a weakness for poetry. To be sure, if they themselves are really poets or orators, perhaps there is nothing so shocking in that, but if in the guise of philosophers they do these things with a few to their own profit and reputation, and not to improve you, that indeed is shocking. For it is as if a physician when visiting patients should disregard their treatment and their restoration to health, and should bring them flowers and courtesans and perfume.

But there are only a few who have displayed frankness [*parrhēsia*] in your presence, and that but sparingly, not in such a way as to fill your ears therewith nor for any length of time; nay, they merely utter a phrase or two, and then, after berating rather than enlightening you, they make a hurried exit, anxious lest before they have finished you may raise an outcry and send them packing, behaving in very truth quite like men who in winter muster up courage for a brief and hurried voyage out to sea. But to find a man who in plain terms, and without guile, speaks his mind with frankness, and neither for the sake of reputation nor for gain makes false pretension, but out of good will and concern for his fellow-men stands ready, if need be, to submit to ridicule, and the disorder and uproar of the mob—to find such a man is not easy, but rather the good fortune of a very lucky city, so great is the dearth of noble, independent souls and such the abundance of toadies, mountebanks, and sophists.

In my own case, for instance, I feel that I have chosen that role, not of my own volition, but by the will of some deity. For when divine providence is at work for men, the gods provide, not only good counselors who need no urging, but also words that are appropriate and profitable to the listener.

(Dio Chrysostom, *Discourses* 32.11, trans. Cohoon and Crosby, LCL)

5. Self-restraint as the mark of the good citizen (Musonius Rufus)

In Paul's time, one of the most current themes among popular philosophers was that of self-restraint or self-mastery (*enkrateia*), which was perceived as the virtue most seemly in rulers and also in those who aspired no higher than to rule themselves. As Stanley K. Stowers notes, Paul's contemporaries regarded self-mastery as distinguishing the civilized from the barbarian. Slaves and women as well were seen as incapable of proper self-control (and naturally required the "rule" of a superior, more reasonable male).[13]

Further, by practicing disciplines of self-control regarding food and sex and maintaining proper household decorum, elite males from subordinated peoples could "claim a place among the ruling classes of the empire." Augustus made self-mastery an important theme of his new order and "socially mobile" individuals sought to display self-mastery as the means to advancing themselves. Although Jews could not participate in the imperial cult (an important medium of social integration and assimilation for subjected peoples), "they could ally themselves with philosophy and present themselves as a uniquely self-mastered people."[14] Stowers considers Philo of Alexandria an important example of this claim to self-mastery. He argues that in Romans (and other letters as well), one of Paul's purposes is to compete with rival teachers by showing that his gospel provides the means to achieving self-mastery.

The Stoic Musonius Rufus addresses the importance of self-control for a king. As Stowers shows, however, such arguments would have been appealing to those with more moderate ambitions as well.

In the next place it is essential for the king to exercise self-control over himself and demand self-control of his subjects, to the end that with sober rule and seemly submission there shall be no wantonness on the part of either. For the ruin of the ruler and the citizen alike is wantonness. But how would anyone achieve self-control if he did not make an effort to curb his desires, or how could one who is undisciplined make others temperate? One can mention no study except philosophy that develops self-control. Certainly it teaches one to be above pleasure and greed, to admire thrift and to avoid extravagance; it trains one to have a sense of shame, and to control one's tongue, and it produces discipline, order, and courtesy, and in general what is fitting in action and in bearing. In an ordinary man when these qualities are present they give him dignity and self-command, but if they be present in a king they make him preeminently godlike and worthy of reverence.

(Musonius Rufus, *Fragment 8, That Kings Also Should Study Philosophy*, trans. Lutz)

6. The self-restraint of the philosopher (Athenaeus)

Might Paul have presented himself in terms associated with popular philosophers? In 1 Cor 9:27 he wrote that he punished and enslaved his body, language that probably suggested self-restraint or self-denial with regard to food. From the ascetic through the connoisseur and on to the glutton, various subcultures within the Greek and Roman worlds exhibited a full variety of approaches to the consumption of food and wine. In 1 Cor 6:13, Paul seems to quote a saying that some knew in the Corinthian church—"Food is for the stomach and the stomach for food"—before correcting it ("but . . ."). In Phil 3:18-19, Paul describes some rivals as enemies of Christ whose "god is their belly," and in Rom 16:18 he similarly describes some who are "enslaved not to our Lord Christ but to their own belly."

This caricature of worshiping or serving one's own belly seems to have had antecedents in Greek literature. It occurs in a compilation of anecdotes known as *The Learned Banqueters*, attributed to Athenaeus (late second or early third century c.e.). The phrase is used in an exchange in which a colleague (or teacher?) accuses the Cynic Cynulcus of drinking too much at dinners; Cynulcus seems to return the criticism in kind. Later in the compilation Cynulcus is challenged to come up with the literary source for the phrase.

> "This is what you Cynics do, Cynulcus. When you drink—or, rather, when you drink too much—you prevent pleasant conversation in the same way pipe-girls and dancing-girls do, and you live in the style this same Plato refers to, when he says in his *Philebus* [21c]: 'not the life of a human being, but that of a jellyfish or one of the shellfish that live in the sea.'" Cynulcus got angry and said: "Glutton! Worshipper of your own belly!"
>
> . . .
>
> "These, then, are the citations I have ready at hand for you at the moment, Cynulcus. But tomorrow or *enēphi*—because Hesiod [*Op.* 410] refers this way to the day after tomorrow—I will fodder you with blows, unless you tell me in what author the phrase 'Worshipper of your own belly' is attested."

Cynulcus was silent, and Ulpian said: "Well, my dog, I myself will tell you this too; Eupolis [fr. 187] refers this way to flatterers, in the play by the same name."[15]

(Athenaeus, *Learned Banqueters* 3.97c, 100b, trans. Olson, LCL)

7. The Philosopher's denial of eloquence (Socrates)

In the Corinthian assembly Paul encountered individuals who considered his oratorical performance inadequate ("his bodily presence is weak, and his speech contemptible," 2 Cor 10:10). Earlier Paul had defended the simplicity of his speech as a deliberate decision not to depend on "lofty words or wisdom" (1 Cor 2:1-5). This claim should not deceive us into thinking that the apostle was untrained or incapable of well-crafted rhetoric, however. Similar disavowals of eloquence were a mainstay of the orator's repertoire, as we see in one of the best-known speeches in Hellenistic culture: Socrates' defense as he stood accused of the capital charge of "corrupting" the youth of Athens.

How you, men of Athens, have been affected by my accusers, I do not know; but I, for my part, almost forgot my own identity, so persuasively did they talk;

Fig. 1.3. *The philosopher Socrates: Fresco from a home in Roman Ephesus, first to fifth century* c.e. *Museum of Ephesus. Photo: P. Vasiliadis.*

and yet there is hardly a word of truth in what they have said. But I was most amazed by one of the many lies that they told—when they said that you must be on your guard not to be deceived by me, because I was a clever speaker. For I thought it the most shameless part of their conduct that they are not ashamed because they will immediately be convicted by me of falsehood by the evidence of fact, when I show myself to be not in the least a clever speaker, unless indeed they call him a clever speaker who speaks the truth; for if this is what they mean, I would agree that I am an orator—not after their fashion.

Now they, as I say, have said little or nothing true; but you shall hear from me nothing but the truth. Not, however, men of Athens, speeches finely tricked out with words and phrases, as theirs are, nor carefully arranged, but you will hear things said at random with the words that happen to occur to me. For I trust that what I say is just; and let none of you expect anything else. For surely it would not be fitting for one of my age to come before you like a youngster making up speeches. And, men of Athens, I urgently beg and beseech you if you hear me making my defense with the same words with which I have been accustomed to speak both in the marketplace at the bankers' tables, where many of you have heard me, and elsewhere, not to be surprised or to make a disturbance on this account. For the fact is that this is the first time I have come before the court, although I am seventy years old; I am therefore an utter foreigner to the manner of speech here.

Hence, just as you would, of course, if I really were a foreigner, pardon me if I spoke in that dialect and that manner in which I had been brought up, so now I make this request of you, a fair one, as it seems to me, that you disregard the manner of my speech—for perhaps it might be worse and perhaps better— and observe and pay attention merely to this, whether what I say is just or not; for that is the virtue of a judge, and an orator's virtue is to speak the truth.

(Plato, *Apology of Socrates* 1, trans. Fowler, LCL)

8. A Critic protests the abundance of self-styled Cynics (Lucian)

Dio Chrysostom was not alone in offering critical comments regarding the abundance of philosophers (see above). The phenomenon was widespread enough to evoke sarcasm from observers. In one of his satirical essays, Lucian of Samosata (c. 120–80 c.e.) protested to Zeus the number of philosophers claiming to speak in the name of God. Note the characteristic appearance of such "public" philosophers (and compare Jesus' instructions to his disciples in Matt 10:9-10; Mark 6:9; Luke 10:4—and Luke 22:35-36!—along with 2 Tim 4:13). Lucian seems particularly vexed that the philosophers are drawing the wrong class of people to themselves.

But at present, do you not see how many short cloaks and staves and wallets there are? On all sides there are long beards, and books in the left hand, and everybody preaches in favor of you; the public walks are full of people assembling in companies and in battalions, and there is nobody who does not want to be thought a scion of Virtue. In fact, many, giving up the trades they had before, rush after the wallet and cloak, tan their bodies in the sun to Ethiopian hue, make themselves extemporaneous philosophers out of cobblers or carpenters, and go about praising you and your virtue. Consequently, in the words of the proverb, it would be easier for a man to fall in a boat without hitting a plank than for your eye to miss a philosopher wherever it looks.

(Lucian, *Double Indictment* 6, trans. Malherbe)

9. A Student writes to his father about the lack of good teachers

In a first-century papyrus letter from Roman Egypt, a son writes to his father, who is supporting the son and a number of his friends as they pursue their educations. Recently they have gotten into some trouble at a theater, and one former friend has been arrested and sent back home. The son complains that he has not made much progress. He has not yet found a scholar (*philologos*) worthy of his allegiance; meanwhile he has hoped at least to sign on with a tutor (*kathēgētēs*), as his friends have, but finds that too many who advertise themselves offer only inferior education. The letter gives us a glimpse into the availability of self-styled "scholars" and tutors who offered their services to young men of ambition.

Fig. 1.4. *Funerary portrait of a young man from Fayum, Egypt, c. 160 C.E. Albright-Knox Gallery, Buffalo. Photo in the public domain.*

Neilos to Theon, his lord and father, very many greetings . . .

You have released me from my present despondency by making it plain that the business about the theater was a matter of indifference to you. For my part, I've lost no time in sailing downstream to find distinguished . . . and I have achieved something in return for my eagerness. I was looking for a scholar and for Chaeremon the tutor and Didymus the son of Aristocles, as I thought that with them I, too, might still meet with success, but found them no longer in the city; instead (I found only) trash, in whose hands most pupils have taken the straight road to having their talent spoiled.

I have written to Philoxenus and his friends telling them that they, too, must leave the matter in the hands of the esteemed . . . so that I, after rejecting Theon, may find a teacher as soon as possible, for I myself formed a bad opinion of him . . . as possessing a completely inadequate training. When I informed Philoxenus of your view he began to be of the same opinion, saying that it was on account of a shortage of sophists . . . was in the same condition as the city, but he said that Didymus, who, it appears, is a friend of his and has a school, would be sailing down and would take more care than the others. He persuaded the sons of Apollonius son of Herodes to go to enroll (in the school of Didymus).

And after this they, too, together with Philoxenus, have been searching until now for a more stylish tutor since the scholar to whom they used to go has died. As for myself, if only I had found some decent tutor, I would pray never to set eyes on Didymus, even from a distance—what makes me despair is that this fellow who used to be a mere provincial sees fit to compete with the rest.

However, knowing as I do that apart from paying useless and excessive fees there is no good to be had from a tutor, I am depending on myself. If you have any opinions on the matter, write to me soon. As Philoxenus also says, I have Didymus always ready to spend his time on me and do everything to help within his capabilities, and by hearing the orators declaiming, of whom Posidonius is one, I shall, with the help of the gods, do well for myself.

The cause of my despondency about this, which is making me neglect my health, is that those who have not yet succeeded ought not to concern themselves with these matters, especially when there are none who are bringing in any money. For at that time the useful Heraclas—curse him!—used daily to contribute some obols, but now, what with his being imprisoned by Isidorus, as he deserved, he's escaped and gone back, I think, to you. Be assured that he would never hesitate to intrigue against you, for, of all things, he felt no shame at gleefully spreading reports in the city about the incident in the theater and telling lies such as would not come even from the mouth of an accuser and that too when, so far from suffering what he deserves, he's been released and behaves in every respect like a free man. All the same, if you are not sending him back, you could at any rate hand him over to a carpenter—for I'm told that a young fellow makes two drachmas a day—or put him to some other employment at which he'll earn more money; his wages can then be collected and in due course sent to us, for you know that Diogas, too, is studying. While you are sending the little one, we will look about for more spacious rooms in a private house; for in order to be near to Dionysius we've been living in rooms much too small.

We received the basket containing exactly the articles you mentioned and the vessels together with the half-*cadus* jar in which we found 22 *choes* instead of 18. To each of the people of whom you wrote I have sent a half-*cadua* of lentils accompanied by a letter. I have received the six measures and a full *coion* of vinegar and 126 lbs. of salted meat and contents of the *cadus* and the 30 baked loaves.

Farewell. [dated] Choiak 4.

(*P.Oxy.* 2190, trans. Winter, slightly modified)[16]

Philosophy in the Workplace

In order to avoid the impression that they were mere performers for hire, some philosophers worked with their hands to support themselves and thus to show that they were genuine.[17] Paul repeatedly refers to his practice of supporting himself through manual labor as a sign of his genuineness as an apostle (1 Cor 4:12; 9:4-18; 2 Cor 11:7-11; 12:13; 1 Thess 2:5, 9); in 2 Thess 3:6-10 Paul's self-support is represented as an example to others. His trade—Acts 18:3 identifies Paul as a tentmaker (or leatherworker, or theater set-maker: the word *skēnopoios* is ambiguous)[18]—allowed him some independence from would-be patrons. That strategy apparently gave offense to potential patrons in the Corinthian assembly, to judge from Paul's defensive response in 1 Corinthians 9.

10. A STOIC RECOMMENDS MANUAL LABOR (MUSONIUS RUFUS)

The first-century Stoic Musonius Rufus considered it an advantage to a philosopher's students if they should see him

> at work in the fields, demonstrating by his own labor the lesson which philosophy inculcates—that one should endure hardships, and suffer the pains of labor with his own body, rather than depend upon another for sustenance.
>
> (Musonius Rufus, *Fragment* 11, trans. Lutz)

Fig. 1.5. *Sign advertising a tailor's shop in Pompeii, first century* C.E. *Photo: Alinari/Art Resource, New York.*

11. A RABBI RECOMMENDS SELF-SUPPORT (R. GAMALIEL)

The Mishnah also recommended the practice of self-support; R. Gamaliel is Gamaliel III (early third century).

> Rabban Gamaliel the son of R. Judah the Patriarch said: "Excellent is the study of the Law together with worldly occupation, for toil in them both puts sin out of mind. But all study of the Law without [worldly] labor comes to naught at the last and brings sin in its train. And let all them who labor with the congregation labor with them for the sake of heaven, for the merits of their fathers supports them and their righteousness endures forever. And as for you, [God says,] I count you worthy of great rewards as though you [yourselves] had done it."
>
> (*m. 'Abot* 2.2, trans. Danby, modified)

12. A CRITIC RIDICULES WORKPLACE PHILOSOPHIZING (LUCIAN)

To others, however, the idea that philosophy and the virtuous life could be taught by mere artisans and manual laborers was laughable. Here the second-century writer Lucian of Samosata poses as Philosophy addressing her father, Zeus, and decrying the Cynics as menials who turn themselves into philosophers to make an easy buck.

> There is a vile race upon the earth, composed for the most part of serfs and menials, creatures whose occupations have never suffered them to become acquainted with philosophy; whose earliest years have been spent in the drudgery of the fields, in learning those base arts for which they are most fitted—the fuller's trade, the joiner's, the cobbler's—or in carding wool, that housewives may have ease in their spinning, and the thread be fit for warp and woof.
>
> Thus employed, they knew not in their youth so much as the name of Philosophy. But they had no sooner reached manhood, than they perceived the respect paid to my followers; how men submitted to their blunt speech, valued their advice, deferred to their judgment, and cowered beneath their censure; all this they saw, and held that here was a life for a king. The learning, indeed, that befits a philosopher would have taken them long to acquire, if it was not utterly out of their reach. On the other hand, their own miserly handicrafts barely rewarded their toil with a sufficiency. To some, too, servitude was in itself an oppression: they knew it, in fact, for the intolerable thing it is.
>
> But they bethought them that there was still one chance left; their sheet-anchor, as sailors say. They took refuge with my lady Folly, called in the assistance of Boldness, Ignorance, and Impudence, ever their untiring coadjutors, and provided themselves with a stock of brand-new invectives; these they have ever ready on their tongues; 'tis their sole equipment; noble provision, is it not, for a philosopher? Nothing could be more plausible than the philosophic disguise they now assume, reminding one of the fabled ass of Cyme, in Aesop, who clothed himself in a lion's skin, and, stoutly braying, sought to play the lion's part; the beast, I doubt not, had his adherents. The externals of philosophy, as you know, are easily aped: it is a simple matter to assume the cloak and wallet, walk with a stick, and bawl, and bark, and bray, against all comers. They know that they are safe; their cloth protects them. Liberty is thus within their grasp: no need to ask their master's leave; should he attempt to reclaim them, their

sticks are at his service. No more short commons for them now, no more of crusts whose dryness is mitigated only by herbs or salt fish: they have choice of meats, drink the best of wines, and take money where they will, *shearing the sheep*, as they call it when they levy contributions, in the certainty that many will give, from respect to their garb or fear of their tongues.

They foresee, of course, that they will be on the same footing as genuine philosophers; so long as their exterior is conformable, no one is likely to make critical distinctions. They take care not to risk exposure: at the first hint of a rational argument, they shout their opponent down, withdraw into the stronghold of personal abuse, and flourish their ever-ready cudgels. Question their practice, and you will hear much of their principles: offer to examine those principles, and you are referred to their conduct. The city swarms with these vermin, particularly with those who profess the tenets of Diogenes, Antisthenes, and Crates. Followers of the Dog, they care little to excel in the canine virtues; they are neither trusty guardians nor affectionate, faithful servants: but for noise and greed and thievery and wantonness, for cringing, fawning cupboard-love,—there, indeed, they are perfect.

Before long you will see every trade at a standstill, the workmen all at large: for every man of them knows that, whilst he is bent over his work from morning to night, toiling and drudging for a starvation wage, idle impostors are living in the midst of plenty, commanding charity where they will, with no word of thanks to the giver, and a curse on him that withholds the gift. Surely (he will say to himself) the golden age is returned, and the heavens shall rain honey into my mouth.

(Lucian, *Runaways* 12-17, trans. Fowler and Fowler)

13. A LATER CRITIC SCORNS TEACHING IN WORKPLACES (CELSUS)

In the late second century, the pagan critic Celsus ridiculed Christians. His scorn provides indirect confirmation of the picture of manual laborers like Paul teaching the virtuous life in their workshops—a notion that Celsus found ridiculous. (We have sections of Celsus's treatise only because Origen quoted it extensively in his rebuttal, *Against Celsus*.)

In private houses also we see wool-workers, laundry-workers, and the most illiterate and bucolic yokels, who would not dare to say anything at all in front of their elders and more intelligent masters. . . . (Children, they say,) should leave father and their schoolmasters, and go along with the women and little children who are their play-fellows to the wool-dresser's shop, or to the cobblers or the washerwoman's shop, that they may learn perfection. And by saying this they persuade them.

(Origen, *Against Celsus* 3.55, trans. Malherbe)

Attitudes toward Manual Labor and "Weakness"

One reason for the scorn of "workplace philosophizing" is apparently the contempt in which members of the upper class held the labor of those who were compelled by necessity to work for a living. Such attitudes would influence how elite members of Roman society in a city like Corinth looked upon someone like Paul.

Debate continues regarding Paul's own economic and social status and the status of the congregations he addressed. Against an older consensus that these assemblies were made up of a cross-section of Roman society, including wealthier and poorer individuals, more recent studies have argued that Paul and his congregations would have come from the great majority of poor people.[19] The following texts make it probable that Paul's self-presentation as working with his own hands would have been enough to draw scorn from the upper classes.

14. A Cynic view of holding down a job (Dio Chrysostom)

Someone like Lucian could caricature the Cynics' claim of indifference toward everyday employment. The Cynic Dio Chrysostom insisted that not being tied down to a single job was a mark of true freedom, for the Cynic

> goes about as neither farmer nor trader nor soldier nor general, nor as shoemaker or builder or physician or orator, nor as one engaged in any other customary occupation, but on the other hand comes and goes in this strange fashion and puts in an appearance in places where impulse or chance may lead him.
> (Dio Chrysostom, *Discourses* 80.1, trans. Malherbe)[20]

15. An Epicurean view of employment (Philodemus)

Philodemus of Gadara (first century B.C.E.) expressed a common sentiment among the privileged landowners in traditional agricultural society. Living off the exploitation of others' hard labor was ignoble, hardly better than living off one's own labor. But making a living from "farming"—that is, enjoying estates worked by others—was noble and provided the necessary leisure for philosophy. We encounter a similar romanticization of rural life on the part of those who never plowed a field or milked a cow in the early Principate.

> To derive one's means from the breeding of horses is ridiculous, from the exploitation of mines by servile labor unenviable, from those two sources by working oneself, pure madness. Miserable also is the lot of the farmer who works with his own hands. "But," says he, "to live off the land while others farm it—that is truly in keeping with wisdom. For then one is least entangled in business, the source of so many annoyances; there is indeed found a becoming way of life, a withdrawal into leisure with one's friends, and for those who moderate their desires, the most honorable source of revenue."
> (Philodemus, *On Household Management* 23, trans. Malherbe)

16. Worthy and unworthy occupations (Cicero)

A century before Paul, the orator Cicero, one of the wealthiest and most powerful men in Republican Rome, set down his assessment of worthy and unworthy occupations. Least worthy—equivalent to slavery—are occupations that simply allow one to make a living, for example by providing the food on Cicero's own table. Most worthy are those occupations that allow one to become wealthy and retire to a comfortable estate. (Note that Cicero's recommendation of "agriculture" refers not to working land but to owning the land on which others work.)

> Now in regard to trades and other means of livelihood, which ones are to be considered becoming to a gentleman and which ones are vulgar, we have been taught, in general, as follows. First, those means of livelihood are rejected as undesirable which incur people's ill-will, as those of tax-gatherers and usurers. Unbecoming to a gentleman, too, and vulgar are the means of livelihood of all hired workmen whom we pay for mere manual labor, not for artistic skill; for in their case the very wage they receive is a pledge of their slavery. Vulgar we must consider those also who buy from wholesale merchants to retail immediately; for they would get no profits without a great deal of downright lying; and verily, there is no action that is meaner than misrepresentation. And all mechanics are engaged in vulgar trades; for no workshop can have anything liberal about it. Least respectable of all are those trades which cater for sensual pleasures: fish-mongers, butchers, cooks, and poulterers, and fishermen, as Terence says. Add to these, if you please, the perfumers, dancers, and the whole corps de ballet.

Fig. 1.6. *M. Tullius Cicero. Nineteenth-century copy of a first-century Roman bust. Photo in the public domain.*

But the professions in which either a higher degree of intelligence is required or from which no small benefit to society is derived—medicine and architecture, for example, and teaching—these are proper for those whose social position they become. Trade, if it is on a small scale, is to be considered vulgar; but if wholesale and on a large scale, importing large quantities from all parts of the world and distributing to many without misrepresentation, it is not to be greatly disparaged. Nay, it even seems to deserve the highest respect, if those who are engaged in it, satiated, or rather, I should say, satisfied with the fortunes they have made, make their way from the port to a country estate, as they have often made it from the sea into port. But of all the occupations by which gain is secured, none is better than agriculture, none more profitable, none more delightful, none more becoming to a freeman.

(Cicero, *On Duties* 1.150-51, trans. Miller, LCL)

17. THE INDIGNITY OF MANUAL LABOR (SENECA)

In an essay written to a friend concerning the value of "liberal studies," Paul's contemporary Seneca—himself fabulously wealthy—reveals the prejudice that his own class, "free-born gentlemen," should be above having to work for a living and that preparation for actual work is the basest form of education. His assumption that those who have prepared themselves for labor will be ill-prepared for reflecting on truth, beauty, and honor may have been a prejudice that Paul would have faced from any wealthy individuals in his audience.

You have been wishing to know my views with regard to liberal studies. My answer is this: I respect no study, and deem no study good, which results in money-making. Such studies are profit-bringing occupations, useful only in so far as they give the mind a preparation and do not engage it permanently. One should linger upon them only so long as the mind can occupy itself with nothing greater; they are our apprenticeship, not our real work. Hence you see why "liberal studies" are so called; it is because they are studies worthy of a free-born gentleman. But there is only one really liberal study—that which gives a man his liberty. It is the study of wisdom, and that is lofty, brave, and great-souled. All other studies are puny and puerile. You surely do not believe that there is good in any of the subjects whose teachers are, as you see, men of the most ignoble and base stamp? We ought not to be learning such things; we should have done with learning them. . . .

"What then," you say, "do the liberal studies contribute nothing to our welfare?" Very much in other respects, but nothing at all as regards virtue. For even these arts of which I have spoken, though admittedly of a low grade— depending as they do upon handiwork—contribute greatly toward the equipment of life, but nevertheless have nothing to do with virtue. And if you inquire, "Why, then, do we educate our children in the liberal studies?" it is not because they can bestow virtue, but because they prepare the soul for the reception of virtue. Just as that "primary course," as the ancients called it, in grammar, which gave boys their elementary training, does not teach them the liberal arts, but prepares the ground for their early acquisition of these arts, so the liberal

Fig. 1.7. *A baker sells bread on the public square. First-century-c.e. fresco from Pompeii. Photo: Fotografica Foglia; Museo Archeologico Nazionale, Naples. Art Resource, New York.*

arts do not conduct the soul all the way to virtue, but merely set it going in that direction.

Posidonius divides the arts into four classes: first we have those which are common and low, then those which serve for amusement, then those which refer to the education of boys, and, finally, the liberal arts. The common sort belong to workmen and are mere hand-work; they are concerned with equipping life; there is in them no pretense to beauty or honor. . . . However, those alone are really liberal—or rather, to give them a truer name, "free"—whose concern is virtue.

(Seneca, *Epistle 88, On Liberal and Vocational Studies*,
trans. Gummere, LCL)

The Indignity of Appearing "Weak"

At least from the time of the late republic and on into the early empire, Roman society explicitly noticed and valued social strength. Terms for social strength include *influence* and *power* or their cognates in the selections that follow. With the exception of Rom 15:1, where the term *strong* seems to refer to a specific group who felt free to eat meat and drink wine (Rom 14:2, 21), Paul frequently identifies himself as weak (see 1 Cor 4:10; 9:22; 2 Cor 6:4-10; 11:16-33; 12:1-10; 13:4; Gal 4:13-14). Such self-presentation might have seemed scandalous to people in a society that placed such value on social strength, as two letters from Seneca demonstrate.

18. The importance of avoiding discomfort (Seneca)

Let us, however, as far as we can, avoid discomforts as well as dangers, and withdraw to safe ground, by thinking continually how we may repel all objects of fear. If I am not mistaken, there are three main classes of these: we fear want, we fear sickness, and we fear the troubles which result from the force of the stronger person. And of all these, that which shakes us most is the dread which hangs over us from our neighbor's strength.

(Seneca, *Epistle* 14.3-4, trans. Gummere, LCL, modified)

19. The importance of avoiding contempt (Seneca)

Contempt remains to be discussed. He who has made this quality an adjunct of his own personality, who is despised because he wishes to be despised and not because he must be despised, has the measure of contempt under his control. Any inconveniences in this respect can be dispelled by honorable occupations and by friendships with men who have influence with an influential person; with these men it will profit you to engage but not to entangle yourself, lest the cure may cost you more than the risk.

(Seneca, *Epistle* 105.5, trans. Gummere, LCL)[21]

20. On being intimidated by the powerful (Pliny)

The risk involved in engaging with socially powerful people can be seen in the way the younger Pliny, Roman governor of Bithynia, later described his decision to continue to defend a client before an impressive body of judges—including friends of Caesar—despite being warned in a dream to give it up. (Note that Paul also had contacts with people in Caesar's household, most probably socially powerful slaves who worked for the emperor [Phil 4:22].)

I had undertaken to act on behalf of Junius Pastor when I dreamed that my mother-in-law came and begged me on her knees to give up the case. I was very young at the time and I was about to plead in the Centumviral Court before the most powerful citizens and even before friends of Caesar.[22] Any one of these considerations could have shaken my resolve after such a depressing dream, but I carried on, believing that "the best and only omen is to fight for your country" [*Iliad* 12.243]. For my pledged word was as sacred to me as my country or as anything dearer than that. I won my case, and it was that speech which drew attention to me and set me on the threshold of a successful career.

(Pliny, *Epistle* 1.18.3, trans. Radice, LCL, modified)

In another letter Pliny comments on the challenge of adjudicating legal cases against socially powerful people, in this case a deceased proconsul who was being tried posthumously along with the man's living accomplices.

21. THE WEIGHT OF THE POWERFUL IN COURT (PLINY)

It looked as though we should run short of time and lose our breath and voice if we bundled so many accusations and defendants all together, so to speak, and then the large number of names and charges might exhaust the attention of the magistrates and possibly leave them in confusion. Moreover, the combined influence of the individuals concerned might procure for each the effect of the whole, and, finally, the most powerful might make scapegoats of the humble, and so escape at their expense. Privilege and self-interest are most likely to triumph when they can be concealed behind a mask of severity.

(Pliny, *Epistle* 3.9.9, trans. Radice, LCL, modified)

22. THE "WEAKNESS" OF THE MANY WHO OBSERVE TORAH (HORACE)

"Weakness" could also be associated with particular ethnicities. Horace, writing during the reign of the emperor Augustus, associates weakness with the religious sensitivities of those who practice Jewish observances. In a satire he describes being accosted by an overly talkative acquaintance. When a friend approaches, he tries to signal that he wishes to be rescued from conversation, but the second acquaintance puts him off, claiming respect for the Jewish Sabbath.

Cruelly arch, he laughs, and pretends not to take the hint: anger galled my liver. "Certainly, [said I,] you said that you wanted to communicate something to me in private."

"I remember it very well; but will tell it you at a better opportunity; today is the thirtieth Sabbath. Would you affront the circumcised Jews?"

I reply, "I have no scruple [on that account]."

"But I have. I am something weaker, one of the multitude. You must forgive me: I will speak with you on another occasion." And has this sun arisen so disastrous upon me! The wicked rogue runs away.

(Horace, *Satire* 1.9.68-72)[23]

23. UPPER-CLASS PERCEPTIONS OF AN IMPRISONED CHRISTIAN LEADER (LUCIAN)

If Paul made a great deal of presenting himself as a "slave of Christ," he also emphasized his multiple imprisonments for the sake of Christ (2 Cor 6:5; 11:23; Phil 1:12-18; Phlm 1; compare Eph 3:1; 4:1; 6:20). In Paul's day, imprisonment was not itself a form of punishment, as it often is today. Imprisonment functioned rather as a necessary preliminary to standing trial. One would be imprisoned only until one could be tried in court. The court's verdict might be release, beating and then release, forced labor, exile, or execution, but not more imprisonment.

Paul's self-presentation as prisoner and the care that some of the assemblies showed to him while he was imprisoned (Phil 2:25; 4:10, 18; compare Col 4:18) is consistent with the teaching elsewhere that followers of Jesus should care for the imprisoned (Matt 25:36-45; Mark 13:11; Luke 21:12; Heb 10:34; 13:3; Rev 1:9; 2:10). That expectation became so normative that it could serve as the stereotypical target of satire, as in this biting account from the second century c.e. Lucian of Samosata describes a charlatan, Proteus (or Peregrinus, "Pilgrim"), who masqueraded as a Christian missionary in order to garner support from gullible communities (and thus avoid prosecution for murdering his father). The extract reveals Lucian's contempt for such solicitude toward the imprisoned.

> It was then that [Proteus] learned the wondrous lore of the Christians, by associating with their priests and scribes in Palestine. And—how else could it be?—in an instant he made them all look like children, for he was prophet, cult-leader, head of the synagogue, and everything, all by himself. He interpreted and explained some of their books and even composed many, and they revered him as a god, made use of him as a lawgiver, and set him down as a protector, next after that other, to be sure, whom they still worship, the man who was crucified in Palestine because he introduced this new cult into the world.
>
> Then at length Proteus was arrested for this and thrown into prison, which itself gave him no little reputation as an asset for his future career and the charlatanism and notoriety-seeking that he loved. Well, when he had been imprisoned, the Christians, regarding the incident as a calamity, left nothing undone in the effort to rescue him. Then, as this was impossible, every other form of attention was shown him, not in any casual way but with due diligence, and from the very break of day aged widows and orphan children could be seen waiting near the prison, while their officials even slept inside with him after bribing the guards. Then elaborate meals were brought in, and sacred books of theirs were read aloud, and excellent Peregrinus—for he still went by that name—was called by them "the new Socrates."
>
> Indeed, people came even from the cities in Asia, sent by the Christians at their common expense, to help and defend and encourage the hero. They show incredible speed whenever any such public action is taken; for in no time they lavish their all. So it was then in the case of Peregrinus; much money came to him from them by reason of his imprisonment, and he procured not a little revenue from it. The poor wretches have convinced themselves, first and foremost, that they are going to be immortal and live for all time, in consequence of which they despise death and even willingly give themselves into custody; most of them. Furthermore, their first lawgiver persuaded them that they are all brothers of one another after they have transgressed once for all by denying the Greek gods and by worshipping that crucified sophist himself and living under his laws. Therefore they despise all things indiscriminately and consider them common property, receiving such doctrines traditionally without any definite evidence. So if any charlatan and trickster, able to profit by opportunity, comes among them, he quickly acquires sudden wealth by imposing upon simple folk.

However, Peregrinus was freed by the then governor of Syria, a man who was fond of philosophy. Aware of his recklessness and that he would gladly die in order that he might leave behind him a reputation for it, he freed him, not considering him worthy even of the usual punishment of scourging.

(Lucian, *Passing of Peregrinus* 11-14, trans. Harmon, LCL, modified)

The "Obedience of Faith among the Nations"

Another striking aspect of Paul's self-presentation is that he regularly sounds echoes of what we might consider the *political* language of Roman magistrates and the rhetoric of civic forums. Beyond his use of the term *ekklēsia*, discussed above, scholars have long noted that the Greek term *euangelion*, normally translated "gospel" or "good news" (see Rom 1:1, 16-17; 2:16; 15:19) was also used in connection with the emperor and especially in the celebration of the wondrous benefits that Augustus had brought to the world. As we shall see further in chapter 3, the modern distinction of "political" and "religious" language does not accord with the way these themes were blended in the Roman world.

24. The Priene inscription

In an inscription from Priene in Asia Minor,[24] the leaders of various cities in the province decree that the birthday of Augustus shall be regarded as a holiday and celebrated at the same time that terms of office begin. Although it is known as "the Priene Inscription," copies have been found also in Apamea, Eumeneia, and Dorylaeum. Note the exalted language about the birth of Augustus as the start of a new creation for the world; note also the use of the term *euangelion*, here in the plural, to refer to the "good news" regarding Augustus's reign.

> It seemed good to the Greek cities in Asia, on the recommendation of the high priest Apollonius, son of Menophilos from Arcadia, since providence, in divinely ordering our existence, has shown esteem and a lavish outlay has embellished the good—perfection—onto life by displaying Augustus, whom virtue has filled for the benefit of humankind, while graciously giving us and those after us a Savior who has ended war, setting things right in peace, and since Caesar when revealed surpassed the hopes of all who had anticipated the good news [*euangelia*],[25] not only going beyond the benefits of those who had preceded him, but rather leaving no hope of surpassing him for those who will come, because of him the birthday of God began good news [*euangelia*] for the world.[26]

25. The Emperor Gaius (Caligula) as false herald (Philo)

Some measure of the way "religious" and "political" themes could overlap can be derived from the way Philo of Alexandria (20–54 c.e.) discusses the emperor Gaius's descent into cruelty and madness. Here he describes Gaius's predilection for appearing in public in the figure of one or another of the Greek gods Hermes, Apollo, or Ares. Philo considers the emperor's imposture as Hermes particularly offensive because the true duty of the "interpreter of the gods" is to proclaim benefits to all humanity; but Gaius became, in effect, an antievangelist, a false herald (*kēryx*).

> So great a frenzy possessed him, so wild and delirious an insanity, that leaving the demigods below he proceeded to advance upwards and armed himself to attack the honors paid by their worshippers to the deities held to be greater and divine on both sides [that is, by humans and gods alike], Hermes, Apollo, and Ares. To take Hermes first, he arrayed himself with herald's staffs, sandals and mantles, a grotesque exhibition of order in disorder, consistency in confusion, reason in derangement. . . .
>
> Then those who saw these things were struck with amazement at the strange contradiction, marveling how one whose actions were the opposite of those whose honors he purposed to share as their equal did not think fit to practice their virtues and yet at the same time invested himself with their insignia each in turn. Yet surely these trappings and ornaments are set as accessories on images and statues as symbolically indicating the benefits which those thus honored provide for the human race.
>
> Hermes is shod with sandals like outstretched wings, why? Is it not because it befits the interpreter [*hermēneus*] and spokesman [*prophētēs*] of things divine,

Fig. 1.8. *The emperor Gaius (Caligula), marble bust, c. 40* C.E. *Museo Palazzo Massimo, Rome. Photo: Neil Elliott.*

whence also he gets his name of Hermes, that when he is the harbinger of good [*ta agatha diangellein*], since not even a wise man, much less a god, makes himself the announcer of evil, he should be very swift-footed, traveling with wellnigh the speed of wings in the zeal which brooks no delay. The news of things profitable should be carried quickly, bad news slowly if it is not permitted to leave it untold.

Again Hermes assumes the herald's staff as an emblem of covenants of reconciliation, for wars come to be suspended or ended through heralds establishing peace; wars where no heralds are admitted create endless calamities both for the assailants and the defenders. But for what useful purpose did Gaius assume the sandals? Was it that everything of ill report and evil name, instead of being buried in silence, as it should be, might be noised abroad with impetuous speed and resound on every side? And yet what need was there for this activity in locomotion? Standing where he was, he rained miseries untold one after another as from perennial fountains on every part of the inhabited world. And what need of the herald-staff had he whose every word and deed was not for peace but filled every house and city throughout Greece and the outside world with intestine wars! No, let him shed Hermes, let him purge himself of his lying claim to a title so ill-fitting, the impostor!

(Philo, *Embassy to Gaius* 93-94, 98-102, trans. Colson, LCL)

26. The submission of nations and "gifts of the peoples" (Virgil)

As we shall see in chapter 3, the Greek term *pistis*, like the Latin *fides*, has a broader range than we normally mean by "faith." "Faithfulness" and "loyalty" are better translations. The term was regularly used euphemistically to describe relationships of loyalty between the Roman Empire and the peoples it had conquered.

Paul's particular language about securing "the obedience of faith among the nations" (Rom 1:5) or, more simply, "the obedience of the nations" (Rom 15:18), along with his reference to his "priestly service" in bringing "the offering of the nations" to God (Rom 15:16), might well have struck echoes in his contemporaries' ears of language more customarily used by or about the emperor. One may compare, for example, the claims Augustus made about himself in the *Res Gestae Divi Augusti*, the "achievements" or "works" of the divine Augustus (see chapter 3). One should also compare Virgil's description of the great shield that Venus gave her son, Aeneas, the fabled ancestor of the Roman people. On the shield, Vulcan had depicted scenes prophesying the future of Aeneas's descendants, including the Battle of Actium (at which Octavius would defeat Mark Antony), Augustus's subsequent triumphs, and his acceptance of the tribute of conquered nations.

But [Augustus] Caesar, entering the walls of Rome in triple triumph, was dedicating to Italy's gods his immortal votive gift—three hundred mighty shrines throughout the city. The streets were ringing with gladness and games and shouting; in all the temples was a band of matrons, in all were altars, and before the altars slain steers covered the ground. He himself, seated at the snowy threshold of shining Phoebus, reviews the gifts of nations and hangs them on the proud portals. The conquered peoples move in long array, as diverse in fashion of dress and arms as in tongues. Here Mulciber had portrayed the Nomad race and the ungirt Africans, here the Leleges and Carians and quivered Gelonians. Euphrates moved now with humbler waves, and the Morini were there, furthest of mankind, and the Rhine of double horn, the untamed Dahae, and Araxes chafing at his bridge. Such sights [Aeneas] admires on the shield of Vulcan, his mother's gift, and, though he knows not the events, he rejoices in their representation, raising up on his shoulder the fame and fortunes of his children's children.

(Virgil, Aeneid 8.715-31, trans. Fairclough, LCL)

Paul's "Autobiography"

Paul's letters were written to established assemblies of followers of Jesus. They nevertheless give us some evidence—even if limited and indirect—of what Paul's initial presentation to an audience of potential adherents might have looked and sounded like. Though personal details in the letters are far sketchier than in the dramatic narratives in Acts, Paul did make aspects of his own biography a part of his proclamation.

27. TARSUS (STRABO)

It is Acts that identifies Paul as a "man of Tarsus" (9:11; 21:39; 22:3); Paul himself never mentions the city in his letters (though he does tell the Galatians that after receiving God's "revelation" of Christ he went into "the areas of Syria and Cilicia" (Gal 1:21, of which Tarsus was the capital). We have testimonies to the wealth of Tarsus from the fourth century B.C.E. The Seleucid ruler Antiochus IV made it a Greek city-state in 171 B.C.E.; Mark Antony rewarded the city for its allegiance by giving it independence and tax-free status in 42 B.C.E., a status that Octavian reaffirmed after he defeated Antony in 31 B.C.E. Strabo praised the city for its educational resources.

> The people at Tarsus have devoted themselves so eagerly, not only to philosophy, but also the whole round of education in general, that they have surpassed Athens, Alexandria, or any other place that can be named where there have been schools and lectures of philosophers. But it is so different from other cities that there the men who are fond of learning are all natives, and foreigners are not inclined to sojourn there; neither do these natives stay there, but they complete their education abroad; and when they have completed it they are pleased to live abroad, and but few go back home. . . . Further, the city of Tarsus has all kinds of schools of rhetoric; and in general it not only has a flourishing population but also is most powerful, and thus keeps up the reputation of the mother-city.
>
> (Strabo, Geographica 14.5.13, trans. Reasoner)

A Pharisee

In his letter to the Philippians Paul lists reasons he might have to boast, including being "a member of the people of Israel, of the tribe of Benjamin, a Hebrew born of

Hebrews; as to the law, a Pharisee" (3:5). The Pharisees were, at different times in the Hellenistic era, a powerful party involved in Jerusalem politics. By the Roman era, however, their influence seems to have waned, though they were something of a "loyal opposition" to the power of the Sadducees and the families that controlled the high priesthood. Our sources—Josephus, the New Testament, and later rabbinic literature—offer tantalizing clues that we continue to struggle to fit together. One scholar has written that "recent research on the Pharisees has paradoxically made them and their role in Palestinian society more obscure and difficult to describe"; even more enigmatic is the question how Diaspora Jews—and their non-Jewish neighbors— would have perceived Paul's claim to the role.[27]

Both Josephus and the Mishnah describe the Pharisees in contrast to the Sadducees—Josephus, in terms of their differing beliefs; the Mishnah, in terms of their opposite rulings regarding aspects of Torah observance.

28. Pharisees and Sadducees (Josephus)

Josephus describes three "schools" (*haireseis*) of Judaism in order to disparage a fourth "school" or "fourth philosophy," that of the Zealots, as a betrayal of genuine Jewish principles. In the course of these descriptions he contrasts the Pharisees and the Sadducees. The reference in this extract to "Fate" (*heimarmenē*) might be an effort to represent apocalyptic beliefs in terms of Hellenistic philosophy; Josephus's reference to a Pharisaic belief in the transference of souls (metempsychosis) is otherwise unattested.

> Of the two first-named schools, the Pharisees, who are considered the most accurate interpreters of the laws and hold the position of the leading sect, attribute everything to Fate [*heimarmenē*] and God; they hold that to act rightly or otherwise resets, indeed, for the most part with human beings, but that in each action Fate cooperates. Every soul, they maintain, is imperishable, but the soul of the good alone passes in to another body, while the souls of the wicked suffer eternal punishment.
>
> The Sadducees, the second of the orders, do away with Fate altogether, and remove God beyond, not merely the commission, but the very sight, of evil. They maintain that human beings have the free choice of good or evil, and that it rests with each person's will whether one follows the one or the other. As for the persistence of the soul after death, penalties in the underworld, and rewards, they will have none of them.
>
> (*Jewish War* 2.162-65, trans. Thackeray, LCL, modified)

29. Pharisees and Sadducees (m. Yadayim)

Notice the sorts of concerns that distinguished Pharisees and Sadducees according to this passage from the Mishnah: particular rulings concerning cleanness and uncleanness and concerning liability for damages.

> The Sadducees say, We cry out against you, O Pharisees, for you say, "The Holy Scriptures render the hands unclean," [and] "The writings of Hamiram

[probably Homer] do not render the hands unclean." Rabban Johanan b. Zakkai said, "Have we naught against the Pharisees save this!—for lo, they say, 'The bones of an ass are clean, and the bones of Johanan the High Priest are unclean.'" They said to him, "As is our love for them so is their uncleanness—that no man make spoons of the bones of his father or mother." He said to them, "Even so the Holy Scriptures: as is our love for them so is their uncleanness; [whereas] the writings of Hamiram which are held in no account do not really render the hands unclean.

The Sadducees say, "We cry out against you, O Pharisees, for you declare clean an unbroken stream of liquid" [that is, uncleanness cannot travel "up" the stream]. The Pharisees say, "We cry out against you, O Sadducees, for you declare clean a channel of water that flows from a burial ground." The Sadducees say, "We cry out against you, O Pharisees, for you say, 'If my ox or my ass have done an injury they are culpable, but if my bondman or my bondwoman have done an injury they are not culpable'—if, in the case of my ox or my ass (about which no commandments are laid upon me) I am responsible for the injury that they do, how much more in the case of my bondman or my bondwoman (about whom certain commandments are laid upon me) must I be responsible for the injury that they do!" They [the Pharisees] said to them [the Sadducees], "No!—as you argue concerning my ox or my ass (which have no understanding) would you likewise argue concerning my bondman or my bondwoman which have understanding?—for if I provoke him to anger he may go and set fire to another's stack of corn, and it is I that must make restitution!"

(*m. Yadayim* 4.6-7, trans. Danby, alt.)

A Persecutor of the *Ekklēsia*

Paul writes to the Galatians that they have no doubt heard about his "earlier life in Judaism," that he was "violently persecuting" the *ekklēsia* of God "and trying to destroy it" (Gal 1:13). Luke writes that Paul attended the stoning of Stephen (Acts 7:54-60) and then set about "ravaging" the *ekklēsia*, "entering house after house; dragging off both men and women, he committed them to prison" (8:3). Luke emphasizes Paul's personal antipathy to the followers of Jesus: "Still breathing threats and murder against the disciples of the Lord," he "went to the high priest and asked him for letters to the synagogues at Damascus" authorizing him to bring any followers of Jesus back "bound to Jerusalem" (9:1-2).

Why did Paul persecute the early *ekklēsiai*? Paula Fredriksen has evaluated different explanations that have been offered by interpreters and finds many of them historically improbable. It is unlikely, for example (though it is the view of "an almost universal consensus"), that Paul persecuted Jewish Christians "because they challenged religious principles fundamental to Judaism." Fredriksen finds little or no basis for the assumptions that these believers abandoned the observance of Torah; rather "everything we know about Jesus' original disciples indicates that they kept the Law."[28]

Neither would belief in a risen messiah who had been crucified have constituted a religious offense (despite Paul's argument in Gal 3:13, a "snarled passage" that Fredriksen considers only an impromptu argument directed to a specific situation).[29] The inclusion of non-Jews alongside Jews, even at table fellowship, might have appeared distasteful to individual Jews but was hardly a religious offense, as the widespread acceptance of non-Jews in synagogue life—and traveling to Jerusalem to offer sacrifices in the temple—attest.[30]

Fredriksen argues instead that it was the social and political volatility of the message proclaimed by these Jewish believers that caused alarm: "The enthusiastic proclamation of a messiah executed very recently as a political insurrectionist—a crucified messiah—combined with a vision of the approaching End preached also to Gentiles—this was dangerous. If it got abroad, it could endanger the whole Jewish community."[31] This concern for the precarious stability of Diaspora Jewish communities motivated Paul's efforts to suppress the messianic movement.

Most likely Paul was implementing the synagogue discipline based on Deuteronomy 25 and described in the Mishnah tractate *Makkot*, "Stripes" (or "lashes")—a discipline to which he himself was later subjected (2 Cor 11:24, on Roman civil punishment, 11:25). Although interpreters have offered different explanations for what offense a Jewish court might have found in the proclamation of Jesus, the most likely (and least theologically prejudicial) explanation is that proclaiming as messiah one known to have been executed by Rome would have sounded a politically incendiary note that jeopardized the already precarious situation of Jewish populations in Roman cities (on which see further chapter 4).[32]

30. Synagogue discipline (M. Makkoth)

The Mishnah tractate *Makkot*, "Stripes," lays out the reasons for imposing stripes as a disciplinary penalty, the limitations on the penalty, and the ultimate goal of restoration to the Jewish community.

> These are they who are to be scourged: he that has [sexual] connection with his sister, his father's sister, his mother's sister, his wife's sister, his brother's wife, his father's brother's wife, or a menstruant; a High Priest who married a widow, a common priest who married a woman who was divorced or who had performed *halitzah* [see Deut 25:7-9], an Israelite that married a bastard or a *Nethinah*, or the daughter of an Israelite that married a bastard or a *Nathin* [temple slave]. If a woman was a widow and also divorced [and a High Priest married her], he is thereby culpable on two counts. If a woman was divorced and had also performed *halitzah* [and a common priest married her], he is culpable only on one count. . . .
>
> [These also are to be scourged:] an unclean person who ate Hallowed Things, or who entered the Temple while he was unclean, or who ate the fat or the blood, the Remnant, or the Refuse [of the offerings], or [an offering] that was become unclean; or who slaughtered [an offering] or offered it outside the Temple; or who ate at Passover what was leavened, or who ate or did any act of work on the Day of Atonement.

(Other ritual offenses follow.)

How many stripes do they inflict on a man? Forty save one, for it is written, "By number forty" [Deut 25:2-3]; [that is to say], a number near to forty. R. Judah says: He suffers the forty stripes in full. And where does he suffer the added one? Between the shoulders. . . .

How do they scourge him? They bind his two hands to a pillar on either side, and the minister of the synagogue lays hold on his garments—if they are torn they are torn, if they are utterly rent they are utterly rent—so that he bares his chest. A stone is set down behind him on which the minister of the synagogue stands with a strap of calf-hide in his hand, doubled and re-doubled, and two [other] straps that rise and fall [are fastened] thereto.

The hand-piece of the strap is one handbreadth long and one handbreadth wide; and its end must reach to his navel [the navel of the man being struck on the shoulder]. He gives him one third of the stripes in front [on the chest] and two-thirds behind [on the bared shoulder]; and he may not strike him when he is standing or when he is sitting, but only when he is bending low, for it is written, "The judge shall cause him to lie down" [Deut 25:2]. And he that smites, smites with his one hand with all his might. . . .

All they who are liable to Extirpation, if they have been scourged are no longer liable to Extirpation, for it is written, "And thy brother seem vile unto thee" [Deut 25:3] when he is scourged then he is thy brother. So R. Hanina b. Gamaliel. Moreover R. Hanina b. Gamaliel said: "If he that commits one transgression thereby forfeits his soul, how much more, if he performs one religious duty, shall his soul be restored to him!" R. Simeon says: "From the same place we may learn [the like], for it is written, 'Even the souls that do them shall be cut off'; and it says, 'Which if a man do he shall live by them' [Lev 18:5]; thus to him that sits and commits no transgression is given a reward as to one that performs a religious duty." R. Simeon the son of Rabbi says: "Lo, it says, 'Only be sure that thou eat not the blood, for the blood is the life . . .' [Deut 12:23]; if a man keeps himself apart from blood (which man's soul abhors) he receives a reward, how much more, if he keeps himself apart from robbery and incest (which a man's soul longs after and covets), shall he gain merit for himself and his generations and the generations of his generations to the end of all generations!"

R. Hananiah b. Akashya says: "The Holy One, blessed is he, was minded to grant merit to Israel; therefore hath he multiplied for them the Law and commandments, as it is written. 'It pleased the Lord for his righteousness' sake to magnify the Law and make it honorable' [Isa 42:21]."

(*m. Makkot* 3.1-3, 10-12, trans. Danby, modified)[33]

Witness of the Heavenly Christ

At the heart of Paul's self-understanding as an apostle was a visionary experience: "Have I not seen Jesus our Lord?" (1 Cor 9:1). Christ's appearance qualified Paul to take his place among the other apostles: "Last of all . . . he appeared also to me" (1 Cor 15:8). This visionary experience was, for Paul, a divine revelation (an *apokalypsis*): "God . . . was pleased to reveal [*apokalyptein*] his son to me" (Gal 1:15-16).

Although Acts repeatedly depicts this "revelation" as a terrestrial experience— that is, Paul saw a bright light and heard a voice while traveling along the road to Damascus (Acts 9:1-9; 22:6-11; 26:12-18)—Paul himself never gives such an account in his own letters. Instead, in 2 Corinthians 12, in the midst of a heated argument regarding "visions and revelations" (*optasias kai apokalypseis*), he speaks obliquely of "a person in Christ" who "was caught up to the third heaven" and "heard things that are not to be told" (NRSV). A number of scholars have shown that elements of Paul's language here fit very well with what we know from somewhat later texts as a rich tradition of visionary experience in Hellenistic and later rabbinic Judaism.

This tradition was fueled by tantalizing biblical descriptions of righteous mortals who had been taken up into heaven, like Enoch (Gen 5:24) or Elijah, who was whisked heavenward on a "chariot of fire" (2 Kgs 2:11); of heavenly visions in which human beings were allowed to behold the very presence of God seated upon a heavenly throne (Isa 6:1-2); or of a figure in human form ("like a son of man") similarly enthroned and empowered by God (the Ancient of Days, Dan 7:13-14) or even identified with "the appearance of the likeness of the glory of the LORD" (Ezek 1:26-28). This Jewish visionary tradition also owed much to Hellenistic cosmological speculation.[34]

Much of what would come to be called the *merkavah* tradition of Jewish mysticism (from the chariot, *merkābâ*, in 2 Kings 2 and from the exotic description of a wheeled conveyance for the "living creatures" in Ezekiel 1, later identified as a chariot) is found in writings later than Paul's period. But the constellation of elements— heavenly ascent, visions of paradise, the heavenly worship given to God by angels, and perhaps of greatest importance for understanding Paul, the transformation of the seer through participation in the divine being and the heavenly throne room—are

Fig. 1.9. *The prophet Ezekiel's vision of restored bodies and a restored ark of the covenant. Fresco from the synagogue at Dura Europos, Syria, c. 239 C.E. Josephus's mention of Pharisaic interest in "fate" may refer to apocalyptic traditions concerning a future life beyond death. Photo: Art Resource, New York.*

already present in the Enoch literature, the book of *Jubilees*, and the "angelic liturgy" texts (the *Songs of the Sabbath Sacrifice* [4Q400–407; 11Q17] found at Qumran).

Paul does not identify the vision described in 2 Corinthians 12 with his own first vision of the risen Christ. Indeed, the implication is that Paul experienced several ecstatic encounters with Christ over the course of his apostolic career. But it is nevertheless possible that the first "revelation" of Christ to Paul was one such event.[35] Though Paul's visionary experience is unlike those described in other Jewish texts, in that he identifies the heavenly being to whom dominion shall be given as the crucified Jesus, the vocabulary and imagery Paul uses seem to place him within a broader mystical-apocalyptic tradition as our earliest first-person testimony to it.

31. ANGELIC WORSHIP (*SONGS OF THE SABBATH SACRIFICE*)

Though fragmentary, a number of texts from Cave 4 at Qumran, dated to the first century B.C.E., give evidence of keen interest among some Second-Temple Jews in the heavenly world described in prophetic visionary accounts. These texts describe ongoing angelic worship of God, presumably going on at the same time sacrifices are offered on earth—though the language of an "inner Temple" might suggest that the texts provide an access to heavenly worship distinct from the sacrifices in the (earthly) temple. Note the references to heavenly chariots and a "throne-chariot." These texts are of tremendous importance for interpreting language about angelic worship in 1 Corinthians, Colossians, Ephesians, and other early Christian texts as well. Missing text, in brackets, has been reconstructed on the basis of patterns seen in the same or other fragments; "gods" translates the Hebrew *'lwhym*.

> [To the Master. Song of the holocaust of the] first [Sabba]th, on the fourth of the first month.
> Praise [the God of . . .] the "gods" [*'ĕlōhîm*] of supreme holiness; in [his] divine [kingship, rejoice. For he has established] supreme holiness among the everlastingly holy, the Holy of Holies, to be for him the priests of [the inner Temple in his royal sanctuary], ministers of the Presence in his glorious innermost Temple chamber. In the congregation of all the gods [*'ĕlîm*] of [knowledge, and in the congregation of all the ["gods" of] God, he engraved his precepts for all the spiritual works, and [his glorious] judgments [for all who lay the foundations of] knowledge, the people (endowed with) his glorious understanding, the "gods" who are close to knowledge . . . of eternity and from the fountain of holiness to the sanctuary of supreme [holiness] . . . prie[sts] of the inner Temple, ministers of the Presence of the [most] holy King . . . his glory. They shall grow in strength decree by decree to be seven [eternal councils. For he fo]unded them [for] himself as the most [holy, who minister in the h]oly of holies . . . do not endure [those who per]vert the way. There is [n]othing impure in their sanctuaries. He engraved for them [precepts relating to ho]ly gifts; by them, all the everlastingly holy shall sanctify themselves. He shall purify the [luminously] pure [to repa]y all those who render their way crooked. Their expiations shall obtain his goodwill for all those who repent from sin . . . knowledge among the priests of the inner Temple, and from their mouth (proceed) the teachings of the holy with the judgments of [his glory] . . . his [gra]ces for everlasting

merciful forgiveness. In his zealous vengeance . . . he has established for himself as priests of the inner Temple, the most holy . . . of gods, the priests of the highest heights who are near [to . . .]

(4Q400 frg. 1.1, trans. Vermes)

. . . His glorious chariots. When they go . . . they do not turn aside . . . but advance straight . . .

For the Mas[ter. Song of the holocaust of] the twelfth [S]abbath [on the twenty-first of the third month.]

[Praise the God of . . . w]onder, and exalt Him . . . of glory in the te[nt of the God of] knowledge. The [cheru]bim prostate themselves before Him and bless. As they rise, a whispered divine voice [is heard], and there is a roar of praise. When they drop their wings, there is a [whispere]d divine voice. The cherubim bless the image of the throne-chariot above the firmament, [and] they praise [the majes]ty of the luminous firmament beneath His seat of glory. When the wheels advance, Angels of holiness come and go. From between His glorious wheels, there is as it were a fiery vision of most holy spirits.

About them, the appearance of rivulets of fire in the likeness of gleaming brass, and a work of . . . radiance in many-colored glory, marvelous pigments, clearly mingled. The spirits of the living "gods" ['ĕlîm] move perpetually with the glory of the marvelous chariot(s). The whispered voice of blessing accompanies the roar of their advance, and they praise the Holy One on their way of return. When they ascend, they ascend marvelously and when they settle, they stand still. The sound of joyful praise is silenced and there is a whispered blessing of the "gods" in all the camps of God.

And the sound of praise . . . from among all their divisions . . . and all their numbered ones praise, each in his turn.

(4Q405 frg. 20, col. 2, 21-22, trans. Vermes)

32. HEAVENLY REVELATIONS GIVEN TO ENOCH

Genesis declares that Enoch "walked with God; then he was no more, because God took him" (5:24). That cryptic statement became the headwaters for a torrent of Jewish tradition in the Hellenistic age that claimed Enoch first as its champion, then as a medium of revelation. In *Jubilees* (mid-second century B.C.E.) Enoch is described as taken up into heaven, where he received revelation in the company of the angels for "six jubilees" (three hundred years). He also offered priestly service in a miraculously preserved Garden of Eden. He thus serves in the text as an exemplar of right observance and, as the first author of a divinely inspired text (he "wrote a testimony" and "deposited" it "upon the earth," 4:18-19), becomes a heavenly accreditation for the judgments and opinions presented in the book.

And [Enoch] saw what was and what will be in a vision of his sleep as it will happen among the children of men in their generations until the day of judgment. He saw and knew everything and wrote his testimony and deposited the testimony upon the earth against the children of men and their generations. . . .

And he was therefore with the angels of God six jubilees of years. And they showed him everything which is on earth and in the heavens, the dominion of the sun. And he wrote everything, and bore witness to the Watchers, the ones who sinned with the daughters of men because they began to mingle themselves with the daughters of men so that they might be polluted. And Enoch bore witness against all of them. And he was taken from among the children of men, and we led him to the garden of Eden for greatness and honor. And behold, he is there writing condemnation and judgment of the world, and all of the evils of the children of men. And because of him none of the water of the Flood came upon the whole land of Eden, for he was put there for a sign and so that he might bear witness against all of the children of men so that he might relate all of the deeds of the generations until the day of judgment. And he offered the incense which is acceptable before the Lord in the evening (at) the holy place on Mount Qater. For the Lord has four (sacred) places upon the earth: the garden of Eden and the mountain which you are upon today, Mount Sinai, and Mount Zion, which will be sanctified in the new creation for the sanctification of the earth. On account of this the earth will be sanctified from all sin and from pollution throughout eternal generations.

(*Jubilees* 4:19, 21-26, trans. Wintermute)

33. ENOCH'S HEAVENLY JOURNEY AND TRANSFORMATION (1 ENOCH 70-71)

The explosion of Enochic literature (and of an "Enochic movement") sometime between the mid-second century B.C.E. and the early first century C.E. shows the interest in Judea in finding revelatory figures—mortals who had ascended into the heavens to receive knowledge and wisdom—in the Torah as well as the prophetic writings. The book we call *1 Enoch* is available in its entirety only in Ethiopic translation (in more than forty manuscripts), but much earlier fragments in Aramaic, Greek, and Latin are known to us. The numerous Aramaic fragments from Qumran, which include every section except the "Similitudes" (chapters 37–71), show the popularity of the Enochic library in the late second and early first century B.C.E. Although we cannot establish that the Similitudes were already extant in Paul's day, they show the combination of features that marked what would come to be called the *merkavah* tradition: interest in the heavenly "chariot," the angelic host, the revelation of secret knowledge, and the transformation into a heavenly being of the mortal who is taken up into heaven and receives revelation.

> And after this, while he was living, his name was raised
> into the presence of that son of man
> And into the presence of the Lord of Spirits
> from among those who dwell on the earth.
> He was raised on the chariots of the wind,
> and his name departed <from among them.>

[Enoch's account] And from that day, I was not reckoned among them; and he set me between two winds, between the North and the West, where the angels took cords to measure for me the place of the chosen and the righteous. And there I saw the first fathers and the righteous, who were dwelling in that place from of old.

And after that, my spirit was taken away,
    and it ascended to heaven.
And I saw the sons of the holy angels,
    and they were stepping on flames of fire;
And their garments were white, as were their tunics,
    and the light of their faces was like snow.
And I saw two rivers of fire,
    and the light of that fire shone like hyacinth,
    and I fell on my face before the Lord of Spirits.
And the angel Michael, one of the archangels, took me by my right
    hand and raised me up,
    and he brought me out to all the secrets;
and he showed me all the secrets of mercy,
    and he showed me all the secrets of righteousness.
And he showed me all the secrets of the ends of heaven and all the
    treasuries of the stars,
    and all the luminaries emerge from there before the holy ones.
And he took my spirit—even me, Enoch—to the heaven of heavens,
    and I saw there, as it were, <a house> built of hailstones,
    and between those stones were tongues of living fire.
And my spirit saw <in that light> a circle that encircled that house
    of fire,
    from its four sides (came) rivers full of living fire,
    and they encircled that house.
And around it were Seraphim and Cherubim, and Ophanim,
    and those who do not sleep,
    but guard the throne of his glory.
And I saw angels that could not be counted,
    thousands of thousands and ten thousand times ten thousand;
    they were surrounding that house.
And Michael and Raphael and Gabriel and Phanuel,
    and the holy angels who (are in) the heights of heaven,
    were going in and out of that house.
And out of that house came
    Michael and Raphael and Gabriel and Phanuel
    and many holy angels without number.
And with them was the Head of Days,
    and his head was white and pure as wool,
    and his apparel was indescribable.
And I fell on my face,
    and all my flesh melted,
    and my spirit was transformed.
                       (*1 Enoch* 70–71, trans. Nickelsburg and VanderKam)

34. ENOCH IN PARADISE (2 ENOCH)

Another Enoch text, 2 Enoch, similarly cannot be dated with any certainty earlier than the late first century.[36] Nevertheless, it is at least intriguing because, as Paul does in 2 Corinthians 12, it locates paradise in "the third heaven."

> And those men took me from there, and they brought me up to the third heaven, and set me down [there]. Then I looked downward, and I saw Paradise. And that place is inconceivably pleasant. And I saw the trees in full flower. And their fruits were ripe and pleasant-smelling, with every food in yield and giving off profusely a pleasant fragrance.
>
> And in the midst (of them was) the tree of life, at that place where the Lord takes a rest when he goes into paradise. And that tree is indescribable for pleasantness and fine fragrance, and more beautiful than any (other) created thing that exists. And from every direction it has an appearance which is gold-looking and crimson, and with the form of fire. And it covers the whole of Paradise. And it has something of every orchard tree and of every fruit. And its root is in Paradise at the exits that leads to the earth. . . .
>
> And there are three hundred angels, very bright, who look after Paradise; and with never-ceasing voice and pleasant singing they worship the Lord every day and hour. And I said, "How very pleasant is this place!"
> And those men said to me . . . "This place, Enoch, has been prepared for
>   the righteous,
> who suffer every kind of calamity in their life
> and who afflict their souls,
> and who avert their eyes from injustice,
> and who carry out righteous judgment,
> and who give bread to the hungry,
> and who cover the naked with clothing,
> and who lift up the fallen,
> and who help the injured and the orphans,
> and who walk without a defect before the face of the Lord,
> and who worship him only: even for them this place has been prepared
>   as an eternal inheritance."
>
> (2 Enoch 8–9, trans. Andersen)

35. MOSES AS RECIPIENT OF HEAVENLY REVELATION (PHILO)

Philo of Alexandria wrote a little earlier than Paul. Relying in part on creative interpretation of the Greek scriptures, he could describe Moses as having been taken up into heaven, set at God's side, and shown unutterable mysteries, being himself transformed into a divine being, a "god" (theos).

> And so, as [Moses] abjured the accumulation of lucre, and the wealth whose influence is mighty among men, God rewarded him by giving him instead the greatest and most perfect wealth. That is the wealth of the whole earth and sea and rivers, and of all the other elements and the combinations which they form. . . . For if, as the proverb says, what belongs to friends is common, and the prophet is called the friend of God [Exod 33:11], it would follow that he shares

also God's possessions, so far as it is serviceable. . . . Again, was not the joy of his partnership [*koinōnia*] with the Father and Maker of all magnified also by the honor of being deemed worthy to bear the same title? For he was named god [*theon*, Exod 7:1 LXX] and king of the whole nation, and entered, we are told, into the darkness where God was [Exod 20:21], that is, into the unseen, invisible, incorporeal and archetypal essence of existing things. Thus he beheld what is hidden from the sight of mortal nature and, in himself and his life displayed for all to see, he has set before us, like some well-wrought picture, a piece of work beautiful and godlike, a model for those who are willing to copy it.

(Philo, *Life of Moses* 155-59, trans. Colson, LCL, adapted)

36. The assumption of Moses (Philo)

There is also another proof that the mind is immortal, which is of this nature: There are some persons whom God, advancing to higher degrees of improvement, has enabled to soar above all species and genera, having placed them near himself; as he says to Moses, "But stand thou here with me" [Deut 5:31]. When, therefore, Moses is about to die, he is not added to one class, nor does he forsake

Fig. 1.10. *Moses and the burning bush. Fresco from the synagogue at Dura Europos, Syria, c. 239 c.e. Photo: Art Resource, New York.*

another, as the men before him had done; nor is he connected with "addition" or "subtraction," but "by means of the word of the Cause of all things, by whom the whole world was made" [Deut 34:5]. He departs to another abode, that you may understand from this that God accounts a wise man as entitled to equal honor with the world itself, having both created the universe, and raised the perfect man from the things of earth up to himself by the same word.

But when [God] gave him the use of all earthly things and suffered him to dwell among them, he assigned to him not such a power as he might exercise in common with an earthly governor or monarch, by which he should forcibly rule over the passions of the soul, but he appointed him to be a sort of god, making the whole of the body, and the mind, which is the ruler of the body, subjects and slaves to him; "For I give thee," says he, "as a god to Pharaoh" [Exod 7:1].

But God is not susceptible of any subtraction or addition, inasmuch as he is complete and entirely equal to himself. In reference to which it is said of Moses, "That no one is said to know of his tomb" [Deut 34:6]; for who could be competent to perceive the migration of a perfect soul to the living God? Nor do I even believe that the soul itself while awaiting this event was conscious of its own improvement, inasmuch as it was at that time becoming gradually divine; for God, in the case of those persons whom he is about to benefit, does not take him who is to receive the advantage into his counsels, but is accustomed rather to pour his benefits ungrudgingly upon him without his having any previous anticipation of them.

(Philo, *On the Sacrifices of Abel and Cain* 8-9, trans. Yonge)

37. The Dangers of visionary speculation (the Mishnah)

In the midst of a discussion of the Festal Offering, the Mishnah tractate *Ḥagigah* sounds a cautionary note regarding controversial, lurid, or dangerously speculative topics, including Ezekiel's fantastic vision of a heavenly chariot (*merkavah*) in Ezekiel 1, from which the Jewish tradition of *merkavah* mysticism derives its name.

J. W. Bowker points out that the concern the rabbis express here is halakhic: that is, it has to do with the risk of approaching the holy God in a state of impurity. It is not a "doctrinal" concern: figures as "orthodox" as Yohanan ben Zakkai are also attested as the recipients of such visions. On the other hand, Alan F. Segal has argued that speculation about a second "power" in heaven ultimately was rejected as unacceptable by the rabbinic tradition.[37]

> The forbidden degrees [of sexual contact: Lev 18:6-23] may not be expounded before three persons, nor the Story of Creation before two, nor the Chariot [that is, Ezekiel 1] before one alone, unless he is a Sage who understands of his own knowledge. Whoever gives his mind to four things, it were better for him if he had not come into the world: what is above? What is beneath? What was beforetime? And what will be hereafter? And whoever takes no thought for the honor of his Maker, it were better for him if he had not come into the world.
>
> (*m. Ḥagigah* 2.1, trans. Danby, modified)

38. Concerns about specific biblical texts (the Mishnah)

Similarly, the tractate *Megillah* discourages the public interpretation of certain potentially controversial or provocative passages, including Ezekiel's vision, in worship.

> The story of Reuben [Gen 35:22] is read out but not interpreted; the story of Tamar [Gen 38:10-30] is read out and interpreted. The first story of the calf [Exod 2:1-20] is read out and interpreted, and the second [Exod 32:21-25] is read out but not interpreted. The Blessing of the Priests [Num 6:24-26] and the story of David [2 Sam 11:2-17] and of Amnon [2 Sam 13:1-39] are read out but not interpreted. They may not use the chapter of the Chariot [Ezekiel 1] as a reading from the Prophets; but R. Judah permits it. R. Eliezer says: "They do not use the chapter 'Cause Jerusalem to know' [Ezek 16:1] as a reading from the Prophets."
>
> (*m. Megillah* 4.10, trans. Danby, modified)

39. A revelatory dream from the Hellenistic world (Hippocrates)

Dreams or revelatory visions (see Acts 16:9) were commonplace in Hellenistic literature. Here Hippocrates, a physician from the age of Socrates, describes the beginning of such a revelation, occasioned by the god Asclepius and mediated by the goddess Truth.

> In that night . . . I had a dream, from which, I believe, nothing dangerous will come. But I woke up terrified, for I thought I saw Asclepius himself, and he came near to me. . . . But Asclepius did not look as he usually does in pictures, gentle and mild, but his gestures were wild and quite terrible to behold. Dragons followed behind him . . . but the god stretched out his hand to me, and I took it and asked him to heal me and not to leave me. However, he said, "At the moment you need nothing from me, but this goddess . . . will lead you. . . ." So I turned around and saw a large woman, with a simple hairdo, splendidly clothed. Pure light streamed forth from the pupils of her eyes, like lightning from stars. And the god withdrew from me, but the woman grasped my hand. . . . As she then turned around, I said, "Please tell me who you are and how I should address you." She replied, "'Truth' . . . which you see appearing: 'shine.'"
>
> (Hippocrates, *Letter* 15, trans. Boring)

40. A Roman general dreams of his destiny (Cicero)

The Roman world also knew its portentous visions of heaven and of the future. In the sixth book of his *De Republica*, Cicero narrates the dream of the Roman general Publius Cornelius Scipio (185–129 B.C.E.), which Cicero places some two years before his decisive defeat of Carthage (in 146).

Note the "revelatory" character of the dream, in Cicero's telling. Scipio's grandfather, the general Scipio Africanus, assures Scipio of his own impending military conquests and of the glorious future of the Roman people but also warns him that he will be required to assume the responsibilities of dictator of Rome and reverse the reforms of Tiberius Gracchus, which Cicero considered odious. Cicero apparently recognizes the popularity of the Gracchian reforms, however, allowing the protests of his implied readers almost to interrupt his narration and awaken Scipio from his dream! It is, at last, a vision of the infinite expanse of the heavens that gives Scipio the assurance he needs to perform his duty. The narration begins as Scipio has been welcomed by the Numidian king, who had been given his throne by Scipio's own grandfather.

> At a later hour, after an entertainment of royal magnificence, we prolonged our conversation far into the night, while the old man talked to me about nothing else but Africanus, rehearsing not only all that he had done, but all that he had said. When we parted to go to our rest, sleep took a stronger hold on me than usual, on account both of the fatigue of my journey and of the lateness of the hour.
>
> In my sleep, I suppose in consequence of our conversation . . . Africanus appeared to me, with an aspect that reminded me more of his bust than of his real face. I shuddered when I saw him. But he said: "Preserve your presence of mind, Scipio; be not afraid, and commit to memory what I shall say to you.
>
> "Do you see that city, which was brought through me into subjection to the Roman people, but now renews its old hostility, and cannot remain quiet,"—and he showed me Carthage from a high place full of stars, shining and splendid,—"against which you, being little more than a common soldier, are coming to fight? In two years from now, you, as Consul, will overthrow this city, and you will obtain of your own right the surname which up to this time you hold as inherited from me. When you shall have destroyed Carthage, shall have celebrated your triumph over it, shall have been Censor, and shall have

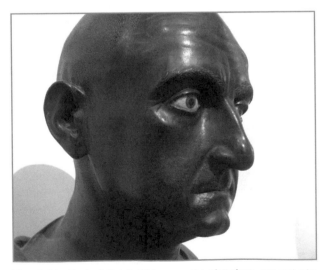

Fig. 1.11. *Bust of Scipio Africanus, the victorious general who appeared to his grandson in a dream; first century* C.E., *excavated from Herculaneum. Museo Archeologico Nazionale, Naples. Photo in the public domain.*

traversed, as an ambassador, Egypt, Syria, Asia, and Greece, you will be chosen a second time Consul in your absence, and will put an end to one of the greatest of wars by extirpating Numantia. But when you shall be borne to the Capitol in your triumphal chariot after this war, you will find the State disturbed by the machinations of my grandson [that is, Tiberius Gracchus].

"In this emergency, Africanus, it will behoove you to show your country the light of your energy, genius, and wisdom. But I see at that time, as it were, a double way of destiny. For when your age . . . shall have completed for you in the course of nature the destined period, to you alone and to your name the whole city will turn; on you the Senate will look, on you all good citizens, on you the allies, on you the Latini. You will be the one man on whom the safety of the city will rest; and, to say no more, you, as Dictator, must re-establish the State, if you escape the impious hands of your kindred."

Here, when Laelius had cried out, and the rest of the company had breathed deep sighs, Scipio, smiling pleasantly upon them, said, "I beg you not to rouse me from sleep and break up my vision. Hear the remainder of it."

Africanus continues to address his grandson:

"But that you, Africanus, may be the more prompt in the defense of the State, know that for all who shall have preserved, succored, enlarged their country, there is a certain and determined place in heaven where they enjoy eternal happiness; for to the Supreme God who governs this whole universe nothing is more pleasing than those companies and unions of men that are called cities. Of these the rulers and preservers, going hence, return hither."

Here I, although I had been alarmed, not indeed so much by the fear of death as by that of the treachery of my own kindred [that is, Tiberius Gracchus], yet asked whether Paulus, my father, and others whom we supposed to be dead were living. "Yes, indeed," he replied, "those who have fled from the bonds of the body, like runners from the goal, live; while what is called your life is death. But do you see your father Paulus coming to you?" When I saw him, I shed a flood of tears; but he, embracing and kissing me, forbade my weeping.

Then as soon as my tears would suffer me to speak, I began by saying, "Most sacred and excellent father, since this is life, as Africanus tells me, why do I remain on the earth, and not rather hasten to come to you?"

Scipio's father explains that it is every noble soul's duty to perform its proper obligations on earth before it may be released in death.

"But, Scipio, like this your grandfather, like me, your father, cherish justice and that sacred observance of duty to your kind, which, while of great worth toward parents and family, is of supreme value toward your country. Such a life is the way to heaven, and to this assembly of those who have already lived, and, released from the body, inhabit the place which you now see,"—it was that circle that shines forth among the stars in the most dazzling white,—"which you have learned from the Greeks to call the Milky Way."

And as I looked on every side I saw other things transcendently glorious and wonderful. There were stars which we never see from here below, and all the stars were vast far beyond what we have ever imagined. The least of them

was that which, farthest from heaven, nearest to the earth, shone with a bor-
rowed light. But the starry globes very far surpassed the earth in magnitude.
The earth itself indeed looked to me so small as to make me ashamed of our
empire, which was a mere point on its surface."

(Cicero, *De republica* 6.1-9, trans. Peabody)

Arabia

Paul declares that after his vision of the risen Christ he did not consult with other
apostles but "went away at once into Arabia" (Gal 1:17). We know nothing else of this
period; but in his account of Moses' life, Philo ascribes special significance to Moses'
sojourn in Arabia ("Midian," Exod 2:15).

41. Moses' sojourn in Arabia (Philo)

> When those in authority [in Egypt] who suspected the youth's [Moses'] inten-
> tions, knowing that he would remember their wicked actions against them and
> take vengeance when the opportunity came, had thus once got a handle, they
> poured malicious suggestions by the thousand from every side into the open
> ears of his grandfather, so as to instill the fear that his sovereignty might be
> taken from him. . . .
>
> While such talk was in circulation, Moses retired [*hypanechōrēsen*] into
> the neighboring country of Arabia, where it was safe for him to stay, at the
> same time beseeching God to save the oppressed from their helpless, miserable
> plight, and to punish as they deserved the oppressors who had left no form of
> maltreatment untried, and to double the gift by granting to himself that he
> should see both these accomplished. God, in high approval of his spirit, which
> loved the good and hated evil, listened to his prayers, and very shortly judged
> the land and its doings as became His nature. But, while the divine judgment
> was still waiting, Moses was carrying out the exercises of virtue with an admi-
> rable trainer, the reason within him, under whose discipline he labored to fit
> himself for life in its highest forms, the theoretical and the practical. He was
> ever opening the scroll of philosophical doctrines, digested them inwardly with
> quick understanding, committed them to memory never to be forgotten, and
> straightway brought his personal conduct, praiseworthy in all respects, into
> conformity with them; for he desired truth rather than seeming, because the
> one mark he set before him was nature's right reason, the sole source and foun-
> tain of virtues.

(Philo, *Life of Moses* 1.46-48, trans. Colson, LCL)

Paul at Corinth

One fixed point on which scholars attempt to construct at least the skeleton of a
chronology of Paul's life is the so-called Gallio inscription at Delphi. According to
Acts, Paul was brought before Gallio when the latter was proconsul of Achaia (Acts
18:12-17). The inscription, in which the Emperor Claudius greets the city of Delphi
and, in the course of settling a civic affair about which we have no other information,

refers to the proconsul Gallio, allows us to date Paul's appearance before him to the year 51.

42. THE GALLIO INSCRIPTION

> Tiberius Claudius Caesar Augustus Germanicus Pontifex Maximus, in his tribunician power year twelve, acclaimed emperor the twenty-sixth time, father of the country . . . sends greetings to the city of Delphi. I have long been zealous for the city of Delphi and favorable to it from the beginning, and I have always observed the cult of the Pythian Apollo, but with regard to the present stories, and those quarrels of the citizens of which a report has been made by Lucius Junio Gallio, my friend and proconsul of Achaia . . . will still hold the previous settlement.
>
> (Gallio inscription, trans. Foakes-Jackson and Lake)

Paul's Death in Rome

In what may well have been the last of his letters known to us, Paul declares to the Romans his plans to come to Rome and be sent by them on his way farther west, to Spain (Rom 15:23-24). According to Acts, Paul did travel to Rome, but in Roman custody in the wake of mob violence in Jerusalem (Acts 21–28). He was to make his appeal to Caesar himself (25:10-12). But Acts does not tell this story; it ends instead with Paul waiting for that hearing, in Roman custody, and having relative freedom to preach to Jews and non-Jews "without hindrance" (28:30-31). The implication of the phrase that Paul "lived two whole years" in Rome is that the author of Acts is aware, and expects the reader to be aware, of Paul's death in Rome, but the narrative's silence on that point has long been a puzzle in scholarship.[38] We will return in chapter 6 to early Christian traditions about Paul's death by execution in Rome. Here we present accounts of the "great fire" in Rome in 64 c.e., which the emperor Nero made the pretext for a particularly vicious persecution of "Christians." (This is apparently the earliest occasion in which Christians were distinguished as such by the empire.)

43. THE GREAT FIRE IN ROME (TACITUS)

Writing decades later, the historian Tacitus gave free rein to the popular suspicion that Nero himself was responsible for the fire, recounting rumors that arsonists both stoked the flames and prevented others from extinguishing them and detailing the extravagance of Nero's building projects on the ruins of the burned part of the city.

> A disaster followed, whether accidental or treacherously contrived by the emperor, is uncertain, as authors have given both accounts, worse, however, and more dreadful than any which have ever happened to this city by the violence of fire. It had its beginning in that part of the circus which adjoins the Palatine and Caelian hills, where, amid the shops containing inflammable wares, the conflagration both broke out and instantly became so fierce and so rapid from the wind that it seized in its grasp the entire length of the circus. For here there were no houses fenced in by solid masonry, or temples surrounded by walls,

Fig. 1.12. *The ruins of the octagonal room in the Domus Aurea, Nero's palace on the Palatine Hill, 54–68 c.e. Photo: Luciano Romano Grafiluce; Scala/Art Resource, New York.*

or any other obstacle to interpose delay. The blaze in its fury ran first through the level portions of the city, then rising to the hills, while it again devastated every place below them, it outstripped all preventive measures; so rapid was the mischief and so completely at its mercy the city, with those narrow winding passages and irregular streets, which characterized old Rome.

(Tacitus describes the enormity of suffering and death caused by the fire.)

And no one dared to stop the mischief, because of incessant menaces from a number of persons who forbade the extinguishing of the flames, because again others openly hurled brands, and kept shouting that there was one who gave them authority, either seeking to plunder more freely, or obeying orders.

Nero at this time was at Antium, and did not return to Rome until the fire approached his house, which he had built to connect the palace with the gardens of Maecenas. It could not, however, be stopped from devouring the palace, the house, and everything around it. However, to relieve the people, driven out homeless as they were, he threw open to them the Campus Martius and the public buildings of Agrippa, and even his own gardens, and raised temporary structures to receive the destitute multitude. Supplies of food were brought up from Ostia and the neighboring towns, and the price of corn was reduced to three sesterces a peck. These acts, though popular, produced no effect, since a rumor had gone forth everywhere that, at the very time when the city was in flames, the emperor appeared on a private stage and sang of the destruction of Troy, comparing present misfortunes with the calamities of antiquity. . . .

Nero meanwhile availed himself of his country's desolation, and erected a mansion in which the jewels and gold, long familiar objects, quite vulgarized by our extravagance, were not so marvelous as the fields and lakes, with woods on one side to resemble a wilderness, and, on the other, open spaces and extensive views.

(Nero sought to ingratiate himself to the people by promising an extensive rebuilding program, to include public parks and new housing; he also sought "means of propitiating the gods" through sacrifices.)

Fig. 1.13. *An amethyst depicting Nero in the guise of Apollo, holding a lyre, first century* c.e. *The emperor's flair for theatrical and musical self-promotion was notorious. Cabinet des médailles de la Bibliothèque nationale de France. Photo in the public domain.*

But all human efforts, all the lavish gifts of the emperor, and the propitiations of the gods, did not banish the sinister belief that the conflagration was the result of an order. Consequently, to get rid of the report, Nero fastened the guilt and inflicted the most exquisite tortures on a class hated for their abominations, called Christians by the populace.

Christus, from whom the name had its origin, suffered the extreme penalty during the reign of Tiberius at the hands of one of our procurators, Pontius Pilatus, and a most mischievous superstition, thus checked for the moment, again broke out not only in Judaea, the first source of the evil, but even in Rome, where all things hideous and shameful from every part of the world find their centre and become popular.

Accordingly, an arrest was first made of all who pleaded guilty; then, upon their information, an immense multitude was convicted, not so much of the crime of firing the city, as of hatred against mankind. Mockery of every sort was added to their deaths. Covered with the skins of beasts, they were torn by dogs and perished, or were nailed to crosses, or were doomed to the flames and burnt, to serve as a nightly illumination, when daylight had expired. Nero offered his gardens for the spectacle, and was exhibiting a show in the circus, while he mingled with the people in the dress of a charioteer or stood aloft on a car. Hence, even for criminals who deserved extreme and exemplary punishment, there arose a feeling of compassion; for it was not, as it seemed, for the public good, but to glut one man's cruelty, that they were being destroyed.

(Tacitus, *Annals* 15.38-39, 42-44, trans. Church and Brodribb)

44. Nero's "punishment" of Christians (Suetonius)

Suetonius does not describe the fire, although his reference to new buildings implies it. Neither does he connect the "punishment" of Christians to the fire but lists it among a number of police measures carried out by Nero.

He [Nero] devised a new form for the buildings of the city and in front of the houses and apartments he erected porches, from the flat roofs of which fires could be fought; and these he put up at his own cost. He had also planned to extend the walls as far as Ostia and to bring the sea from there to Rome by a canal.

During his reign many abuses were severely punished and put down, and no fewer new laws were made: a limit was set to expenditures; the public banquets were confined to a distribution of food; the sale of any kind of cooked viands in the taverns was forbidden, with the exception of pulse and vegetables, whereas before every sort of dainty was exposed for sale. Punishment was inflicted on the Christians, a class of men given to a new and mischievous superstition. He put an end to the diversions of the chariot drivers, who from immunity of long standing claimed the right of ranging at large and amusing themselves by cheating and robbing the people. The pantomimic actors and their partisans were banished from the city.

(Suetonius, *Nero* 16, trans. Rolfe, LCL)

QUESTIONS FOR REFLECTION

1. How might a Jewish contemporary have heard Paul's self-description as an "apostle" of Jesus Christ? How might a non-Jew have heard it?
2. What would contemporaries have made of Paul's emphasis on supporting himself by manual labor? How would different life circumstances affect the way others regarded this aspect of Paul's work?
3. In what ways did Paul's self-presentation resemble that of self-styled "philosophers"? What expectations might such a resemblance have inspired in his hearers?
4. How would others have heard Paul's language about his own weakness and about the weakness of the crucified Christ?
5. In what ways might contemporaries have heard Paul's claim to work for the "obedience" or "faithful obedience" of the nations?
6. In what ways might our own social and cultural assumptions regarding what is "political" and what is "religious" affect our understanding of Paul and his world?
7. How important are Paul's references to his own visionary experiences? How should people understand these visionary experiences today?
8. Nero appears to have attacked Christians because they were a convenient target, the objects of popular suspicion, rather than because of specific beliefs. What questions does that raise for you regarding the way we should understand the origins of the Christian religion?

FOR FURTHER READING

Fredriksen, Paula. *From Jesus to Christ: The Origins of the New Testament Images of Jesus.* 2nd ed. New Haven: Yale University Press, 2000. Pages 142–56.

Hock, Ronald F. *The Social Context of Paul's Ministry: Tentmaking and Apostleship.* Minneapolis: Fortress Press, 1995.

Murphy-O'Connor, Jerome. *Paul: A Critical Life* (Oxford: Clarendon, 1996).

On slavery:

Glancy, Jennifer. *Slavery in Early Christianity.* Minneapolis: Fortress Press, 2006.

Harrill, J. Albert. *Slaves in the New Testament: Literary, Social, and Moral Dimensions.* Minneapolis: Fortress Press, 2005.

Martin, Dale B. *Slavery as Salvation: The Metaphor of Slavery in Pauline Christianity.* New Haven: Yale University Press, 1990.

On Paul and philosophy:

Downing, F. Gerald. *Cynics, Paul, and the Pauline Churches: Cynics and Christian Origins II.* New York: Routledge, 1998.

Engberg-Pedersen, Troels. *Paul and the Stoics.* Louisville: Westminster John Knox, 2000.

Malherbe, Abraham J. *Paul and the Popular Philosophers.* Minneapolis: Fortress Press, 1989.

Stowers, Stanley K. *A Rereading of Romans: Justice, Jews, and Gentiles.* New Haven: Yale University Press, 1994.

Winter, Bruce W. *Philo and Paul among the Sophists: Alexandrian and Corinthian Responses to a Julio-Claudian Movement.* 2nd ed. Grand Rapids: Eerdmans, 2002.

On the apocalyptic-mystical tradition in Judaism:

Rowland, Christopher. *The Mystery of God: Early Jewish Mysticism and the New Testament.* CRINT, Section 3: Jewish Traditions in Early Christian Literature 12. Leiden: Brill, 2009.

Segal, Alan F. *Paul the Convert: The Apostolate and Apostasy of Saul the Pharisee.* New Haven: Yale University Press, 1990.

On Paul's "weakness":

Reasoner, Mark. The *Strong and the Weak: Rom. 14.1–15.13 in Context.* SNTSMS 103. Cambridge: Cambridge University Press, 1999.

Wan, Sze-kar. *Power in Weakness: Conflict and Rhetoric in Paul's Second Letter to the Corinthians.* New Testament in Context. Harrisburg, Pa.: Trinity Press International, 2000.

Fig. 2.1. *"Saint Paul: Here he sits and writes." Illustration from a ninth-century manuscript of Paul's letters from the Monastery of Gallen. Württembergische Landesbibliothek Stuttgart, HB II 54. Photo in the public domain.*

2 | Paul's Gospel and Paul's Letters

P aul called his message "the gospel," "the gospel of God," "the gospel of [God's] Son," or at times "my gospel," as if to distinguish it from the teachings of others.[1] In his carefully constructed greeting to the Romans, Paul appeals to his being set apart by God "to the gospel" as the basis of his authenticity and legitimacy. The Greek word *euangelion* is often translated "good news," but as we saw above (no. 24 in chapter 1), the word could also carry political connotations in the context of the accession of an emperor or the appearance of a new order. We do not hear philosophers from the period speaking of their philosophical schools' teachings as "gospels," however. Paul's choice of the term may be significant. Given all that he has to say about the imminent dawning of the rule of God—captured in the subtitle of J. Christiaan Beker's important work *Paul the Apostle: The Triumph of God in Life and Thought*—we might paraphrase the term, rather fully, as "the announcement of God's dawning triumph."[2]

We must acknowledge several complications at the outset of our discussion of Paul's gospel. The first was already mentioned in chapter 1, namely, that Paul's letters are all written to communities of people who have already accepted his "gospel." In them, he reminds his hearers of his initial proclamation; but we should not imagine that any of his letters is a full recapitulation of "the gospel" as he preached it. (As a matter of fact, many scholars regard Romans as just such a recapitulation or "summary" or "presentation" of Paul's gospel to a community of people whom he has not met. That view has been challenged in recent scholarship, however, and we will not presume it here.)[3] This complication motivated the Pauline Theology group of the Society of Biblical Literature to explore each of Paul's letters, in probable chronological order, in order to identify the contours of what "the gospel" or "Paul's theology" might have meant in each one.[4] In the first part of this chapter, then, we turn to texts that may help us understand Paul's letters in the context of ancient letter writing and to the roles that letters played in shaping the character of individuals and communities.

A second complication: Christian theology has long posed the question of Paul's gospel as an antithesis or antidote to Judaism, as the "solution" to a Jewish "plight." That presupposition is now hotly contested and is intertwined with how we understand ancient Judaism and Paul's relation to it. We will put off discussion of these issues to chapter 4.

Finally, Paul's landscape was filled with many people offering good news, necessary antidotes to the ills of the world. The Bible as we know it today can give the false impression that the Christian gospel first appeared on a landscape where Israel's scriptures were the most prominent feature. While it is true that the earliest followers of Jesus of Nazareth were Jews and that Paul's apostolic activities were closely related to synagogues in different cities, those facts should not obscure the tremendous diversity of practices related to "the gods" in Paul's world. The most pervasive "gospel" (*euangelion*) proclaimed in Paul's day—quite literally, as we saw in chapter 1—was the announcement of a glorious new age that had dawned in the figure of Augustus. Aspects of the Augustan "gospel," then, will occupy us in chapter 3.

Paul the Writer of Letters

In one of the early portraits of Paul that the book of Acts gives us, he is known as Saul and carries letters authorizing him to arrest followers of Jesus and bring them back to Jerusalem (Acts 9:2). In contrast, our primary sources for understanding Paul are his own letters, written after his call as an apostle of Christ, addressed to the assemblies in different cities.

Interestingly, Acts never describes Paul writing a letter to an assembly. That is one of several differences that Richard I. Pervo observes between Acts and the genuine letters of Paul.[5]

Paul's Undisputed Letters	Acts
Paul imitates Christ by suffering.	Paul imitates Christ by working miracles.
Paul is an apostle.	Saul/Paul is not called an apostle.
Paul is a missionary to Gentiles.	Paul is a missionary to Jews first.
Paul has conflicts with his communities.	Paul has no conflicts with his communities.
Paul's theological opponents are other believers.	Paul's opponents are primarily Jews.
Paul has difficult relations with other leaders; he is not subordinate to Jerusalem.	Paul and other leaders have no conflicts; he is subordinate to Jerusalem.
Paul engages in conflict over Torah.	Conflict with Jews involves resurrection.
Paul's colleagues are important figures in his mission.	Paul's colleagues are very junior assistants.
Natural theology shows that everyone is without excuse.	Natural theology levels playing field between Jews and Gentiles.

Paul does not claim benefits pertinent to his worldly status.	Paul is a Roman citizen of high status who makes use of his privileges.
Paul is known as a letter writer.	Paul is not depicted writing letters.

Paul's is the best represented voice in the New Testament because of the number of letters that bear his name. In churches that use a common lectionary (that is, a set of assigned readings for worship) today, Paul's letters are read more regularly than any other portion of the Bible.

Some, at least, of Paul's letters were soon collected and shared among assemblies. His letters were also soon imitated, not only by pseudonymous writers who claimed Paul's authority for their own writings (for examples of pseudonymous letters that were not included in our New Testament, see chapter 6) but also by other early Christian writers who wrote in their own names but adopted and adapted the form of Paul's letters.

Paul was influential, then, in no small part because of the very fact that he wrote letters.[6] We can learn more from Paul's letters if we understand the purposes of letter writing in his time.[7]

Our sources: Scholars distinguish the undisputedly genuine letters of Paul from New Testament letters that bear his name but may have been written by others, perhaps after his death. There is no sure consensus regarding which letters are **pseudepigrapha** (writings bearing false attributions), but here is a widely accepted division of genuine and disputed writings.

Undisputed letters	Disputed letters
Romans	Ephesians
1 Corinthians	Colossians
2 Corinthians*	2 Thessalonians
Galatians	1 Timothy
Philippians*	2 Timothy
1 Thessalonians	Titus
Philemon	

*Many scholars consider 2 Corinthians and Philippians to be combinations of parts of several earlier letters.

Among the disputed letters, some letters are more doubtful than others. A good introduction to Paul's letters or a Bible dictionary will provide discussion of the issues related to each letter. On pseudepigraphy in general, see J. H. Charlesworth, "Pseudonymity and Pseudepigraphy," *ABD* 5:540-41.

The Purpose of Letters: Connection

The point may seem obvious: people write letters as a substitute for being present in person with others with whom they wish to communicate. It is clear that Paul writes letters as an expression of his desire to be present to the assemblies (see Rom 1:9-13, for example) and to maintain personal connection with them.[8] Letters also have a "philophronetic" function, that is, to sustain a connection of friendly feeling and relationship, even without any other immediate purpose.

All of Paul's letters are meant to serve other purposes as well, but the measure of this friendly or philophronetic purpose in his letters is the proportion of each letter given over to expressing affection and thanksgiving for one or another assembly. This feature is most notable in Philippians. We have already seen the example of a personal letter from a son to his father (no. 9 above) and, in much more formal language, letters from a philosopher and a Roman governor corresponding with his emperor (nos. 20–21 above). Other examples also show the philophronetic function of ancient letters.

Fig. 2.2. *An educated young woman writer. Fresco from Herculaneum, c. 50 c.e.; Museo Archeologico Nazionale, Naples. Photo in the public domain.*

45. Seneca thanks a correspondent for his letters

I thank you for writing to me so often; for you are revealing your real self to me in the only way you can. I never receive a letter from you without being in your company forthwith. If the pictures of our absent friends are pleasing to us, though they only refresh the memory and lighten our longing by a solace that is unreal and unsubstantial, how much more pleasant is a letter, which brings us real traces, real evidences, of an absent friend! For that which is sweetest when we meet face to face is afforded by the impress of a friend's hand upon his letter—recognition [*agnoscere*].

(Seneca, *Epistle* 40.1, trans. Gummere, LCL)[9]

46. Seneca on unaffected letter writing

You have been complaining that my letters to you are rather carelessly written. Now who talks carefully unless he also desires to talk affectedly? I prefer that my letters should be just what my conversation would be if you and I were sitting in one another's company or taking walks together,—spontaneous and easy; for my letters have nothing strained or artificial about them. If it were possible, I should prefer to show, rather than speak, my feelings. Even if I were arguing a point, I should not stamp my foot, or toss my arms about, or raise my voice; but I should leave that sort of thing to the orator, and should be content to have conveyed my feelings toward you without having either embellished them or lowered their dignity.

(Seneca, *Epistle* 75.1-2, trans. Gummere, LCL)

47. Cicero's letters to a friend

I have nothing to write. There is no news that I have heard, and all your letters I answered yesterday. But as a sick heart not only robs me of sleep, but will not allow me even to keep awake without the greatest pain, I have begun to write to you something or other without any definite subject, that I may have a sort of talk with you, the only thing that gives me relief.

(Cicero, *Letter to Atticus* 9.10.1, trans. Winstedt, LCL)

Though I have nothing to say to you, I write all the same, because I feel as though I were talking to you. Nicias and Valerius are here with me. I am expecting a letter from you early today. Perhaps there will be another in the afternoon, unless your letter to Epirus hinders you: I don't want to interrupt that. I have sent you letters for Marcianus and for Maontanus. Please put them in the same packet, unless you have sent it off already.

(Cicero, *Letter to Atticus* 12.53, trans. Winstedt, LCL)

Letters of Exhortation

Unlike the moral and philosophical epistles written by some of his contemporaries—Seneca, for example—Paul's letters are written to congregations, not individuals.

They nevertheless share with those other letters—and with oral rhetoric such as the speeches of the philosopher Epictetus—a profound concern for moral exhortation.

Adaptation, Protreptic, and Paraenesis

We have already seen in chapter 1 that Paul's self-presentation could be compared to that of a philosopher, which suggests that the assemblies might be compared to philosophical schools or at least to groups of students gathered around a teacher. The philosophical school in the first century did not simply teach theory. Students were trained in how to live, with exercises and punishments designed to help them live in ways that a given philosophical school valued.

Clarence Glad has suggested that early Christian communities had some similarities to Epicurean schools that taught students how to adapt in different situations of life. The sort of adaptation to others that Paul held out as his own goal in 1 Cor 9:22 ("I have become everything in turn to people of every sort") resembled a tradition in Greco-Roman society that emphasized "the importance of adaptability in conduct and speech in the unreserved association with all." Glad described this tradition as "psychagogic adaptation,"[10] arguing that "in both the Pauline and the Epicurean schools, psychagogy is non-dogmatic and perceptive, aimed at molding and consolidating the recipients for purposes of communal solidarity."[11]

In recent decades, students of Paul's letters have given increasing attention also to ancient rhetoric. The study of Paul's rhetoric has moved from efforts to label discrete argumentative units in his letters to understanding how the texture of his letters represents persuasive speech and how that speech can be understood in the wider context of rhetoric as it was practiced in his day.[12] The difficulty we face is that Paul's letters appear to be devoted primarily to exhortation, which was not the focus of the ancient rhetorical handbooks.

Rhetoric is the study and practice of the means of persuasion. Beginning with Aristotle's *Art of Rhetoric*, ancient rhetorical handbooks described the premises and strategies of successful argumentation and gave specific titles to a variety of strategies and techniques. The handbooks customarily distinguished three types of rhetoric, answering three kinds of occasion:

deliberative rhetoric addressed the advantages and disadvantages of a particular public decision;
judicial rhetoric addressed questions of guilt or innocence;
epideictic rhetoric affirmed shared values on ceremonial occasions.

As Stanley K. Stowers points out in his discussion of letters of exhortation and advice, it can be difficult to align ancient classifications of *epistolary* styles, which were concerned with writing, with ancient discussions of *rhetoric* or *oratory*, which were concerned with speaking. Stowers observes, "There is much overlapping and ambiguous terminology, which is partly due to the fact that exhortation was never systematically treated by the rhetoricians"—even though exhortation played an important part in popular moral pedagogy, philosophy, and rhetoric.[13]

Discussions of classical rhetoric usually distinguished between "deliberative" or "advisory" (*symbouleutikos*) speech, which "calls for a specific course of action," and "epideictic" (*epideiktikos*) rhetoric, which "seeks to increase adherence to a value or to cultivate a character trait." Exhortation often involves both sorts of persuasive speech.[14]

Stowers finds another distinction more useful: between *protreptic speech* (and writing) and *paraenesis*. Stowers notes that these terms were not distinguished consistently by Greek and Roman writers—indeed, the terms could be used interchangeably—but the distinction is nonetheless valuable for contemporary discussion. *Protreptic* speech (or letter writing), on the one hand, "calls the audience to a new and different way of life." By *paraenesis*, on the other hand, Stowers means "advice and exhortation to *continue* in a certain way of life."[15]

We should imagine that Paul's initial proclamation in a city would have relied on protreptic rhetoric. Protreptic speeches and protreptic letters sought to exhort an audience to adopt a new way of life by describing, often in harsh terms, the disadvantages of their current way of life or other alternatives to the way of life being advocated. Writing later to established communities in his letters, he explicitly reminded his audiences of values they had *already* embraced and encouraged them to adhere even more closely to those values. This is characteristic of paraenetic speech.[16] (When some interpreters have suggested that Romans is protreptic speech, they emphasize the indications that Paul had never been to Rome and suggest that he intended his letter to function in the place of the initial presentation of his gospel.)

The following readings help to illustrate the distinction Stowers proposes. Though much later than Paul, the treatise on letter styles by pseudo-Libanius (fourth to sixth century C.E.) bears on the categorization of Paul's letters because of the distinction the author makes between the "advisory" letter (*symbouleutikē*) and the paraenetic letter. Here the paraenetic style is understood as reinforcing widely accepted values; the advisory style addresses practical matters in occasional circumstances where there may be controversy. (Note that this distinction is different from that made by Stowers.)

48. The paraenetic letter (Pseudo-Libanius)

> The paraenetic style (*parainetikē*) is that in which we exhort (*parainein*) someone by urging him (*protrepein*) him to pursue something or to avoid something. Paraenesis is divided into two parts, encouragement (*protropē*) and dissuasion (*apotropē*). Some also call it the advisory (*symbouleutikē*) style, but do so

incorrectly, for paraenesis differs from advice. For paraenesis is hortatory speech that does not admit of a counter-statement, for example, if someone should say that we must honor the divine. For nobody contradicts this exhortation were he not mad to begin with. But advice (*symbouleuein*) is advisory speech that does admit of a counter-statement, for example, if someone should say that we must wage war, for much can be gained by war. But someone else might counter that we should not wage war, for many (bad) things result from war, for example, defeat, captivity, wounds, and frequently the razing of a city.

(Pseudo-Libanius, *Epistolary Styles* 5, trans. Malherbe)

49. On the protreptic style of speech (Epictetus)

Epictetus described the "protreptic style" by opposing it to the sort of speech of the would-be philosopher who seeks flattery rather than a change in the hearer.

Does a philosopher invite people to a lecture?—Is it not rather the case that, as the sun draws its own sustenance to itself, so he also draws to himself those to whom he is to do good? What physician ever invites a patient to come and be healed by him? Although I am told that in these days the physicians in Rome *do* advertise; however, in my time they were called in by their patients. . . .

Men, the lecture room of the philosopher is a hospital; you ought not to walk out of it in pleasure, but in pain. For you are not well when you come; one man has a dislocated shoulder, another an abscess, another a fistula, another a headache. And then am I to sit down and recite to you dainty little notions and clever little mottoes, so that you will go out with words of praise on your lips, one man carrying away his shoulder just as it was when he came in, another his head in the same state, another his fistula, another his abscess? . . .

But isn't there such a thing as the right style for exhortation [*protreptikos charaktēr*]? . . . Why, what *is* the style for exhortation? The ability to show to the individual, as well as to the crowd, the warring inconsistency in which they are floundering about, and how they are paying attention to anything rather than what they truly want. For they want the things that conduce to happiness, but they are looking for them in the wrong place. . . . Who that ever heard you reading a lecture or conducting a discourse felt greatly disturbed about himself, or came to a realization of the state he was in, or on going out said, "The philosopher brought it home to me in fine style; I must not act like this any longer"?

(Arrian, *Discourses of Epictetus* 3.23, passim, trans. Oldfather, LCL)

50. Adaptive methods of exhortation (Dio Chrysostom)

Dio Chrysostom describes how a Cynic teaches others.

[The Cynic] will strive to preserve his individuality in seemly fashion . . . always honoring and promoting virtue and sobriety and trying to lead all men thereto, partly by persuading and exhorting, partly by abusing and reproaching, in the hope that he may thereby rescue somebody from folly . . . and soft living, taking them aside privately one by one and also admonishing them in groups every time he finds opportunity, "with gentle words at times, at others harsh."

(Dio Chrysostom, *Discourse* 77/78.38, trans. Glad)

Fig. 2.3. *A page from Arrian's* Discourses of Epictetus *from the eleventh- or twelfth-century Codex Bodleianus (Cod. Misc. Graec. 521). Bodleian Library. Photo in the public domain.*

51. Frank speech versus flattery (Philodemus)

In a discussion of flattery, the Epicurian philosopher Philodemus offers advice on teaching students the importance of correction.

> Let us make it clear to them that the goods of friendship are very durable and that flattery is the antagonist of friendship; let us also consider well the goods that rise from frank speech, both (the frank speech) directed towards one's intimate associates, and (the frank speech) directed towards all men, and let us avoid as vain the company of adulators, and still more let us not mix with them but seek cohabitation with those who speak candidly.
>
> (Philodemus, *On Flattery, Herc.* 1082, col. 2.1-14, trans. Glad)

52. Exhortation and "the rod"

In another place Philodemus depicts a student describing how he might be openly criticized or beaten if he makes a mistake. Compare 1 Cor 4:21, where Paul threatens to come among the Corinthians "with a stick"!

I did not sin then, but now he will deem me deserving of frank criticism if he catches me. . . . For I declare that I did not sin before, but I fell of my own will into the ignorance of youth; and on account of that he had to give me a beating.

(Philodemus, *On Frank Criticism*, PHerc, fragment 83.7-10, trans. Glad)

53. A Protreptic letter (Crates)

In this brief letter, the Cynic Crates (first or second century c.e.) urges his friend Aper to adopt the Cynic lifestyle. Brief and to the point, the letter nevertheless exemplifies the protreptic function of contrasting one way of life as superior to another, however popular, and urging its adoption.

To Aper, do well. The oracle of the ancients, honored Sir, has given advice that is concise and fitting in regard to every circumstance: Do not flee from what is necessary. For the one who flees from what is inevitable must be unhappy, and the one who desires what is impossible must fail to obtain it. Perhaps, then, I shall seem to you to be rather importunate and pedantic, and I do not defend myself against this charge. And yet, if it does seem so to you, condemn me, but pay attention to the ancients. For I have concluded from my own case that we men are distressed precisely when we wish to live a life without hardship. But this wish is impossible. For we must live with the body, and we must live with men as well, and most hardships issue from the folly of those who live in society,

Fig. 2.4. *The fourth-century-b.c.e. philosophers Crates and Hipparchia are depicted in a first-century-c.e. fresco from the Villa Farnesina. For marrying Crates and joining him in the Cynic lifestyle on the streets of Athens, Hipparchia was disowned by her parents. Their life together became a popular theme in later literature and art. Museo delle Terme, Rome. Photo in the public domain.*

and in turn, from the body. If, therefore, a wise man lives by these principles, he is free from pain and confusion, a happy man.

But if he is ignorant of these principles, he will never cease from being dependent on vain hopes and from being constrained by desires. As for you, then, if you are satisfied with the life of the masses, make use of those advisors, for in fact they are more expert in these matters. But if the life of Socrates and Diogenes pleases you, leave the writings of the tragic poets to others and devote yourself to emulating those men.

(Crates, Letter 35, trans. Hock)

The Effects of Protreptic Rhetoric

To the extent that a philosopher or self-declared emissary from heaven called hearers to adopt a dramatically different way of life, those who responded to that call would have experienced a degree of distress. Old habits would have to change; the fabric of social relationships would be strained, even to the breaking point, as family members and neighbors wondered and worried about new behaviors and abrupt withdrawal from long-familiar interactions. One purpose of paraenesis (such as we find in Paul's letters), then, was to support new members and to reinforce the transition they had made. As Abraham J. Malherbe observes, "The pedagogical concerns of the philosophic subculture represented by such persons as Epictetus and Plutarch reveal the constant attention that was given to the nurture of those who had embarked on a new way of life"; the same attention, Malherbe argues, informs Paul's letters.[17]

54. The distress of new students of philosophy (Epictetus)

The Stoic Epictetus took a severe line with those who had committed themselves to a life of philosophy under his direction.

> You sit trembling for fear that something will happen, and lamenting, and grieving, and groaning about other things that are happening.... Although you have these faculties free and entirely your own, you do not use them, nor do you realize what gifts you have received, and from whom, but you sit sorrowing and groaning, some of you blinded toward the giver himself and not even acknowledging your benefactor, and others—such is their ignoble spirit—turning aside to fault-finding and complaints against God.
>
> (Arrian, Discourses of Epictetus 1.6.38, 41-42, trans. Oldfather, LCL)

55. The temptation to return to old ways (Epictetus)

On another occasion, Epictetus scolded his students for returning to old ways:

> You go back to the same things again; you have exactly the same desires as before, the same aversions, in the same way you make your choices, your designs, and your purposes, you pray for the same things and are interested in the same things. In the second place, you do not even look for anybody to give you advice, but you are annoyed if you are told what I am telling you. Again you say, "He is an old man without the milk of human kindness in him."
>
> (Arrian, Discourses of Epictetus 2.17.36-38, trans. Oldfather, LCL)

Types of Letters

From a general consideration of the purpose of Paul's letters we turn to the specific types of letters recognized by ancient or modern writers.

Letter-Essays

As we have seen, a philosopher like Seneca could use the sort of direct address customary in a letter to compose a thematic essay (no. 17 above). As Stanley K. Stowers notes, some protreptic letters were quite extensive, launching into discussions of the philosophical system the author was advocating. In many such philosophical or moral treatises from the Hellenistic and Roman world, the epistolary form was used as a literary device by authors who presented their ideas to friends, acquaintances, and patrons. Such "letter-essays" often appeared under a title "on" or "concerning" their topic. They could also employ the epistolary form of responding to a request to introduce their topic: for example, "I write because you asked me to discuss . . ."

Paul uses a similar form in 1 Corinthians, addressing questions "concerning" which the Corinthians inquired (using the Greek preposition *peri*: 7:1; 8:1; 12:1).[18] But that similarity must be weighed against the differences between Paul's letters and the letter-essay. Formally, in 1 Corinthians, the topical introduction ("concerning . . .") is used several times for different topics within a single letter. Further, the purpose of Paul's letter is more clearly anticipated in the opening chapters, where the topical introduction is absent. Finally, the letter-essay was normally addressed, however artificially, to a single individual, while Paul's letters all address immediate situations in actual communities. (For another sort of letter addressed to a community, see no. 145 in chapter 4.)

Types of Letters Recognized in Ancient Handbooks

We have two well-known "manuals" for letter writing from the Roman world, *Epistolary Types* by pseudo-Demetrius (written between the second century B.C.E. and the third century C.E.) and *Epistolary Styles* by pseudo-Libanius, mentioned above. Both authors describe and give an example of each type of letter. (This chapter opened with letters that may be taken as examples of what pseudo-Demetrius calls the "friendly" type of letter.)

These are ideal types, reflecting different sorts of rhetoric. Longer, more complex letters, like some of Paul's, may include aspects of different kinds of rhetoric, which may make it difficult to assign a letter to a single classification. For this reason, Stowers refers to Paul's letters as "complex hortatory letters."[19] The letter types described here may help identify the overall character of one or another of Paul's letters. More often, perhaps, they may help us identify the rhetorical function of a component part of a letter.

Fig. 2.5. *P46, from about 200 c.e., is the earliest extant manuscript of Paul's letters; this page contains 2 Corinthians 11:33—12:9. Papyri Collection of the University of Michigan. Photo in the public domain.*

56. Epistolary Types (Pseudo-Demetrius)

According to the theory that governs epistolary types, . . . (letters) can be composed in a great number of styles, but are written in those which always fit the particular circumstance. . . .

There are, then, twenty-one kinds that we have come across. Perhaps time might produce more than these, since it is a highly gifted inventor of skills and theories. But as far as we are concerned, there is no other type that properly pertains to the epistolary mode. Each of them is named after the form of style to which it belongs. . . .

The friendly type [*philikos*], then, is one that seems to be written by a friend to a friend. But it is by no means (only) friends who write (in this manner). For frequently those in prominent positions are expected by some to write in a friendly manner to their inferiors and to others who are their equals, for example, to military commanders, viceroys, and governors. There are times, indeed, when they write to them without knowing them (personally). They do so, not because they are close friends and have (only) one choice (of how to write), but because they think that nobody will refuse them when they write in a friendly manner, but will rather submit and heed what they are writing. . . .

The commendatory type [*systatikos*], which we write on behalf of one person to another, mixing in praise, at the same time also speaking of those who had previously been unacquainted as though they were (now) acquainted. . . .

The blaming type [*memptikos*] is one that undertakes not to seem harsh. . . .

It is the reproachful type [*oneidistikos*] when we once more reproach, with accusations, someone whom we had earlier benefited, for what he has done. . . .

The consoling type [*paramythētikos*] is that written to people who are grieving because something unpleasant has happened (to them). . . .

The censorious type [*epitimētikos*] is that written with rebukes on account of errors that have already been committed. . . .

The admonishing type [*nouthetētikos*] is one which indicates by its name what its character is. For admonition is the instilling of sense [*noun entithēnai*] in the person who is being admonished, and teaching him what should and should not be done.

It is the threatening type [*apeilētikos*] when with intensity we instill fear in people for what they have done or would do.

It is the vituperative type [*psektikos*] when we bring to light the badness of someone's character or the offensiveness of (his) action against someone. . . .

It is the praising type [*epainetikos*] when we encourage someone and express our approval of what he has done or has proposed to do. . . .

It is the advisory type [*symbouleutikos*] when, by offering our own judgment, we exhort (someone to) something or dissuade (him) from something. . . .

The supplicatory type [*axiōmatikos*] consists of requests, supplications, and so-called entreaties; sometimes it consists of a petition. . . .

It is the inquiring type [*erōtēmatikos*] when we inquire about something and urge that a reply be sent to us. . . .

The responding type [*apophantikos*] responds to the person making an inquiry. . . .

It is the allegorical type [*allēgorikos*] when we wish the person to whom we write to be the only one to understand (what we mean), and when we intimate one thing by means of something else. . . .

It is the accounting type [*aitiologikos*] when we give the reasons why something has not taken place or will not take place. . . .

The accusing type [*katēgorikos*] is that which consists of an accusation of things that have been done beyond the bounds of propriety. . . .

The apologetic type [*apologētikos*] is that which adduces, with proof, arguments which contradict charges that are being made. . . .

It is the congratulatory type [*syncharētikos*] when we write and rejoice with someone over the important and wonderful things that have happened to him. . . .

It is the ironic type [*eirōnikos*] when we speak of things in terms that are their opposites, and when we call bad men noble and good. . . .

The thankful type [*apeucharistikos*] calls to mind the gratitude that is due (the reader). . . .

(Pseudo-Demetrius, *Epistolary Types*, passim; trans. Malherbe)

Letters of Recommendation

Letter writing often serves the purpose of giving a recommendation for someone, very often the person carrying the letter. Though Paul had to contend with the fact that, unlike the rival teachers in Corinth, he had no letter of recommendation for himself that he could produce for the Corinthians (2 Cor 3:1-3), his letters contain many recommendations for others—for example, for Phoebe (Rom 16:1-2). The recommendation achieves the same function as what pseudo-Demetrius called the "commendatory" letter.

In *Form and Structure of the Familiar Greek Letter of Recommendation*, Chan-Hie Kim identifies the standard components of recommendation letters as follows:

+ an opening that contains a greeting and a health wish
+ the "background," containing an identification of the person being recommended and some description of this person
+ a "request" section, containing the actual request, a description of what is requested, and some sort of purpose or result that will be accomplished if the request is completed
+ a "closing" that includes a friendly regard for the recipient's health and a farewell greeting[20]

As pseudo-Demetrius suggests, the letter of recommendation overlaps in function with the letter of introduction, since every letter of recommendation both introduces and commends to the reader a person whom they have not met. Some letters of introduction supply a recommendation of the person's experience or qualities.

Here are a series of letters of recommendation, the first two from the same person. Kim notes that a common element in the letter of recommendation is a phrase that asks the recipient to provide for whatever the recommended person might need—what we might call a "request for a blank check."[21] Note that some letters have additional elements: an address (to direct the letter carrier) and a date.

57. A Greek letter of recommendation for Heraclides

Address: To Tyrannus the treasurer
From Theon to the most honored Tyrannus, special greetings.
Heraclides who delivers this letter to you is my brother. So I beg you to stand by him with all the influence you have. And I also asked Hermes your

brother in a letter to inform you about him. You will do me a big favor if you follow through on this note's request.

I pray above all that you are well, without pain, and that things are going for the best for you.

Farewell.

(*P.Oxy.* 292, trans. Reasoner)[22]

58. A letter of recommendation for Hermophilus

To Heraclides, royal scribe of Oxyrhyncynopolis

From Theon to Heraclides his brother,

Warmest greetings and wishes for good health! Hermophilus, who delivers this letter to you, is [. . .] and asked me to write to you. It has come up that he has a little business in Cercemon. So if it pleases you, please do him right in this.

Take care to keep yourself in good health.

Farewell.

In the third year of Tiberius Caesar Sebastos, third day of Phaophi

(*P.Oxy.* 746; trans. Reasoner)[23]

59. A Letter of introduction for Dioskoros

Address: To dearest Moussios

Heracles to dearest Moussios, greetings. I ask you to treat as my very close friend the introduced Dioskoros, who is presenting this letter to you. You will gratify me by doing this.

Date: Pharmouthi 13

(*P.Hermo.* 1, trans. Reasoner)[24]

60. A Letter of introduction for Isodoros

Apollonius to Serapion, strategos and gymnasiarch, warmest greetings and may Zeus always keep you well.

Isodoros who is carrying this letter to you is my household servant. If he should require something for support that you can offer, do it for him, marking it in my account. If you do this you will really be doing me a favor. And perform the same services without hesitation for those whom he designates.

Take care to keep yourself well. Farewell.

In the 36th year of Caesar, Phaōpi 26

(*P.Merton* 62, trans. Reasoner)[25]

Letters of Admonition

The Greek word *nouthetein*, "admonish," carries the connotation of "setting one's mind right" (*noun tithein*), according to pseudo-Demetrius. It follows that admonition can take different forms and be expressed in different tones. Pseudo-Demetrius also allows that letters of admonition can be phrased softly, expressing confidence in the recipient even while encouraging a change in behavior for the better. Several of Paul's letters might be described as including "admonitory" sections; note too Paul's expression of confidence in Rom 15:14-16 that he has written to the Roman congregations by way of "reminder," despite his confidence that they can "admonish" (*nouthetein*) one another. The following very personal example comes from Egypt in the second century C.E.

61. An admonition from one brother to another

Sempronius to Maximus his brother, many greetings.

Before all I pray for your welfare. I learned that you are treating our revered mother harshly. Please, sweetest brother, do not cause her grief in any way. If any of the brothers talk back to her, you ought to hit them. For now you should be called father. I know that you are able to please her without me writing this letter, but do not take my letter of admonition in the wrong way. For we ought to worship her who bore us as a god, especially since she is good.

I have written these things to you, brother, knowing the sweetness of our revered parents. Please write to me about your welfare.

Farewell, brother.

(Papyrus letter, *SB3*, 62643, trans. Stowers)[26]

Fig. 2.6. *Two brothers. Funerary portrait from Roman Egypt, second century C.E. Corbis Images.*

62. Seneca admonishes a friend's grief

In the following letter to a friend grieving the loss of his child, Seneca offers both consolation and admonition, showing that the ideal "types" described by pseudo-Demetrius and pseudo-Libanius are rather theoretical and can be combined in a single epistle. Seneca's letter also speaks volumes about his expectations regarding "manliness," the expression of emotion, and the relationship between father and children.

> Seneca to his own Lucilius, greeting.
>
> I enclose a copy of the letter which I wrote to Marullus at the time when he had lost his little son and was reported to be rather womanish in his grief—a letter in which I have not observed the usual form of condolence: for I did not believe that he should be handled gently, since in my opinion he deserved criticism rather than consolation. When a man is stricken and is finding it most difficult to endure a grievous wound, one must humor him for a while; let him satisfy his grief or at any rate work off the first shock; but those who have assumed an indulgence in grief should be rebuked forthwith, and should learn that there are certain follies even in tears.

(The letter to Marullus)

> Is it solace that you look for? Let me give you a scolding instead! You are like a woman in the way you take your son's death; what would you do if you had lost an intimate friend? A son, a little child of unknown promise, is dead; a fragment of time has been lost. We hunt out excuses for grief; we would even utter unfair complaints about Fortune, as if Fortune would never give us just reason for complaining! But I had really thought that you possessed spirit enough to deal with concrete troubles, to say nothing of the shadowy troubles over which men make moan through force of habit. Had you lost a friend (which is the greatest blow of all), you would have had to endeavor rather to rejoice because you had possessed him than to mourn because you had lost him.
>
> But many men fail to count up how manifold their gains have been, how great their rejoicings. Grief like yours has this among other evils: it is not only useless, but thankless. Has it then all been for nothing that you have had such a friend?
>
> Let us say this also to him who mourns and misses the untimely dead: that all of us, whether young or old, live, in comparison with eternity, on the same level as regards our shortness of life. For out of all time there comes to us less than what any one could call least, since "least" is at any rate some part; but this life of ours is next to nothing, and yet (fools that we are!), we marshal it in broad array!
>
> These words I have written to you, not with the idea that you should expect a cure from me at such a late date—for it is clear to me that you have told yourself everything that you will read in my letter—but with the idea that I should rebuke you even for the slight delay during which you lapsed from your true self, and should encourage you for the future, to rouse your spirit against Fortune and to be on the watch for all her missiles, not as if they might possibly come, but as if they were bound to come. Farewell.

(Seneca, *Epistle* 99, trans. Gummere, LCL)

Petitions

Under letters of "supplication" pseudo-Demetrius includes formal petitions, of which a number are extant from the Roman world. John L. White has identified four basic elements of official petition letters: opening, background, request, and closing.[27] It is helpful to consider Paul's requests in his letters in light of these expected parts of a petition.

63. LETTER OF PETITION TO THE POLICE CAPTAIN

Here is a letter of petition written in the year 42 C.E.

> To the police captain of Euhemeria.
> To Tiberius Claudius Philoxenus, strategus and chief of police, from Paes, gardener of Thermoutharion.
> The shepherds of Ophelion, and his sons Papontos and Ophelion, of Euhemeria in the division of Themistes, let their flocks into the pasturage which I have in the olive-yard of Thermoutharion daughter of Lycarion, and overran, cropped, and utterly destroyed it, doing no slight damage. I beg you to write instructions to the police captain of the village. And they cut the heads off very many young trees.
> (Endorsed) To the police captain: send them up.
> The 22nd year of Tiberius Claudius Caesar Augustus Germanicus Imperator. Pharmouthi 9
>
> > (*P.Ryl.* 152, trans. White, adapted)

64. LETTER OF PETITION TO THE PREFECT OF EGYPT, CLAUDIUS BALBILLUS[28]

> To Tiberius Claudius Balbillus from Nemesion, collector of poll-tax for Philadelphia, . . . all six collectors for the aforesaid villages in the division of Heraclides in the Arsinoite nome. The once numerous inhabitants of the aforesaid villages have now been reduced to a few, because some have fled for lack of means and others have died without leaving heirs-at-law, and for this reason we are in danger owing to impoverishment of having to abandon the collectorship; wherefore resorting to you (in order not to have to abandon it) we request you, who are the savior and benefactor of all, to write, if it please you, to Asinianus the strategus of the nome to keep us free from molestation and await your decision at the assize of the nome up here, in order that we may enjoy your beneficence.
> Farewell.
>
> > (*P.Graux* 2, trans. White)

65. A PETITION FROM A VILLAGE SEEKING RELIEF

The following petition from fourth-century-Egypt villagers addresses a magistrate who apparently has threatened to lay a claim on the bodies of some in the village, perhaps forcing them into labor (slavery?) in payment of some debt. Note the peculiar combination of pride and subdued defiance—the villagers insist they have never surrendered more than what they owed and note that no one can steal into their village unseen—but also abject subservience that may express despair: They are ready to offer up a few of their "best young fellows." (See also nos. 107–9 in chapter 3).

> To our master and patron, . . . from [several signatories and] all the people of the village of Euhemeria. We wish you to know, Lord, that even in your father's day, as under Your Beneficence, we have never handed over our bodies—rather, year in and year out, that we have completed our due services but surrender ourselves to no one. There is no stranger in our village, and there are two watch-towers, so no one can ride or walk into the village [unobserved]. But if [any] should come for the best of our young fellows, we would not say you nay. Do whatever seems best to you to do.
>
> (*P.Ross.Georg.* 3.8, trans. MacMullen)

The "Apologetic" Letter (Letter of Defense)

From the first century comes the following pseudepigraphic letter, attributed to Socrates, in which the philosopher is made to answer accusations regarding his refusal to accept payment from others for philosophizing. Thus, Socrates becomes an advocate of the Cynic way of life. Note that similar concerns appear to have arisen regarding Paul's refusal of patronage in Corinth, eliciting defensive statements in 2 Corinthians.

66. Socrates defends his refusal of support (pseudepigraphic)

> I have taken care of the two visitors, as you urged me to do, and I have sought out one of our companions who will plead their cause before the people. He said that he would serve quite readily because he, too, desires to please you.
>
> But concerning the money and the things you wrote about so mockingly, there is perhaps nothing unusual about some people inquiring, first of all, why I have chosen a life of poverty while others zealously pursue wealth, and then why, although it is possible for me to get large sums of money from many people, I willingly refuse gifts not only from living friends, but also from friends who have died and left gifts to me. And it is not surprising that other people consider one who is thus inclined to be insane.
>
> Yet one must consider not only this feature, but also the rest of our way of life, and if we appear different from others in regard to bodily practices, one must not be surprised if we also stand apart in our attitude toward material gain. Therefore, I am satisfied to have the plainest food and the same garment summer and winter, and I do not wear shoes at all, nor do I desire political fame except to the extent that it comes from being prudent and just.
>
> But those who pursue the luxurious life forgo nothing in their diet, and they seek to wear different garments not only during the same year, but even in the same day, and they take great delight in forbidden pleasures.
>
> But concerning my children, and your statement that I should provide for them, all men can learn what I think about them. I consider the one origin of happiness to be right thinking. But he who has no understanding, but trusts in gold and silver, first thinks that he possesses the good which he does not have,

and then becomes much more wretched than others. It is the same as if one person, although oppressed by poverty, will, even if not now, then certainly at some later time come to his senses, while another person, laboring under false notions of what it is to be truly happy, neglects what is truly beneficial, and being corrupted by affluence, in addition to the truly human goods which he has already failed to obtain, is defrauded of the hope of future good. For it is not possible for such a man to come safely to virtue, who is held captive by the flattery of men who are clever at speaking, and who is held captive by the sorcery of pleasures, which attack the soul through every sense organ and gradually drive out every bit of good or moderation.

(Socrates, *Epistle* 6 [pseudepigraphic], trans. Stowers)

The Ambassadorial Letter

In discussing Paul's letter to the Romans, Robert Jewett has proposed that the tone of respect that Paul strikes in Romans (see 1:8-12; 15:14-16) best fits the genre of the ambassadorial letter.[29] He proposes as a prime example of that genre the letter that King Agrippa of Judea wrote to the emperor Gaius (Caligula) to protest Gaius's plan to install a statue of himself in the Jerusalem temple.

67. King Agrippa's letter to Emperor Gaius (Philo)

Philo of Alexandria presents a transcript of the letter in his account of his own embassy of protest and petition to Gaius. The circumstances were desperate: the emperor had sadistically surprised Agrippa with the baleful news of his plans, causing the king such distress that he collapsed and had to be removed from court. Agrippa composed this letter only after he had begun to recover two days later. Note here, in the beginning and end of the letter, the tone that Agrippa adopts, expressing submission, honor, and gratitude to a benefactor even under such duress as causes him to offer his own life to protect the sanctity of the temple. (Other excerpts from the letter are included in nos. 118 and 122 in chapter 4, below.)

O Master,

Fear and shame have taken from me all courage to come into your presence to address you since fear teaches me to dread your threats; and shame, out of respect for the greatness of your power and dignity, keeps me silent. But a writing will show my request, which I now here offer to you as my earnest petition.

In all men, O emperor! a love of their country is innate, and an eagerness for their national customs and laws. I am, as you know, a Jew; and Jerusalem is my country, in which there is erected the holy temple of the most high God. And I have kings for my grandfathers and for my ancestors, the greater part of whom have been called high priests, looking upon their royal power as inferior to their office as priests; and thinking that the high priesthood is as much superior to the power of a king, as God is superior to man; for that the one is occupied in rendering service to God, and the other has only the care of governing them. Accordingly I, being one of this nation, and being attached to this country and to such a temple, address to you this petition on behalf of them all....

Fig. 2.7. *Coin of Agrippa I, minted in Caesarea, 42–43* c.e. *The inscription around Agrippa's portrait reads "Great King (Agrippa, Friend of Caesar)"; obverse, an image of Tychē (Fortuna) and "Caesarea [dedicated to] Augustus." Photo by courtesy of the Classical Numismatic Group.*

You have thought the native countries of some of your friends worthy of being admitted to share all the privileges of the Roman constitution; and those who but a little while ago were slaves, became the masters of others who also enjoyed your favor in a higher, or at all events not in a lower degree, and they were delighted too at the causes of your beneficence. And I indeed am perfectly aware that I belong to the class which is in subjection to a lord and master, and also that I am admitted to the honor of being one of your companions, being inferior to you in respect of my birthright and natural rank, but inferior to no one whomsoever, not to say the most eminent of all men, in good will and loyalty towards you, both because that is my natural disposition, and also in consequence of the number of benefits with which you have enriched me; so that if I in consequence had felt confidence to implore you myself on behalf of my country, if not to grant to it the Roman constitution, at least to confer freedom and a remission of taxes on it, I should not have thought that I had any reason to fear your displeasure for preferring such a petition to you, and for requesting that most desirable of all things, your favor, which it can do you no harm to grant, and which is the most advantageous of all things for my country to receive. For what can possibly be a more desirable blessing for a subject nation than the good will of its sovereign? . . .

If I were to enumerate the benefits which I myself have received at your hands, the day would be too short for me; besides the fact that it is not proper for one who has undertaken to speak on one subject to branch off to a digression about some other matter. And even if I should be silent, the facts themselves speak and utter a distinct voice. You released me when I was bound in chains and iron. Who is there who is ignorant of this? But do not, after having done so, O emperor! bind me in bonds of still greater bitterness: for the chains from which you released me surrounded a part of my body, but those which I am now anticipating are the chains of the soul, which are likely to oppress it wholly and in every part; you abated from me a fear of death, continually suspended over my head; you received me when I was almost dead through fear; you raised me up as it were from the dead. Continue your favor, O master, that your Agrippa may not be driven wholly to forsake life; for I shall appear (if you do not do so) to have been released from bondage, not for the purpose of being saved, but for that of being made to perish in a more conspicuous manner.

You have given me the greatest and most glorious inheritance among mankind, the rank and power of a king, at first over one district, then over another and a more important one, adding to my kingdom the district called Trachonitis and Galilee. Do not then, O master! after having loaded me with means of superfluity, deprive me of what is actually necessary. Do not, after you have raised me up to the most brilliant light, cast me down again from my eminence to the most profound darkness. I am willing to descend from this splendid position in which you have placed me; I do not deprecate a return to the condition in which I was a short time ago; I will give up everything; I look upon everything as of less importance than the one point of preserving the ancient customs and laws of my nation unaltered; for if they are violated, what could I say, either to my fellow countrymen or to any other men? It would follow of necessity that I must be looked upon as one of two things, either as a betrayer of my people, or as one who is no longer accounted a friend by you. And what could be a greater misery than either of these two things? For if I am still reckoned among the company of your friends, I shall then receive the imputation of treason against my own nation, if neither my country is preserved free from all misfortune, nor even the temple left inviolate. For you, great men, preserve the property of your companions and of those who take refuge in your protection by your imperial splendor and magnificence.

And if you have any secret grief or vexation in your mind, do not throw me into prison, like Tiberius, but deliver me from any anticipation of being thrown into prison at any future time; command me at once to be put out of the way. For what advantage would it be to me to live, who place my whole hopes of safety and happiness in your friendship and favor?

(Philo, *Embassy to Gaius* 276-79, 285-88, 323-29, trans. Yonge)

The "Amicus Domini" Letter

The genre of the *amicus domini* letter has received increasing attention especially in relation to Paul's letter to the owner of the slave Onesimus. (Although Paul addresses the letter to three people whom he names—Philemon, Apphia, and Archippus—and to "the assembly in your house," the letter is customarily known as Philemon.) Because a runaway slave was in grave danger, at the very least of harsh punishment if captured and returned to the master, a slave who wished to return to his master could often do so only by pleading with a "friend of the master" to intercede on his or her behalf. Characteristic of such letters are a plea that the slave is genuinely remorseful for fleeing and for any other insubordination; that the slave resolves to be even more obedient; and that the master's friend is so convinced of the slave's plea that he is willing to stake his friendship with the master on the slave's future behavior.

68. PLINY INTERCEDES FOR A FREEDMAN IN DISFAVOR

The following example, from Pliny, is especially remarkable, since the person for whom the governor intercedes is not a slave but a "freedman"—that is, a *former* slave, now legally manumitted but still clearly obligated to his former master.

> Your freedman, whom you lately mentioned to me with displeasure, has been with me, and threw himself at my feet with as much submission as he could have fallen at yours. He earnestly requested me with many tears, and even with all the eloquence of silent sorrow, to intercede for him; in short, he convinced me by his whole behavior that he sincerely repents of his fault. I am persuaded he is thoroughly reformed, because he seems deeply sensible of his guilt. I know you are angry with him, and I know, too, it is not without reason; but clemency can never exert itself more laudably than when there is the most cause for resentment. You once had an affection for this man, and, I hope, will have again; meanwhile, let me only prevail with you to pardon him. If he should incur your displeasure hereafter, you will have so much the stronger plea in excuse for your anger as you show yourself more merciful to him now. Concede something to his youth, to his tears, and to your own natural mildness of temper: do not make him uneasy any longer, and I will add, too, do not make yourself so; for a man of your kindness of heart cannot be angry without feeling great uneasiness. I am afraid, were I to join my entreaties with his, I should seem rather to compel than request you to forgive him. Yet I will not scruple even to write mine with his; and in so much the stronger terms as I have very sharply and severely reproved him, positively threatening never to interpose again in his behalf. But though it was proper to say this to him, in order to make him more fearful of offending, I do not say so to you. I may perhaps, again have occasion to entreat you upon his account, and again obtain your forgiveness; supposing, I mean, his fault should be such as may become me to intercede for, and you to pardon. Farewell.
>
> (Pliny, *Epistle* 103, *to Sabinianus*, trans. Melmoth)

The Gospel in Paul's Letters

We turn next to a consideration of specific themes that sound in Paul's letters, themes that were evidently core elements of his proclamation. In his earliest letter known to us, 1 Thessalonians, Paul declares that believers in Macedonia and Achaia praise the Thessalonians for having "turned to God from idols, to serve a living and true God, and to wait for his Son from heaven, whom he raised from the dead—Jesus, who rescues us from the wrath that is coming" (1:9-10).

As we will see in chapter 4, the distinction between "idols" (the images of the gods of the Greek and Roman world) and the one "true God," and the attribution of immoral behavior to idolatry, were commonplaces in Jewish apologetic literature. Even among Greek and Roman philosophers who speculated about the actual nature of the gods, however, the importance of worshiping the gods by participating in public cult—joining in prayers and sacrifices before images of the gods—was rarely questioned.

Fig. 2.8. *Portrait of Seneca, first century. Museo Palazzo Massimo, Rome. Photo: Neil Elliott.*

"To Turn from Idols": Idolatry and the Belief in a Supreme God

Luke offers a very different depiction of Paul's encounter with idolatry in Athens (Acts 17). Here Paul gives ostensible respect (however ironically Luke may intend the reader to take these lines) to the piety of the Athenians, whose streets are filled with temples and altars and who even worship an "unknown god" (17:23). Paul takes the opportunity to present himself as the herald of this unknown god who is the true creator of all things, "in whom we live and move and have our being" (17:28).

That phrase is set in quotation marks in some modern translations because we find it in the thought of the Stoic philosopher Aratus (c. 310 B.C.E.). We have no way of knowing whether Paul (or Luke) was familiar with the teaching of Aratus, since the New Testament text does not cite him by name. Interestingly, however, we find the same quotation in the work of another Hellenistic Jew, the apologist Aristobolus (second century B.C.E.), and it might seem more likely that Paul (or rather, Luke) knew it from Aristobolus's writing or from a similar use of the phrase in Jewish propaganda.[30] (Aristobolus is mentioned also in 2 Macc 1:10—2:18.)[31]

Fig. 2.9. *Inscription on an altar, from the time of the republic, discovered on the Palatine Hill in Rome in 1820. In the fifth century* B.C.E. *Pausanius described an altar dedicated "to unknown gods" in Athens* (Description of Greece *5.14.8). Photo: Philip Rickerby. The inscription reads:*

SEI · DEO · SEI · DEIVAE · SAC(RVM)/
G(AIUS) · SEXTIVS · C(AII) · F(IIVS) · CALVINVS · PR(AETOR)/
DE · SENATI · SENTENTIA/
RESTITVIT
Be it consecrated to a god or goddess,
G(aius) Sextius Calvinus, s(on of) G(aius), pr(aetor),
By order of the Senate,
Restored (this altar).

69. Aristobulus, fragment 4

We have the following fragment of Aristobolus's works from a citation in the fourth-century Christian writer Eusebius. Eusebius points out that, although he finds the pagan philosopher useful, he has edited Aratus's text by replacing the words *Dis* and *Zeus* with *theos*, the generic Greek word for "God."

> . . . But he himself [i.e., God] is in every way heavenly, and brings everything on earth to fulfillment, because he controls their beginning, middle, and end. So the word of the ancients; so the one born in the water [i.e., Moses] set it forth, after receiving the teaching from God in statements on the two-tablet law. It

is forbidden to speak in any other way; and, indeed, I am trembling in body and soul. From the heights he rules over all in order. But you, O child, draw near with your mind, after gaining full mastery over your tongue, and lay this account in your heart.

And Aratus has this to say about the same subject: "Let us start with God, and may men never leave him without mention. But all the streets are full of God and all market-places of men; the sea is full and the harbors, and all of us need God in every way. For we are his offspring and the gentle God shows men signs of good fortune. He stirs people to work, reminding them of the means of living. He says when the best clod of earth should be given over to oxen and mattocks. He says when seasons are favorable to plant a circle of trees and to sow the various seeds."

I think it has been demonstrated clearly that the power of God permeates all things. And as was necessary, we have signified this by removing the divine names Dis and Zeus used throughout the verses; for their inherent meaning relates to God, and for this reason we have expressed it this way. We have presented these things therefore in a way not unsuited to the things being discussed. All philosophers agree that it is necessary to hold devout convictions about God, something which our school prescribes particularly well. And the whole structure of our law has been drawn up with concern for piety, justice, self-control, and other qualities that are truly good.

(Eusebius, *Praeparatio Evangelica* 13.12, 666a–667a, trans. Holladay)

70. Praise of the supreme God (Cleanthes)

The Stoic Cleanthes (third century b.c.e.) exemplifies a lofty understanding of a supreme God who has created all things and governs them according to a divine and universal reason or word (*logos*). It is with such conceptions of a single supreme God that we may presume Luke sought to make connection. Note, however, that Cleanthes' reverence for the supreme God, whom he identifies with Zeus, requires neither the refusal to recognize other deities nor the avoidance of their worship.

Most glorious of the immortals, invoked by many names, ever all-powerful,
Zeus, the First Cause of Nature, who rules all things with Law,
Hail! It is right for mortals to call upon you,
since from you we have our being, we whose lot it is to be God's image,
we alone of all mortal creatures that live and move upon the earth.
Accordingly, I will praise you with my hymn and ever sing of your might.
The whole universe, spinning around the earth,
goes wherever you lead it and is willingly guided by you.
So great is the servant which you hold in your invincible hands,
your eternal, two-edged, lightning-forked thunderbolt.
By its strokes all the works of nature came to be established,
and with it you guide the universal Word of Reason which moves through all
    creation,
mingling with the great sun and the small stars.
O God, without you nothing comes to be on earth,
neither in the region of the heavenly poles, nor in the sea,

Fig. 2.10. *Marble bust of Zeus, second-century-c.e. Roman copy of a fifth-century-b.c.e. Greek original. Palazzo Massimo, Rome. Photo in the public domain.*

except what evil men do in their folly.

But you know how to make extraordinary things suitable,

and how to bring order forth from chaos; and even that which is unlovely is
    lovely to you.

For thus you have joined all things, the good with the bad, into one,

so that the eternal Word of all came to be one.

This Word, however, evil mortals flee, poor wretches;

though they are desirous of good things for their possession,

they neither see nor listen to God's universal Law;

and yet, if they obey it intelligently, they would have the good life.

But they are senselessly driven to one evil after another:

some are eager for fame, no matter how godlessly it is acquired;

others are set on making money without any orderly principles in their lives;

and others are bent on ease and on the pleasures and delights of the body.

They do these foolish things, time and again,

and are swept along, eagerly defeating all they really wish for.

O Zeus, giver of all, shrouded in dark clouds and holding the vivid bright
    lightning,

rescue men from painful ignorance.
Scatter that ignorance far from their hearts,
and deign to rule all things in justice,
so that, honored in this way, we may render honor to you in return,
and sing your deeds unceasingly, as befits mortals;
for there is no greater glory for men
or for gods than to justly praise the universal Word of Reason.

(Cleanthes, *Hymn to Zeus*, trans. Ellery)

71. Isis as the single supreme God (Apuleius)

One way to make sense of the potentially bewildering multitude of deities brought together in the Roman world (and beyond it) is to notice similarities between the way different peoples conceived of various gods and worshiped them and to understand these similarities as evidence that in fact the same deity was being worshiped. This is the message Isis brings to Lucius, the long-suffering protagonist of the *Metamorphoses* of Apuleius (second century c.e.). Lucius's curiosity in magic took an unfortunate turn when he was turned into an ass (thus the title under which the story is perhaps better known, *The Golden Ass*). At length Isis delivers him and reveals herself as the true God hailed by many peoples under different names.

Isis was originally one of the national gods of Egypt, but in the Hellenistic age she became widely popular in the Eastern Mediterranean. In the Roman era she was worshiped in Rome, Pompeii (where a temple to her has been excavated), and elsewhere. She was honored by civic cults and inspired tremendous personal devotion as well, not as an "Egyptian" deity but as the supreme God. Note again that honoring Isis does not prevent one from honoring her by other names. Nevertheless, at times different emperors suppressed "Egyptian" rites (including the cult of Isis) in Rome.

> Behold, Lucius, I am come; your weeping and prayer have moved me to succor you. I am she that is the natural mother of all things, mistress and governess of all the elements, the initial progeny of worlds, chief of the powers divine, queen of all that are in hell; the principal of them who dwell in heaven, manifested alone and under one form of all the gods and goddesses. At my will the planets of the sky, the wholesome winds of the seas, and the lamentable silences of hell be disposed; my name, my divinity is adored throughout all the world, in divers manners, in variable customs, and by many names. For the Phrygians who are the first of all call me the Mother of the gods of Pessinus; the Athenians, who are sprung from their own soil, Cecropoian Minerva; the Cyprians, who are girt about the sea, Paphian Venus; the Cretans who bear arrows, Dictynnian Diana; the Sicilians, who speak three tongues, infernal Proserpine; the Eleusinians their ancient goddess Ceres; some Juno, others Bellona, others Hecate, other Rhamnusia, and principally both sort of the Ethiopians who dwell in the Orient and are enlightened by the morning rays of the sun, and the Egyptians, who are excellent in all kind of ancient doctrine, and by their proper ceremonies accustomed to worship me, do call me by my true name, Queen Isis.
>
> (Apuleius, *Metamorphoses* 11.4, trans. Hanson, LCL)

Fig. 2.11. *Roman statue of Isis, early second century* c.e., *from the Villa Adriana near Tivoli. Museo Capitolino, Rome. Photo in the public domain.*

The Public Face of Piety

Paul's demand that the Thessalonians "turn from idols" would have required much more than that they conceive of a single supreme God. He required that they turn away from the regular, public worship of gods that their neighbors would have considered not only normal and salutary but necessary for the welfare of the city. Despite considerable discussion and debate among Roman philosophers and orators regarding the line between proper religious observance and excessive scrupulosity, there was wide consensus that the gods of a Roman city required and deserved worship.

72. Fear of the gods and the Roman state (Polybius)

In the second century B.C.E., the Roman citizen Polybius remarked on the superiority of Roman religiosity. The Greek word *deisidaimonia*, literally "reverence" or "fear of the gods" (the *daimones*), could be evaluated positively (as here) or negatively (as "superstition," as by Cicero, no. 73, or the second-century-C.E. writer Plutarch in his treatise *On Superstition*).

> The quality in which the Roman commonwealth is the most distinctly superior is in my opinion the nature of their religious convictions. I believe that it is the very thing which among other peoples is an object of reproach. I mean superstition [*deisidaimonia*], which maintains the cohesions of the Roman state.
> (Polybius, *Histories* 6.56, trans. Paton, LCL)

73. On the distinction between *religio* and *superstitio* (Cicero)

In contrast to the later Christian theological emphasis on right belief concerning the nature of God, Roman religion in general was less concerned with theoretical questions than with the practical issue of how mortals should offer worship to whatever gods there were. Cicero's essays *On Divination* and *On the Nature of the Gods* provide the exceptions that prove the rule. In the first he is concerned to promote *religio* but to discourage *superstitio*, an obsessively fearful approach to the gods as potential enemies:

> Wherefore, just as it is a duty to extend the influence of true religion, which is closely associated with the knowledge of nature, so it is a duty to weed out every root of superstition. For superstition is ever at your heels to urge you on; it follows you at every turn. It is with you when you listen to a prophet, or an omen; when you offer sacrifices or watch the flight of birds; when you consult an astrologer or a soothsayer; when it thunders or lightens or there is a bolt from on high; or when some so-called prodigy is born or is made. And since necessarily some of these signs are nearly always being given, no one who believes in them can ever remain in a tranquil state of mind.
> (Cicero, *On Divination* 2.149, trans. Falconer, LCL)

74. That worshiping the gods is a universal impulse (Cicero)

Although Cicero's treatise *On the Nature of the Gods* includes a lengthy survey and critique of various philosophical views of the gods, his ultimate point is simply to show that traditional worship of the gods is reasonable. We may thus speak of a certain "ambivalence" on Cicero's part: as a philosopher, he is skeptical toward specific arguments regarding the existence of the gods, but he is nevertheless attached to their worship.[32]

> Any one who should reflect how unthinkingly and recklessly these ideas are advanced, ought to reverence Epicurus and place him among the number of those very beings that form the subject of this inquiry, for it was he alone who perceived, in the first place, the fact of the existence of the gods from the idea of them which nature herself had implanted in all men's minds. For what nation or race of men is there that does not possess, independently of instruction, a certain preconception of them? . . .
>
> You see, then, that what constitutes the foundation of this inquiry is excellently well laid, for since the belief in question was determined by no ordinance, or custom, or law, and since a steadfast unanimity continues to prevail amongst all people without exception, it must be understood that the gods exist.
>
> . . . Since their existence is pretty universally admitted not only among philosophers but also among those who are not philosophers, let us own that the following fact is also generally allowed, namely, that we possess a "preconception," to use my former word, or "previous notion" of the gods. . . . For nature that gave us the idea of gods as such, has also engraved in our minds the conviction that they are blessed and eternal. . . .
>
> Enough would have now been said, if our aim were only to worship the gods with piety, and to be freed from superstition, for a divine nature of this exalted kind, being eternal and supremely blessed, would receive the pious worship of humanity (everything that is of surpassing excellence inspiring a just reverence), and also all fear arising from the violence and anger of the gods would have been dispelled, now that it is understood that anger and favor have no place in a blessed and immortal nature, and that, when those feelings have been removed, no terrors threaten us from the powers above.
>
> (Cicero, *On the Nature of the Gods* 1.16-17, trans. Rackham, LCL, adapted)

75. The civic importance of honoring the gods (Cicero)

Theoretical reservations regarding the nature of the gods aside, Cicero emphasized the importance of offering them worship in order to maintain the health, peace, and prosperity of the city. He considered traditional religious rites the foundation of the Roman state:

> I ought to uphold the beliefs about the immortal gods which have come down to us from our ancestors, and the rites and ceremonies and duties of religion. For my part I always shall uphold them . . . and no eloquence . . . shall ever dislodge me from the belief as to the worship of the immortal gods which I have inherited from our forefathers. . . .
>
> The religion of the Roman people comprises ritual, auspices, and the third additional division consisting of all such prophetic warnings as the interpreters of the Sibyl or the soothsayers have derived from portents and prodigies. Well, I have always thought that none of these departments of religion was

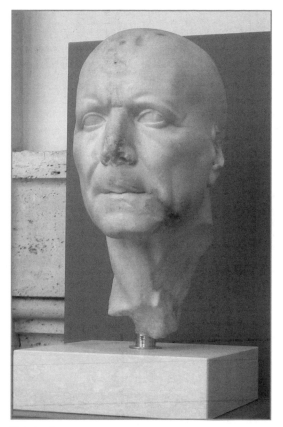

Fig. 2.12. *A priest of Isis. Marble bust, first century c.e. Although Egyptian priests were occasionally expelled from Rome, the portrait (from a wealthy villa in the city) conveys Roman propriety. Museo Palazzo Massimo. Photo: Neil Elliott.*

to be despised, and I have held the conviction that Romulus by his auspices and Numa by his establishment of our ritual laid the foundations of our state, which assuredly could never have been as great as it is had not the fullest measure of divine favor been obtained for it.

(Cicero, *On the Nature of the Gods* 3.2.5, trans. Rackham, LCL)

76. The danger of skepticism toward the gods (Epictetus)

More than a century later, the Stoic Epictetus, too, showed a traditional Roman circumspection toward the gods. Here he chastises other philosophers (Epicurus in particular, but also those of the Academy) for promoting a skepticism that he believes undermines the piety that is both an expression of human nature and a necessity for the welfare of the city. Note, first, the rhetorical technique, common in the *diatribe*, of putting words into an imaginary interlocutor's mouth (here set in quotation marks). Note too the intensity of Epictetus's sarcasm at the end of the excerpt.

> **Diatribe** is a style of teaching and moral exhortation in which the speaker uses dialogue and questions directed to an imaginary opponent to lead hearers away from possible errors and toward greater insight and right behavior. The technique of sustained speech-in-character was called *prosōpopoiia*.[33]

Ah, what a misfortune! A man has received from nature measures and standards for discovering the truth, and then does not go on and take the pains to add to these and to work out additional principles to supply the deficiencies, but does exactly the opposite, endeavoring to take away and destroy whatever faculty he does possess for discovering the truth. What do you say, philosopher? What is your opinion of piety and sanctity?

"If you wish, I shall prove that it is good."

By all means, prove it, that our citizens may be converted and may honor the Divine and at least cease to be indifferent about the things that are of supreme importance. Do you, then, possess the proofs?

"I do."

Thank heaven.

"Since, then, you are quite satisfied with all this, hear the contrary: The gods do not exist, and even if they do, they pay no attention to men, nor have we any fellowship with them, and hence this piety and sanctity that the multitude talk about is a lie told by impostors and sophists, or, I swear, by legislators to frighten and restrain evildoers."

Well done, philosopher! You have conferred a service upon our citizens, you have recovered our young men who were already inclining to despise things divine.

"What then? Does not all this satisfy you? Learn now how righteousness is nothing, how reverence is folly, how a father is nothing, how a son is nothing."

Well done, philosopher! Keep at it; persuade the young men, that we may have more who feel and speak as you do. It is from principles like these that our well-governed states have grown great! Principles like these have made Sparta what it was! These are the convictions which Lycurgus wrought into the Spartans by his laws and his system of education, namely, that neither is slavery base rather than noble, nor freedom noble rather than base! Those who died at Thermopylae died because of these judgments regarding slavery and freedom! And for what principles but these did the men of Athens give up their city?

And then those who talk thus marry and beget children and fulfill the duties of citizens and get themselves appointed priests and prophets! Priests and prophets of whom? Of gods that do not exist! And they themselves consult the Pythian priestess—in order to hear lies and to interpret the oracles to others! Oh what monstrous shamelessness and imposture!

(Arrian, *Discourses of Epictetus* 2.20.21-27, trans. Oldfather, LCL, alt.)

77. That impiety toward the gods leads to immorality (Epictetus)

Later in the same speech Epictetus continues his attack on skeptical philosophers, now suggesting that one of the dire consequences of impiety (the refusal to honor the gods) is the temptation to all sorts of immoral behavior. Compare this view with Paul's—or the author of Wisdom of Solomon—for whom it is precisely the worship of (false) gods that generates immorality.

Grateful mortals indeed and reverential: Why if nothing else, at least they eat bread every day, and yet have the audacity to say, "We do not know if there is a Demeter, or a Kore, or a Pluto";[34] not to mention that, although they enjoy night and day, the changes of the year and the stars and the sea and the earth and the co-operation of mortals, they are not moved in the least by any one of these things, but look merely for a chance to belch out their trivial "problem"

Fig. 2.13. *A priest presides over worship at a temple of Isis. Fresco from Herculaneum, first century* c.e. *Photo in the public domain.*

and after thus exercising their stomach to go off to the bath. But what they are going to say, or what they are going to talk about, or to whom, and what their hearers are going to get out of these things that they are saying, all this has never given them a moment's concern.

I greatly fear that a noble-spirited young man may hear these statements and be influenced by them, or, having been influenced already, may lose all the bits of nobility that he possessed; that we may be giving an adulterer reasons for strengthening his behavior; that some embezzler of public funds may lay hold of a faulty argument based upon these theories; that some who neglects his own parents may gain even more boldness from them.

(Arrian, *Discourses of Epictetus* 2.20.32-35, trans. Oldfather, LCL)

78. Rome officially welcomes Cybele (Ovid)

One indication that religion in the Roman world was a very public phenomenon can be found in Ovid's account of how the Phrygian goddess Cybele, the Great Mother,

Fig. 2.14. *A crowned and enthroned Cybele, offering grain to a devotee and holding the tympanum, the drum used in worship; her crown represents the walls of a city under her protection; a lion lies at her feet. Relief from Phrygia, early fourth century* B.C.E. *Pergamon Museum. Photo: Marcus Cyron.*

Fig. 2.15. *A Roman image of Cybele shows traditional features, now transformed into the image of an aristocratic Roman matron. White marble, about 50 C.E. The Getty Villa. Photo: Marshall Astor.*

vcame to be worshiped in Rome. Religions in the first-century Mediterranean world were very conscious of their beginnings. In his poem *Fasti*, Ovid provides explanations for the feasts and fasts of the Roman religious calendar; in the following selection, he asks the Muse Erato to recount how an ostensibly foreign goddess was brought to Rome in 204 B.C.E.

Note the importance here not only of the cult's antiquity but also of oracles from Apollo and from the Sibylline books, cherished in Rome; of portents including an earthquake; and of claimed connections with Aeneas, fabled survivor of the Trojan War and ancestor of Julius Caesar. These claims and the implied connection with the Vestal Virgins in effect make Cybele's cult authentically "Roman." Note too the ceremonial roles played by key civic officials, including a Roman delegation to the Phrygian king Attalus and, in Italy, the equestrian and senatorial classes en masse.

> "Teach this also, I beg you, O escort, from where was she sought,
> from where did she come. Or was she ever in our city?"
> (The Muse responds)

"[Mount] Dindymus and Cybele and [Mount] Ida with her lovely fonts
and the kingdom of Ilium [i.e., Troy], the Mother ever loved.[35]
When Aenas brought Troy to the Italian lands,
the goddess almost trailed the rafts bearing sacred stuff,
but not yet was her spirit sought by Fate for Latium [Italy].
So aware of this, she stayed instead in her usual place.
Later, after strong Rome the works of five centuries
saw, and raised its head over the routed world,
the destining words of the Euboean song [the Sibylline books] the priest
studied; what he studied went like this:
'The Mother is out—O Roman, I charge you—ask for Mother.
when she arrives, she must be welcomed with a pure hand.'
The elders went round and round with this clouded prophecy—
Who was the missing parent? Where should she be pursued?
Apollo was asked. 'Summon the gods' Mother,'
he said. 'She must be found, in the yoke, on Mt. Ida.'
Princes were dispatched. At that time, Attalus ruled Phrygia.
He refused the request of the Ausonian [Roman] leaders.[36]
I sing of a miracle, though. The earth quaked with a long roar,
and thus the diva declared from her shrine,
'I myself wanted to be sought; let there be no delay, carry out my will.
Rome is a fitting place where every god may go.'
In a terrified panic at her voice, Attalus said, 'Proceed.
You'll still be ours—Rome registers her forebears among the Phrygians.'
Many axes cut the pines right away,
those which the devout Phrygian [the ancestor Aeneas] had used when
   fleeing.[37]
A thousand hands put together, and in colorful, glowing designs,
the heavenly Mother has a hollowed ship.
She is transported most securely through her son's waters.

(The craft bearing an image of Cybele at last reaches Ostia. There the planned welcoming ceremony goes awry when the boat runs aground—until the goddess performs a miracle.)

All equestrians and serious senators joined with the masses
to greet her as she arrived at mouth of Tuscan stream
along with mothers, daughters, and young married women advancing,
and those who kept the holy hearths in their virginity.[38]
The men wear out their eager arms, straining on the rope,
while the alien vessel barely advances up the stream.
Long had the soil been in a dry spell; crops scorched and thirsty
though pushed hard, the boat sank to miry bottom.
All hands present drove beyond their powers,
assisting the effort with loud sounding voice.
But like an ocean isle, it sat firmly in the middle.
The men stood and trembled, surprised by the sign.

(A noblewoman whose chastity has been impugned by her neighbors, Claudia Quinta, approaches the goddess and appeals to be vindicated. Cybele thus enters Italy by a portent that disproves false accusations against a virtuous devotee.)

> Claudia Quinta drew her lineage from ancient Clausus,[39]
> 　nor were her looks unequal to her elite line.
> She was pure, though not believed to be. An awful rumor
> 　had injured her; she'd been falsely accused.
> In fancy dress and varied hairdos she'd go out;
> 　this didn't help; nor did her unrelenting, sharp talk toward old men.
> Knowing she was right, she laughed at her fraudulent fame,
> 　though we in the public hold fast to others' faults.
> When she then walked out of the proper ladies' line,
> 　and drew clean river water into her hands,
> three times sprinkling her head, three times raising hands skyward—
> 　everyone watching thought her crazy—
> and falling to her knees, with face to the goddess' figure
> 　fastened, with hair now tousled, she poured out this saying:
> 'Nourishing, fertile womb of the gods—
> 　your petitioner's prayers please accept under this firm provision.
> My chastity is doubted. If you sentence me, I will admit what I deserve;
> 　I will pay the atoning punishment by death, defeated by the goddess'
> 　　judgment.
> But if I am innocent, a pledge of my life
> 　and chastity please give—give way to my chaste hand!'
> Saying this, she tugged a little on the rope—
> 　weird, but what I say is witnessed by the theater—[40]
> the goddess dislodged now accompanied the pilot, and by following she
> 　applauded Claudia.

(Ovid, *Fasti* 4, trans. Reasoner)

The people then welcomed Cybele to Italy with a night of feasting and public sacrifices.[41]

"The Word of the Cross"

In Acts 19 Luke narrates Paul's attempt to convince a group of Stoic and Epicurean philosophers of his message on the Hill of Mars (the Areopagus) in Athens. His appeal to belief in a single, benevolent creator who rules the world justly is apparently successful until he mentions Jesus' resurrection from the dead, at which point some of the philosophers scoff (17:32).

In Paul's own letters, in contrast, it is not the resurrection per se but Paul's insistence on proclaiming "nothing . . . except Jesus Christ, and him crucified" (1 Cor 2:2) that he considers the true scandal in his message, "a stumbling block to Jews and foolishness to Greeks" (1:23). Although he can also write to the Corinthians that he passed on to them what he had received, "that Christ died for our sins in accordance with the scriptures" (15:3), Paul never offers a summary of which scriptures he (or anyone else in the early apostolic community) had in mind.

Nor could he: Nothing in Jewish scripture suggested on its own that the death of a messiah would be "necessary" to achieve God's purposes. The "discovery" of scriptural "prophecies" of the messiah's divinely ordained death must then have occurred after Jesus' crucifixion, when his followers went looking for them. (Even the Gospels—which repeatedly show Jesus declaring plainly to his disciples that the messiah "must" die—show that the disciples did not understand this necessity until after Easter: see, for example, Luke 24:13-27; John 20:9.)[42]

Jesus' death by crucifixion was not scandalous because it was unusual. To the contrary, he shared the fate of tens of thousands of Jews and innumerable others, most of them slaves, subjects of Roman conquest and of Roman law alike. Nor was his death scandalous because it was extraordinarily painful (despite its customary depiction in Hollywood films). To the contrary, victims of crucifixion routinely suffered for days on the cross.

The Roman Use of Crucifixion

Crucifixion was "the most wretched of deaths" (Josephus, *War* 7.203), the severe form of execution practiced by the Romans against slaves and conquered peoples not only to punish but to humiliate the victim and thus to teach a terrible lesson to the conquered. As the first-century orator Quintilian exclaimed, "Whenever we crucify the guilty, the most crowded roads are chosen, where the most people can see and be moved by this fear. For penalties relate not so much to retribution as to their exemplary effect" (*Decl.* 274).[43]

Roman officials had long used crucifixion to punish slave conspiracies or to deter slave revolts on the expanding estates of the Roman patricians (Livy, 22.33.2; 33.36.3). After the first slave revolt in Sicily, 450 slaves were crucified; after the revolt led by Spartacus in 71 B.C.E., more than six thousand slaves were crucified along the Appian Way. In the first century C.E., under Nero, the Senate revived the custom of executing all the slaves of a household (which might be hundreds) if a single slave killed his master (Tacitus, *Ann.* 13.32.1).

The Romans used crucifixion also to terrorize subject peoples into submission. In his suppression of revolts in Judea after the death of Herod the Great, the Roman general Varus destroyed villages, slaughtered their residents, and then rounded up accused leaders of the insurrection and crucified some two thousand men (Josephus, *War* 2.75; *Ant.* 17.295). Just before the mid-first century C.E., the governor Tiberius Alexander crucified the sons of the rebel Judas of Gamala (*Ant.* 20.102). A few years later, Quadratus, legate of Syria, crucified Samarians and Judeans who had been taken prisoner by the governor Cumanus in suppression of their internecine battles (*War* 2.241; *Ant.* 20.129). Later in the 50s, the governor Felix crucified many other "brigands" involved in the insurgency of the rebel Eleazar (*War* 2.253; *Ant.* 20.160-61). Still later, in the increasingly volatile atmosphere of the mid-60s, the governor Florus put down protests of his provocations in Jerusalem by ordering a retaliatory

Fig. 2.16. *The heel bone of a young Jewish man, crucified during the reign of Herod, discovered in a tomb outside Jerusalem in the first century* c.e. *The iron nail could not be removed by those who buried him. Israel Museum, Jerusalem. Photo: Erich Lessing/Art Resource, New York.*

massacre in the upper city; he had several eminent citizens, including priests, beaten and crucified (*War* 2.293-308).

At last, during the Roman siege of Jerusalem toward the end of the revolt of 66–70, the Roman general Titus ordered the capture of desperate men and women who crept outside the walls of the city to look for food. These refugees were "scourged and subjected to torture of every description, before being crucified opposite the walls. . . . His main reason [for crucifying many each day] was the hope that the spectacle might perhaps induce the Judeans to surrender, for fear that continued resistance would involve them in a similar fate" (*War* 5.446-51).

Already decades before the defeat of Jerusalem, however, crucifixion was well established as a device of torture and terror. For Paul to have proclaimed as a deliverer one who had been subjected to so humiliating and debasing a death— a death in "the form of a slave" (Phil 2:7-8)—was on its face both scandalous and incomprehensible.[44]

The following quotations speak to elite Roman perceptions of crucifixion and the crucified.

79. The indignity of crucifixion (Cicero)

Cicero came to public prominence when he prosecuted Gaius Verres, a warlord who had combined brutality, treachery, and corruption to profit from the civil war between Gaius Marius and Sulla (87–86 B.C.E.). As a junior officer in Marius's army, Verres had stolen the cashier's box and defected to Sulla's lines; later, as governor of Sicily, his profiteering included extortion from temples, falsifying security contracts, and close collaboration with pirates.

All this was treasonous, but in his indictment Cicero built up to what he considered Verres' most heinous crime: when one of his prisoners escaped and threatened to expose the governor's corruption, Verres recaptured the man—a Roman citizen named Publius Gavius—and flogged and crucified him publicly. However affected, Cicero's horror at the crime speaks volumes about the function of crucifixion to distinguish rulers from ruled.

> For why should I speak of Publius Gavius, a citizen of the municipality of Cosa, O judges? or with what vigor of language, with what gravity of expression, with what grief of mind shall I mention him? But, indeed, that indignation fails me. I must take more care than usual that what I am going to say be worthy of my subject, worthy of the indignation which I feel. For the charge is of such a nature, that when I was first informed of it I thought I should not avail myself of it. . . .
>
> In the middle of the forum of Messana, a Roman citizen, O judges, was beaten with rods; while in the mean time no groan was heard, no other expression was heard from that wretched man, amid all his pain, and between the sound of the blows, except these words, "I am a citizen of Rome." He fancied that by this one statement of his citizenship he could ward off all blows, and remove all torture from his person. He not only did not succeed in averting by his entreaties the violence of the rods, but as he kept on repeating his entreaties and the assertion of his citizenship, a cross—*a cross*, I say—was got ready for that miserable man, who had never witnessed such a stretch of power. . . .
>
> And you, Verres, . . . you confess that he did cry out that he was a Roman citizen; but that the name of citizenship did not avail with you even so much as to cause the least hesitation in your mind, or even any brief respite from a most cruel and ignominious punishment. This is the point I press, this is what I dwell upon, O judges; with this single fact I am content. I give up, I am indifferent to all the rest. By his own confession he must be entangled and destroyed. You did not know who he was; you suspected that he was a spy. I do not ask you what were your grounds for that suspicion, I impeach you by your own words. He said that he was a Roman citizen.
>
> If you, Verres, being taken among the Persians or in the remotest parts of India, were being led to execution, what else would you cry out but that you were a Roman citizen? And if that name of your city, honored and renowned as it is among all men, would have availed you, a stranger among strangers, among barbarians, among men placed in the most remote and distant corners of the earth, ought not he, whoever he was, whom you were hurrying to the cross, who was a stranger to you, to have been able, when he said that he was a Roman citizen, to obtain from you, the praetor, if not an escape, at least a respite from death by his mention of and claims to citizenship?
>
> (Cicero, *Ad Verrem* 2.5.61, 64, trans. Yonge)

80. Crucifixion "the most pitiable thing in the world" (Seneca)

In a letter to his friend Lucilius, Seneca contemplates the sudden death of a mutual acquaintance. Because one cannot determine one's own future or avoid the inevitability of death, Seneca advises that one should live each day "as a separate life," "as a rounded whole," and thus live unafraid of death. By contrast, he derides as contemptible a poem in which Maecenas prays that his death may be postponed, his life extended, as long as possible, even should he endure injury, deformity, or crucifixion. Better, Seneca admonishes, to seek an immediate death than to endure the excruciating pain of crucifixion. Clearly, for Seneca, the notion of nobly facing death by crucifixion is an impossibility.

> For he only is anxious about the future, to whom the present is unprofitable. But when I have paid my soul its due, when a soundly-balanced mind knows that a day differs not a whit from eternity—whatever days or problems the future may bring—then the soul looks forth from lofty heights and laughs heartily to itself when it thinks upon the ceaseless succession of the ages. For what disturbance can result from the changes and the instability of Chance, if you are sure in the face of that which is unsure? Therefore, my dear Lucilius, begin at once to live, and count each separate day as a separate life. He who has thus prepared

Fig. 2.17. *A Roman graffito, from the second or third century* c.e., *depicts a donkey being crucified; the caption, presumably referring to a Christian, reads "Alexamenos worships God" (or, in the imperative, "worship [your] God!"). Drawing by Neil Elliott after the original in the Museum of the Palatine, Rome.*

himself, he whose daily life has been a rounded whole, is easy in his mind; but those who live for hope alone find that the immediate future always slips from their grasp and that greed steals along in its place, and the fear of death, a curse which lays a curse upon everything else.

(From that fear) came that most debased of prayers, in which Maecenas does not refuse to suffer weakness, deformity, and as a climax the pain of crucifixion, provided only that he may prolong the breath of life amid these sufferings:

Fashion me with a palsied hand,
   Weak of foot, and a cripple;
Build upon me a crook-backed hump,
   Shake my teeth till they rattle—
All is well, if my life remains.
   Save, oh, save it, I pray you,
   Though I sit on the piercing cross!

—There he is, praying for that which, if it had befallen him, would be the most pitiable thing in the world! And seeking a postponement of suffering, as if he were asking for life! I should deem him most despicable had he wished to live up to the very moment of crucifixion: "Nay," he cries, "you may weaken my body if you will only leave the breath of life in my battered and ineffective carcass! Maim me if you will, but allow me, misshapen and deformed as I may be, just a little more time in the world! You may nail me up and set my seat upon the piercing cross!" Is it worth while to weigh down upon one's own wound, and hang impaled upon a gibbet, that one may but postpone something which is the balm of troubles, the end of punishment? Is it worth all this to possess the breath of life, only to give it up? What would you ask for Maecenas but the indulgence of Heaven? What does he mean by such womanish and indecent verse? What does he mean by making terms with panic and fear? What does he mean by begging so vilely for life? He cannot ever have heard Virgil read the words:

Tell me, is Death so wretched as that?

He asks for the climax of suffering, and—what is still harder to bear— prolongation and extension of suffering; and what does he gain thereby? Merely the boon of a longer existence. But what sort of life is a lingering death? Can anyone be found who would prefer wasting away in pain, dying limb by limb, or letting out his life drop by drop, rather than expiring once for all? Can any man be found willing to be fastened to the accursed tree, long sickly, already deformed, swelling with ugly tumors on chest and shoulders, and draw the breath of life amid long-drawn-out agony? I think he would have many excuses for dying even before mounting the cross!

Deny, now, if you can, that Nature is very generous in making death inevitable. Many men have been prepared to enter upon still more shameful bargains: to betray friends in order to live longer themselves, or voluntarily to debase their children and so enjoy the light of day which is witness of all their sins. We must get rid of this craving for life, and learn that it makes no difference when your suffering comes, because at some time you are bound to suffer. The point is, not how long you live, but how nobly you live. And often this living nobly means that you cannot live long. Farewell.

(Seneca, *Epistle* 101, *On the Futility of Planning Ahead*,
trans. Gummere, LCL)

Death as Atonement

Although the Letter to the Hebrews dwells at length on typological arguments concerning the death of Jesus, making extended comparisons with the sacrifices of the Jerusalem temple and offering the theological principle (not attested in Torah) that "without the shedding of blood there is no forgiveness of sins" (Heb 9:22), Paul in his own letters never describes *how* the death of Jesus provides atonement. Indeed, Paul uses a variety of ritual metaphors to describe Jesus' death: the slaughter of a Passover lamb (1 Cor 5:7), the offering of firstfruits (1 Cor 15:20), the regular sin offerings of Exodus 29 or Leviticus 4 (Rom 8:3, perhaps 2 Cor 5:21: the LXX often translates the Hebrew *ḥaṭṭat* with *hamartia*), or the sprinkling of a goat's blood on the lid of the ark of the covenant on the Day of Atonement (Rom 3:25; compare Leviticus 16).

As scholars have often noted, none of these metaphors is developed or explained. (For example, the Passover lamb is not considered a "sacrifice" in the Torah; again, if Christ's blood represents the blood of a goat on the Day of Atonement, then what in the narrative of Christ's death corresponds to the *second* goat in that ritual, onto whom the people's sins are transferred?) As James D. G. Dunn observes, these metaphors are used in very formulaic ways, pointing to Paul's use of earlier Christian tradition.[45] Further, the brevity of these references suggests that Paul's intention was to connect with other believers whom he expected to share this common repertoire of metaphors; it was apparently *not* Paul's purpose to offer a particular "theology of atonement," let alone one that was distinctively his own.[46]

It is nevertheless appropriate to ask where Paul's ideas about the atoning power of Jesus' death (or, behind him, the ideas developed in the earliest assemblies) came from, even if such an inquiry is beyond the scope of this textbook. In the foreground of such an inquiry must be the sacrificial system of the Jerusalem temple as laid out in Torah and as understood by Hellenistic Jews in Paul's own day. But Paul's use in Rom 3:25 of the Greek word *hilastērion* may point in another direction. The word was used in the LXX to translate *kapporet*, the "mercy seat" (NRSV) that was the lid of the ark of the covenant. But it also was used in a Hellenistic Jewish text, much closer to Paul's time, to refer to the atoning value of the deaths of martyrs.

81. Atonement through the deaths of the faithful (4 Maccabees)

Fourth Maccabees relates the grisly narrative of the torture and execution of a faithful Jewish elder, Eleazar, and of a courageous mother who was forced to watch her seven sons put to death before her eyes by the tyrant Antiochus IV Epiphanes. Remarkably, this narrative is framed as a "most philosophical" treatise on the supremacy of "devout reason" over the emotions (4 Macc 1:1-6). The martyrs each defied the tyrant, proclaiming their steadfast faith in God who would vindicate their obedience and punish the king. The narrator's summary of the account refers to the atoning nature of their action.

> The tyrant himself and all his council marveled at their endurance, because of which they now stand before the divine throne and live the life of eternal blessedness. For Moses says, "All who are consecrated are under your hands." These, then, who have been consecrated for the sake of God, are honored, not only with this honor, but also by the fact that because of them our enemies did not rule over our nation, the tyrant was punished, and the homeland purified—they have become, as it were, a ransom for the sin of our nation. And through the blood of those devout ones and their death as an atoning sacrifice [*hilastērion*], divine Providence preserved Israel that previously had been mistreated. . . .
>
> Therefore those who gave over their bodies in suffering for the sake of religion were not only admired by mortals, but also were deemed worthy to share in a divine inheritance. Because of them the nation gained peace, and by reviving observance of the law in the homeland they ravaged the enemy. The tyrant Antiochus was both punished on earth and is being chastised after his death. Since in no way whatever was he able to compel the Israelites to become pagans and to abandon their ancestral customs, he left Jerusalem and marched against the Persians. . . .
>
> O bitter was that day—and yet not bitter—when that bitter tyrant of the Greeks quenched fire with his fire in his cruel caldrons. . . . For these crimes divine justice pursued and will pursue the accursed tyrant. But the sons of Abraham with their victorious mother are gathered together into the chorus of the fathers, and have received pure and immortal souls from God, to whom be glory forever and ever. Amen.
>
> (4 Maccabees 17:17-22; 18:3-5, 20, 22-24 NRSV)

"This Present Evil Age"

At the very beginning of his address to the Galatian assemblies, Paul praises Christ "who set us free from the present evil age" (Gal 1:4). In Romans Paul decries the immorality of the age (Rom 1:18-32) and calls the assemblies to put away "reveling and drunkenness, . . . debauchery and licentiousness, . . . quarreling and jealousy" (13:13). The appeal to turn away from a wicked age was not unusual in the early empire; but turn away—to what?

Stanley K. Stowers describes the commonality of "decline narratives" or "myths of degeneration" in Roman culture, by means of which various leaders sought to evoke an earlier, more virtuous age and promised to restore it.[47] Karl Galinsky similarly observes in his discussion of "Augustan culture" that the "golden age" perceived by poets like Virgil and Horace was an age of work, of the ongoing effort that could alone lead "to the accomplishment of a lasting, civilized order."[48] In Roman imperial ideology, then, the point of describing how bad things had been was to point to how good things were about to become—once the populace is mobilized under the benevolent rule of Augustus.

82. Hope for a Golden Age (Virgil)

Virgil's *Fourth Eclogue* is often read as an expression of the "realized eschatology" that a triumphant Augustus could later seize upon in crafting an ideology of Roman destiny. The *Eclogue* explicitly celebrates the rise of a different figure, however—Gaius Asinius Pollio, who was made consul in 40 b.c.e.—and the short-lived peace between Antony and Octavian. The hopes for a wondrous child may have been inspired by Antony's similarly short-lived liaison with Cleopatra, whatever later generations (Roman and Christian alike) would make of the prophecy; or the child may have been "no more than a symbol or personification" of a new "time of prosperity and happiness," a relief from ongoing civil strife.[49]

Note that even this utopian description of a golden age—reminiscent of the messianic prophecies in Isaiah 9 and 11—yields to the recognition that elements

Fig. 2.18. *Ancient (first century b.c.e.?) Roman bust of a young man, from the tomb of Virgil in Naples. Photo: A. Hunter Wright.*

of "old-time sin" still remain, requiring the exertions of noble Romans on military expeditions.

> Now is come the last age of Cumaean song: the great line of the centuries begins anew. Now the Virgin returns, the reign of Saturn returns; now a new generation descends from heaven on high. Only do you, pure Lucina, smile on the birth of the child, under whom the iron brood shall at last cease and a golden race spring up throughout the world! Your own Apollo now is king![50]
>
> And in your consulship, Pollio, yes, yours, shall this glorious age begin, and the mighty months commence their march; under your sway any lingering traces of our guilt shall become void and release the earth from its continual dread. He shall have the gift of divine life, shall see heroes mingled with gods, and shall himself be seen by them, and shall rule the world to which his father's prowess brought peace.
>
> But for you, child, the earth untilled will pour forth its first pretty gifts, gadding ivy with foxglove everywhere, and the Egyptian bean blended with the laughing briar; unbidden it will pour forth for you a cradle of smiling flowers. Unbidden, the goats will bring home their udders swollen with milk, and the cattle will not fear huge lions. The serpent, too, will perish, and perish will the plant that hides its poison; Assyrian spice will spring up on every soil.
>
> But as soon as you can read of the glories of heroes and your father's deeds, and can know what valor is, slowly will the plains yellow with the waving corn, on wild brambles the purple grape will hang, and the stubborn oak distill dewy honey.
>
> Yet will a few traces of old-time sin live on, to bid men tempt the sea in ships, girdle towns with walls, and cleave the earth with furrows. A second Tiphys will then arise, and a second Argo to carry chosen heroes; a second war will be fought, and great Achilles be sent again to Troy.
>
> Next, when now the strength of years has made you a man, even the trader will quit the sea, nor will the ship of pine exchange wares; every land will bear all fruits. Earth will not suffer the harrow, nor the vine the pruning hook; the sturdy plowman, too, will now loose his oxen from the yoke. No more will wool be taught to put on varied hues, but of himself the ram in the meadows will change his fleece, now to sweetly blushing purple, now to a saffron yellow; and scarlet shall clothe the grazing lambs at will.
>
> "Ages so blessed, glide on!" cried the Fates to their spindles, voicing in unison the fixed will of Destiny.
>
> O enter upon your high honors—the hour will soon be here—dear offspring of the gods, mighty seed of a Jupiter to be! See how the world bows with its massive dome—earth and expanse of sea and heaven's depth! See how all things rejoice in the age that is at hand!
>
> I pray that the twilight of a long life may then be vouchsafed me, and inspiration enough to hymn your deeds. Then shall neither Thracian Orpheus nor Linus vanquish me in song, though mother give aid to the one and father to the other, Calliope to Orpheus, to Linus fair Apollo. Even were Pan to compete with me and Arcady be judge, then even Pan, with Arcady for judge, would own himself defeated.

Begin, baby boy, to recognize your mother with a smile; ten months have brought your mother long travail. Begin, baby boy! The child who has not won a smile from his parents, no god ever honored with his table, no goddess with her bed!

(Virgil, Fourth Eclogue, trans. Fairclough, LCL)

83. The present as an era of toil (Virgil)

The previous vision of an effortless paradise, crops yielding their fruits, livestock giving their milk and their many-colored wool spontaneously, is fantastic. A new tone emerges a few years later in Virgil's *Georgics*. Here Jupiter sends difficulties precisely to provoke human effort. In the *Georgics*, Karl Galinsky sees an important element in what will soon be the Augustan cultural program: "the Golden Age is the result of *labor*. . . . It is a Golden Age which, in contrast to that of *Eclogue* 4, is based on agriculture and includes the fortification of cities. . . . In other words, it is a Golden Age based on blood, sweat, and tears. It is not a paradisiac state, but implies both a social order and an ongoing effort."[51]

> The Father himself has willed that the way of cultivation should not be easy, and he was the first to cause the land to be cultivated by men's skill, sharpening men's minds with cares, not letting his realm be sluggish in heavy lethargy. Before Jupiter no tillers subdued the land. Even to mark the field or divide it with boundaries was unlawful. Men strove for the common property of all, and the earth herself used to bring forth things more freely when no one begged for her gifts. He added hurtful venom to the black snakes; he commanded wolves to be predators and the sea to swell; he shook honey from the leaves and hid the fire away; he held back the wine that was running everywhere in streams, to that experience by taking thought might gradually hammer out the various arts, might seek to produce corn by plowing, and might strike forth fire hidden in the veins of flint. Then did the rivers first feel hollowed-out alder trees; then did the sailor number the stars and name them—the Pleiades, the Hyades, and Lycaon's offspring, the gleaming Great Bear. Then men found out how to snare game in traps, and birds with lime, and to surround vast mountain glades with hounds. And now one lashes a wide stream with a casting net, seeking the depths, and another drags his dripping net through the seas. Then came iron's stiffness and the blade of the shrill saw (for early man cleft the splitting wood with wedges); then came the remaining arts. Unrelenting toil has come to occupy all areas of existence and want that is pressing when life is hard.

(Virgil, Georgics 1.121-40, trans. Galinsky)

84. The lingering guilt of the Roman people (Horace)

In one of his "Roman odes," written in 23 b.c.e., Horace laments the "moral degeneration" of the Roman people. The current neglect of shrines and temples has offended the gods, who have sent repeated defeats and ill-fortune to Rome; meanwhile Roman homes are defiled by a sexual profligacy unworthy of Rome's pious ancestors. As Galinsky writes, this degeneracy "had to be remedied before there could be any hope for better times."[52]

Fig. 2.19. *Agricultural laborers. Relief from Roman Gaul, first to fourth century* c.e.; *Trier. Photo in the public domain.*

Your fathers' guilt you still must pay,
    Till, Roman, you restore each shrine,
Each temple, mouldering in decay,
    And smoke-grimed statue, scarce divine.
Revering Heaven, you rule below;
    Be that your base, your coping still;
'Tis Heaven neglected bids o'erflow
    The measure of Italian ill.
An evil age erewhile debased
    The marriage-bed, the race, the home;
Thence rose the flood whose waters waste
    The nation and the name of Rome.
Not such their birth, who stain'd for us
    The sea with Punic carnage red,
Smote Pyrrhus, smote Antiochus,
    And Hannibal, the Roman's dread.[53]
Theirs was a hardy soldier-brood,
    Inured all day the land to till
With Sabine spade, then shoulder wood
    Hewn at a stern old mother's will,
When sunset lengthen'd from each height
    The shadows, and unyoked the steer,
Restoring in its westward flight
    The hour to toilworn travail dear.
What has not cankering Time made worse?
    Viler than grandsires, sires beget
Ourselves, yet baser, soon to curse
    The world with offspring baser yet.

        (Horace, *Ode* 3.6, trans. Conington)

85. Prayer that a new age might dawn with Augustus (Horace)

In his *Carmen Saeculare*, "Hymn for the Age," written only a few years later on the occasion of Augustus's Secular Games, Horace's tone is decidedly brighter, though still cautious. A golden age is at hand *if* the gods behold a virtuous Roman people and a pious city. To that end, significantly, Horace gestures to Augustus's legislation regarding marriage, couched here as a prayer for the fecundity of the Roman people.

> O Phoebus and Diana, ruler of the woods,
>   Fair ornaments of heaven, O ever worshipful
> And to be worshiped, give what we beseech you
>   At this sacred time;
> For which, the Sibylline verses instruct
>   That chosen virgins and most chaste youths
> Should to those who delight in the seven hills
>   Sing out their praise.
> O gracious Sun, in your radiant carriage
>   You bring forth day and cast it in shadow,
> Each day new yet the same; greater than Rome
>   May you ne'er see.

Fig. 2.20. *Apollo and Diana. Ceramic tile from the Temple of Apollo on the Palatine Hill, Rome; first century c.e. Photo: Werner Forman/Art Resource, New York.*

Protect in their labor to timely birth,
    O gracious Ilithyia, your matrons;
Or if you care to be hailed as Lucina,
    Or Genitalis:
O Goddess, prosper our children,
    And prosper the laws as decreed that govern
The joining with women, and marriage;
    Give them new life.
May each return of ten elevens of years
    Refresh our city with hymns and with games,
Three days in the bright clear light of the sun
    And as welcome by night.
And you, O Fates, having chanted in truth
    What has been ordained what now is established
In order: to past good deeds,
    Add now good fortune.
Let fertile earth, full of fruits and of flocks,
    Bestow upon Ceres a crown of grain;
May life-giving rains and Jove's clear air
    Nourish young life.
Gentle Apollo, belay your weapons,
    Heed our youths' prayers;
Horned queen of stars, O sovereign Moon,
    Heed you our maidens.
If Rome was your doing—if Trojan troops
    On Tuscan soil landed, by you commanded
To abandon their homes and even their city
    To wend their way here;
For whom pure Aeneas, who wholly unharmed
    Through Troy, burning (no fault of his),
Did find his way free, yet bound to give
    More than he left;
O Gods, to our pliable youth give sound teaching;
    O Gods, to their elders, give peaceable rest;
To the children of Romulus, wealth and prosperity
    And all good fame.
Whatever he asks you, the glorious issue
    of Anchises and Venus,[54] offering white bulls,
O give him: to conquer his enemy, but the defeated
    To welcome in mercy.
Now, by both sea and land, Parthians fear him,
    Our armies as well, the axes of Rome;
The Scythians beg terms, so recently proud,
    And those of India.
Now good faith, and peace, and honor, and modesty
    Ancient, and virtue long-abandoned, do dare
To return; and blessed Plenty appears,
    Her horn quite full.

Phoebus, the Augur, radiant with his bow,
    Beloved of nine muses, who with his own art
To the wearied limbs of the body
    Gives healthful balm—
That he now might look upon Palatine altars
    With favor, and bless our affairs with good will,
    The welfare of Italy further to profit for now
    and to better age;
And Diana, who rules Mounts Aventine
    and Algidus, that she hear the prayers
Of the Fifteen, and to those of our youths
    Lend her ears;
To Jupiter, with all the gods, in hope
    Good and certain, that they do hear and heed us,
We, the choir, in the praises of Phoebus and Diana instructed
    Do also our praises speak.

          (Horace, *Carmen Saeculare*, trans. Elliott)

These last texts convey the intense and exuberant expectation that greeted the ascendancy of Augustus. We turn in the next chapter to explore the contours of what may be called the Augustan "gospel."

QUESTIONS FOR REFLECTION

1. The "advisory" letter gives practical advice sometimes in response to questions. Paul writes in 1 Corinthians that he is responding to questions or concerns from the Corinthian assembly (1 Cor 7:1; compare 8:1; 12:1). To what extent can that letter be read as a letter of advice?

2. Some interpreters have read Romans as a letter of politely phrased admonition; others, as an ambassadorial letter. How do you understand the polite tone in the letter frame (chapters 1 and 15)? What kind of letter is Romans?

3. Paul strikes notes of reproach in Galatians, notes of consolation and of self-defense in 2 Corinthians, and notes of commendation and friendship in Philippians. What else is going on in each letter? Do any of these categories describe the primary function of one or another of these letters?

4. What aspects of the *amicus domini* letter are present in Philemon? What aspects are missing? Is that letter type a compelling analogy for Philemon?

5. How should we go about determining what "Paul's gospel" was? Was it a single set of beliefs? How consistent was "his gospel" as he responded to very different situations in his letters? Should we expect to find "his gospel" all contained in a single letter? Should we try to reconstruct it from all of his letters? What role should other writings (for example, Acts, texts containing the sayings of Jesus, etc.) play? If we define Paul's "gospel" as

what he first proclaimed to an audience orally, what relationship does that proclamation have to his letters?

6. What difference does it make for our understanding of Paul's letters that the English word *gospel* is almost exclusively a *religious* term, without political connotations? If the Greek word *euangelion* could be used in celebration of the emperor's accession, how should that change the way we understand the word *gospel* in Paul's letters?

7. Given the importance in Roman society of paying honor to the Roman gods, how would Paul's insistence on "turning from idols" have sounded to people in different social locations? What tensions or conflicts might have arisen as a result of his proclamation?

8. How would Paul's language about a "present evil age" and a future reversal have sounded next to language about a "golden age" having already arrived? How would people in different social locations have heard the two messages?

FOR FURTHER READING

On letters:

Klauck, Hans-Josef. *Ancient Letters and the New Testament: A Guide to Context and Exegesis.* Translated by Daniel Bailey. Waco: Baylor University Press, 1998.

Malherbe, Abraham J., ed. and trans. *Ancient Epistolary Theorists.* SBLSBS 19. Atlanta: Scholars, 1988.

Stowers, Stanley K. *Letter Writing in Greco-Roman Antiquity.* Library of Early Christianity 5. Philadelphia: Westminster, 1986.

On rhetoric:

Kennedy, George A. *New Testament Interpretation through Rhetorical Criticism.* Studies in Religion. Chapel Hill: University of North Carolina Press, 1984.

Mack, Burton L. *Rhetoric and the New Testament.* Guides to Biblical Scholarship, New Testament. Minneapolis: Fortress Press, 1990.

On exhortation to the philosophical life:

Malherbe, Abraham J. *Moral Exhortation: A Greco-Roman Sourcebook.* Library of Early Christianity 4. Philadelphia: Westminster, 1986.

―――. *Paul and the Popular Philosophers.* Minneapolis: Fortress Press, 1989.

―――. *Paul and the Thessalonians: The Philosophic Tradition of Pastoral Care.* Philadelphia: Fortress Press, 1987.

On Roman religion:

Beard, Mary, John North, and Simon Price. *Religions of Rome.* Vol. 1, *A History.* Vol. 2, *A Sourcebook.* Cambridge: Cambridge University Press, 1998.

Ferguson, John. *The Religions of the Roman Empire.* Aspects of Greek and Roman Life. Ithaca, N.Y.: Cornell University Press, 1970.

Klauck, Hans-Josef. *The Religious Context of Early Christianity: A Guide to Graeco-Roman Religions.* Translated by Brian McNeil. Minneapolis: Fortress Press, 2003.

Kraemer, Ross S., ed. *Maenads, Martyrs, Matrons, Monastics: A Sourcebook on Women's Religions in the Greco-Roman World.* Philadelphia: Fortress Press, 1988.

Meyer, Marvin W., ed. *The Ancient Mysteries: A Sourcebook; Sacred Texts of the Mystery Religions of the Ancient Mediterranean World.* San Francisco: Harper & Row, 1987.

On Paul's gospel:

Bassler, Jouette, ed. *Pauline Theology.* Vol. 1, *Thessalonians, Philippians, Galatians, Philemon.* Minneapolis: Fortress Press, 1991.

Beker, J. Christiaan. *Paul's Apocalyptic Gospel: The Coming Triumph of God.* Philadelphia: Fortress Press, 1982.

Brondos, David A. *Paul on the Cross: Reconstructing the Apostle's Story of Redemption.* Minneapolis: Fortress Press, 2006.

Campbell, Douglas A. *The Quest for Paul's Gospel: A Suggested Strategy.* JSNTSup 274. New York: T&T Clark, 2005.

Donfried, Karl, ed. *The Romans Debate.* Rev. and exp. ed. Peabody, Mass.: Hendrickson, 1991.

Dunn, James D. G. *The Theology of Paul the Apostle.* Grand Rapids: Eerdmans, 1998.

Hay, David M., ed. *Pauline Theology.* Vol. 2, *1 and 2 Corinthians.* Minneapolis: Fortress Press, 1993.

Hay, David M., and E. Elizabeth Johnson, eds. *Pauline Theology.* Vol. 3, *Romans.* Minneapolis: Fortress Press, 1995.

Jervis, L. Ann, and Peter Richardson, eds. *Gospel in Paul: Essays on Corinthians, Galatians, and Romans for Richard N. Longenecker.* JSNTSup 108. Sheffield: Sheffield Academic, 1994.

Wright, N. T. *The Climax of the Covenant: Christ and the Law in Pauline Theology.* Minneapolis: Fortress Press, 1992.

Fig. 3.1. *Virgil seated between Clio, the Muse of history, and Melpomene, the Muse of tragedy. Mosaic from Tunisia, third century C.E. In his hand he holds the Aeneid, his epic poem describing the founding of Rome by Aeneas, the divinely destined ancestor of Augustus. Virgil's epic was the best-known account of the gods' dealings with humanity in the Roman world. Bardo Museum, Tunis, Tunisia. Photo by Effi Schweitzer, released in the public domain.*

3 | The Gospel of Augustus

With the last readings in chapter 2, we touched on themes that became ever more prominent after Octavian's victory over Mark Antony in the Battle of Actium (31 B.C.E.) and his being given unprecedented power by the Senate and hailed as "Augustus" (or in Greek, *Sebastos*, "sacred one"). These themes were picked up and elaborated by his successors in the Julio-Claudian house—the dynasts reaching from Julius Caesar through Augustus, Tiberius, Gaius (Caligula), and Claudius to Nero in a lineage constituted largely through adoption (see fig. 3.21 below). Together these themes wove a ubiquitous and powerful fabric of meaning for citizens and subjects of the Roman Empire, a veritable Augustan "gospel." As such they were a large part of the environment in which Paul and the members of his assemblies lived, moved, and had their being.

The Gospel according to Virgil

The most renowned expression of these themes was Virgil's *Aeneid*, commissioned by Augustus himself. A masterpiece of epic poetry, the *Aeneid* revisits the era of Homer's *Iliad* and *Odyssey*: the Trojan War and its aftermath. But instead of following the Greek warrior Odysseus, Virgil focuses his epic on a Trojan hero, Aeneas, who through exemplary courage and piety rescues his father, Anchises, his son Ascanius, and his ancestral gods (Lares) from the flames of the destroyed city. Aeneas's long voyage brings him not to Greece but to Italy (called Latium, hence "Latin," or Lavinium), where the gods reward his piety by allowing him to found a race who are destined to rule the world.

The *Aeneid* weaves the memory of Etruscan origins, legends of Numa and Romulus, the fairly recent emergence of Rome as a Mediterranean power surpassing Greece, and the dizzying accession of Augustus into an epic that evokes hallowed antiquity. More, it provides a powerful ideological message: that Romans have become "lords of the world" not just through military power but through divine destiny (for the gods have decreed for them an "empire without end"), earned through the virtue they have inherited from their pious ancestor Aeneas. Destiny and loyalty are recurrent themes throughout the poem; so are Roman might and the innocence of Roman power. Note the "prophecy" at the end of the following extract of Augustus's shutting up the doors of the temple of Janus in 29 B.C.E., ceremonially bringing an end to war.

86. The destiny of Aeneas and his progeny (Virgil)

At a point in the narrative when Aeneas and his companions seem lost, Virgil narrates a heavenly conversation in which Jupiter assures Venus that her favorite, Aeneas, will prevail. (Compare the roles of Zeus and Athena in the *Odyssey*.)

Fig. 3.2. *Aeneas rescues his father and son from the sack of Troy. First-century-c.e. Roman figurine. Museo Archeologico Nazionale, Naples. Photo: Fotografica Foglia, Scala/Art Resource, New York.*

Smiling on her [Venus] with that look wherewith he clears sky and storms, the Father of men and gods gently kissed his daughter's lips, and then spoke thus:

"Spare your fears, Lady of Cythera; your children's fates abide unmoved. You will see Lavinium's city and its promised walls; and great-souled Aeneas you will raise on high to the starry heaven. No thought has turned me. This your son—for since this care gnaws at your heart, I will speak and, further unrolling the scroll of fate, will disclose its secrets—shall wage a great war in Italy, shall crush proud nations, and for his people shall set up laws and city walls, till the third summer has seen him reigning in Latium and three winters have passed in camp since the Rutulians were laid low. But the lad Ascanius, now surnamed Iulus—Ilus he was, while the Ilian state [Troy] stood firm in sovereignty—shall fulfill in empire thirty great circles of rolling months, shall shift his throne from Lavinium's seat, and, great in power, shall build the walls of Alba Longa.

Here then for thrice a hundred years unbroken shall the kingdom endure under Hector's race, until Ilia, a royal priestess, shall bear to Mars her twin offspring. Then Romulus, proud in the tawny hide of the she-wolf, his nurse, shall take up the line, and found the walls of Mars and call the people Romans after his own name. For these I set no bounds in space or time; but have given empire without end. Spiteful Juno, who now in her fear troubles sea and earth and sky, shall change to better counsels and with me cherish the Romans, lords of the world, and the nation of the toga. Thus is it decreed. There shall come a day, as the sacred seasons glide past, when the house of Assaracus [The Trojan

Fig. 3.3. *Romulus and Remus, twin ancestors of the Romans, nursed by a she-wolf. The Iconography, known as the Lupa Capitolina, is ancient; the bronze wolf is Etruscan, sixth or fifth century* B.C.E. *The twins were restored sometime during the Renaissance. Museo Capitolino, Rome. Photo: Vanni/Art Resource, New York.*

lineage] shall bring into bondage Phthia and famed Mycenae, and hold lordship over vanquished Argos. From this noble line shall be born the Trojan Caesar, who shall extend his empire to the ocean, his glory to the stars, a Julius, name descended from the great Iulus! Him, in days to come, shall you, anxious no more, welcome to heaven, laden with Eastern spoils; he, too, shall be invoked in vows. Then wars shall cease and savage ages soften; hoary Faith [Fides] and Vesta, Quirinus with his brother Remus, shall give laws. The gates of war, grim with iron and close-fitting bars, shall be closed; within, impious Rage, sitting on savage arms, his hands fast bound behind with a hundred brazen knots, shall roar in the ghastliness of blood-stained lips.

(Virgil, Aeneid 1.255-97, trans. Fairclough, LCL)

87. A prophecy of Augustus (Virgil)

In book 6 of the *Aeneid*, in a scene reminiscent of Odysseus's journey to the underworld in the *Odyssey*, Aeneas is given a visionary tour of the afterlife and the future. There he meets his father, Anchises, now deceased, who shows him the fate of souls and the torments awaiting evildoers (*Aeneid* 6.679-755), and then "the glory henceforth to attend the Trojan race." Anchises points out hallowed ancestors in a line from Aeneas's own sons to Romulus, then introduces two more descendants: Julius Caesar, who would be deified after his death, and his adopted son Augustus. The prophecy (for so Virgil intends it to be understood) shows that Augustus's glory will surpass the renown of Alexander's conquests, Hercules' labors, and the sway of Bacchus—who as the Greek god Dionysos was taken by Mark Antony as his protector until he was defeated by Octavian.

> Turn hither now your two-eyed gaze, and behold this nation, the Romans that are yours. Here is Caesar and all the seed of Iulus destined to pass under heaven's spacious sphere. And this in truth is he whom you so often hear promised you, Augustus Caesar, son of a god, who will again establish a golden age in Latium amid fields once ruled by Saturn; he will advance his empire beyond the Garamants and Indians to a land which lies beyond our stars, beyond the path of year and sun, where sky-bearing Atlas wheels on his shoulders the blazing star-studded sphere. Against his coming both Caspian realms and the Maeotic land even now shudder at the oracles of their gods, and the mouths of sevenfold Nile quiver in alarm. Not even Hercules traversed so much of earth's extent, though he pierced the stag of brazen foot, quieted the woods of Erymanthus, and made Lerna tremble at his bow; nor he either, who guides his car with vine-leaf reins, triumphant Bacchus, driving his tigers down from Nysa's lofty peak. And do we still hesitate to make known our worth by exploits or shrink in fear from settling on Western soil?

(Other ancestors pass before Anchises and Aeneas: Numa the lawgiver and Roman generals who conquered Greece and Carthage, last of these Quintus Fabius Maximus, who fought Hannibal of Carthage. To the last of these Anchises speaks an injunction directed beyond him to the whole Roman people):

Fig. 3.4. *Aeneas rescues father and son from Troy. Denarius minted by Julius Caesar in 47/46 B.C.E. Staatliche Münzsammlung, Munich. Photo: Bibi Saint-Pol, released into the public domain.*

"You [Fabius], are he, the mightiest. . . . You, Roman, be sure to rule the world (be these your arts), to crown peace with justice, to spare the vanquished and to crush the proud."

(Virgil, *Aeneid* 6.788-807, 847, 851-53, trans. Fairclough, LCL)

The Achievements of Augustus

A cardinal element of the Augustan gospel was that the hopes expressed by the likes of Virgil and other poets were not dreamy wistfulness: they had been fulfilled through the virtue and industry of Augustus himself, with the cooperation of a Senate who recognized both. The first of Augustus's achievements was simply bringing and end to the civil war that he had waged against his father's murderers and then against his rival Mark Antony. The defeat and forced suicides of Antony and Cleopatra brought an end to combat and a tremendous sense of relief to hard-pressed Italy; a grateful Senate was swift to reward the victor with honors and the bestowal of unprecedented authority.

In succeeding years, it was Augustus who would come to define the expectations people held for their emperor. Acclaimed Augustus by the Senate in 27 B.C.E. and ruling until his death in 14 C.E., he sought from the beginning to stabilize the Roman Republic and to extend its influence worldwide. Because he exerted his own power so decisively, historians sometimes describe his accomplishments as a political revolution, in which he transformed the Roman Republic into the Roman Empire.[1]

88. The *Pax Augustana* (Augustan peace: Horace)

Under Augustus, Horace could write of an imperturbable peace. Note here that the god Bacchus is viewed as less of a threat than he was 150 years earlier (compare no. 174 below).

When I wished to sing of fights and cities won, Apollo checked me, striking loud his lyre, and forbade my spreading tiny sails upon the Tuscan Sea. Your time, O Caesar, has restored to farms their plentiful crops and to our Jupiter the standards stripped from the proud columns of the Parthians; free of war, it has closed Quirinus's temple, has put a check on license by passing a just order, banished crime and called back home the ancient ways by which the Latin name and might of Italy grew great, and the fame and majesty of our dominion were stretched from the sun's western bed to its rising.

While Caesar guards the state, not civil rage, nor violence, nor wrath that forges swords, embroiling hapless towns, shall banish peace. Not they that drink the Danube deep shall break the Julian laws, nor Getae, Seres, unbelieving Parthians, nor they by Tanais born. On common and on sacred days, amid the gifts of merry Bacchus, with wife and child we first will duly pray the god; then after our leading fathers' custom, in measures joined to strains of Lydian flutes, we will hymn the glories of the heroic dead, Troy and Anchises and benign Venus's offspring.

(Horace, *Odes* 4.15, trans. Bennett, LCL, adapted)

89. Prayer at the altar of Peace (Ovid)

Earlier (no. 78) we encountered Ovid's *Fasti*, the calendrical poem for the first six months of the Roman year. Here are Ovid's lines regarding the festive day on which *Pax*, deified Peace, is celebrated and worshiped.[2]

The song now has brought us to the very altar of Peace.
  Its day will be the penultimate day of the month.
Your ribboned hair crowned with laurels from Actium,
  O Peace, be near and stay gentle in the whole world.
So now may there be no enemies and no occasion for victory parade;
  may you be for our princes a higher prize than war.
Let the soldier arm himself only to restrain armed threats
  and let the war bugle be blown only in parade.
Let those near and far in the world dread Aeneas' scions
  and if some land fears Rome too little, let it love Rome instead.
O priests, join incense to the peace-flames,
  and may a white sacrifice fall, pierced in the head,
That this country, which guarantees peace, may endure in peace,
  ask the favorable gods with devout prayers.

(Ovid, *Fasti* 1.709-22, trans. Reasoner)

The Virtues of Augustus

The idea that the Roman emperor was the source or embodiment of divine virtues had roots in the political thought of Greece and of the Roman Republic (where Pompey

Fig. 3.5. *The Ara Pacis, Altar of Peace, commissioned by the Senate and completed in 9 B.C.E.; now housed in the Museo Ara Pacis built by Mussolini. Reliefs depict, first, the sacrifice of Aeneas upon landing in Italy; then a sacred procession that includes Senators, the emperor's ally Marcus Agrippa, and Augustus himself. Photo: Manfred Heyde.*

and Julius Caesar had already been regarded as embodying particular virtues). The emperor was viewed, not least in the provinces, as a divine guarantor of good things to the world. All humanity, not just Roman citizens, were the beneficiaries of the emperor's generosity and paternal care. His victories over Roman enemies, his conquests of barbarian peoples, and his suppression of piracy were all viewed as the basis for all other benefits of his rule; but in Roman propaganda these were understood to be the results not of his resort to superior military force but to the favor that the gods had bestowed upon him (and, through him, on the Roman people) because of his virtues. These virtues were given divine honors (in a way that the emperor himself could not be, at least in Rome) in what is now called the "cult of virtues."

Victoria, the emperor's power to conquer barbarians and rule over any enemies who threatened the stability of the Mediterranean world, was the foundational virtue. Next in popular consciousness and closely associated with the virtue of victory was *Pax*, or Peace.[3] Sometimes *Securitas*, Security, was associated with *Pax* (just as police forces today sometimes use the motto "Safety and Security"). Other deified virtues in imperial propaganda were *Concordia* (social Harmony), *Felicitas* (Happiness), *Clementia* (Mercy), *Fides* (Faith in the sense of loyalty), *Iustitia* (Justice), *Salus* (Health), and *Spes* (Hope). These deified virtues were almost ubiquitous in Paul's world in literature and theatrical performance, on coins, in sculptures and monumental architecture, and in official inscriptions (to name only the cultural expressions that have left tangible evidence to us on parchment or stone).

90. THE EMPEROR'S VIRTUES HONORED (THE PRIENE INSCRIPTION)

Nor was the enthusiasm for Augustus's achievements limited to Rome; if anything it was greater in the eastern provinces, where Hellenistic rulers had long been revered in ways that Romans themselves considered extravagant. We have already seen (no. 24 above) that cities in Asia Minor dedicated copies of this inscription, known from the copy in Priene, to celebrate the "good news" of Augustus's rise to power and to honor him on his birthday as the beginning of a new age. The preamble to the declaration contains a Roman proconsul's letter extolling the dawn of a new age with Augustus.

> Paulus Fabius Maximus, proconsul, sends greetings to the cities of Asia . . . [The next few lines are fragmentary.] It is difficult to say . . . whether the birthday of the very divine Caesar is more of pleasure or more of service, which we may rightly take as equal to the foundation of everything, even in service, if not in nature; when indeed there was nothing that was not crumbling and changed into ruin that he did not restore to proper form. In another way he gave a boon to all the world though it would have blithely accepted destruction if the general blessing of all, Caesar, had not been born.
>
> So one may rightly take this day as the time when the beginning of existence and of life has come to be, which is the limit and end for any regret that

Fig. 3.6. *A coin dedicated CLEMENTIAE CAESARIS, "To the Mercy of Caesar," 44 B.C.E. The title surrounds the temple of Clementia, which was dedicated in 44, inside which stood statues of Julius Caesar and the goddess with their hands clasped in unity. The obverse names P[ublius] Sepullius Macer as the person who minted the coin. Image courtesy of Numismatica Ars Classica.*

one has been born. And because, besides this day, there is no other that is so beneficial in both public and private life—one may consider the more fortunate opportunities or the good fortune that has come for all—occurring, as it does, nearly at the same time that rulers take office in the cities of Asia, which makes clear that a pattern was formed beforehand according to some divine purpose in order that there may be an occasion of worship for Augustus; and since it is difficult to give thanks equal to such benefits as his, unless we were to consider some new way of repayment for each one, while people should delight in a birthday that is a shared day of enjoyment for all, if some pleasure might come to them and their people because it is inauguration day:

It seems to me that the birthday of the most godlike Caesar should be held by all the citizens to be identical with the first of the new moons. On that day let all enter their magistracy, which is on the ninth day before the calends of October, so that when the specific ritual is adopted, there may be even greater worship from outside the province and it may become more well known to all, which I think will cause even greater advantage to emerge for our district. There should be a decree by the council of Asia to write out all his virtues, so that what we have conceived for the worship of Augustus may endure forever. I order that the decree be engraved on a stele to be erected in the temple. Let the decree be displayed, written in both languages [Greek and Latin].[4]

(trans. Reasoner)

91. Concordia, social concord (Ovid)

In his *Fasti*, Ovid addressed the celebration on January 16 of Concordia, which Augustus had brought to the Roman people. Note also here what was a common phenomenon in Roman iconography, the sexualization of the conquest of a people: Germany's submission is compared to sexual surrender.

> Fair goddess . . .
> Concordia, now you take good care of the Latin crowd,
>   now the dedicated hand has established you.
> Furius—conqueror of the Etruscan people—the old temple
>   had vowed, and he kept faith on that vow.
> The story is that the commoners took up weapons to secede from the nobility,
>   and Rome was then in fear of her own power.
> The recent story is better yet—Germany let down
>   her unkempt hair (at your bidding, honored prince [Augustus];
> Then you sacrificed the booty of the conquered people
>   and built the temple for the goddess whom you yourself honor).
> Your mother established her by both her business affairs and the altar,
> who alone was considered worthy of great Jupiter's bed.[5]

(Ovid, Fasti 1.639-50, trans. Reasoner)

92. Deeds Accomplished by the Divine Augustus (Res Gestae)

Toward the end of his life, Augustus had the record of his accomplishments, in Latin the *Res Gestae Divi Augusti*, inscribed on the walls of temples in several cities

Fig. 3.7. *A common decorative motif: a disconsolate woman represents a conquered nation. Statue pedestal, first century* C.E. *Museo Palazzo Massimo, Rome. Photo: Neil Elliott.*

throughout the empire; the following text is excerpted from the inscription on the wall of a temple devoted to the worship of the Augustan family in Ankyra in Galatia. (The superscription is not from Augustus himself.) Note the ways the emperor claims to have exhibited various virtues—justice (in punishing the wicked), mercy (in pardoning the submissive), piety (in restoring temples), and so on—and also to have avoided receiving extravagant honors for himself. All he has done, he implies, has been done for the welfare of the Roman people.

(Superscription)

This is a copy of the deeds of the divine Augustus by which he subjected the whole world to the rule of the Roman people; also of the amounts he spent on the Republic and on the Roman people; as he engraved them on two bronze pillars set up in Rome.

1. When only nineteen years old, I initiated and funded an army by which I won liberty for the Republic when it was domineered by a faction.[6] Because of this, the Senate with honor-bestowing resolutions added me to its rolls, in the

consulship of Gaius Pansa and Aulus Hirtius, granting both the right to vote as a consul and the office of propraetor over soldiers. Because I was a propraetor the Republic charged me, along with the consuls, to make sure no harm came to the Republic. On top of this, when both consuls fell in war that same year, the people made me consul and a member of the ruling trio [*trium virum*], because I consolidated the Republic.

2. I exiled those who killed my father [that is, Julius Caesar], bringing their crime under proper judgment, and later when they warred against the Republic, I defeated them twice.[7]

3. I spearheaded civil and foreign wars throughout the whole earth, on land and sea, and after winning them I always let those citizens who asked for pardon live. I chose to save rather than kill foreign peoples who could safely be spared. . . .

4. I celebrated minor triumphs twice, curule triumphs three times, and I was saluted as "Imperator" twenty-one times.[8] The Senate even designated more triumphs for me, but I am not counting them. . . .

5. I did not accept the title "dictator" offered me by the people and Senate of Rome, either once when I was absent or again when I was present. . . . I did not avoid responsibility for the supply of grain when grain was most scarce, which I administered so that in a few days I rescued the people with my own

Fig. 3.8. *"I always let those citizens who asked for pardon live." Silver cup from a villa in Boscoreale, first century c.e. The mercy (clementia) of Augustus was a premiere theme in imperial ideology. It meant not only beneficence to the needy (the predominant meaning in later Christianity) but also magnanimity toward the conquered, as when he shows mercy toward captured barbarians. Photo: Erich Lessing/Art Resource, New York. Reconstruction by Micah Thompson.*

funds from the dread and danger they were experiencing. I did not accept the offer of being consul for a year or for life then made to me.

6. (On three different occasions . . .) when the Senate and Roman people together consented that I should be in charge of legislation and morality alone and with complete authority, I rejected any power that went against the customs of the fatherland. I fulfilled what the Senate wanted me to oversee using my tribunician authority. And even for this change, I asked and received a co-ruler five times from the Senate.

7. I was one of the ruling trio for ten consecutive years for the restoration of the assembly. As of this day on which I write, I have been first man [*princeps*]

Fig. 3.9. *Statue of Augustus as military victor, erected at Prima Porta (copy of a bronze original from 20 B.C.E.). Augustus's military victories and the resulting supremacy of Rome were the base upon which Augustus built the authority of the emperor's person. The spear he originally held was "the sign of imperium" that guaranteed* Fides, *the "obligation of the powerful to all those entrusted to them" (Karl Galinsky,* Augustan Culture, 61). *Museo Chiaramonti, the Vatican. Photo: Till Nierman.*

Fig. 3.10. *The most widely copied image of Augustus in his own age (some time after 12 B.C.E.) depicted not his military exploits but his piety—his reverence for the gods of Rome, his ancestors, and his household. His toga is pulled over his head in the gesture of worship; he extends his hands to offer sacrifice. Both his revitalization of Roman temples and his legislation concerning marriage were intended as reforms expressing his concern for traditional Roman values. Museo Palazzo Massimo, Rome. Photo: Neil Elliott.*

of the Senate for forty years. I was high priest, augur, member of the council of Fifteen for sacred matters, one of the Seven for religious feasts, a brother of the Arval council, a member of the society of Titius, and a fetial priest. . . .

9. The Senate ordered that sacred vows be taken for my well being every five years. As a result of these sacred vows, games have often been held in my life, at times sponsored by the highest four groups of priests, at other times sponsored by the consuls. All citizens by common consent, both private and those who held municipal posts, consistently sought the gods for my welfare at all the sacred meals they held in the presence of the ancient Greek gods.

10. My name, by senatorial order, was added into the hymn of the Salii; legislation was passed that I should be regarded as inviolable forever; and to me the tribunician power was assigned for as long as I would live. I refused to

be designated "pontifex maximus"[9] in the place of my colleague who was still alive, at the time that people offered me the priesthood that my father held. After some years, when the man died who had occupied the office at a time of civil agitation, I accepted that priesthood, such a crowd flowing to Rome from everywhere in Italy for my installation as never before accounted. . . .

12. . . . When I returned to Rome from Spain and Gaul, having completed matters in those provinces so that they prospered, the Senate passed a resolution that an altar of the Augustan Peace [the *Ara Pacis*] should be dedicated by the field of Mars for my return, when Tiberius Nero and Publius Quintilius were consuls, ordering that magistrate, priests, and Vestal Virgins offer sacrifice on it for the anniversary.

13. While I was first man, the Senate ordered that the door of Janus Quirinus, which our ancestors wanted to be shut when peace was attained by victories through the whole territory of the Roman people, on land and sea, should be shut on three occasions, though before I was born it was only recorded to have been shut twice during all the time since the foundation of the city.

(Augustus next recounts occasions on which he gave out donations, of money or of grain, to every member of the Roman plebs from his father's will or his own inheritance [15-16]; his establishing colonies of his retired troops by gifts of money and land, whether from the spoils of war or his own fortune [17]; his supplementing the imperial treasury on occasions of distress from his own funds [18]; his construction or restoration of numerous civic buildings and temples in Rome [19-21]; his provision of gladiator shows, mock naval battles, and other entertainments [22-23]. Note that in the next paragraph he accuses his rival Mark Antony of having committed sacrilege by plundering temples in Asia; his own restoration of stolen goods is, again, an indication of his piety.)

24. After the conquest, I returned the items to the temples of all the provinces of Asia which the one against whom I had been warring had stolen from temples and privately held.[10] They put up about eighty silver statues of me on foot, on horse, and in chariot in the city, which I myself removed. I set up golden gifts from the money that these statues brought, in Apollo's temple, in my name and in the name of those who had honored me with those statues.[11]

25. I brought peace to the sea from pirates. I captured about 30,000 slaves who had fled from their masters and taken up arms against the Republic, returning them to their masters for the necessary punishment. All Italy voluntarily swore allegiance to me after the war I won at Actium, begging me to be their leader. The provinces of Gaul, of Spain, Africa, Sicily, and Sardinia swore the same. . . .

26. I enlarged the boundaries of all the provinces of the Roman people that bordered peoples not obedient to our empire.[12] I pacified the Gallic and Spanish provinces. . . . I pacified the Alps . . . not waging an unjust war against any people. . . . The Cimbrians and Charydians and Semnonians and other peoples of the Germans in the same area sought via their representatives a friendly relationship with me and the Roman people. At my bidding and under my guidance two armies were led almost simultaneously into Ethiopia reaching as far

Figs. 3.11-13. *Reliefs on the* Ara Pacis *(completed in 9 B.C.E.): Aeneas sacrifices upon landing in Italy; Augustus (figure partly destroyed) walks in sacred procession; Marcus Agrippa follows the flamines, the priests of Rome's official cults. Photos: Neil Elliott.*

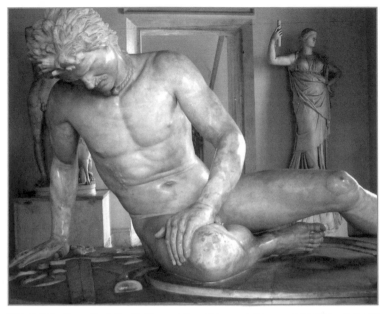

Fig. 3.14. *"I pacified the Gallic and Spanish provinces. . . ." Nations that did not resist conquest were brought into "friendship" (amicitia) with the Roman people. Those that resisted were immortalized in images depicting their defeat. Formidable warriors like the Dying Gaul (pictured; first-century-*C.E.* copy of a third-century-*B.C.E.*. Hellenistic original)—were especially important elements in Roman propaganda. This image is now in the Louvre; numerous images like it once adorned the temple of Zeus in Pergamon. See "For Further Reading" below. Photo in the public domain.*

as Nabata village, near Meroë, and an army advanced into the part of Arabia called "happy." . . . Large numbers of the enemy from both peoples were slain on the battlefield and several towns were captured.

27. I added Egypt to the empire of the Roman people. I could have made greater Armenia a province, when its king Artaxes was slain, but I wished rather, in the example of our ancestors and by means of Tiberius Nero, who was my stepson then, to pass the kingdom on to Tigranes. . . . I recovered all the provinces, most of them then held by kings, that verge on the Adriatic Sea toward the east and Cyrene; before then I recovered Sicily and Sardinia, which had been possessed in the slave war.

28. I planted colonies of soldiers in Africa, Sicily, Macedonia, both Spains, Achaea, Asia, Syria, Gaul in the area of Narbo and Pisidia. And Italy has twenty-eight colonies that were founded by my initiative and have become crowded and very filled while I live. . . .

30. I subjected the peoples of the Pannonians—whom no army of the Roman people ever approached before I became first man—to the empire of

the Roman people . . . and I advanced the territory of Illyricum as far as the riverbank of the Danube.[13] . . . (My army) forced the peoples of the Dacians to endure the commands of the Roman people.

31. Envoys from the kings of India were often sent to me; at no time before this had they appeared beside a Roman leader.[14] . . .

32. Kings claimed political asylum with me as suppliants. . . . And while I was *princeps*, many other peoples experienced the good faith of the Roman people, who before had no exchange of ambassadors and friendship with the Roman people. . . .

33. The nations of the Parthians and Medes received from me through envoys their requested nobles to be kings of their nations.[15] . . .

34. When consul for the sixth and seventh times, after I put down the civil war and when all agreed that I was completely in control of all the affairs of state, I transferred the Republic out of my control and into the authority of the Senate and Roman people. In return for my contribution, I was called "Augustus" by decree of the Senate, the doorposts of my home were covered with laurels, a city crown was placed over my door and a golden shield was placed in the Curia Julia, on which the Senate and the Roman people gave an inscription for me, attesting that the reason for this very shield was my excellence, mercy, righteousness and piety. After that time I advanced before all in reputation, though I had no more authority than the others who shared state offices with me.[16]

35. When I was fulfilling my thirteenth consulship, the Senate, equestrian order, and whole Roman people named me "father of the fatherland" and resolved that this should be inscribed on the porch of my residence, in the Curia Julia and in the Augustan forum under the chariot that by decree of the Senate was placed there for me. I am in my 76th year while writing this.

Postscript

1. All of the money that I gave, whether to the treasury or to the Roman populace or to the pension funds for soldiers was 600 million denarii.

2. New constructions he [i.e., Augustus] completed: temples of Mars, of Thundering Jupiter, of Jupiter Feretrius, of Apollo, of Julius, of Quirinus, of Minerva, of Queen Juno, of Jupiter god of Liberty, of the Lares, of the gods of the Penates, of Iuvenes, of the Great Mother, the Lupercal; the government suite at the circus, the Senate chamber with the Chalcidicum, the Augustan forum, the Julian basilica, the theater of Marcellus, the Octavian porch, the Caesars' woodlands across the Tiber.

3. He rebuilt the Capitol and sacred temples to the total number of eighty-two, the theater of Pompey, aqueducts, the Flaminian way. His outlays for entertaining extravaganzas; gladiator shows; athletic games; animal hunts; naval battles; gifts of money to colonies, cities, and towns destroyed by earthquake and fire, or to specific friends and senators whose required level of net worth he subsidized, are incalculable.

(*Res Gestae Divi Augusti*, trans. Reasoner)

Fig. 3.15. *Marble copy, from Arles, of the clupeus virtutis, the golden Shield of Virtues awarded by the Senate to Augustus, perhaps in 27 B.C.E. The inscription on this copy reads:*

SENATVS/ POPVLVSQVE ROMANVS/
IMP. CAESARI DIVI F. AVGVSTO/
COS. VIII DEDIT CLVPEVM/ VIRTVTIS CLEMENTIAE/
IVSTITIAE-PIETATIS-ERGA/
DEOS PATRIAMQVE.
The Senate/and Roman people/
to Emperor Augustus, Caesar and Son of God,/
in his eighth consulship gave this shield,/
[to recognize his] works of virtue, mercy, justice, and piety/
to the Gods and his fatherland.

The sixth line uses the Greek term erga, "works," rather than Latin, suggesting that the word had a technical usage in what Frederick W. Danker has called the "theology of benefaction" (Benefactor: Epigraphic Study of a Graeco-Roman and New Testament Semantic Field [St. Louis: Clayton, 1982]). Photo: Cl. M. Lacanaud; by permission of the Musée de l'Arles et dela Provence antiques. Photo: Erich Lessing/Art Resource, New York.

Patronage is the term scholars use to describe a set of roles and expectations in highly stratified Roman society, governed by rules of obligation according to "asymmetrical reciprocity." A powerful and wealthy person (like Augustus) could provide benefits to social inferiors that they were incapable of providing for themselves. The **patron** thus put **clients** under virtually limitless obligation to show honor in return. Unlike contemporary capitalist society, where many people aspire to make money for its own sake, the Romans were very clear that wealth was often a means to attain something of arguably greater value: honor.

Patronage thus "naturalized" inequalities by making it appear that the powerful were the only recourse to which the powerless (or "weak") could appeal. Augustus could also refuse specific honors because he did not wish to accept even implicit obligations to others. For a peer to refuse a benefaction, however, could be construed as an insult—as may well explain the tension between Paul and some of the Corinthians evident in 2 Corinthians, especially chapters 8–9.

See John H. Elliott, "Patronage and Clientage," in *The Social Sciences and New Testament Interpretation*, ed. Richard Rohrbaugh (Peabody, Mass.: Hendrickson, 1996), 144–56. For more detailed studies, see G. E. M. de Ste. Croix, *The Class Struggle in the Ancient Greek World: From the Archaic Age to the Arab Conquests* (Ithaca, N.Y.: Cornell University Press, 1980), esp. 241–42, 341–43, 364–67; Frederick W. Danker, *Benefactor: Epigraphic Study of a Graeco-Roman and New Testament Semantic Field* (St. Louis: Clayton, 1982); Peter Marshall, *Enmity in Corinth: Social Conventions in Paul's Relations with the Corinthians*, WUNT 2.23 (Tübingen: Mohr, 1987); John K. Chow, *Patronage and Power: A Study of Social Networks in Corinth*, JSNTSup 75 (Sheffield: JSOT Press, 1992).

93. A priest of Augustus in Roman Corinth

The following inscription was made on a monument, erected in the mid-first century c.e., to honor Julius Spartiaticus, a Roman aristocrat who had been made an equestrian (note, given a "public horse") and given other prestigious political and sacred responsibilities, including priesthood in the cults of Julius Caesar and Augustus, by the emperor Claudius. He was thus in a position to provide patronage for "the tribe Calpurnia," who made the inscription. The inscription illustrates both the important civic role of the imperial cult and the way in which patronage was intertwined with that cult: Julius Spartiaticus had obviously expended tremendous wealth in public benefactions and was duly recognized and honored for his efforts.

Gaius Julius, Son of Laco,
Grandson of Eurycles [of the tribe] Fabia, Spartiaticus,
Procurator of Caesar and Augusta
Agrippina, Tribune of the Soldiers, Awarded a Public Horse
By the Deified Claudius, Flamen [priest]
Of the Deified Julius, Pontifex, Duovir Quinquennalis twice,
Agonothete of the Isthmian and Caesar-
Augustan Games, High-Priest of the House of Augustus
In Perpetuity, First of the Achaeans.
Because of his virtue and eager
And all-encompassing munificence toward the divine house
And toward our colony, the tribesmen
Of the Tribe Calpurnia
[dedicated this] to their patron.[17]

The Imperial Gospel in Coins

Currency was one of the most prevalent and efficient means of communicating the themes of imperial ideology visually. We have already seen a coin of Julius Caesar expressing themes that would become important in the principate of Augustus (see fig. 3.6). Such themes were taken up by successive emperors as well, as their coinage illustrates. Here we discuss a few representative examples.

> The study of ancient coins, **numismatics,** is an important resource for scholarship on the Roman Empire.

Figure 3.16 shows a coin commemorating the justice of the emperor Tiberius. The Roman Empire claimed that the deified virtue of righteousness (*iustitia*; *dikaiosynē*) was especially found in its emperors. A coin minted during the reign of the emperor Tiberius (14–37 C.E.) reads:

TI(BERIVS) CAESAR DIVI AVG(VSTI) F(ILIVS) AVGVSTVS
Tiberius Caesar, Augustus, son of the divine Augustus

On the reverse side is an image of the deified virtue Iustitia, enthroned and holding a laurel branch and scepter. Around her reads the emperor's title that this coin announces as most linked to the virtue of justice:

Fig. 3.16. *Coin of the Emperor Tiberius. Photo courtesy of Classical Numismatics Group, Inc.*

PONTIF(EX) MAXIM(VS)
highest priest

Figure 3.17 shows a coin celebrating Nero's achievement of peace. The Romans' political presence in the Mediterranean had long held the larger world in view, as we have seen already in Augustus's *Res Gestae*. This coin, possibly minted in Nero's reign shortly after the great fire and persecution of Christians in 64 C.E., celebrates how Nero has "gained peace on land and sea." On one side of the coin we see the emperor Nero, with the curly hair for which he was known. Around his portrait we read:

NERO CLAVD(IVS) CAESAR AVG(VSTVS) GER(MANICVS)
P(ONTIFEX) M(AXIMVS) TR(IBVNICIA) P(OTESTAS) IMP(ERATOR)
P(ATER) P(ATRIAE)
Nero Claudius Caesar Augustus Germanicus,
Highest Priest, holding tribunician power, emperor, father
of the fatherland.

On the reverse side of the coin, the inscription moves around a picture of the temple of Janus Quirinus with its doors closed. As we have seen in *Res Gestae* 13, the doors of this temple were closed ceremonially only when Rome was not fighting anyone on land or sea.

The inscription reads:

PACE P(OPVLO) R(OMANO) TERRA MARIQ(VE)
PARTA IANVM CLVSIT
Peace on land and sea having been brought forth for the Roman people,
he shut the gate of Janus.

Fig. 3.17. *Coin of the Emperor Nero, 65 c.e. Photo courtesy of Stack's LLC.*

The S and C on either side of the closed temple stand for *Senātūs Consultō*, or "by decree of the Senate," showing that the Senate approved that the coin be minted and perhaps also that they approved the closure of the temple doors.[18]

Figure 3.18 depicts a coin issued shortly after Paul's death and the forced suicide of Nero by the emperor Otho, who reigned for only three months. The imperial gospel included the announcement that peace and security had been achieved. The inscription on the obverse reads

IMP(ERATOR) M(ARCVS) OTHO CAESAR AVG(VSTVS)
TR(IBVNICIA) P(OTESTAS)
Emperor Marcus Otho, Caesar Augustus, [holds] tribunician power

Fig. 3.18. *Coin of the emperor Otho, 68 c.e. Photo courtesy of Stack's LLC.*

The curls in Otho's hair are meant to remind people of Nero's hairstyle. On the reverse side, around the deified virtue Securitas (Security), who holds a wreath and a scepter to show her absolute rule, the inscription implicitly equates Otho's imperial rule with the Roman people's safety:

SECVRITAS P(OPVLAE) R(OMAE)
The security of the Roman people

The Imperial "Son of God"

From Augustus onward, a new phrase entered the Roman political vocabulary as he and several of his descendants were honored as *Divi Filius*—son of God. This does not mean that the emperor himself was worshiped, at least not in Rome, where such a practice would have been scandalous. Julius Caesar had accepted many divine honors in Rome while alive; but this was a tactical mistake that his adopted son Octavius, as Augustus, was careful not to repeat.[19]

Nevertheless, as early as Cicero's justification for Pompey's rule, the Romans had made use of the Hellenistic idea that the gods had predestined their rulers to hold power over them. This idea came to be focused on the person of the emperor. Even when Augustus or one of his descendants did not claim worship, they were often addressed in terms that evoked their divinity. After the assassination of Julius Caesar, the Senate honored him as a divine being who had been taken up into heaven (called *apotheosis*); thus his adopted son Octavian became "son of God."

Upon his own death, Augustus too was deified, and his adopted son Tiberius thus came to be called "son of the Divine Augustus." Not all the emperors in the early empire were so fortunate: only Augustus, Tiberius, Claudius, Vespasian, Titus, and Nerva were deified in the first century.

94. Augustus second only to Jupiter (Horace)

Already in Horace's *Odes*, we see extravagant language in praise of Augustus. In one Ode, praises to Bacchus and Phoebus Apollo as gods beneath the rule of Jupiter are followed by direct address to Jupiter. Note the mention here of Justice as Augustus's chief virtue; also the division of labor: Jupiter may reign in the realm of the gods, but on earth, it is Augustus:

> O father and guardian of the human race, you son of Saturn, to you by fate has been entrusted the charge of mighty Caesar; may you be lord of all, with Caesar next in power! Whether he lead in well-earned triumph the humbled Parthians, that now threaten Latium, or the Seres and Indians lying along the borders of the East, second to you alone shall he with justice rule the broad earth; be it yours to shake Olympus with your ponderous chariot, yours to hurl your angry bolts on polluted groves!
>
> (Horace, *Odes* 1.12.5-6, trans. Bennett, modified)

Fig. 3.19. *The Grande Camée de France. Sardonyx cameo, c. 20–23 c.e. At the center, Tiberius, depicted as divine, sits next to Livia, his mother; above them, the deified Augustus, holding a scepter, welcomes Germanicus into heaven. At the bottom, barbarians sit in defeat. Paris, Bibliothèque nationale. Photo: Marie-Lan Nguyen.*

95. "God of triumph" (Horace)

In another *Ode*, Horace's exuberant language is ambiguous: Is Augustus himself the "god of triumph"? Note too the idea of a restoration of the "ancient age of gold" in connection with the earlier discussion.

> You, a poet of loftier strain, shall sing of Caesar, when, honored with the well-earned garland, he shall lead in his train along the sacred slope the wild Sygambri; a sovereign than whom nothing greater, nothing better, have the fates and gracious gods bestowed upon the world, nor shall bestow, even though the centuries roll backward to the ancient age of gold.
>
> You shall sing of the festal days, of the city's public games to celebrate the return of brave Augustus in answer to our prayers, and of the forum free from strife. Then, if I have anything deserving to be heard, the best powers of my voice shall swell the acclaim, and happy at Caesar's homecoming I'll sing: "O

glorious day, to be linked with honor!" And as you take the lead along the ways, "Hail! God of triumph!" we will shout all of us together, and not only once, "Hail, God of triumph!" and incense we will offer to the kind gods.

(Horace, *Odes* 4.2.33-52, trans. Bennett, modified)

96. The deification of Julius Caesar (Vitruvius)

The following selection, from about 22 B.C.E., addressed to Augustus by an architect proposing an impressive building project, combines the ideas that the heavenly council had brought Augustus to power and that his father, Julius Caesar, had been assumed into their company. The divinity of the emperor's person could be described in literature or depicted in images even in the absence of formal cult.

Fig. 3.20. *Winged Victory. Bronze statue from Brescia, first century* c.e. *Coins from the third century* b.c.e. *depict Victoria laying a wreath of palms, signaling Rome's supremacy in the First Punic War. Horace associated the goddess with Augustus. Photo: Stefano Bolognini.*

When your highness's divine mind and power, O Caesar, gained the empire of the world, Rome gloried in your triumph and victory. For all her enemies were crushed by your invincible courage and all mankind obeyed your bidding; the Roman people and Senate were not only freed from fear but followed your guidance, inspired as it was by a generous imagination. Amid such affairs I shrank from publishing my writings on architecture in which I displayed designs made to a large scale, for I feared lest by interrupting at an inconvenient time, I should be found a hindrance to your thoughts.

But I observed that you cared not only about the common life of all men, and the constitution of the state, but also about the provision of suitable public buildings; so that the state was not only made greater through you by its new provinces, but the majesty of the empire also was expressed through the eminent dignity of its public buildings. Hence I conceived that the opportunity should be taken at once of bringing before you my proposals about these things: the more so, because I had been first known to your father here, whose virtues I revered. When, however, the council of heaven gave him an abode in the mansion of the immortals and placed in your power your father's empire, that same zeal of mine which had remained faithful to his memory found favor with you.

(Vitruvius, Preface to *On Architecture*, trans. Granger, LCL)[20]

97. Nero "son of the divine Claudius"

A final example concerns Nero, who throughout his reign would combine claims to his descent from Augustus and to being, upon the apotheosis of his father, "son of the divine Claudius." The combination is ubiquitous in inscriptions:

> [Dedicated] To Nero, son of the divine Claudius,
> descendant of Tiberius Caesar Augustus
> and Germanicus Caesar,
> [themselves] sons of the divine Augustus.
> (*IG* 5.1.1450. Trans. Elliott)[21]

These examples should suffice to show that the language of "sonship" (Greek *hyiothesia*, see Romans 8–9) had a wide currency in Paul's world. (See also nos. 101 and 102 below.) It was wrapped up with themes of ancestry and destiny, power and the right to rule, especially as these were focused on the dynasty of Julius Caesar, his adopted son Augustus, and his descendants through sonship (including adoption). Figure 3.21 diagrams the familial relationships in the Julio-Claudian dynasty.

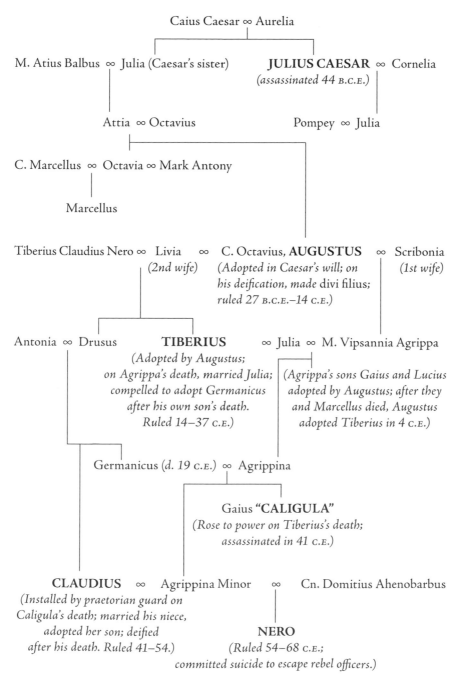

Caius Caesar ∞ Aurelia

M. Atius Balbus ∞ Julia (Caesar's sister)   **JULIUS CAESAR** ∞ Cornelia
                                                 (assassinated 44 B.C.E.)

Attia ∞ Octavius   Pompey ∞ Julia

C. Marcellus ∞ Octavia ∞ Mark Antony

Marcellus

Tiberius Claudius Nero ∞ Livia ∞ C. Octavius, **AUGUSTUS** ∞ Scribonia
                        (2nd wife) *(Adopted in Caesar's will; on* *(1st wife)*
                                      his deification, made divi filius;
                                      ruled 27 B.C.E.–14 C.E.)

Antonia ∞ Drusus   **TIBERIUS**   ∞ Julia ∞ M. Vipsannia Agrippa
                     (Adopted by Augustus;
           on Agrippa's death, married Julia; *(Agrippa's sons Gaius and Lucius*
           compelled to adopt Germanicus   *adopted by Augustus; after they*
              after his own son's death.   *and Marcellus died, Augustus*
                 Ruled 14–37 C.E.)   *adopted Tiberius in 4 C.E.)*

Germanicus *(d. 19 C.E.)* ∞ Agrippina

Gaius **"CALIGULA"**
(Rose to power on Tiberius's death;
assassinated in 41 C.E.)

CLAUDIUS ∞ Agrippina Minor ∞ Cn. Domitius Ahenobarbus
(Installed by praetorian guard on
Caligula's death; married his niece,
adopted her son; deified   **NERO**
after his death. Ruled 41–54.)   *(Ruled 54–68 C.E.;*
                             committed suicide to escape rebel officers.)

Fig. 3.21. *The Julio-Claudian House*

Claudius's Death and Nero's Accession

In 54 c.e. the emperor Claudius died after falling sick in the theater and then being fed a plate of mushrooms at home by his wife (and niece), Agrippina. Her son from a previous marriage, Nero, whom she had compelled Claudius to adopt as his own son, came to power as the next emperor and called on the Senate to declare his stepfather ascended into heaven as a god. The Senate complied, arranging for the requisite ceremony (including sworn oaths from witnesses).

This transfer of power—only a few years, at most, before Paul wrote his letter to the Romans—presented something of an anomaly to the pattern just described. Writing decades later, Suetonius and Tacitus reported considerable suspicion at the time that Claudius may in fact have been murdered; Suetonius observed that Nero would come to neglect the divine honors for his stepfather. Tacitus scoffed at the "duly counterfeited" mourning of widow and bereaved son. L. Junius Gallo, brother of Nero's advisor Seneca and formerly the proconsul of Corinth (before whom Paul had appeared according to Acts 18), quipped that if Claudius were among the immortals it was because he had been "hauled into heaven on a hook."[22]

Because of the peculiar circumstances attending this particular apotheosis, the unusual abundance of responses to it, and the importance that has been attributed to the character of Nero's reign in discussions of Paul's political views, several aspects of Nero's accession and reign merit attention here.

98. Nero's clemency (Seneca)

Members of Nero's court were duly enthusiastic about his accession. His longtime tutor, the philosopher Seneca, became his close advisor (until he too fell under suspicion and was compelled to commit suicide). In a speech addressed to the young emperor (Nero was nineteen) Seneca extols his clemency—or, on another interpretation, subtly pleads for the dissolute young emperor to curb his worst inclinations.

Fig. 3.22. *An unusual bust of the young Nero, first century c.e. His toga is pulled over his head in the gesture of worship. Museum of Fine Arts, Boston. Photo in the public domain.*

You are distinguished, Caesar, by a state free of bloodshed, and this, by your great pride in which you glory that no drop of human blood has been shed, for this is very significant and miraculous, since no one ever was granted the sword at a younger age.

(Seneca, *On Mercy* 1.11.3, trans. Reasoner)

99. A new golden age (Calpurnius Siculus)

Another member of Nero's court, Calpurnius Siculus, penned a poem in which two shepherds stumble upon a prophecy carved into a tree by Faunus, god of the forest. The poem borrows shamelessly—and transparently—from Virgil: its theme is that the golden age inaugurated by Augustus now sees "a second birth" with Nero, who surpasses even Augustus by coming to power without force of arms. The poem also implies sharp criticism of Claudius as corrupt and brutal: Nero, "a kinder god," restores both justice and clemency. Note that the last lines of this selection accept as fact the deification of Claudius. Here is the prophecy:

Amid untroubled peace, the Golden Age springs to a second birth; at last kindly Themis [Justice], throwing off the gathered dust of her mourning, returns to the earth; blissful ages attend the youthful prince who pleaded a successful case for the Iuli of the mother town.[23] While he, a very God, shall rule the nations, the unholy War-Goddess shall yield and have her vanquished hands bound behind her back, and stripped of weapons, turn her furious teeth into her own entrails; upon herself shall she wage the civil wars which of late she spread o'er all the world: no battles like Philippi shall Rome lament henceforth;[24] no triumph o'er her captive self shall she celebrate. All wars shall be quelled in Tartarean durance: they shall plunge the head in darkness, and dread the light.

Fair peace shall come, fair not in visage alone—such as she often was when, though free from open war, and with distant foe subdued, she yet mid the riot of arms spread national strife with secret steel. Clemency has commanded every vice that wears the disguise of peace to betake itself afar: she has broken every maddened sword-blade. No more shall the procession of a fettered Senate weary the headsman at his task; no more will crowded prison leave only a Senator here and there for the unhappy Curia to count.[25]

Peace in her fullness shall come; knowing not the drawn sword, she shall renew once more the reign of Saturn in Latium, once more the reign of Numa who first taught the tasks of peace to armies that rejoiced in slaughter and still drew from Romulus' camp their fiery spirit—Numa who first hushed the clash of arms and bade the trumpet sound 'mid holy rites instead of war.[26]

No more shall the consul purchase the form of a shadowy dignity or, silenced, receive worthless fasces and meaningless judgment-seat. Nay, laws shall be restored; right will come in fullest force; a kinder god will renew the former tradition and look of the Forum and displace the age of oppression.[27]

Let all the peoples rejoice, whether they dwell furthest down in the low south or in the uplifted north, whether they face the east or west or burn beneath the central zone. Do ye mark how already for a twentieth time the night is agleam in an unclouded sky, displaying a comet radiant in tranquil light? And how brightly, with no presage of bloodshed, twinkles its undiminished luster?

Is it with any trace of blood-hued flame that, as is a comet's way, it besprinkles either pole? Does its torch flash with gory fire?

But aforetime it was not such, when, at Caesar's taking off, it pronounced upon luckless citizens the destined wars. Assuredly a very god shall take in his strong arms the burden of the massive Roman state so unshaken, that the world will pass to a new ruler without the crash of reverberating thunder, and that Rome will not regards the dead as deified in accord with merit ere the dawn of one reign can look back on the setting of the last.

(Calpurnius Siculus, Eclogue 1, 37-88, trans. Duff and Duff, LCL)

Nero's "Good Years"

It is something of a commonplace in biblical studies that the beginnings of Nero's reign were exemplary—and therefore that Paul's endorsement of the ruling authorities as "set in place by God" (Rom 13:1-7), written during those years, should not surprise us.[28] The commonplace relies, however, on only a single anecdote, reported in two fourth-century historical epitomes, in which the second-century emperor Trajan quipped that all of the preceding emperors together were not as good as "five years of Nero."

Fig. 3.23. *The apotheosis of Claudius. Cut sardonyx gem, c. 54 C.E. Despite such respectful treatments, the fact that a satire concerning Claudius's official deification was written within Nero's own court (see below) shows contempt at least for Claudius and, perhaps, more generally for the notion of deification by decree. Photo: Sailko.*

Fig. 3.24. *A coin of Nero's early reign celebrates his harmony with his mother, Agrippina; he later had her put to death. The inscription is devoted to her:*

AGRIPP. AVG. DIVI CLAVD. NERONIS CAES.
MATER,
Agripp(ina), Mother of Nero Claudius Caesar, (son of) the divine Augustus.

Reverse, NERONI CLAVD. DIVI F. CAES. AVG. GERM. IMP. TR. P.; around, EX S. C.
(Coin of) the Emperor Nero, son of the divine Claudius,
Augustus Germanicus, holding tribunal power,
by the Senate's decree.

Miriam T. Griffin observes, however, that historians closer to Nero himself agreed on a catalogue of vices and ills that "come from all periods of Nero's reign." Suetonius remarked that omens at Nero's birth had warned his father that "any child born to himself and Agrippina was bound to have a detestable nature and become a public danger," an assessment Suetonius clearly shared (*Nero* 6). In Suetonius's view, the wickedness of "the true Nero" was evident from his adolescence (26); at last the historian turns to Nero's death by declaring that "after nearly fourteen years of misrule"—that is, his entire reign—"the earth rid herself of him" (40). Tacitus described those years as a decline from better rule into worse, but regarded the earlier years as only "a *relatively* innocent time"; his governing theme is that "vice appears when the restraints on a person are removed" (in Nero's case, by exile and murder), "thus releasing his true nature."[29]

100. Nero's achievement (Martial)

It would seem, then, that the ancient historians do not present a picture of Nero's early "good years," before things "went bad"; rather, they show a mixed picture of a wicked emperor who nevertheless accomplished some good things. For the satirist Martial, the latter could be summed up rather quickly.

Do you ask, Severus, how it could come to pass that Charinus, the very worst of men, has done one thing well? I will tell you at once. Who was ever worse than Nero? Yet what can be better than Nero's warm baths? But hark, there is not wanting some ill-natured individual to say, immediately, in a sour tone, "What, do you prefer the baths of Nero to the munificent structures of Domitian, our lord and master?" I prefer the warm baths of Nero to the baths of the debauched Charinus.

(Martial, *Epigram* 7.34, trans. Bohn)

101. Popular barbs aimed at Nero (Suetonius)

Suetonius arranges his account of Nero's life by treating first his "less atrocious acts—some deserving no criticism, some even praiseworthy—from the others" (*Nero* 19). His list of the emperor's "follies and crimes" is formidable (20-39). Nero was so arrogant about his own musical and theatrical talents as to prove an international embarrassment for Rome (20-25). His "insolent, lustful, extravagant, greedy, or cruel early practices" might have been written off as youthful indiscretion, Suetonius writes, but "this was clearly the true Nero, not merely Nero in his adolescence" (26). As Suetonius's catalogue of the emperor's crimes demonstrates, he "practiced every kind of obscenity" (29). "There was no family relationship that Nero did not criminally abuse" (35), and he "was no less cruel to strangers than to members of his own family" (36). Nor did he show any greater mercy "to the common folk, or to the very walls of Rome": so Suetonius introduces the account of Nero setting the great fire of 64 (38).

> History "from below" or **"people's history"** is a twentieth-century school of historiography that seeks, first, to read "elite" sources—monuments, official inscriptions, literature—"against the grain," and second, to give priority to more prosaic evidence (for example, the Egyptian papyri) or expressions of popular sentiment—such as graffiti, mob demonstrations, or other collective practices—that provide the cover of anonymity for the participants. In recent years some Pauline scholars have sought to incorporate the concepts of such partially "hidden transcripts" into their accounts of Paul's environment.
>
> See Justin J. Meggitt, *Paul, Poverty, and Survival*, Studies of the New Testament and Its World (Edinburgh: T&T Clark, 1998), chapter 2; Richard A. Horsley, ed., *Christian Origins*, vol. 1 of *A People's History of Christianity*, ed. Denis R. Janz (Minneapolis: Fortress Press, 2007).

Rather than quote the entire account here, we present Suetonius's quotations of popular jokes made at Nero's expense—gestures of hostility necessarily made anonymously. (There were also two recorded conspiracies to assassinate Nero as well as the rebellion mounted against him by Vindex, the Roman governor of Gaul.) Such contemporary reactions provide evidence that Nero's crimes, including sexual assault, sacrilege, and murder (for Suetonius considers Nero guilty of Claudius's death as well as the murder of his own mother), were popular knowledge, not private matters known only to palace insiders.

Also targeted are Nero's pretensions at musical ability, lack of military prowess, and ambition for his own building programs.

> Not satisfied with seducing free-born boys and married women, Nero raped the Vestal Virgin Rubria. He nearly contrived to marry the freedwoman Acte, by persuading some friends of consular rank to swear falsely that she came of royal stock. Having tried to turn the boy Sporus into a girl by castration, he went through a wedding ceremony with him—dowry, bridal veil and all—took him to his palace with a great crowd in attendance, and treated him as a wife. A rather amusing joke is still going the rounds:

Fig. 3.25. Agrippina, Claudius's niece, wife, and possible murderer; Nero's mother and eventual victim. Bust, first century C.E. Museo Palazzo Massimo, Rome. Photo: Neil Elliott.

> The world would have been a happier place had Nero's
> father Domitius married that sort of wife.

. . . It was strange how amazingly tolerant Nero seemed to be of the insults that everyone cast at him, in the form of jokes and lampoons. Here are a few examples of verses, in Greek or Latin, posted on city walls or current orally:

> Alcmaeon, Orestes, and Nero are brothers,
> Why? Because all of them murdered their mothers.

—

> Count the numerical values
> Of the letters in Nero's name,
> And in "murdered his own mother":
> You will find their sum is the same.[30]

—

> Aeneas the Trojan hero
> Carried off his aged father;
> His remote descendant Nero
> Likewise "carried off" his mother:
> Heroes worthy of each other.

—

> Though Nero may pluck the chords of a lyre
> And the Parthian King the string of a bow,
> He who chants to the lyre with heavenly fire
> Is "Apollo" as much as his far-darting foe.[31]

—

> The Palace is spreading and swallowing Rome!
> Let us all flee to Veii and make it our home.
> Yet the Palace is growing so damnably fast
> That it threatens to gobble up Veii at last. . . .

Once, as he crossed a street, Isidorus the Cynic loudly taunted him with: "In your song about Nauplius you make good use of ancient ills, but in all practical matters you make ill use of modern goods." Again, the comedian Datus, acting in an Atellan farce, illustrated the first line of the song "Goodbye Father, goodbye Mother" with gestures of drinking and swimming—Claudius had been poisoned, Agrippina nearly drowned—and the last line, "Hell guides your feet," with a wave of his hand towards the Senators whom Nero planned to massacre.

Later, during a severe shortage of food—compounded by the threat of the Gallic uprising under Vindex—Nero was found to have profiteered in grain. Suetonius reports the popular abuse only intensified.

Nero was now so universally loathed that no bad enough abuse could be found for him. Someone tied a tress of hair to the head of one of his statues, with a note attached in Greek:

> This is a real contest for once,
> And you are going to lose!

A sack was draped around the neck of another statue, with a similar note reading:

> I have done what I could,
> But you deserve the sack!

Insults were scrawled on columns that

> Nero's crowing has aroused the *galli!*

—for *Galli* means both "cocks" and Gauls—and several people played the same trick, pretending to have trouble with their slaves at night and shouting out,

> Vengeance is coming!

—a reference to Vindex's name. . . .

Again, while his speech against Vindex was being read in the Senate, a passage running ". . . the criminals will soon incur the punishment, and die the death which they so thoroughly deserve," was hailed on all sides with cries of

> Augustus, you will do it! . . .

At last Suetonius recounts Nero's last days, as Roman generals in Spain and Africa as well as Gaul rose against him and he was forced to flee Rome. He finally committed suicide when he saw that he was about to be captured. Suetonius's summary points out that, despite his general unpopularity, there were some who cherished his memory long afterward.

> Nero died at the age of thirty-one, on the anniversary of Octavia's murder. In the widespread general rejoicing, citizens ran through the streets wearing caps of liberty. But there were people who used to lay spring and summer flowers on his grave for a long time, and had statues made of him, wearing his fringed toga, which they put up on the Rostra; they even continued to circulate his edicts, pretending he was still alive and would soon return to confound his enemies.
> (Suetonius, *Nero* 28; 39; 45-46; 57, trans. Graves)

102. The "Pumpkinification" of Claudius (Seneca)

One of the most surprising texts from Nero's early reign is a harsh satire, penned in all probability by Seneca himself (the text is anonymous but Dio Cassius attributed an *Apokolokyntōsis* to him). The text subjects the deceased Claudius to merciless ridicule. Nero had showed contempt for his stepfather, making crude jokes about his death that raised suspicions about himself—referring, for example, to mushrooms as "the food of the gods" because mushrooms had, in effect, ushered Claudius into their company (Suetonius, *Nero* 33). It is therefore reasonable to suppose that this satire was written precisely for the amusement of Nero's inner circle.

What is especially remarkable about the text is its comic premise: the machinery of apotheosis is a hoax; the solemn testimony of sworn witnesses has been suborned. The gods into whose presence Claudius has been commended through pious prayers,

Augustus chief among them, find the newcomer wholly repulsive and unworthy of their company. The title is a play on the Greek *apotheōsis*: the *apokolokyntōsis* of Claudius means he has been made not god, but gourd.

> I wish to place on record the proceedings in heaven last October 13 of the new year which begins this auspicious age. It shall be done without malice or favor. This is the truth.
>
> Ask, if you like, how I know it? . . . Who has ever made the historian produce a witness to swear for him? But if an authority must be produced, ask of the man who saw Drusilla translated to heaven: the same man will affirm for sure that he saw Claudius on the road.[32] All that happens in heaven he must see. He is the custodian of the Appian Way; by that route, you know, both Tiberius and Augustus went up to the gods. Question him, he will tell you the tale when you are alone; with groups of people he is silent. You see, he swore in the Senate that he beheld Drusilla mounting heavenwards, and all he got for his good news was that everybody considered him a liar; since then, he solemnly swears he will never bear witness again to what he has seen, not even if he had seen a man murdered in open market. What he told me I report plain and clear, as I hope for his health and happiness. . . .
>
> Claudius began to breathe his last, and could not make an end of the matter. Then Mercury, who had always been much pleased with his wit, drew aside one of the three Fates, and said: "Cruel dame, why do you let the poor wretch be tormented? After all this torture cannot he have a rest? Four and sixty years it is now since he began to pant for breath. What grudge is this you bear against him and the whole empire? . . . Do what has to be done: Kill him, and let a better man rule in empty court."[33]

The three Fates set to work, spinning short life-threads for Claudius and two other prominent Romans who died in the same year; then turn their task to weaving a thread of pure gold for Nero. Phoebus, that is, Apollo, joins them and urges more than a young life for the emperor; Nero should bear his own divine likeness. The speech involves the sort of fawning flattery we should expect within the imperial court.)

> Then Phoebus says, "O sister Fates! I pray take none away,
> But suffer this one life to be longer than mortal day.
> Like me in face and lovely grace, like me in voice and song,
> He'll bid the laws at length speak out that have been dumb so long,
> Will give unto the weary world years prosperous and bright. . . .
>
> As the bright sun looks on the world, and speeds along its way
> His rising car from morning's gates: so Caesar doth arise,
> So Nero shows his face to Rome before the people's eyes,
> His bright and shining countenance illumines all the air,
> While down upon his graceful neck fall rippling waves of hair."
> . . .

Fig. 3.26. *Bust of Nero, after 64* c.e. *Museo Palazzo Massimo, Rome. Photo: Neil Elliott.*

(After a derisive recapitulation of Claudius's last hours, the satire turns to his reception into heaven.)

> Word comes to Jupiter that a stranger had arrived, a man well set up, pretty gray; he seemed to be threatening something, for he wagged his head ceaselessly; he dragged the right foot. They asked him what nation he was of; he answered something in a confused mumbling voice: his language they did not understand. He was no Greek and no Roman, nor of any known race. On this, Jupiter bids Hercules go and find out what country he comes from; you see Hercules had traveled over the whole world, and might be expected to know all the nations in it. But Hercules, the first glimpse he got, was really much taken aback, although not all the monsters in the world could frighten him; when he saw this new kind of object, with its extraordinary gait, and the voice of no terrestrial beast, but such as you might hear in the leviathans of the deep, hoarse and inarticulate, he thought his thirteenth labor had come upon him. When he looked closer, the thing seemed to be a kind of man.

The gods begin to debate whether to accept Claudius as a god on Mount Olympus and what sort of god he should be. It almost looks as though Claudius will be made a god when the deified Augustus rises to press an indictment and moves to remove Claudius from heaven and send him to the underworld.

> "I call you to witness, my lords and gentlemen," said he, "that since the day I was made a god I have never uttered one word. I always mind my own business. But now I can keep on the mask no longer, nor conceal the sorrow which shame makes all the greater. Is it for this I have made peace by land and sea? For this have I calmed civil wars? For this, laid a firm foundation of law for Rome, adorned it with buildings, and all that—my lords, words fail me; there are none can rise to the height of my indignation. I must borrow that saying of the eloquent Messala Corvinus, 'I am ashamed of my authority.'[34]
>
> "This man, my lords, who looks as though he could not hurt a fly, used to chop off heads as easily as a dog sits down.[35] But why should I speak of all those men, and such men? There is no time to lament for public disasters, when one has so many private sorrows to think of. . . . This man you see, who for so many years has been masquerading under my name, has done me the favor of murdering two Julias, great-granddaughters of mine, one by cold steel and one by starvation; and one great grandson, L. Silanus—see, Jupiter, whether he had a case against him (at least it is your own if you will be fair).
>
> "Come, tell me, blessed Claudius, why of all those you killed, both men and women, without a hearing, why you did not hear their side of the case first, before putting them to death? Where do we find that custom?[36] It is not done in heaven. Look at Jupiter: all these years he has been king, and never did more than once to break Vulcan's leg, 'Whom seizing by the foot he cast from the threshold of the sky,'[37] and once he fell in a rage with his wife and strung her up: did he do any killing? Yet you killed Messalina, whose great-uncle I was no less than yours. . . .

(Augustus turns again to his fellow gods.)

> "Is this the one you want now to make a god? Look at his body, born under the wrath of heaven! In fine, let him say the three words quickly, and he may have me for a slave.[38] God! who will worship this god, who will believe in him? If you make gods of such as him, no one will believe *you* to be gods. To be brief, my lords: if I have lived honorably among you, if I have never given plain speech to any, avenge my wrongs. This is my motion."
>
> Then he read out his amendment, which he had committed to writing:
>
> "Inasmuch as the blessed Claudius murdered his father-in-law Appius Silanus, his two sons-in-law, Pompeius Magnus and L. Silanus, Crassus Frugi his daughter's father-in-law, as like him as two eggs in a basket, Scribonia his daughter's mother-in-law, his wife Messalina, and others too numerous to mention: I propose that strong measures be taken against him, that he be allowed no delay of process, that immediate sentence of banishment be passed on him, that he be deported from heaven within thirty days, and from Olympus within thirty hours."

Fig. 3.27. *Bronze head of Claudius, from Britain (41–54 C.E.). Photo: Trustees of the British Museum/Art Resource, New York.*

(In the next paragraphs, the ideal of justice drives the evaluation of Claudius's reign. Notice, again, the rejoicing of the Roman people as well as early jabs at the lawyers' profession. The funeral dirge is unremitting sarcasm.)

This motion was passed without further debate. Not a moment was lost: Mercury seized [Claudius's] neck and haled him to the lower regions, to that destination "from which they say no traveler returns."[39]

As they passed downwards along the Sacred Way, Mercury asked what was that great concourse of men. Could it be Claudius's funeral? It was certainly a most gorgeous spectacle, got up regardless of expense, clear it was that a god was being borne to the grave: tooting of flutes, roaring of horns, an immense brass band of all sorts, such a din that even Claudius could hear it. Joy and rejoicing on every side, the Roman people walking about like free men. Agatho and a few idle lawyers were weeping for grief, and for once they sort of meant it. . . .

When Claudius saw his own funeral train, he understood that he was dead. For they were chanting his dirge in anapests, with much mopping and mouthing:

"Pour forth your laments, your sorrow declare,
   Let the sounds of grief rise high in the air:
For he that is dead had a wit most keen,
   Was bravest of all that on earth have been.
Racehorses are nothing to his swift feet:
   Rebellious Parthians he did defeat;
Swift after the Persians his light shafts go:
   For he well knew how to fit arrow to bow,
Swiftly the striped barbarians fled:
   With one little wound he shot them dead.
And the Britons beyond in their unknown seas,
   Blue-shielded Brigantians too, all these
He chained by the neck as the Romans' slaves.
   He spoke, and the Ocean with trembling waves
Accepted the axe of the Roman law.
   O weep for the man! This world never saw
One quicker a troublesome suit to decide,
   When only one part of the case had been tried,
   (He could do it indeed and not hear either side).
Who'll now sit in judgment the whole year round?
   Now he that is judge of the shades underground
Once ruler of a hundred cities in Crete,
   Must yield to his better and take a back seat.[40]
Mourn, mourn, idle lawyers, you bribe-taking crew,
   And you, minor poets, woe, woe is to you!
And you above all, who get rich quick
   By the rattle of dice and the three card trick."[41]

(Claudius, oblivious to the sarcasm, is "charmed to hear his own praises sung," but Mercury hastens to deliver him to the gates of hell, where Claudius is alarmed to encounter the great black hound Cerberus. A second trial now takes place. Claudius, surrounded by a multitude of his own victims, cannot find a defender. The judge, Aeacus, condemns him without hearing his self-defense—a surprising move to all but Claudius, for whom it had become a routine practice—then various horrific sentences are considered.)

There was a long discussion as to the punishment he ought to endure. Some said that Sisyphus had done his burden-carrying long enough; Tantalus would be dying of thirst, if he were not relieved; the drag must be put at last on wretched Ixion's wheel. But it was determined not to let off any of the old stagers, lest Claudius should dare to hope for any such relief. It was agreed that some new punishment must be devised: they must devise some new task, something senseless, to suggest some craving without result. Then Aeacus decreed he should rattle dice for ever in a box with no bottom. At once the poor wretch began his fruitless task of hunting for the dice, which for ever slipped from his fingers.[42] . . .

   All of a sudden who should turn up but Caligula, and claims the man for a slave: brings witnesses, who said they had seen him being flogged, caned, fisticuffed by him.[43] He is handed over to Caligula, and Caligula makes him a present to Aeacus. Aeacus delivers him to his freedman Menander, to be his law-clerk.

(Seneca, The Apocolocyntosis, trans. Rouse, adapted)

Nero's Bloodless Rule

In stark contrast to Suetonius's morbid review of Nero's reign (no. 101), the official propaganda of the era dwelled at length on Nero's having come to power without resort to force—something even the great Augustus could not have boasted. We have already seen (no. 98) Seneca marvel at Nero's accomplishment, since "no one ever was granted the sword at a younger age," and heard the theme of Nero's innocent rule extolled in the *First Eclogue* of Calpurnius Siculus in mythic terms (no. 99): "Clemency has commanded every vice that wears the disguise of peace to betake itself afar: she has broken every maddened sword-blade. . . . Peace in her fullness shall come; knowing not the drawn sword."

The theme of Nero's disavowal of the sword may be relevant for discussions of Rom 13:1-7, written during the early years of Nero's reign. There Paul declares, in part, that the ruling authority (*exousia*) "does not bear the sword idly" (or "in vain," NRSV: *ou gar eikēi tēn machairan phorei*, 13:4). By implication, Paul is saying that the sword remains active and dangerous.

Some scholars have attempted to read these statements as Paul's deliberate use of irony—as if he intends his audience to know that he does not mean what he is saying—or as a veiled critique of the claims of Neronian propaganda.[44] There is no way to know whether Paul had that propaganda in view; but the strength and consistency of the "signal" from Nero's court bear consideration. That message is particularly ironic, first, because Nero was certainly able to find other creative alternatives to the sword in his murderous career; second, because Nero's empire continued to wage war on its frontiers and against rebellious provinces—including the brutal war on Judea begun in 66 c.e.; and third, because, according to early church tradition, Paul himself was executed by the sword under Nero. Here we call attention to other semiofficial expressions of admiration for Nero's "idle sword."

103. PRAISE OF NERO'S MERCY (SENECA)

The first selection comes from that same speech by Seneca, *On Mercy* (*De clementia*), addressed to the young emperor. Whether the speech was meant sincerely to congratulate the emperor for his innate virtues or to try to dissuade him from acting impulsively out of innate cruelty is a matter of debate (see below).

> It is a pleasure to subject a good conscience to a round of inspection, then to cast one's eyes upon this vast throng—discordant, factious, and unruly, ready to run riot alike for the destruction of itself and others if it should break its yoke—and finally to commune with oneself thus:
> "Have I of all mortals found favor with Heaven and been chosen to serve on earth as vicar of the gods? I am the arbiter of life and death for the nations;

Fig. 3.28. *The gladius, the short sword issued to Roman Infantry. Modern replica. Photo in the public domain.*

it rests in my power what each man's lot and state shall be; by my lips Fortune proclaims what gift she would bestow on each human being; from my utterance peoples and cities gather reasons for rejoicing; without my favor and grace, no part of the wide world can prosper; all those many thousands of swords which my peace restrains will be drawn at my nod; what nations shall be utterly destroyed, which banished, which shall receive the gift of liberty, which have it taken from them, what kings shall become slaves and whose heads shall be crowned with royal honor, what cities shall fall and which shall rise—this it is mine to decree.

"With all things thus at my disposal, I have been moved neither by anger nor youthful impulse to unjust punishment, nor by the foolhardiness and obstinacy of men which have often wrung patience from even the serenest souls, nor yet by that vainglory which employs terror for the display of might—a dread but all too common use of great and lordly power. With me the sword is hidden, nay, is sheathed: I am sparing to the utmost of even the meanest blood; no man fails to find favor at my hands though he lack all else but the name of man. Sternness I keep hidden, but mercy ever ready at hand."

Seneca continues with praise that Nero's virtues surpass those of Augustus or Tiberius; there is no model to which Nero should aspire other than himself (1.6). Some clue to the purpose of the speech may be perceived in Seneca's admission that the Roman people were anxious about the nature of the young prince's rule:

Great was the hazard that the Roman people faced so long as it was uncertain what course those noble talents of yours would take; today the prayers of the state are assured, for there is no danger that you will be seized by sudden forgetfulness of yourself. . . . Yet today your subjects one and all are constrained to confess that they are happy, and, too, that nothing further can be added to their blessings, except that these may last. Many facts force them to this confession . . . : a security deep and abounding, and justice enthroned above all injustice; before their eyes hovers the fairest vision of a state which lacks no element of complete liberty except the license of self-destruction. Above all . . . alike to the highest and the lowest, extends the same admiration for your quality of mercy."

(Seneca, *On Mercy* 1.1-4, 7-9, trans. Basore, LCL)

104. An age when swords are obsolete (Einsiedeln *Eclogue*)

In a third, anonymous eclogue (named one of the "Einsiedeln Eclogues" because the tenth-century manuscript containing them was discovered in Einsiedeln, Switzerland), two shepherds pause to look over a peaceful landscape of pious cities and ripened fields. The extravant description of a bountiful and peaceful golden age, ruled by the goddess Justice, sounds themes that we have already heard from Virgil and Calpurnius Siculus. Note in particular the theme that wars are a thing of the past—so much that children marvel at the swords hanging over the mantlepiece.

> Do you see how the villagers, outspread o'er the well-worn turf, offer their yearly vows and begin the regular altar-worship? Temples reek of wine; the hollow drums resound to the hands; the Maenalids[45] lead the youthful ring-dances amid the holy rites; joyful sounds the pipe; from the elm hangs the he-goat doomed to sacrifice, and with neck already stripped lays his vitals bare. Surely then the offspring of today fight with no doubtful hazard?
>
> Surely the blockish herd denies not to these times the realms of gold? The days of Saturn have returned with Justice the Maid: the age has returned in safety to the olden ways. With hope unruffled does the harvester garner all his corn-ears; the Wine-god betrays the languor of old age; the herd wanders on the lea; we reap with no sword, nor do towns in fast-closed walls prepare unutterable war: there is not any woman who, dangerous in her motherhood, gives birth to an enemy. Unarmed our youth can dig the fields, and the boy, trained to the slow-moving plough, marvels at the sword hanging in the abode of his fathers. Far from us is the luckless glory of Sulla and the threefold crisis when dying Rome despaired of her final resources and sold her martial arms.[46] Now doth earth untilled yield fresh produce from the rich soil, now are the wild waves no longer angry with the unmenaced ship; tigers gnaw their curbs, lions endure the cruel yoke; be gracious, chaste Lucina: thine own Apollo now is king.[47]

(Einsiedeln *Eclogue* 2, 18–35, trans. Duff and Duff, LCL)

The "Vast Unruly Throng"

Seneca's description of Nero's subjects as "this vast throng—discordant, factious, and unruly," or the Einsiedeln *Eclogue*'s reference to the "blockish herd" (*stolidum pecus*), like Cicero's earlier disdain for the Roman plebs as the "dirt and shit" of the city (*sordes urbis et faex, To Atticus* 1.16.11), all show the contempt of the propertied upper class for their inferiors.[48] An elaborate vocabulary distinguished the honorable rich and powerful from the contemptible poor and powerless.[49] Furthermore, the reigning ideology of the day insisted that it was simply natural for those at the top of the social pyramid to wield power over those beneath them—who were so inferior they could hardly be expected to serve their own interests capably. Roman rule was inevitably beneficial to the ruled, and if the latter failed to perceive the fact it was because of their innate incomprehension or unstinting ingratitude.[50]

Speaking of **order, class, and social status** in Roman society is complicated. Roman citizens were divided into three **orders** (Latin *ordo*, plural *ordines*), the Senate (and those families with sufficient wealth and pedigree to aspire to it), the Equestrian ("calvalry" or "knights, Equites), who with the Senate held most wealth and power, and the *plebs*, the common Roman citizens. (Noncitizens and slaves were not included as "orders.") Economic **class** refers to relations between those who lived from the surplus wealth produced by others and laborers who did not control the wealth they produced in what Ramsay MacMullen has called a "very steep social pyramid." (Roman society knew nothing of what we would recognize as a "middle class.")

Wayne A. Meeks has shown that **social status** depended on the interaction of a number of factors: whether one were slave or free; ordo, citizenship, family background, ethnic origins, gender, wealth, occupation, age, and—to a lesser degree—personal achievement. **Status ambivalence** resulted when a person held high status in one factor but lower status in another.

See Ramsay MacMullen, *Roman Social Relations, 50 B.C. to A.D. 284* (New Haven: Yale University Press, 1974); G. E. M. de Ste. Croix, *The Class Struggle in the Ancient Greek World: From the Archaic Age to the Arab Conquests* (Ithaca, N.Y.: Cornell University Press, 1980); Wayne A. Meeks, *The First Urban Christians: The Social World of the Apostle Paul* (New Haven: Yale University Press, 1983); Peter Garnsey and Richard Saller, *The Roman Empire: Economy, Society, and Culture* (Berkeley and Los Angeles: University of California Press, 1987), chapter 6; Martin Goodman, *The Roman World, 44 BC—AD 180*, Routledge History of the Ancient World (London: Routledge, 1997), chapter 17; Justin J. Meggitt, *Paul, Poverty, and Survival*, Studies of the New Testament and Its World (Edinburgh: T&T Clark, 1998); Steven Friesen, "Poverty in Pauline Studies: Beyond the So-Called New Consensus," *JSNT 26* (2004): 323–61; Todd D. Still and David G. Horrell, eds., *After the First Urban Christians: The Social-Scientific Study of Pauline Christianity Twenty-Five Years Later* (London: T&T Clark, 2009).

Frank Talk about Economic Exploitation

Among their peers, however, the "rulers of the world" could be candid enough about the fact that they ruled in order to extract wealth from those under their control. Such remarks are in tension with the more formal claims of imperial benefaction.

105. Augustus buys his way to power (Tacitus)

Looking back on the beginnings of the empire, Tacitus—himself no friend of commoners—recognized that from the beginning Augustus had used bribery and class antagonism to secure his position.

> Augustus won over the soldiers with gifts, the populace with cheap corn, and all men with the sweets of repose, and so grew greater by degrees, while he concentrated in himself the functions of the Senate, the magistrates, and the laws. He was wholly unopposed, for the boldest spirits had fallen in battle, or in the proscription, while the remaining nobles, the readier they were to be slaves, were raised the higher by wealth and promotion, so that, aggrandized by revolution, they preferred the safety of the present to the dangerous past. Nor did the provinces dislike that condition of affairs, for they distrusted the government of the Senate and the people, because of the rivalries between the leading men and the rapacity of the officials, while the protection of the laws was unavailing, as they were continually deranged by violence, intrigue, and finally by corruption.
>
> (Tacitus, *Annals* 1.2.2, trans. Church and Brodribb)

106. Roman governors as bloodsuckers (Tiberius)

Through taxation, "the Romans wrung ultimately from the provincial peasants all that could be economically extracted."[51] The emperor Tiberius rebuked his governor in Egypt when he taxed the populace more than Rome required: "I want my sheep shorn, not shaved" (Dio Cassius 57.10.5). On another occasion, Josephus reports, Tiberius was asked by friends why he delayed so long in replacing his governors; his answer was that if a provincial governor knew he might be replaced sooner, he would press his subjects harder to enrich himself—and bleed the people dry.

> He told them this fable by way of illustration. Once a man lay wounded, and a swarm of flies hovered about his wounds. A passerby took pity on his evil plight, and, in the belief that he did not raise a hand because he could not, was about to step up and shoo them off. The wounded man, however, begged him to think no more of doing anything about it. At this the man spoke up and asked him why he was not interested in escaping from his wretched condition.
>
> "Why," said he, "you would put me in a worse position if you drove them off. For since these flies have already had their fill of blood, they no longer feel such a pressing need to annoy me but are in some measure slack. But if others were to come with a fresh appetite, they would take over my now weakened body and that would indeed be the death of me."

> He [Tiberius] too, he said, for the same reason, took the precaution of not dispatching governors continually to the subject peoples who had been brought to ruin by so many thieves; for the governors would harry them utterly like flies. Their natural appetite for plunder would be reinforced by their expectation of being speedily deprived of that pleasure. The record of Tiberius' acts will bear out my account of his humor in such matters.
>
> (Josephus, *Ant.* 18.172-75, trans. Feldman, LCL)

The emperor Nero was more blunt as he gave instructions to his provincial governors: "You know my requirements. See that no one is left with anything!" (Suetonius, *Nero* 32).

Some scholars have marveled that the Roman Empire could efficiently govern so vast a territory without a massive military presence in every province. Surely the loyalty it attracted was a response to the perceived benefits of Roman rule (and even the frank recognition on the part of subject peoples that they were unfit for self-rule).[52] Other scholars observe, however, that it was the local aristocracies who promoted the imperial cult in the provinces as a way of reinforcing their own position. The imperial cult provided a way to represent "otherwise unmanageable" Roman power locally.[53] The Roman historian Livy observed that Rome was able to conquer the Greek cities because everywhere it was "the leading men and all the aristocracy" who favored alliance with Rome and the status quo, even though "the multitude and those in poor circumstances desired complete change" (*History of Rome* 35.34).

It is also relevant that instead of garrisoning the provinces, the Romans relied on a system of contracted tax farmers who could rely on their own ingenuity and brute force to fill the empire's tax quotas. Rome's requirements were only a part of what a resourceful governor and the tax collectors might appropriate for themselves.[54] "Peasants were visited by an affliction worse than locusts, worse than drought: the man from the city, come to collect rents or taxes," writes Ramsay MacMullen. Abundant evidence from petitions on papyri testify to "a regular war, . . . carried on between the rural inhabitants who had nothing but their powers to endure, and the tax collector backed by the ultimate powers of the state."[55] The latter enjoyed remarkable impunity, to judge by the brutality used to meet quotas.

107. A LANDHOLDER PROTESTS THE TAX COLLECTOR'S BRUTALITY

From two papyri letters we may reconstruct a petition from a small landholder in Egypt. (See also the letters of petition above, nos. 64 and 65 in chapter 2.)

> To the prefect of Egypt,
>   From Gemellus of Antinoë, landholder at Karanis . . .
>   I appeal, my lord, against Kastor, tax collector's assistant of the village of Karanis. This person, who held me in contempt because of my infirmity—for I have only one eye and I do not see with it though it appears to have sight, so that I am utterly worthless in both—first publicly abused me and my mother, after maltreating her with numerous blows and demolishing all four doors of mine with an axe so that our house is wide open and accessible to every

malefactor—although we owed nothing to the fiscus, and for this reason he dared not even produce a receipt, lest he be convicted through it of injustice and extortion.

(*P.Mich.* 422, 424, trans. MacMullen)

108. The violence of tax collectors (Philo)

Another protest against the breathtaking cruelty of tax collectors comes from Philo of Alexandria. His general topic is the prohibition of oppression which he finds in Exod 23:11 and Lev 25:2 (concerning letting land lay fallow). His comments suggest that sadistic violence was not the work of a few rogue tax collectors.

> So too let rulers of cities cease from racking them with taxes and tolls as heavy as they are constant. Such rulers both fill their own coffers and while hoarding money hoard also illiberal vices which defile the whole of civic life. For they purposely choose as tax-gatherers the most ruthless of men, brimful of inhumanity, and put into their hands resources for overreaching.
>
> These persons add to their natural brutality the immunity they gain from their masters' instructions, and in their determination to accommodate every action to those masters' pleasure they leave no severity untried, however barbarous, and banish mercy and gentleness even from their dreams. And therefore in carrying out their collecting they create universal chaos and confusion and apply their exactions not merely to the property of their victims but also to their bodies, on which they inflict insults and outrages and forms of torture quite original in their savagery.
>
> Indeed, I have heard of persons who, actuated by abnormal frenzy and cruelty, have not even spared the dead, persons who become so utterly brutalized that they venture even to flog corpses with whips. And when anyone censured the extraordinary cruelty shown . . . [they responded that] they treated the dead . . . with such contempt not for the useless purpose of insulting the deaf and senseless dust but in order to excite the pity of those who were related to them by birth or some other tie of fellowship, and thus urge them to ransom the bodies of their friends by making a final gift in payment for them.
>
> (Philo, *On the Special Laws* 2.92-95, trans. Colson, LCL)

109. Villages ravaged by the tax collector (Philo)

In another place, discussing Deut 24:16, Philo turns again to rapacious tax collectors as examples of "the cruel of heart and bestial of nature" who are the targets of the law's condemnation. Note the astonishing cruelty used not only to extract taxes but to terrorize a region.

> An example of this was given a little time ago in our own district by a person who was appointed to serve as a collector of taxes. When some of his debtors whose default was clearly due to poverty took flight in fear of the fatal consequences of his vengeance, he carried off by force their womenfolk and children and parents and their other relatives and beat and subjected them to every kind of outrage and abuse in order to make them either tell him the whereabouts of the fugitive or discharge his debt themselves. As they could do neither the first

for want of knowledge, nor the second because they were as penniless as the fugitive, he continued this treatment until while wringing their bodies with racks and instruments of torture he finally dispatched them by newly-invented methods of execution.

He filled a large basket with sand and having hung this enormous weight by ropes round their necks set them in the middle of the market-place in the open air, in order that while they themselves sank under the cruel stress of the accumulated punishments, the wind, the sun, the shame of being seen by the passers-by and the weights suspended on them, the spectators of their punishments might suffer by anticipation.

Some of these, whose souls saw facts more vividly than did their eyes, feeling themselves maltreated in the bodies of others, hastened to take leave of their lives with the aid of sword or poison or halter, thinking that in their evil plight it was a great piece of luck to die without suffering torture.

The others who had not seized the opportunity to dispatch themselves were brought out in a row, as is done in the awarding of inheritances, first those who stood in the first degrees of kinship, after them the second, then the third and so on till the last. And when there were no kinsmen left, the maltreatment was passed on to their neighbors and sometimes even to villages and cities which quickly became desolate and stripped of their inhabitants who left their homes and dispersed to places where they expected to remain unobserved.

(Philo, *On the Special Laws* 3.159-63, trans. Colson, LCL)

110. PUBLIC OUTCRY OVER FOOD PRICES (TACITUS)

Tacitus records unrest during Tiberius's reign over the price of corn:

During the same consulship a high price of corn almost brought on an insurrection. For several days there were many clamorous demands made in the theatre with an unusual freedom of language towards the emperor. This provoked him to censure the magistrates and the Senate for not having used the authority of the State to put down the people. He named too the corn-supplying provinces, and dwelt on the far larger amount of grain imported by himself than by Augustus. So the Senate drew up a decree in the severe spirit of antiquity, and the consuls issued a not less stringent proclamation. The emperor's silence was not, as he had hoped, taken as a proof of patriotism, but of pride.

(Tacitus, *Annals* 6.12, trans. Church and Brodribb)

111. PUBLIC PROTESTS PUT DOWN WITH FORCE (TACITUS)

Later, during Nero's reign, Tacitus records public protest in Puteoli, near Rome, over the excessive corruption and greed of their local government. The Senate heard both sides of the dispute—but responded with military action against the protesters.

During the same consulship a hearing was given to two conflicting deputations from Puteoli, sent to the Senate by the town council and by the populace. The first spoke bitterly of the violence of the multitude; the second, of the rapacity of the magistrates and of all the chief citizens. That the disturbance, which had gone as far as stoning and threats of fire, might not lead on to bloodshed

Fig. 3.29. *Rioters in the amphitheater. Fresco from a house in Pompeii, first century. Muzeo Archéologico Nazionale, Naples. Photo in the public domain.*

and armed fighting, Caius Cassius was appointed to apply some remedy. As they would not endure his rigor, the charge of the affair was at his own request transferred to the brothers Scribonii, to whom was given a praetorian cohort, the terror of which, coupled with the execution of a few persons, restored peace to the townspeople.

(Tacitus, Annals 13.48, trans. Church and Brodribb)

Defiance at the Frontiers

Along with unrest in Italy, we have indirect evidence of the sentiments of other men and women in the provinces—including local aristocrats—who declined the "friendship of the Roman people." We will see in chapter 4 evidence that Jews in Judea and elsewhere had different attitudes to Roman rule. Tacitus records two speeches made by Celtic leaders in Britain who rallied armies to throw off the Roman yoke. There is no way of knowing, of course, how much of these speeches—if anything—goes back to the sources themselves; Tacitus is less interested in taking their side than in showing the ferocity of rebels who eventually fell to Roman power.

112. A Celtic queen rallies an army (Tacitus)

In 61 c.e., Boudicca, queen of the Iceni, led an army into battle against the Roman invaders. She held close to her two daughters, who had been raped by Roman soldiers. The battle went against her; at length she took poison to escape being captured alive. Tacitus records that the Romans killed eighty thousand Iceni, men and women alike—"a great glory." (The Iceni had also committed atrocities, Tacitus reports. Our purpose is less to take sides than to compare Boudicca's characterization of Roman rule with the way Roman propagandists described it.)

> Boudicca, with her daughters before her in a chariot, went up to tribe after tribe, protesting that it was indeed usual for Britons to fight under the leadership of women. "But now," she said, "it is not as a woman descended from noble ancestry, but as one of the people that I am avenging lost freedom, my scourged body, the outraged chastity of my daughters. Roman lust has gone so far that not our very persons, nor even age or virginity, are left unpolluted.
>
> But heaven is on the side of a righteous vengeance; a legion which dared to fight has perished; the rest are hiding themselves in their camp, or are thinking anxiously of flight. They will not sustain even the din and the shout of so many thousands, much less our charge and our blows. If you weigh well the strength of the armies, and the causes of the war, you will see that in this battle you must conquer or die. This is a woman's resolve; as for men, they may live and be slaves."
>
> (Tacitus, *Annals* 14.35, trans. Church and Brodribb)

113. "Where they make a desert, they call it peace" (Tacitus)

More than two decades later, the Romans still pressed the last vestiges of British resistance against the northern coast of Scotland. The chieftain Calgacus mustered his people—drawn, in part, from Celtic nobility, people who had for years sought to avoid direct military confrontation—with the prospect not only of driving the Romans from Britain but of inspiring an empire-wide rebellion, beginning within the Roman ranks themselves. His army failed; the next day, Tacitus reports, the Romans indeed created a desolation. Here is Calgacus's speech.

> We are all undebased by slavery; and there is no land behind us, nor does even the sea afford a refuge, whilst the Roman fleet hovers around. Thus the use of arms, which is at all times honorable to the brave, now offers the only safety even to cowards. In all the battles which have yet been fought, with various success, against the Romans, our countrymen may be deemed to have reposed their final hopes and resources in us: for we, the noblest sons of Britain, and therefore stationed in its last recesses, far from the view of servile shores, have preserved even our eyes unpolluted by the contact of subjection. . . .

But (now) there is no nation beyond us; nothing but waves and rocks, and the still more hostile Romans, whose arrogance we cannot escape by obsequiousness and submission. These plunderers of the world, after exhausting the land by their devastations, are rifling the ocean: stimulated by avarice, if their enemy be rich; by ambition, if poor; unsatiated by either the East or West: the only people who behold wealth and indigence with equal avidity. To ravage, to slaughter, to usurp under false titles, they call empire; and where they make a desert, they call it peace.

Our children and relations are by the appointment of nature the dearest of all things to us. These are torn away by levies to serve in foreign lands. Our wives and sisters, though they should escape the violation of hostile force, are polluted under names of friendship and hospitality. Our estates and possessions

Fig. 3.30. *A Gallic warrior kills himself to avoid capture after having killed his wife; first-century-c.e. Roman copy of a third-century-b.c.e. Hellenistic original from the Temple to Zeus in Pergamum. Images of dying and defeated Gauls were a favorite motif in Roman monumental art (see fig. 3.14 above). Museo Alltemps, Rome. Photo in the public domain.*

are consumed in tributes; our grain in contributions. Even our bodies are worn down amidst stripes and insults in clearing woods and draining marshes. Wretches born to slavery are once bought, and afterwards maintained by their masters: (but) Britain every day buys, every day feeds, her own servitude. . . .

Can you imagine that the Romans are as brave in war as they are licentious in peace? Acquiring renown from our discords and dissensions, they convert

Fig. 3.31. *Here Nero is presented as a partially nude warrior subduing the nation of Armenia, represented as a helpless woman. Despite official professions of faithfulness and "friendship" for subject peoples, the Romans were not above celebrating their conquests in more forceful terms. The Sebasteion, or Temple of Augustus, in Aphrodisias (early second century* c.e.*) contained numerous such sculptures, conveying the message that Roman conquest was as "natural" as the subjection of women to men. Photo courtesy of the New York University Excavations at Aphrodisias.*

the faults of their enemies to the glory of their own army; an army compounded of the most different nations, which success alone has kept together, and which misfortune will as certainly dissipate. Unless, indeed, you can suppose that Gauls, and Germans, and (I blush to say it) even Britons, who, though they expend their blood to establish a foreign dominion, have been longer its foes than its subjects, will be retained by loyalty and affection! Terror and dread alone are the weak bonds of attachment; which once broken, they who cease to fear will begin to hate.

"Every incitement to victory is on our side. The Romans have no wives to animate them; no parents to upbraid their flight. Most of them have either no home, or a distant one. Few in number, ignorant of the country, looking around in silent horror at woods, seas, and a heaven itself unknown to them, they are delivered by the gods, as it were imprisoned and bound, into our hands. Be not terrified with an idle show, and the glitter of silver and gold, which can neither protect nor wound. In the very ranks of the enemy we shall find our own bands. The Britons will acknowledge their own cause. The Gauls will recollect their former liberty. The rest of the Germans will desert them, as the Usipii have lately done.

Nor is there anything formidable behind them: ungarrisoned forts; colonies of old men; municipal towns distempered and distracted between unjust masters and ill-obeying subjects. Here is a general; here an army. There, tributes, mines, and all the train of punishments inflicted on slaves; which whether to bear eternally, or instantly to revenge, this field must determine. March then to battle, and think of your ancestors and your posterity.

(Tacitus, *Agricola* 30-32, trans. Brooks, modified)

The Roman imperial context—including not only the brute facts of conquest but the ideological claims of imperial propaganda as well—shaped the world in which Paul and his fellow Jews lived. We turn in chapter 4 to specific aspects of Jewish reality in the Roman world.

QUESTIONS FOR REFLECTION

1. In light of the texts in chapter 2 and this chapter, what connotations might the following words or phrases have carried in the ears of Paul's contemporaries? Would what Paul had to say about these themes have sounded different from the messages dominant in Roman culture?

    a. "faith"; "the obedience of faith" among nations (see Rom 1:5, 16)
    b. "justice" or "righteousness"; "mercy" (see, for example, Rom 3:21-26)
    c. "peace" (Rom 5:1-2; Phil 4:4-9; "peace and security," 1 Thess 5:3)

2. Given the official declarations that one or another emperor had been taken up into heaven and that his adopted son had become "son of God," how might Paul's language about being made "children" (literally, "sons") of God in Romans (chapters 4; 8; 9) or Galatians (chapters 3–4) have sounded? What might his contemporaries have heard when he spoke of

Jesus Christ being raised from the dead? (See Rom 1:1-4; Titus 2:11-14.) How would language about Jesus as "lord," as one who "rises to rule the nations" (Rom 15:12), or as one to whom "every knee shall bend" (Phil 2:10) have sounded?

3. Given the different attitudes presented toward Roman rule in general or toward specific emperors, how might contemporaries have heard Paul's exhortation to "be subject to the ruling authorities" and to pay taxes (Rom 13:1-7) have sounded?

4. What difference might it have made that Paul used a Greek word, ekklēsia, that was normally used for public rather than private assemblies?

5. Compare the idea of a new world order described in the *Res Gestae* of Augustus with the new creation language in Rom 8:18-25 or 2 Cor 5:16-21. What is similar; what is different?

FOR FURTHER READING

On social realities in the Roman Empire:

de Ste. Croix, G. E. M. *The Class Struggle in the Ancient Greek World: From the Archaic Age to the Arab Conquests.* Ithaca, N.Y.: Cornell University Press, 1980.

Garnsey, Peter, and Richard Saller. *The Roman Empire: Economy, Society, and Culture.* Berkeley and Los Angeles: University of California Press, 1987.

Goodman, Martin. *The Roman World 44 BC–AD 180.* Routledge History of the Ancient World. London: Routledge, 1997.

Lefkowitz, Mary R., and Maureen B. Fant, eds. *Women's Life in Greece and Rome: A Source Book in Translation.* Baltimore: Johns Hopkins University Press, 1982.

MacMullen, Ramsay. *Roman Social Relations, 50 B.C. to A.D. 284.* New Haven: Yale University Press, 1974.

On the imperial cult, propaganda, and imagery:

Alcock, Susan E. *Graecia Capta: The Landscapes of Roman Greece.* Cambridge: Cambridge University Press, 1983.

Ando, Clifford. *Imperial Ideology and Provincial Loyalty in the Roman Empire.* Classics and Contemporary Thought 6. Berkeley and Los Angeles: University of California Press, 2000.

Galinsky, Karl. *Augustan Culture: An Interpretive Introduction.* Princeton: Princeton University Press, 1996.

Price, Simon R. F. *Rituals and Power: The Roman Imperial Cult in Asia Minor.* Cambridge: Cambridge University Press, 1984.

Zanker, Paul. *The Power of Images in the Age of Augustus*. Translated by Alan Shapiro. Jerome Lectures, 16th Series. Ann Arbor: University of Michigan Press, 1988.

On Paul in the context of Roman Empire:

Georgi, Dieter. *Theocracy in Paul's Praxis and Theology*. Translated by David Green. Philadelphia: Fortress Press, 1991. Ex Libris edition with new foreword by Helmut Koester, Minneapolis: Fortress Press, 2009.

Horsley, Richard A., ed. *Paul and Empire: Religion and Politics in the Roman Empire*. Harrisburg, Pa.: Trinity Press International, 1997.

————, ed. *Paul and Politics: Ekklesia, Israel, Imperium, Interpretation: Essays in Honor of Krister Stendahl*. Harrisburg, Pa.: Trinity Press International, 2000.

————, ed. *Paul and the Roman Imperial Order*. Harrisburg, Pa.: Trinity Press International, 2003.

Kahl, Brigitte. *Galatians Re-imagined: Reading with the Eyes of the Vanquished*. Paul in Critical Contexts. Minneapolis: Fortress Press, 2009.

Lopez, Davina C. *Apostle to the Conquered: Reimagining Paul's Mission*. Paul in Critical Contexts. Minneapolis: Fortress Press, 2008.

Marchal, Joseph A. *The Politics of Heaven: Women, Gender, and Empire in the Study of Paul*. Paul in Critical Contexts. Minneapolis: Fortress Press, 2009.

Stowers, Stanley K. *A Rereading of Romans: Justice, Jews, and Gentiles*. New Haven: Yale University Press, 1994.

Tamez, Elsa. *The Amnesty of Grace: Justification by Faith from a Latin American Perspective*. Translated by Sharon H. Ringe. Nashville: Abingdon, 1991.

Fig. 4.1. *Menorah, with etrog and shofar. Third-century-c.e. mosaic from the synagogue at Maon, Israel. Photo: Deror Avi.*

4 | Paul's People: Israel

Writing to the assembly in Philippi, Paul described his reasons to "be confident in the flesh": he had been "circumcised on the eighth day, a member of the people of Israel, of the tribe of Benjamin, a Hebrew born of Hebrews; as to the law, a Pharisee; as to zeal, a persecutor of the church; as to righteousness under the law, blameless" (Phil 3:4-6). Writing to the assemblies in Rome, he expressed "great sorrow and unceasing anguish" for his own people, wishing he could be "accursed and cut off from Christ" for their sake, for "they are Israelites, and to them belong the adoption, the glory, the covenants, the giving of the law, the worship, and the promises; to them belong the patriarchs, and from them, according to the flesh, comes the Messiah, who is over all, God blessed forever" (Rom 9:2-5 NRSV). On the basis of such statements, we should hardly be surprised by the answer Paul gave to his own rhetorical question in Rom 3:1-2: "Then what advantage has the Jew? Or what is the value of circumcision? Much, in every way."

But Paul went on to qualify all of those statements. Yes, he had much to boast about as a Hebrew, "yet whatever gains I had, these I have come to regard as loss because of Christ," as "rubbish" (Phil 3:7, 8). Now he sought to be found "not having a righteousness of my own that comes from the law, but one that comes through faith in Christ, the righteousness from God based on faith" (3:9). One way of understanding that language—the way the Christian tradition has led most readers to understand that language, until relatively recently—is to infer that as a Jew, Paul *had* sought "a righteousness of [his] own that comes from the law," indeed, that (so far as Paul was concerned) *all* Jews did so. In Romans, Paul wrote that "Israel, who did strive for the righteousness that is based on the law, did not succeed in fulfilling that law. Why not? Because they did not strive for it on the basis of faith, but as if it were based on works" (Rom 9:31-32 NRSV).

Further, the "anguish" Paul expressed in Romans for his fellow Jews was clearly motivated by the assumption that in some way, many of them were "lost." Thus, even when Paul emphasized that the ultimate horizon of his apostleship to the nations (or "Gentiles," as the NRSV translates *ethnē*) was the well-being *of Israel*—"Inasmuch then as I am an apostle to the Gentiles, I glorify my ministry in order to make my own people jealous"—his purpose was "thus [to] save some of them" (Rom 11:13-14 NRSV). Paul understood that some failure had overtaken Israel: "they have stumbled over the stumbling stone" (Rom 9:32); their zeal for God was "not enlightened," and so they sought "to establish their own" righteousness, not recognizing that "Christ is the end of the law" (10:2-4). To the Corinthians, Paul writes about Israel that "to this very day, whenever Moses is read, a veil lies over their minds; but when one turns to the Lord, the veil is removed" (2 Cor 3:14-16).

Questions, Questions

The way the Christian tradition has usually made sense of these very different statements has been to speak of Paul's movement from life as a Jew to life as a Christian: that is, in the language used since Augustine, to speak of Paul's "conversion" from Judaism to Christianity (or, less charitably, of his "defection" or "apostasy" from Judaism).[1] Paul *used* to think as a Jew; after his encounter with the reality of the risen Christ, he came to think as a Christian, no longer as a Jew. But this way of thinking about Paul raises questions. Paul himself spoke of being "called," as Israel's prophets had been—but the prophets were not "converts." Is speaking of Paul's conversion from one religion to another anachronistic?[2] There clearly was a "before" and an "after" Christ for Paul, but to what extent is the language of "conversion" helpful for describing the difference? Was the transition from "before" to "after" precipitated by some crisis, some experience of dissatisfaction or frustration *as a Jew*? Paul's soliloquy on the law in Romans 7—"I was once alive apart from the law, but when the commandment came, sin revived and I died," and so on—has often been read this way, but does that reading project too much of subsequent Christian theology back onto Paul? If Paul had experienced some fundamental frustration as a Jew, why did *other* Jews not talk that way? Was Paul simply spiritually sensitive beyond any of his peers? Or was he mistaken about his own ancestral religion? Further, to the extent that Paul's experience was unique, how realistic was it for him (or anyone else in the early "Christian" movement) to expect that he could convince other Jews of his perspective?

Such questions have been asked for decades, but since the 1970s they have received far more attention from interpreters, including an increasing number of Jewish Pauline scholars. In *Paul and Palestinian Judaism*, E. P. Sanders showed, by a careful survey of Jewish literature from the Second Temple period, that Jews in Paul's day simply did not think of the law as a way to "seek their own righteousness" before God. But that demonstration immediately called into question the basis of much Christian interpretation of Paul. If Jews did *not* believe in or practice works-righteousness, then what was Paul at such pains to oppose? "What, in Paul's view, was wrong with Judaism"—and did that view have any connection with reality?[3]

Fig. 4.2. *A Byzantine fresco from the fourteenth century illustrates the predominant Christian understanding of Paul's conversion, dependent on Acts 9. At left, Saul receives letters from the high priest in Jerusalem authorizing his persecution of the churches; in the center, the heavenly Christ intervenes; at right, a blinded Paul is led into the home of Ananias—and into the Christian church. Decani Monastery, Bosnia-Herzegovina. Photo: Erich Lessing/Art Resource, New York.*

Sanders's own answer, at last, was that *"this is what Paul finds wrong in Judaism: it is not Christianity."*[4] That is, "Paul was not trying accurately to represent Judaism on its own terms, nor need we suppose that he was ignorant on essential points. He simply saw the old dispensation as worthless in comparison with the new."[5] If we ask *how* Paul came to hold such a view—if not through penetrating introspection of his own experience as a Jew—we confront, in the wake of Sanders's discussion, the proposal from other scholars that it was Paul's social experience, as a Christian in the company of non-Jewish ("Gentile") Christians, that determined his reevaluation of his past as a Jew. As Heikki Räisänen put it, "In the course of his work among Gentiles he had fully internalized the Gentile point of view and identified himself with it." The consequences had less to do with the apostle's keen theological acumen than with his felt need for *"secondary rationalization."* Paul's statements about the impossibility of achieving righteousness through works of law are, on this proposal, only rationalizations for a break with the law that he made for other, less irrational reasons.[6]

On the other hand, other scholars have protested that such a view improperly renders Paul a Jew only ethnically, or as Pamela Eisenbaum has put it, only *kata sarka* ("according to the flesh"). In terms of halakhah, he had "moved outside the bounds of

Judaism, or at least he moved so far to the margins that he ventured into something no longer recognizably Jewish."[7] But just that conclusion—which a number of Christian interpreters might readily affirm—is disputed by scholars who argue that Paul *as an apostle of Christ* must still be understood on fundamentally Jewish premises.

The phrase **"New Perspective on Paul"** is used in two different ways in scholarship today. In a broad sense, it refers to the range of questions and challenges posed to the long-standing Protestant interpretation of Paul by E. P. Sanders, James D. G. Dunn (who coined the phrase in a famous 1983 essay), and others. In a more narrow sense, it identifies the specific counterproposals offered by Sanders and Dunn. A helpful entrée to the ever-growing literature on the New Perspective is "the Paul Page," online at http://www.thepaulpage.com.

Addressing these fiercely contested issues is far beyond the scope of this chapter. It is nevertheless important to recognize how many questions of interpretation are bound up together here. *Why* did Saul the Pharisee persecute the early assemblies (Gal 1:13-24)? Was it because they somehow transgressed the halakhic norms of Judaism? *How* did the "revelation" of Christ convince Paul that Christ was "the end of the law" (Rom 10:4)?—or did that sequence of thought run the other way?

Did Paul warn the non-Jewish members of the assemblies not to seek circumcision because he thought they could not keep the whole law, or because he did not want them to boast of keeping it, or because the effort would put them outside of Christ? Did Paul himself observe Torah, for example, by eating only kosher food? Did he teach Jews within the assemblies (or even outside them) to abandon Torah observance, for example, by eating nonkosher food or ceasing to circumcise their newborn sons? Is that what his confrontation with Cephas in Antioch (Galatians 2) was about?

Did Paul respect temple worship and the system of purity that the Torah put in place to protect its sanctity, or did he consider the temple (and with it, purity laws) obsolete and irrelevant? According to Acts, already in the early days of the Jesus movement, "thousands" of Jewish believers had already heard that Paul taught Jews "to forsake Moses"—but the elders of the Jerusalem "church" knew that was a false accusation (Acts 21:20-24). Is that report historically accurate, or an instance of Luke's tendentious defense of Paul?

A "sociological" interpretation seeks to move away from Paul's view of individual salvation to ask about Paul's concern for the integrity of the "law-free church" as a group. Here again, questions arise: Was Paul concerned to keep the "law-free church" safe from the pressure of the synagogue, or did he want to preserve connections with the synagogue?[8]

Fig. 4.3. *A Greek inscription from the wall separating the Court of the Women from the Court of the Nations in the temple precinct (also described by Josephus, War 5.193-94): "No foreigner is to go inside the fence and enclosure around the sanctuary. Whoever is caught doing so will deserve his death." The author of Ephesians declares that in his death Christ "has broken down the dividing wall, that is, the hostility between us" (2:14). This is taken by many interpreters as an allusion to the temple barrier—though the letter might well have been written some time after the temple itself was destroyed by the Romans. National Archaeological Museum, Istanbul. Photo: Tamar Hayardeni.*

All of these questions are the subjects of lively debate today. All of them involve comparisons between Paul and other Jews of his time. The selections gathered in this chapter are intended to provide only a sample of relevant texts for such comparisons. There are a number of invaluable reference and sourcebooks available on Judaism in the Second Temple period; we will not try to duplicate those resources here. (See "For Further Reading" at the end of the chapter.)

We will look first at texts illustrating the experience of Jews under the Roman Empire and then at aspects of Jewish belief and practice that may bear on questions of "Paul and the law." In the following chapter we turn to aspects of Jewish interaction with the non-Jewish environment that would have been part of the context of the *ekklēsiai*.

The Diaspora

Since the conquests of Alexander the Great in the fourth century B.C.E., Jews living in the Diaspora (that is, outside the homeland of Judea: the Greek word means "scattering") spoke Greek, read their scriptures in Greek translation, and often conducted their prayers and worship in Greek. Their synagogue buildings were regular parts of the civic landscape throughout the Hellenistic world; inscriptions in Greek and, occasionally, Hebrew honored donors and synagogue officials (*archisynagōgoi*) and reserved sections of the theater for Jews and God-fearers, as was done for other ethnic and trade groups.

Scholars use the term **Septuagint** to refer to the Greek translation (and, in some books, expansion) of Hebrew scriptures, a process that most likely took place in stages, over time. The name, and the Roman numeral LXX, refer to the seventy Jewish scholars who, according to legend, did the translation at the request of King Ptolemy of Egypt (probably Ptolemy II Philadelphus) in the third century B.C.E. (see the *Letter of Aristeas*). The most complete textual witnesses to a Greek translation are the ancient Christian Bibles, Codex Vaticanus (B, fourth century C.E.) and Alexandrinus (A, fifth century). See Melvin K. H. Peters, "Septuagint," *ABD* 5:1093–1104.

---

114. "Colonies" of Judea (Agrippa I)

Although most Jews in Paul's day lived in the Diaspora and were unlikely ever to have traveled to Jerusalem, it is clear that they nevertheless felt a strong connection with Judea as their homeland and with the temple as a central place of worship, in which they participated by sending agricultural tithes and monetary contributions. This strong connection to Judea and the temple is evident in a letter to the emperor Gaius (Caligula) that Philo attributed to King Agrippa I (ruled 41-44 C.E.). Agrippa wrote to implore the emperor not to violate the temple's sanctity by erecting his own statue in the holy of holies. In the course of that argument, he defended the loyalty of Jews throughout the empire and suggested that, by offering Jerusalem relief, the emperor would win the gratitude of Judea's "colonies" in the Diaspora as well.

> I, being one of this nation, and being attached to this country and to such a temple, address to you this petition on behalf of them all. On behalf of the nation, [first], that it may not be looked upon by you in a light contrary to the true one; since it is a most pious and holy nation, and one from the beginning most loyally disposed to your family. For in all the particulars in which mortals are enjoined by the laws, and in which they have it in their power to show their piety and loyalty, my nation is inferior to none whatever in Asia or in Europe, whether it be in respect of prayers, or of the supply of sacred offerings, or in the abundance of its sacrifices, not merely of such as are offered on occasions of the public festivals, but in those which are continually offered day after day; by which means they show their loyalty and fidelity more surely than by their

mouth and tongue, proving it by the designs of their honest hearts, not indeed saying that they are friends to Caesar, but being so in reality.

Concerning the holy city, I must now say what is necessary. It, as I have already stated, is my native country, and the metropolis, not only of the one country of Judaea, but also of many, by reason of the colonies [apoikias] which it has sent out from time to time into the bordering districts of Egypt, Phoenicia, Syria in general, and especially that part of it which is called Coele-Syria, and also with those more distant regions of Pamphylia, Cilicia, the greater part of Asia Minor as far as Bithynia, and the furthermost corners of Pontus. And in the same manner into Europe, into Thessaly, and Boeotia, and Macedonia, and Aetolia, and Attica, and Argos, and Corinth and all the most fertile and wealthiest districts of Peloponnesus. And not only are the continents full of Jewish colonies, but also all the most celebrated islands are so too; such as Euboea, and Cyprus, and Crete. I say nothing of the countries beyond the Euphrates, for all of them except a very small portion, and Babylon, and all the satrapies around, which have any advantages whatever of soil or climate, have Jews settled in them.

So that if my native land is, as it reasonably may be, looked upon as entitled to a share in your favor, it is not one city only that would then be benefited by you, but ten thousand of them in every region of the habitable world, in Europe, in Asia, and in Africa, on the continent, in the islands, on the coasts, and in the inland parts. And it corresponds well to the greatness of your good fortune, that, by conferring benefits on one city, you should also benefit ten thousand others, so that your renown may be celebrated in every part of the habitable world, and many praises of you may be combined with thanksgiving.

(Philo, *Embassy to Gaius* 279-84, trans. Yonge)

115. The superiority of the Jewish law (Josephus)

Diaspora Jews sought to present their way of life as embodying the highest values of Hellenistic culture. Their laws—honored equally by Jews in every land—were based on the wisdom and insight miraculously given to Moses. They required a superior piety in worship of the one true God and promoted exemplary self-control and virtuous behavior within the Jewish community and to the benefit of the cities in which Jews made their home. Further, because all Jews everywhere knew and practiced these laws in the same way, Jewish communities were characterized by a unique harmony. In all these ways the Jewish *politeia* (sometimes translated "polity," "constitution," or "way of life") showed itself, in that competition among neighboring *politeiai* that was ubiquitous in Hellenistic civilization, to be superior to its rivals.

Josephus made just such a case in his apology of the Jewish way of life, *Against Apion*. (That Josephus, writing in the early second century c.e., framed his argument as a refutation of the anti-Semitic slanders of Apion—an Egyptian scholar who had been active in Rome in the early decades of the *first* century, against whom Philo had had to contend as an antagonist before the imperial court—shows the long duration of hostility on the part of at least some Romans contemporary with Paul. Indeed, historian Theodor Mommsen wrote that "hatred of Jews and Jew-baiting are as old as the Diaspora itself.")[9]

Persons who have espoused the cause of order and law—one law for all—and been the first to introduce them may fairly be admitted to be more civilized and virtuously disposed than those who lead lawless and disorderly lives. In fact, each nation endeavors to trace its own institutions back to the remotest date, in order to create the impression that, far from imitating others, it has been the one to set its neighbors an example of orderly life under law.

That being so, the virtue of a legislator is to have insight to see what is best and to win over to the laws which he introduces those who are to live under them; the virtue of the masses is loyally to abide by the laws adopted and, in prosperity or in adversity, to make no change in them.

Now, I maintain that our legislator is the most ancient of all legislators in the records of the whole world. Compared with him, your Lycurguses and Solons, and Zaleucus, who gave the Locrians their laws, and all who are held in such high esteem by the Greeks, appear to have been born but yesterday. Why, the very word *law* was unknown in ancient Greece. Witness Homer, who nowhere employs it in his poems.[10] In fact, there was no such thing in his day; the masses were governed by maxims not clearly defined and by the orders of royalty, and continued long afterwards the use of unwritten customs, many of which were time to time altered to suit particular circumstances.

On the other hand, our legislator, who lived in the remotest past (that, I presume, is admitted even by our most unscrupulous detractors), proved himself the people's best guide and counselor; and after framing a code to embrace the whole conduct of their life, induced them to accept it, and secured, on the firmest footing, its observance for all time.

(Josephus, *Against Apion* 2.151-56, trans. Thackeray, LCL, adapted)

An "**apology**" (Greek *apologia*) is a defense speech: Plato's *Apology of Socrates* is the best-known ancient example. References to Jewish "apologetic" literature imply that writers sought to defend Jews and Judaism against detractors and opponents, but that does not mean that they addressed those opponents directly. (Josephus's *Against Apion* was written decades after Apion's death.) The same writings could serve an epideictic or paraenetic function, reinforcing values and convictions within Jewish communities.

---

116. ORAL TRADITION (M. 'ABOT)

Paul claimed in 1 Corinthians to have "passed on" what he "received" concerning appearances of the risen Jesus (1 Cor 15:3-7) and the Lord's supper (1 Cor 11:23-25). Similar language appears in the *Pirqe 'Avot*, "the sayings of the fathers," in the Mishnah (compiled, according to tradition, c. 200 C.E., though the final form of the tractate may be much later). It is possible that Paul already provides evidence for a wider Jewish practice of "passing on" tradition (note that the Gamaliel who appears in this sequence is the same rabbi from whom Paul claims to have learned the law according to Acts 22:3).

The *Pirqe 'Avot* describes how the "oral Torah" was handed down from Moses through a carefully maintained tradition. This work functions, by its presence in the Mishnah, to present the teachings of the Mishnah as authoritative tradition going back to Moses himself and thereby authorizes the rabbis responsible for the Mishnah's promulgation. The compilation of memorable aphorisms resembles the way Hellenistic philosophical schools epitomized the tradition of teachers going back to the founder and the Christian notion of apostolic succession, which developed in the same period. Curiously, the sayings in the *Pirqe 'Avot* touch very little on ritual aspects of the Torah. This first portion of the tractate follows the tradition to roughly the time of Paul.

> Moses received the Law from Sinai and committed it to Joshua, and Joshua to the elders, and the elders to the Prophets; and the Prophets committed it to the men of the Great Synagogue [in Ezra's day]. They said three things: Be deliberate in judgment, raise up many disciples, and make a fence around the Law.
>
> Simeon the Just was of the remnants of the Great Synagogue. He used to say: "By three things is the world sustained: by the Law, by the [Temple-] service, and by deeds of loving-kindness."
>
> Antigonus of Soko received [the Law] from Simeon the Just. He used to say: "Be not like slaves who minister to the master for the sake of receiving a bounty, but be like slaves who minister to the master not for the sake of receiving a bounty; and let the fear of Heaven be upon you."
>
> Jose b. Joezer of Zeredah and Jose b. Johanan of Jerusalem received [the Law] from them. Jose b. Joezer of Zeredah said: "Let your house be a meeting-house for the Sages and sit amid the dust of their feet and drink in their words with thirst."

Fig. 4.4. *This silver fragment, dated to 600 B.C.E., one of two discovered at Ketef Hinnom in Israel in 1979, contains the priestly blessing in Numbers 26. These fragments are the oldest known texts of Torah. Israel Museum. Photo in the public domain.*

Jose b. Johanan of Jerusalem said: "Let your house be opened wide and let the needy be members of your household; and talk not much with womankind." They said this of a man's own wife: how much more of his fellow's wife! Hence the Sages have said: "He who talks much with womankind brings evil upon himself and neglects the study of the Law and at the last will inherit Gehenna."

Joshua b. Perahyah and Nittai the Arbelite received [the Law] from them. Joshua b. Perahyah said: "Provide yourself with a teacher and get yourself a fellow [disciple]; and when you judge any man incline the balance in his favor."

Nittai the Arbelite said: "Keep far from an evil neighbor and consort not with the wicked and lose not belief in retribution."

Judah b. Tabbai and Simeon b. Shetah received [the Law] from them. Judah b. Tabbai said: "Do not become like them who would influence the judges; and when the suitors stand before you let them be in your eyes as wicked men, and when they have departed from before you let them be in your eyes as innocent, so soon as they have accepted the judgment."

Simeon b. Shetah said: "Examine the witnesses diligently and be cautious in your words lest from them they learn to swear falsely."

Shemaiah and Abtalion received [the Law] from them. Shemaiah said: "Love labor and hate mastery and seek not acquaintance with the ruling power."

Abtalion said: "You Sages, give heed to your words lest you incur the penalty of exile and you be exiled to a place of evil waters, and the disciples that come after you drink [of them] and die, and the name of Heaven be profaned."

Hillel and Shammai received [the Law] from them. Hillel said: "Be of the disciples of Aaron, loving peace and pursuing peace, loving mankind and bringing them nigh to the Law."

He used to say: "A name made great is a name destroyed, and he who increases not decreases, and he who learns not is worthy of death, and he who makes worldly use of the crown shall perish."

He used to say: "If I am not for myself who is for me? And being for mine own self what am I? And if not now, when?"

Shammai said: "Make your [study of the] Law a fixed habit; say little and do much, and receive all men with a cheerful countenance."

Rabban Gamaliel said: "Provide yourself with a teacher and remove yourself from doubt, and tithe not overmuch by guesswork."

Simeon his son said: "All my days have I grown up among the Sages and I have found naught better for a man than silence; and not the expounding [of the Law] is the chief thing but the doing [of it]; and he who multiplies words occasions sin."

Rabban Simeon b. Gamaliel said: "By three things is the world sustained: by truth, by judgment, and by peace, as it is written, 'Execute the judgment of truth and peace' [Zech. 8:16]."

(m. 'Abot 1.1-18, trans. Danby, modified)

Our **primary sources for Second Temple Judaism** include 1 and 2 Maccabees, Philo, and Josephus, all of which betray clear biases and agendas; the rather diverse writings included in the Dead Sea Scrolls, which involve their own problems of interpretation related to their discovery near the ruins at Qumran and to ancient descriptions of the "Essenes"; and the vast rabbinic literature, including Mishnah, Tosefta, and midrashic writings, which was compiled much later than the Second Temple but includes much earlier material. The use of any of these sources requires careful consideration of the purposes of the writers or, in the case of rabbinic material, those who gave particular anecdotes their final form. On the "methodological crisis" attending the contemporary use of rabbinic material and the fundamental methodological importance of Jacob Neusner's work, see Shaye J. D. Cohen, "The Political and Social History of the Jews in Greco-Roman Antiquity: The State of the Question," in *Early Judaism and Its Modern Interpreters,* ed. Robert A. Kraft and George W. E. Nickelsburg, Bible and Its Modern Interpreters 2 (Atlanta: Scholars, 1986), 33–56; Anthony J. Saldarini, "Reconstructions of Rabbinic Judaism," in ibid., 437–77 (a revised edition of the volume is in preparation); and H. L. Strack and G. Stemberger, *Introduction to the Talmud and Midrash,* trans. Markus Bockmuehl (Minneapolis: Fortress Press, 1992). See also "For Further Reading" at the end of this chapter.

117. The Synagogue as site of training in the law (Josephus)

Moses not only wrote exemplary legislation, according to Josephus. He also designed the ideal pedagogical system for "practical training in morals": the synagogue.

> For ignorance [of the law, Moses] left no pretext. He appointed the Law to be the most excellent and necessary form of instruction, ordaining, not that it should be heard once for all or twice or on several occasions, but that every week people should desert their other occupations and assemble to listen to the Law and to obtain a thorough and accurate knowledge of it, a practice which all other legislators seem to have neglected. . . . But, should any of our nation be questioned about the laws, they would repeat them all more readily than their own names. The result, then, of our thorough grounding in the laws from the first dawn of intelligence is that we have them, as it were, engraved on our souls. A transgressor is a rarity; evasion of punishment by excuses an impossibility.
>
> To this cause above all we owe our admirable harmony. Unity and identity of religious belief, perfect uniformity in habits and customs, produce a very beautiful concord in human character. Among us alone will be heard

no contradictory statements about God, such as are common among other nations, not only on the lips of ordinary individuals under the impulse of some passing mood, but even boldly propounded by philosophers; some putting forward crushing arguments against the very existence of God, others depriving Him of His providential care for humankind. Among us alone will be seen no difference in the conduct of our lives. With us all act alike, all profess the same doctrine about God, one which is in harmony with our Law and affirms that all things are under [God's] eye. Even our womenfolk and dependents would tell you that piety must be the motive of all our occupations in life.

(Josephus, *Against Apion* 2.175-81, trans. Thackeray, LCL)

The origins of the **synagogue**—variously described in ancient Greek sources as the "gathering (-place": *synagōgē*) or "prayer-house" (*proseuchē*) and in rabbinic Hebrew as the "house of study" (*bêt midrāš*)—remain controversial, but Josephus notwithstanding, most scholars would date it no earlier than the Persian period. See Rachel Hachlili, "Synagogue," *ABD* 6:251–63; Anders Runesson, *The Origins of the Synagogue: A Socio-Historical Study*, Coniectanea biblica, New Testament 37 (Lund: Almqvist & Wiksell, 2001).

Diaspora Synagogues and Reverence for the Temple

"They are Israelites, and to them belong . . . the worship," Paul declared (Rom 9:4). The Greek *latreia*, "worship," corresponded to the Hebrew *ʿăbōdâ* and pointed specifically to the sacrificial worship and prayers conducted in the temple.[11] In this, Paul echoed the reverence many Diaspora Jews showed for the temple—some part at least of which was heightened by the grandeur of Herod's impressive expansion and renovation of the site, which elicited awe from Jesus' disciples (Mark 13:1 and par.) and from the rabbis as well ("Whoever has not seen Herod's Temple has never seen a beautiful building," *b. B. Bat.* 4a; *b. Sukkah* 51b). But others, too, acknowledged the beauty and solemnity of the temple.

118. "Schools of temperance and justice" (Agrippa I)

In the rest of the letter of Agrippa I that was cited above (no. 114), the king went to great lengths to point out the respect shown to the temple by prominent Romans, including Marcus Agrippa and Augustus himself. (The king glossed over Pompey's violation of the temple in 63 B.C.E. and mentioned Pontius Pilate's provocative installation of golden shields on the temple's walls as a scandalous exception to his theme.) M. Agrippa had frequented the temple while in Judea and had extolled its beauty; he, like Augustus after him, had made lavish gifts to the temple; and Augustus had

Fig. 4.5. *This first-century-c.e. synagogue inscription—from Jerusalem, in Greek—identifies a donor to a Jerusalem synagogue, and tells us something of the function of this synagogue for hospitality as well as study and community life. Photo courtesy of Bibleplaces.com. The inscription reads:*

> *Theodotos (son of) Vettenos, a priest and a ruler of the synagogue, the son of a ruler of the synagogue (himself the son of a ruler of the synagogue), built [this] synagogue for the reading of law and for teaching the commandments; also the hostel, and the rooms, and the baths, for lodging those in need. Its foundation stone was laid by his fathers, the elders, and Simonides. (trans. Elliott)*

"commanded perfect sacrifices of whole burnt offerings to be offered up to the most high God every day, out of his own revenues" (*Embassy* 317).

Agrippa's letter shows that Jews in the Diaspora sought the right to send the required tithes and firstfruits offering to Jerusalem (see Exod 23:16-19; Lev 23:9; Deut 26:2); that these contributions were collected in synagogues; and that Augustus's own guarantee that those contributions would not be hindered was a cherished promise. Note the description of the synagogue's role in Jewish life.

> And though I might be able to establish this fact, and demonstrate to you the feelings of Augustus, your great grandfather, by an abundance of proofs, I will be content with two. For, in the first place, he sent commandments to all the governors of the different provinces throughout Asia, because he heard that the sacred first fruits were neglected, enjoining them to permit the Jews alone to assemble together in the synagogues, for that these assemblies were not revels, which from drunkenness and intoxication proceeded to violence, so

as to disturb the peaceful condition of the country, but were rather schools of temperance and justice, as the men who met in them were studiers of virtue, and contributed the first fruits every year, sending commissioners to convey the holy things to the Temple in Jerusalem.

And, in the next place, he commanded that no one should hinder the Jews, either on their way to the synagogues, or when bringing their contributions, or when proceeding in obedience to their national laws to Jerusalem, for these things were expressly enjoined, if not in so many words, at all events in effect.

(Philo, *Embassy to Gaius* 311-13, trans. Yonge)

119. Imperial guarantees of Jewish rights (Josephus)

The texts under consideration show that Jewish apologetic writings appealed not only to the merits of the Torah (*nomos*) for promoting virtue and social harmony but also to the precedent of official decrees by earlier emperors and governors. These decrees guaranteed the rights of Diaspora communities to collect and transmit funds and gifts for the temple; to secure, prepare, and distribute kosher food; and to be exempted from legal and military requirements on the Sabbath. These decrees, Josephus emphasized, were a matter of public record, "laid up in the public places of the cities and . . . extant still in the capitol."

Fig. 4.6. *Remains of the courtyard of the Sardis synagogue in Asia Minor (Turkey), second or third century* c.e. *One of the best-preserved synagogues from the Roman world, it was an impressive building on the civic landscape. Photo: A. G. Baydin.*

As Leonard V. Rutgers has shown, however, these decrees were "essentially *ad hoc* measures" issued "in response to the requests of the Jewish communities" in various parts of the Eastern Mediterranean "to help them protect their traditional Jewish way of life against the constant attacks of their Greek neighbors." These responses did not constitute—despite the impression Josephus might have wished to leave!—anything like "a Magna Carta or formal document that aimed at defining the legal status of all Jewish communities . . . once and for all."[12]

Many of the decrees cited by Josephus hark back to Julius Caesar's promises to the Hasmonean king Hyrcanus II, whose grandfather Simon had fought with his brother Judas Maccabeus ("the Hammer") against Seleucid tyranny. Hyrcanus had been deposed by his brother Aristobolus II, but on his invasion of Judea in 63 B.C.E. Pompey had sided with Hyrcanus, restoring him as high priest; in 47 B.C.E. Caesar made him ethnarch ("ruler of his people," but less than king).

> It seems to me to be necessary here to give an account of all the honors that the Romans and their Emperor paid to our nation, and of the leagues of mutual assistance they have made with it, that all the rest of mankind may know what regard the kings of Asia and Europe have had for us, and that they have been abundantly satisfied of our courage and fidelity. . . . Out of these evidences will I demonstrate what I say; and will now set down the decrees made both by the senate and by Julius Caesar, which relate to Hyrcanus and to our nation.
>
> (Josephus, *Antiquities* 14.10.1 [§§186-89], trans. Whiston)

Josephus cites a number of decrees of Caesar, including this copy dispatched to Sidon.

> "The decrees of Caius Caesar, consul, containing what has been granted and determined, are as follows: That Hyrcanus and his children bear rule over the nation of the Jews, and have the profits of the places to them bequeathed; and that he, as himself the high priest and ethnarch of the Jews, defend those that are injured; and that ambassadors be sent to Hyrcanus, the son of Alexander, the high priest of the Jews, that may discourse with him about a league of friendship and mutual assistance; and that a table of brass, containing the promises, be openly proposed in the capitol, and at Sidon, and Tyre, and Ascalon, and in the Temple, engraved in Roman and Greek letters: that this decree may also be communicated to the quaestors and praetors of the several cities, and to the friends of the Jews; and that the ambassadors may have presents made them; and that these decrees be sent everywhere."
>
> (Josephus, *Antiquities* 14.10.3 [§§196-98], trans. Whiston)

Caesar's decrees further included a Sabbath-year respite from tribute for the city of Jerusalem; requirements that "tithes" be paid to Hyrcanus and his sons; and the promise that no external force would be allowed to raise military auxiliaries or to extract funds for quartering soldiers in Judea (*Ant.* 14.203-4). Such promises made to the Jews could require warning or rebuking local governments that had taken actions to restrict Jewish community life. Caesar offered one such rebuke to the government of the island of Paros regarding the Jews on nearby Delos.

Julius Caius, praetor of Rome, to the magistrates, senate, and people of the Parians, sends greeting. The Jews of Delos, and some other Jews that sojourn there, in the presence of your ambassadors, signified to us that, by a decree of yours, you forbid them to make use of the customs of their forefathers and their way of sacred worship. Now it does not please me that such decrees should be made against our friends and confederates, whereby they are forbidden to live according to their own customs, or to bring in contributions for common suppers and holy festivals, while they are not forbidden so to do even at Rome itself; for even Caius Caesar, our imperator and consul, in that decree wherein he forbade the Bacchanal rioters to meet in the city, did yet permit these Jews, and these only, both to bring in their contributions, and to make their common suppers. Accordingly, when I forbid other Bacchanal rioters, I permit these Jews to gather themselves together, according to the customs and laws of their forefathers, and to persist therein. It will be therefore good for you, that if you have made any decree against these our friends and confederates, to abrogate the same, by reason of their virtue and kind disposition towards us.

(Josephus, *Antiquities* 14.10.8 [§§213-16], trans. Whiston)

Another decree, from the Roman consul Publius Cornelius Dolabella (44 B.C.E.) to the Ephesians, grants Jews exemption from being pressed into military service and rights concerning access to kosher food.

When Artermon was *prytanis*, on the first day of the month Lenaeon; Dolabella, *imperator*, to the senate, and magistrates, and people of the Ephesians, sends greeting.

Alexander, the son of Theodorus, the ambassador of Hyrcanus [II] the son of Alexander, the high priest and ethnarch of the Jews, appeared before me to show that his countrymen could not go into their armies because they are not allowed to bear arms or to travel on the sabbath days; nor there to procure themselves those sorts of food which they have been used to eat from the times of their forefathers. I do therefore grant them a freedom from going into the army, as the former prefects have done, and permit them to use the customs of their forefathers, in assembling together for sacred and religious purposes, as their law requires, and for collecting oblations necessary for sacrifices; and my will is, that you write this to the several cities under your jurisdiction.

(Josephus, *Antiquities* 14.10.12 [§§225-27], trans. Whiston)

Josephus goes on to record the responses of various Greek cities agreeing to the decrees—and occasional letters of censure to those who did not.

Publius Servilius, the son of Publius, of the Galban tribe, the proconsul, to the magistrates, senate, and people of the Milesians, sends greeting. Prytanes, the son of Hermes, a citizen of yours, came to me when I was at Tralles, and held a court there, and informed me that you used the Jews in a way different from my opinion, and forbade them to celebrate their Sabbaths, and to perform the Sacred rites received from their forefathers, and to manage the fruits of the land, according to their ancient custom; and that he had himself been the promulgator of your decree, according as your laws require: I would therefore have

you know, that upon hearing the pleadings on both sides, I gave sentence that
the Jews should not be prohibited to make use of their own customs.

(Josephus, *Antiquities* 14.10.21 [§§244-46], trans. Whiston)

At length Josephus summarizes this lengthy recital by indicating that "there are
many such decrees of the senate and imperators of the Romans . . . which have been
made in favor of Hyrcanus, and of our nation; as also, there have been more decrees
of the cities, and rescripts of the praetors, to such epistles as concerned our rights and
privileges," but that the ones he has brought forward should suffice to demonstrate
"that friendship and confederacy that we [have] had with the Romans" (*Ant.* 14.10.26
[§§265-67]).

> John J. Collins described **"a common ethic"** in Diaspora Juda-
> ism. Although different commandments might be emphasized or
> defended in different ways, especially in representing Judaism to
> non-Jews, "the Mosaic law always retained an authoritative posi-
> tion"; the varieties of Judaism remained "deeply rooted in customs
> and observances which ultimately derived from the Mosaic law"
> (*Between Athens and Jerusalem: Jewish Identity in the Hellenistic
> Diaspora* [New York: Crossroad, 1983], 137). Philosopher Jacob
> Taubes spoke of "a general Hellenistic aura, an apotheosis of
> nomos" in the Roman world in which Diaspora Jews sought both
> to participate and to maintain their own distinctiveness (*The Politi-
> cal Theology of Paul*, trans. Dana Hollander, Cultural Memory in the
> Present [Stanford: Stanford University Press, 2004], 23).

The Rejection of Idols

Any number of Hellenistic Jewish texts could be cited that decried the evils that characterized the pagan world and attributed them to the primary vice of non-Jews: the
worship given to images of the gods. The inherent absurdity of idolatry was a target
of the Second Isaiah's parodies (Isa 40:18-20; 41:7; 44:9-20; 46:6-7; 48:3-5). It later
became a mainstay of Jewish propaganda in the Hellenistic and Roman periods.

120. The Evils of idolatry (Wisdom of Solomon)

The Wisdom of Solomon, produced perhaps in Alexandria between 150 and 50 b.c.e.,
offers an extensive parody of idolatry within Solomon's praise of Wisdom. Beginning
in chapter 9, Solomon directs a long prayer to God, offering praise for the benefit of
Wisdom given to Israel and for the punishment accruing to the ungodly. The passage
has long been recognized as a close conceptual parallel to Rom 1:18—2:16.[13]

In return for their foolish and wicked thoughts,
> which led them astray to worship irrational serpents and worthless animals,

you sent upon them a multitude of irrational creatures to punish them,
> so that they might learn that one is punished by the very thing by which one sins.

. . .

For all people who were ignorant of God were foolish by nature;
> and they were unable from the good things that are seen to know the one who exists,

nor did they recognize the artisan while paying heed to his works;
> but they supposed that either fire or wind or swift air,

or the circle of the stars, or turbulent water,
> or the luminaries of heaven were the gods that rule the world.

. . .

But miserable, with their hopes set on dead things, are those
> who give the name "gods" to the works of human hands,

gold and silver fashioned with skill, and likenesses of animals,
> or a useless stone, the work of an ancient hand.

("Solomon" ridicules the devotion the idolater shows to inanimate figures made by his own hands.)

He takes thought for it, so that it may not fall,
> because he knows that it cannot help itself,
> for it is only an image and has need of help.

When he prays about possessions and his marriage and children,
> he is not ashamed to address a lifeless thing.

For health he appeals to a thing that is weak;
> for life he prays to a thing that is dead;

for aid he entreats a thing that is utterly inexperienced;
> for a prosperous journey, a thing that cannot take a step;

for money-making and work and success with his hands
> he asks strength of a thing whose hands have no strength.

. . .

Equally hateful to God are the ungodly and their ungodliness;
> for what was done will be punished together with the one who did it.

Therefore there will be a visitation also upon the heathen idols,
> because, though part of what God created, they became an abomination,
> snares for human souls and a trap for the feet of the foolish.

For the idea of making idols was the beginning of fornication,
> and the invention of them was the corruption of life;

for they did not exist from the beginning,
> nor will they last forever.

. . .

For the worship of idols [which are] not to be named
> is the beginning and cause and end of every evil.

> (Wisdom of Solomon 11:15-16; 13:1-2, 10-19; 14:8-11, 27 NRSV)

121. THE FOLLY OF IDOL WORSHIP (PHILO)

In his discussion of the *Special Laws* Philo of Alexandria offers a similar critique of idol worship that is typical of Hellenistic Judaism:

> There are some who put gold and silver in the hands of sculptors as though they were competent to fashion gods; and the sculptors taking the crude material and furthermore using mortal form for their model, to crown the absurdity shape gods, as they are supposed to be. And after erecting and establishing temples they have built altars and in their honor hold sacrifices and processions with other religious rites and ceremonies conducted with the most elaborate care, and the vain show is treated by priests and priestesses with the utmost possible solemnity. Such idolaters are warned by the Ruler of All in these words: "Ye shall not make with Me gods of silver and gold," and the lesson conveyed is little less than a direct command, "Neither shall ye make gods the work of your hands from any other material if you are prevented from using the best."
> (Philo, *On the Special Laws* 1.21-22, trans. Colson, LCL)

Jewish Circumspection regarding Idols

If the absurdity of idol worship was an important theme in Jewish teaching, however, the point had to be made cautiously. Honoring the city's gods and thus ensuring the city's welfare were important social values in Roman culture. Because Jews were a minority population in most cities outside of Judea, they had to take care not to appear as enemies of public order and thus draw antagonism to themselves.

In Acts 19 Luke narrates an extraordinary episode that illustrates the possible consequences. When Paul's preaching in Ephesus over a two-year period finds great success ("all the residents of Asia, both Jews and Greeks, heard the word of the Lord," 19:10), a silversmith named Demetrius mobilizes the city's artisans to oppose Paul on the pretext that his proclamation that "gods made with hands are not gods" (19:26) is drawing people away from worship of the city's gods—and thus hurting the metal-working business. Typical of Luke's apologetic narrative are the base ulterior motives of Paul's opponents (Demetrius rouses his colleagues by declaring, "Men, you know that we get our wealth from this business," 19:25) and the crude irrationality of the mob (19:32). Also typical is the clear implication that the charges against Paul are false. Previously we have not heard Paul say anything like the words Demetrius attributes to him; further, the town clerk (NRSV; Greek *grammateus*) exonerates Paul and his companions, "who are neither temple robbers [*hierosylous*] nor blasphemers [*blasphēmountas*] of our goddess" (19:37). Indeed, the clerk's speech indicates that it is the agitation and false charges brought by Demetrius, rather than anything in Paul's proclamation, that have imperiled the civic order (19:35-41).

Despite what may be tendentious aspects of this dramatic narrative, it serves indirectly to illustrate the tensions that we may presume accompanied Paul's own work. His appeal to the residents of Roman cities to "turn from idols" would have required their conspicuous withdrawal from important aspects of everyday civic life and would thus inevitably have made them the focus of unwanted attention, suspicion, and pressure from neighbors and family. Indeed, one of Paul's purposes in

Fig. 4.7. *The Nash papyrus, from Egypt, 200–201* B.C.E. *(discovered in 1930), includes the Ten Commandments and the Shema ("Hear, O Israel," Deut 6:4-5) in Hebrew, though the text more closely resembles the Greek. Before the discovery of the Dead Sea Scrolls this was the earliest known manuscript of the Hebrew Bible. Cambridge University Library. Photo in the public domain.*

1 Thessalonians is to remind his hearers that "when we were with you, we told you beforehand that we were to suffer persecution; so it turned out, as you know" (3:4).

We know from Romans that Paul's message included a polemical critique of idol worship (1:18-32). Like other Jews, however, Paul may have sought to walk a fine line, criticizing the worship of images and calling people to abandon them without directly denouncing the popular gods. Note the shift in tone in 1 Corinthians 8. Paul says first, "We know that 'no idol in the world really exists,' and that 'there is no God but one'" (8:4; the NRSV inserts quotation marks as if Paul is quoting slogans known to the Corinthians). Then he moderates those declarations: "Indeed, even though there may be so-called gods in heaven or on earth—as in fact there are many gods and many lords—yet for us there is one God." (8:5-6). Then he speaks (8:7-13) as if only those with "weak consciences" perceive any reality behind idols. Later, in chapter 10, he insists that his hearers "flee from the worship of idols" (10:14), not because "an idol is anything" but because "what pagans sacrifice, they sacrifice to demons [*daimoniois*] and not to God" (10:19-20).

These passages are some of the most difficult in Paul's letters. Making sense of what Paul is trying to say—and, perhaps, trying *not* to say!—in the context of the letter's argument is the focus of considerable scholarly attention but is beyond the scope of our discussion here. Our purpose rather is to note that what we might call Paul's circumspection, equivocation, or hesitation to speak a single clear condemnation of the gods of Corinth was something he shared with other Jews living in minority communities in cities throughout the Hellenistic world. (As we shall see in chapter 5, however, later portraits of Paul reenvisioned him as an unabashed iconoclast!)

Already in the third century B.C.E., the translators of the Septuagint had changed the meaning of the commandment in Exod 22:27, which in Hebrew reads

'elōhîm lō' t^eqallēl w^enāśî b^e'amm^ekā lō' tā'ōr
You shall not revile God or curse a leader of your people (NRSV),
to read in Greek:
theous ou kakologēseis kai archontas tou laou sou ou kakōs ereis.
You shall not revile gods or speak evil of the rulers of your people.

Elsewhere the Greek translators rendered *'elohim* (which is grammatically plural) with the singular *theos*. The use here of the plural, "gods," and the change from "leader" to "rulers" were made by translators living in Hellenistic Egypt, under circumstances very different from those imagined in the earlier Hebrew text, where the people were called to honor their own God and respect their own leader. The change arguably produced a more sensible modus operandi for a new situation. That, at any rate, is how the Greek text was understood in the first century c.e., as the following excerpts illustrate.

122. THAT PROSELYTES SHOULD NOT REVILE IDOLS (PHILO)

In what follows the preceding extract, Philo addresses proselytes and sympathetic non-Jews (compare no. 178, below). He argues that the search for the true God, "the Father and Ruler of all," is a worthy goal, though the nature of God is "doubtless hard to unriddle and hard to apprehend," demanding "the consideration of the genuine philosopher" (*Spec. Laws* 1.32). Moses provides the example of just such a philosopher. His cry to God, "reveal yourself to me" (Exod 33:13 LXX: Hebrew "show me your ways"), was the culmination of an extended philosophical meditation on the nature of the universe (1.41-44). Philo similarly rephrases God's gracious response in philosophical terms: God declares, "I . . . am discerned by mind and not by sight" (1.46). The revelation to Moses is thus the paradigmatic call to Jews and to proselytes alike: "Let there be the constant and profound longing for wisdom which fills its scholars and disciples with verities glorious in their exceeding loveliness."

Despite the philosophical force of his argument, in the third paragraph below Philo warns new proselytes to refrain from deprecating their own former gods. That injunction no doubt reflected the situation of minority Jewish populations in Roman cities; it may rely as well on the LXX translation of Exod 22:27.

> All of like sort to [Moses], all who spurn idle fables and embrace truth in its purity, whether they have been such from the first or through conversion to the better side have reached that higher state, obtain [God's] approval, the former because they were not false to the nobility of their birth, the latter because their judgment led them to make the passage to piety. These last [Moses] calls "proselytes," or newly-joined, because they have joined the new and godly commonwealth.
>
> Thus, while giving equal rank to all in-comers with all privileges which he gives to the native-born, he exhorts the old nobility to honor them [proselytes] not only with marks of respect but with special friendship and with more than

ordinary goodwill. And surely there is good reason for this; they have left, he says, their country, their kinsfolk, and their friends for the sake of virtue and religion [di'aretēn kai hosiotēta]. Let them not be denied another citizenship or other ties of family and friendship, and let them find places of shelter standing ready for refugees to the camp of piety. For the most effectual love-charm, the chain which binds indissolubly the goodwill which makes us one, is to honor the one God.

Yet he counsels them [the proselytes] that they must not, presuming on the equal privilege and equal rank which he grants them because they have denounced the vain imaginings of their fathers and ancestors, deal in idle talk or revile with an unbridled tongue the gods whom others acknowledge, lest they on their part be moved to utter profane words against Him Who truly is. For they know not the difference, and since the falsehood has been taught to them as truth from childhood and has grown up with them, they will go astray.

(Philo, *On the Special Laws* 1.51-53, trans. Colson, LCL, adapted)

123. On using the name "god" with utmost respect (Philo)

Philo shows a similar understanding of the scene in Leviticus 14 wherein God commands that the congregation stone to death a man—the son of an Egyptian man and

Fig. 4.8. *The cult statue of the Philistine god Dagon lies in pieces before the ark of the covenant (see 1 Samuel 5). Fresco from the synagogue at Dura Europos, early third century c.e. Artistic representation of triumph over pagan idols may have provided a satisfaction unavailable on the landscape of a Roman city. Fresco preserved in the National Museum of Damascus. Photo: Erich Lessing/Art Resource, New York.*

an Israelite woman—who had blasphemed "the name" (of the Lord). The Septuagint translated the command in Lev 14:15-16 as follows:

> Any person who curses a god [*theon*] will receive sin; one naming the name of the Lord [*kyriou*] will be put to death; with stones let the whole congregation of Israel stone the person; whether proselyte or native, because of their naming the name of the Lord [*kyriou*] let them die. (Lev 14:15-16 LXX)

Though it might seem that the extreme penalty is unfairly given here to "naming" rather than "cursing," Philo argues that that is not the point. His exegesis here aligns with his discussion of Exod 22:27, seen above.

> No, clearly by "God" [*theon*] he is not here alluding to the Primal God, the Begetter of the Universe, but to the gods [*theous*] of the different cities who are falsely so called, being fashioned by the skill of painters and sculptors. For the world as we know it is full of idols of wood and stone, and suchlike images. We must refrain from speaking insulting of these, lest any of Moses' disciples get into the habit of treating lightly the name "god" in general, for it is a title worthy of the highest respect and love. But if anyone, I will not say blasphemes the Lord of gods and men, but even ventures to utter His Name unseasonably, let him suffer the penalty of death.
>
> (Philo, *Life of Moses* 2.205-6, trans. Colson, LCL, adapted)

124. On respect for pagan temples and shrines (Josephus)

In *Questions on Exodus* Philo offered three explanations for the command he finds in the Septuagint translation of Exod 22:27 (discussed above): Moses understood that praise was always preferable to reviling; criticism of the gods of others leads to conflict and to war, and the Torah is meant as a source of peace; and refraining from reviling the gods of others may attract them to the God of Israel.

Writing decades later, Josephus presented a similar interpretation of the same command as he sought to answer the anti-Jewish calumnies of one of Philo's opponents, the Alexandrian Apion. Josephus expressed an initial hesitation to embark on comparisons that would prove unflattering to other nations.

> Gladly would I have avoided an investigation of the institutions of other nations; for it is our traditional custom to observe our own laws and to refrain from criticism of those of aliens. Our legislator has expressly forbidden us to deride [*chleuazein*] or blaspheme [*blasphēmein*] the gods recognized by others, out of respect for the very word "God."
>
> (Josephus, *Against Apion* 2.237, trans. Thackeray, LCL)

In his *Antiquities*, Josephus offered a summary of the "constitution" (*politeia*) given by Moses (4.196-301). His phrasing of Exod 22:27 is consistent with the Septuagint and Philo but includes language similar to—but also markedly different from—the language found in Deut 7:25. In Deuteronomy 7, the Lord commands Israel to destroy the shrines of the Canaanites:

The images of their gods you shall burn with fire. Do not covet the silver or the gold that is on them and take it for yourself, because you could be ensnared by it; for it is abhorrent to the LORD your God. Do not bring an abhorrent thing into your house, or you will be set apart for destruction like it. You must utterly detest and abhor it, for it is set apart for destruction. (Deut 7:25-26)

In this case the Septuagint is consistent with the meaning of the Hebrew. But Josephus, eager to show that observing the Jewish law promotes the maintenance of harmonious relations with neighbors, offers a paraphrase that elides the references to destruction, conflates the Exodus passage with this one, and changes the meaning of the second passage in the direction of the Septuagint translation of the first.

> Let none blaspheme the gods which other cities revere, nor rob foreign temples, nor take treasure that has been dedicated in the name of any god.
> (Josephus, *Antiquities* 4.207, trans. Thackeray and Marcus, LCL)

Tensions between Rome and Jewish Communities

Despite the circumspection on the part of Jews that we have just sampled, and despite favorable attitudes on the part of Julius Caesar and Augustus, later emperors showed greater willingness to act with indifference or antagonism to Jews in Rome and other cities. (Indeed, even the favorable decrees cited by Josephus often were issued to counter the hostile actions of non-Jewish neighbors in one or another region.) Anti-Semitism in the Roman world may have owed something to the general disposition of groups to form boundaries separating insiders from outsiders; it clearly was related on some occasions, at least, to Roman suspicion of other "foreign" religions (see below, nos. 174–76); and in the case of Caligula especially it seems to have been aggravated by the Jewish refusal to worship Roman gods.[14]

As we will see in chapter 5, the Roman Senate not infrequently took action to suppress non-Roman rites or even to expel practitioners of foreign worship from Rome (see fig. 5.9). On occasion these actions included Jews. We should not imagine, however, that Rome had a specific policy regarding the Jews as such. Rather, as Leonard V. Rutgers has argued, "Roman magistrates responded to situations." When there was social unrest—whatever its cause—Rome expelled one or another group. This does not necessarily mean that the targeted group was responsible for the civic disturbance; it could be that they were "just a convenient group whose expulsion could serve as an example to establish peace and quiet among the city populace at large."[15] When Roman Jews were persecuted, often "the main motive was the wish to suppress unrest. The fact that Roman authors use disparaging terms such as *superstitio* and 'impious [*profani*] rites' in describing these events reflects a general antipathy to un-Roman religious practices," but in these incidents, Rutgers argues, Roman authorities were simply applying "a well-tried formula that can be traced back as far as the Bacchanalia affair of 186 B.C.E." That formula was the "expulsion of those who on the basis of their un-Roman rituals and practices could easily be represented as threatening the boundaries of Roman society."[16]

125. An expulsion of Jews under Tiberius (Tacitus)

An incident under Tiberius in 19 c.e. illustrates the point just made. Writing almost a century later, Tacitus is scornful of both Egyptians and Jews, but says nothing specific to explain the hostility to Jews.

> There was a debate too about expelling the Egyptian and Jewish worship, and a resolution of the Senate was passed that four thousand of the freedmen class who were infected with those superstitions and were of military age should be transported to the island of Sardinia, to quell the brigandage of the place, a cheap sacrifice should they die from the pestilential climate. The rest were to quit Italy, unless before a certain day they repudiated their impious rites.
> (Tacitus, *Annals* 2.85, trans. Church and Brodribb)

Other ancient authors refer to what was apparently the same incident and offer different explanations. We will turn to Josephus's account below. The historian Dio Cassius, writing two centuries later, attributed the expulsion to Jewish proselytizing activities, but his distance from the event and the stereotyped nature of the charge leave room for doubt.[17] There was nevertheless considerable anxiety among some in Rome regarding the attractions of Judaism.

126. The expulsion of 19 c.e. due to a woman's weakness (Josephus)

Referring to the expulsion of Jews from Rome under Tiberius to which both Tacitus and Dio also referred (see above), Josephus argues that the Jews of Rome were collectively punished for the misdeeds of a few, both Jews and Egyptians. Note that conversion to Judaism plays a role in his account, but Josephus emphasizes the gullibility of the Roman noblewomen who fell for the fraudulent inducements of unscrupulous conmen.

> About the same time also another sad calamity put the Jews into disorder, and certain shameful practices happened about the temple of Isis that was at Rome. I will now first take notice of the wicked attempt about the temple of Isis, and will then give an account of the Jewish affairs.

Josephus relates that a Roman noblewoman named Paulina, though married, was courted by an undeterrable suitor named Decius Mundus, whose lavish gifts she refused. He knew that she was also a devotee of Isis, however, and so he bribed the priests of Isis to assist him in a plot cooked up by his slavewoman Ida. The priests came to Paulina's home and swore that the god Anubis had revealed his desire to sleep with Paulina. Flattered, Paulina convinced her husband of the sincerity of the proposal. She spent the night at the temple, alone (she believed) behind locked doors, being ravished in the dark by Decius Mundus and "supposing he was the god." Still deceived the next day, she boasted to friends of the honor she had received— until Mundus confronted her in public and taunted her with having spared him the expense of additional gifts for her sexual favors. Humiliated, but married to a senator, she went to her husband for vengeance. He went to the emperor, whereupon Tiberius inquired into the matter thoroughly by examining the priests about it, and ordered them to be crucified, as well as Ida, who was the occasion of their perdition, and who had contrived the whole matter, which was so injurious to the woman. He also demolished the temple of Isis, and gave order that her statue should be thrown into the river Tiber; while he only banished Mundus, but did no more to him, because he supposed that what crime he had committed was done out of the passion of love. And these were the circumstances which concerned the temple of Isis, and the injuries occasioned by her priests.

(Josephus, *Antiquities* 18.3.4 [§§65-80], passim, trans. Whiston)

Josephus does not expand on what seems an incredible tale; instead he turns to relate a similar account of an extortion attempt on a Roman noblewoman on the part of some unscrupulous Jews.

There was a man who was a Jew, but had been driven away from his own country by an accusation laid against him for transgressing their laws, and by the fear he was under of punishment for the same; but in all respects a wicked man. He, then living at Rome, professed to instruct men in the wisdom of the laws of Moses. He procured also three other men, entirely of the same character with himself, to be his partners.

These men persuaded Fulvia, a woman of great dignity, and one that had embraced the Jewish religion, to send purple and gold to the temple at Jerusalem; and when they had gotten them, they employed them for their own uses, and spent the money themselves, on which account it was that they at first required it of her. Whereupon Tiberius, who had been informed of the thing by Saturninus, the husband of Fulvia, who desired inquiry might be made about it, ordered all the Jews to be banished out of Rome; at which time the consuls listed four thousand men out of them, and sent them to the island Sardinia; but punished a greater number of them, who were unwilling to become soldiers, on account of keeping the laws of their forefathers. Thus were these Jews banished out of the city by the wickedness of four men.

(Josephus, *Antiquities* 18.3.5 [§§81-84], trans. Whiston)

Josephus's account may seem "hardly possible to accept." Philo, for his part, glossed over the episode as the result of transparently false accusations made by Tiberius's advisor Sejanus, whom Philo characterizes as viciously anti-Jewish and driven "to root out the people." Philo admits, nevertheless, that "a few" of the Jews were guilty of some unmentioned offense (*Embassy* 155-61). Josephus's much more detailed account seems to blame the expulsion not just on four devious conmen but also on a woman's "natural" gullibility, perhaps playing to elite Roman men's prejudices regarding "women's religion" (see chapter 3, nos. 115-17).

Trouble under Gaius (Caligula)

If repressive measures against Jews under Tiberius could be attributed to a more general pattern of reaction against foreign groups, the actions of the emperor Gaius (known to us by his nickname Caligula) were "bitterly hostile" to the Jews (Philo, *Embassy* 346). As we have seen, King Agrippa I wrote to Gaius imploring him not to erect a statue of himself in the Jerusalem temple (see no. 67). That letter won a brief reprieve from Gaius, but the blessing was mixed: the emperor also decreed that no one should be prevented from installing his images anywhere outside of Jerusalem—a

Fig. 4.9. *Funerary inscription in Greek, third century* c.e.: *"Here lies Salo, daughter of Gadias, father of the synagogue of the Hebrews; she lived forty-one years; may her rest be in peace." The synagogue of the Hebrews was the oldest synagogue in Rome. Museo delle Terme de Diocleziano, Rome. Photo in the public domain.*

virtual invitation to mob attacks on synagogues and, Philo expected, to Jewish reprisals that would then be used to justify resumption of the installation of a statue in the temple itself (*Embassy* 334-35).

127. Gaius receives the Jews from Alexandria (Philo)

Philo describes the emperor's reception of the Jewish delegation from Alexandria in which he participated. From the start, Gaius made clear his plans to make a public spectacle of the humiliation of the Jews.

> It is worth while to make mention of what we both saw and heard, when we were sent for to fight the fight for citizenship. For the moment that we entered into the presence of the emperor we perceived from his gaze and from his movement that we had come not before a judge but before an accuser, or rather the enemy of those set against him.
>
> We, as soon as we were introduced into his presence, the moment that we saw him, bent to the ground with all imaginable respect and adoration, and greeted him, calling him the Emperor Augustus; and he replied to us in such a gentle and courteous and humane manner that we not only despaired of attaining our object, but even of preserving our lives.
>
> For, said he, "You are haters of god, inasmuch as you do not think that I am a god, I who am already confessed to be a god by every other nation, but who am refused that appellation by you." And then, stretching up his hands to heaven, he uttered an outburst that was neither righteous to hear nor to translate literally. And immediately the ambassadors of the opposite portion were filled with all imaginable joy, thinking that their embassy was already successful, on account of the first words uttered by Gaius, and so they clapped their hands and danced for joy, and called him by every title which is applicable to any one of the gods.
>
> And while he was triumphing in these super-human designations, the mean flatterer Isidorus said, "O master, even more will you hate these men whom you see before you and their fellow countrymen, if you are made acquainted with their disaffection and disloyalty towards yourself; for when all other men were offering up sacrifices of thanksgiving for your safety, these men alone refused to offer any sacrifice at all; and when I say, 'these,' I include all the rest of the Jews."

The Jews protested in their defense that sacrifices were offered in the Jerusalem temple in honor of the emperor—a compromise that Augustus had welcomed and underwritten.

> And when we all cried out with one accord, "O Lord Gaius, we are falsely accused; for we did sacrifice, and we offered up entire hecatombs, the blood of which we poured in a libation upon the altar, and the flesh we did not carry to our homes to make a feast and banquet upon it, as is the custom of some people to do, but we committed the victims entire to the sacred flame as a burnt offering: and we have done this three times already, and not once only; on the first occasion when you succeeded to the empire, and the second time when

you recovered from that terrible disease with which all the habitable world was afflicted at the same time, and the third time we sacrificed in hope of your victory over the Germans."

"Let these things be true," said he, "You have sacrificed; but you sacrificed to another god, and not for my sake; and then what good did you do me? For you have not sacrificed to me."

Immediately a profound shuddering came upon us the first moment that we heard this expression, which spread even to our outer appearance. And while he was saying these things he entered into the outer buildings, examining the chambers of the men and the chambers of the women, and the rooms on the ground floor, and all the apartments in the upper story, and blaming some points of their preparation as defective, and planning alterations and suggesting designs, and giving orders himself to make them more costly. Then we who were driven about in this way followed him up and down through the whole place, being mocked and ridiculed by our adversaries like people at a play in the theater; for indeed the whole matter was a kind of farce: the judge assumed the part of an accuser, and the accusers the part of an unjust judge, gazing with personal hostility, not according to the nature of truth.

But when he had given some of his orders about the buildings, he then asked a very important and solemn question; "Why is it that you abstain from eating pork?" And then again at this question such a violent laughter was raised by our adversaries, partly because they were really delighted, and partly as they wished to court the emperor out of flattery, and therefore wished to make it appear that this question was dictated by wit and uttered with grace, that some of the servants who were following him were indignant at their appearing to treat the emperor with so little respect, since it was not safe for his most intimate friends to do so much as smile at his words.

And when we made answer that "different nations have different laws, and there are some things whose use is forbidden both to us and to our adversaries"; and when someone said, "there are also many people who do not eat lamb's flesh, which is the most tender of all meat," he laughed and said, "They are quite right, for it is not nice." Being joked with and trifled with and ridiculed in this manner, we were in great perplexity; and at last in a rapid and peremptory manner, he said, "we wish to be informed by what just principles you deserve citizenship."

And when we began to reply to him and to explain it, he, as soon as he had a taste of our pleading on the principles of justice, and as soon as he perceived that our arguments were not contemptible, before we could bring forward the more significant matters that we had to say, cut us short and ran forward and burst into the large building, and as soon as he had entered he commanded the windows which were around it to be filled up with the transparent pebbles very much resembling white crystal which do not hinder the light, but which keep out the wind and the heat of the sun. Then proceeding on deliberately he asked in a more moderate tone, "What are you saying?" And when we began to connect our reply with what we had said before, he again ran on and went into another house, in which he had commanded some ancient and admirable pictures to be placed.

But when our pleadings on behalf of justice were thus broken up, and cut short, and interrupted, and crushed as one may almost say, we, being wearied and exhausted, and having no strength left in us, but being in continual expectation of nothing else than death, could no longer keep our hearts as they had been, but in our agony we proceeded to beg the one true God, praying him to check the wrath of this falsely called god. And he took compassion on us, and turned his mind to mercy. And he becoming pacified merely said, "These men do not appear to me to be wicked so much as unfortunate and foolish, in not believing that I have been endowed with the nature of God"; and so he dismissed us, and commanded us to depart.

Escaping then from what was rather a theater and a prison than a court of justice (for as in a theater, there was a great noise of people hissing, and groaning, and ridiculing us in an extravagant manner, and as in a prison, there were many blows inflicted on our bodies, and tortures, and things to agitate our whole souls by the blasphemies which those around us uttered toward God, and the threats which they breathed forth against ourselves, and which the emperor himself poured forth with such vehemence, being indignant with us not in behalf of any one else, for in that case he would soon have been appeased, but because of himself and his great desire to be declared a god, to which he considered the Jews to be the only people who did not agree, who were unable to subscribe to it), we at last recovered our breath, not because we loved living and cowered before death, since we would have cheerfully embraced death as immortality if our laws and customs could have been established by such means, but because we knew that we should be destroyed with great ignominy, without any desirable goal being attained by such means, for whatever insults ambassadors are subjected to are always applied to those who sent them.

It was owing to these considerations that we were able to hold up our heads for a while, but there were other circumstances which terrified us, and kept us in great perplexity and distress to hear what the emperor would decide, and what he would pronounce, and what kind of sentence he would ultimately deliver; for he heard the general tenor of our arguments, though he disdained to attend to some of our facts. Wasn't it a terrible thing for the interests of all the Jews throughout the whole world to be thrown into confusion by the treatment to which we, its five ambassadors, were exposed? For if he were to give us up to our enemies, what other city could enjoy tranquility? What city would there be in which the citizens would not attack the Jews living in it? What synagogue would be left uninjured? What state would not overturn every principle of justice in respect of those of their countrymen who arrayed themselves in opposition to the national laws and customs of the Jews? They will be overthrown, they will be shipwrecked, they will be sent to the bottom, with all the particular laws of the nation, and those too which are common to all and in accordance with the principles of justice recognized in every city.

We, then, being overwhelmed with affliction, troubled ourselves in our misery with such thoughts as these; for even those who up to this time had seemed to cooperate with us were now tired of taking our part. At least, then, when they were called on, they did not stay inside, but slunk away, fearfully, knowing well the desire that the emperor had to be looked upon as God.

We have now related in a concise and summary manner the cause of the hatred of Gaius to the whole nation of the Jews; we must now proceed to make our palinode . . .

(Philo, *Embassy to Gaius* 347-73, trans. Yonge)

The term *palinode* (*palinōdian*), or "reversal," indicates that Philo intended next to describe the reversal of fortunes—that is, the assassination of Gaius in 41 and the end of the threat he had posed to the temple and to the synagogues of Alexandria. Philo would presumably have attributed the denouement to God's justice (as he does at *Embassy* 107), thus proving the theme stated at the outset of the *Embassy*: "that the Deity exercises a providential foresight with regard to human affairs, and especially on behalf of a nation which addresses its supplications to him, which belongs especially to the father and sovereign of the universe, and the great cause of all things" (2). That narrative, however, is lost to us.

Philo made much the same argument elsewhere in describing the earlier removal and arrest of Flaccus, the Roman governor of Alexandria, as the public outworking of justice. (That argument might provide a conceptual parallel for Paul's understanding of the "righteousness" or "justice of God" in Rom 1:18-32.[18]) When Gaius had come to power, the Greek citizens of Alexandria had taken advantage of Flaccus's sudden

Fig. 4.10. *Herod's temple. Herod's thirty-year renovation of the Second Temple established it as one of the wonders of the Roman world—and him as one of Rome's most capable clients. Scale model at the Israel Museum, Jerusalem. Photo in the public domain.*

vulnerability. (The governor had been favored by Tiberius.) Some wealthier Jews had sued for rights as citizens of Alexandria (and thus exemption from poll taxes), but the Greeks whipped up anti-Jewish sentiment and pressured Flaccus to acquiesce as they attacked synagogues, forcibly relocated Jews into "the first known ghetto in the world," and beginning first by humiliating community elders publicly, then turning to torture and massacre, carried out "history's first pogrom."[19] It fell to Gaius's successor, Claudius, to quell the violence.

Trouble under Claudius

Upon the removal of Flaccus and then Gaius's death, Jews in Alexandria felt enough of a reprieve to try to rise up and defend themselves against their attackers. Claudius used force to put down the violence, then issued a decree warning "both sides" against resuming the conflict.

128. CLAUDIUS'S EDICT OF 41 C.E.

The decree comes down to us in two forms: first, on the left below, Josephus's account in *Antiquities* 19.5.2-3, the only witness available for centuries; on the right, a transcription of the decree discovered in 1912 (*P. London* lines 1-62, 73-109). Note a number of differences between the two versions: in the second, the emperor addresses the Greek delegation directly and accepts various honors from them (all left out of Josephus's account); different accounts of what is now granted to the Jews; fundamentally different postures taken toward the Jews; and Josephus's addition of a second, empire-wide decree generalizing the rights granted in Alexandria to Jews elsewhere.

Josephus's narrative preface to the decree	*The Roman governor's preface, P. London*
Now about this time there was a sedition between the Jews and the Greeks, at the city of Alexandria; for when Gaius was dead, the nation of the Jews, which had been very much mortified under the reign of Gaius, and reduced to very great distress by the people of Alexandria, recovered itself, and immediately took up their arms to fight for themselves. So Claudius sent an order to the prefect of Egypt to quiet that tumult; he also sent an edict, at the requests of king Agrippa and king Herod, both to Alexandria and to Syria, whose contents were as follows:	Lucius Aemilius Rectus declares: Since the whole city—because of its great population—was unable to attend the reading of the very holy and kind letter, I have considered it necessary to post the letter so that in reading it individually, you may be in awe of the magnificence of our God Caesar and be grateful for his kindness in regard to the city—in year 2 of Tiberius Claudius Caesar Augustus Germanicus the emperor, on the 14th of the month New Augustus.

"Tiberius Claudius Caesar Augustus Germanicus, with tribunician power, declares:

Tiberius Claudius Caesar Augustus Germanicus the Emperor, highest priest, with tribunician power, designated consul, to the city of Alexandria, greetings.

Your ambassadors Tiberius Claudius Barbillus, Artemidorus' son Apollonius, Leonidas' son Chaerēmon, Marcus Julius Asklēpiadēs, Gaius Julius Dionysius, Tiberius Claudius Phanias, Potamōn's son Pasiōn, Sabbiōn's son Dionysius, Tiberius Claudius Archibius, Ariston's son Apollōnius, Gaius Julius Apollōnius, and Apollōnius' son Hermaiscus, after handing over the proposal to me, related in a detailed way many things about the city, clarifying for me your favorable disposition toward us, which from long time past—you are favored here—was cherished by me, since you are naturally pious toward the Augustan rulers, which has become known to me by many circumstances, specifically how you have been earnestly concerned for my house, and you have been shown this concern by me as well, of which circumstances I might mention the last, passing over the others: the highest ranking witness is my brother Germanicus Caesar, who greeted you in rather familiar discourse.

Therefore I happily received the honors given me by you, even though I am not easily swayed in such matters. And first, I grant you permission to observe my birthday as an Augustan holiday in the way you yourselves have initiated, and I consent to the installation of images of me and my kin in each of the places mentioned. For I see that you are ready to dedicate all the records of your devotion toward my house. Regarding the two golden images, the one which is the Claudian Pax Augustus, which my illustrious Barbillus proposed and persisted, though I was refusing because it seemed too offensive, shall be set up in Rome, and the other in the manner you thought best shall go in procession among you on specially named days and a throne shall process along with it, decorated in its appearance as you wish.

It would be inappropriate—while agreeing to these—to deny the establishment of a Claudian clan and sacred grove according to the custom of Egypt, so I permit these for you also, and if you wish you may set up the horse-borne images from my procurator, Vitrasius Pollio. With regard to setting up the four-horse chariot images that you want to place for me around the entry points of the land, I grant this for the place called Taposiris in Libya, for Pharos in Alexandria, and a third for Pelusium in Egypt. I decline a high priest and the construction of temples for me, not wanting to be offensive on my account to people, and considering that temples and such things have been assigned as appropriate only for the gods in every age.

About the petitions you have been eager to receive from me—let them come about in this way: I affirm for all who have been ephebes up until my imperial rule that they may keep the citizenship of the Alexandrians, with all the city's special allowances and benefits, except those who, skirting your policies have sought to become ephebes though being born of slave-women; and I wish that all other provisions given by procurators and kings and prefects before me be confirmed, as even the divine Augustus affirmed. I want the leaders of the temple of the divine Augustus that is in Alexandria to be selected randomly as in the temple of the same divine Augustus in Canopus they are selected randomly. . . .

[*Several omitted lines concern three-year terms of office for city officials and the emperor's decision to make further inquiries regarding the Alexandrians' request for a city senate.*]

As for the matter regarding the Jews, the disorder and rebellion, or rather if one must speak the truth—the war, whichever side people decide may have prompted it, though in the conflict many of our ambassadors strove honorably, especially Theon's son Dionysius, I still did not want to make a detailed inquiry, though treasuring irrevocable anger within myself toward those who began to fight.

Let me say plainly that unless you terminate the destruction, this stubborn anger toward one another, I shall be pressed to show how a beneficent ruler is changed to show righteous anger.

Since I am assured that the Jews of Alexandria, called Alexandrians, have been joint inhabitants in the earliest times with the Alexandrians, and have obtained from their kings equal privileges with them, as is evident by the public records that are in their possession, and the edicts themselves; and that after Alexandria had been subjected to our empire by Augustus, their just rights have been preserved by those prefects who have at various times been sent there; and that no dispute had been raised about those just rights, even when Aquila was governor of Alexandria; and that when the Jewish ethnarch was dead, Augustus did not prohibit the appointment of ethnarchs, since he wanted people to be subject [to Rome] while continuing in the observance of their own customs, and not be forced to

Therefore now I solemnly charge the Alexandrians that they gently and generously bear with the Jews who have been living a long time in the same city and that they do nothing in sacrilege of what has been legislated for them regarding divine worship, but rather let them be according to the accustomed practices allowed them even in the reign of the divine Augustus, which practices I also confirm, after listening to both sides.

And I expressly charge the Jews that they lobby for nothing more than what they formerly had, and in time to come that they not send out a second ambassadorial delegation as if they lived in a second city, which is completely without precedent, nor that they intrude into the games overseen by the public sports officials or city managers, while enjoying transgress the ancient rules of their ancestral religion; but that, in the time of Gaius, the Alexandrians became insolent towards the Jews that were among them, and that this Gaius, out of his great madness and lack of understanding, reduced the nation of the Jews very low, because they would not transgress the religious worship of their country, and call him a god:

I wish therefore that none of the just rights of the Jewish people be removed on account of the madness of Gaius; but that those just rights that they formerly enjoyed be preserved to them, and that they may continue in their own customs.

And I charge both parties to take very great care that no troubles may arise after the posting of this edict."

residents' provisions, savoring also the abundance of generous benefits in a foreign city; and that they neither bring in nor approach Jews sailing in from Syria or Egypt, for which I shall be forced to regard them with greater suspicions, if not even marshalling all resources against them as those who stir up the common cancer that extends through the world.

If, while both sides refrain from these past habits, you choose to live with humility and a humane attitude toward one another, then I will hold the city in the highest regard as though linked to us by ancestral kinship. I attest to my friend Barbillus that he has ever displayed a concern for you before me, and who now with all eagerness has acted regarding the conflict on your behalf, also to my friend Tiberius Claudius Archibius.

Farewell.

(trans. Reasoner)

So the edict to Alexandria on behalf of the Jews was written in this manner. But the one that he had for the rest of the world was as follows:

"Tiberius Claudius Caesar Augustus Germanicus, highest priest, with tribunician power, elected consul the second time, declares: Since Kings Agrippa and Herod, dearest friends of mine, have asked that I should grant that the same just rights should be preserved for the Jews who are in all the Roman empire, as they were even granted for those of Alexandria, I most gladly agree; and this grant I make not only for the sake of the petitioners, but considering those for whom I have been petitioned worthy of such a favor on account of their fidelity and friendship to the Romans. I think it also very just that no Grecian city should be deprived of these just rights, since they were preserved to them under the great Augustus. It will therefore be good to permit the Jews, who are in all the world under us, to keep their ancestral customs without obstruction. And I do charge them also to use this my kindness to them with moderation, and not to disdain the religious scruples of other nations, but to keep their own laws. This decree of mine I will that rulers of cities and colonies and municipalities—both those within Italy and those outside it— kings and others holding power through their own ambassadors have inscribed to have it displayed for not less than thirty days, in a place where it may easily be read from the ground."

(trans. Whiston, modified)

129. The Expulsion of Jews from Rome under Claudius (Suetonius)

An episode during the reign of Claudius is widely considered an important aspect of the historical situation of Romans. Acts declares that in Corinth, Paul met two Jews who had come from Italy "because Claudius had ordered all Jews to leave Rome" (18:2). There are other reports of the incident. Dio Cassius writes that the Jews "had again increased so greatly that by reason of their multitude it would have been hard without raising a tumult to bar them from the city," and so Claudius "did not drive them out, but ordered them, while continuing their traditional mode of life, not to hold meetings" (*History* 60.6.6); the account is different enough to cause scholars to question whether it refers to the same incident.[20]

A third, tantalizingly brief reference in Suetonius (*Claudius* 25.4) has attracted attention because interpreters have tried to glean from it some insight into the character of Judaism in Rome. In Latin, it reads:

Iudaeos impulsore Chresto assidue tumultuantes Roma expulit.

One widely accepted translation (Rolfe, LCL) runs:

Since the Jews constantly made disturbances at the instigation of Chrestus, he [Claudius] expelled them from Rome.

On this translation, it seems that Claudius's action was a response to Jewish unrest. Many scholars take "Chrestus" to be Suetonius's confused reference to "Christus," meaning *Jesus* Christ, and further suppose that Suetonius has mistaken Jewish agitation against the preaching of Jesus Christ for agitation *by* someone named Christ. (Suetonius elsewhere mentions Christians very briefly as a "recent" superstition: *Nero* 16.) Another possible translation has been proposed, however, by H. Dixon Slingerland:[21]

> Chrestus caused Claudius to expel the continuously rebelling Jews.

Here "Chrestus" refers not to Christ but to an otherwise unknown Roman advisor to the emperor. (Chrestus was a common enough name, and Slingerland names possible candidates for the reference here.) Chrestus's agitation is directed toward *Claudius*, not the Jews; and, Slingerland argues, their characterization as "continuously rebelling" is simply a generalization, not a reference to a specific episode of unrest in 49 C.E. Note that on Slingerland's view, Christianity is not an element of the narrative.

130. "Perverse and disgusting" rites (Tacitus)

We mentioned above the assertion in some ancient authors that Jews had been expelled from Rome because of their aggressive proselytizing activity. These allegations have often been taken at face value, but scholars have also wondered whether they express only Roman anxiety about *any* "defections" to a foreign religion, no matter how few.

In his *History*, as he is about to narrate the Roman siege and destruction of Jerusalem in 70 C.E., Tacitus pauses to discuss at some length the origin of the Jews and their "impious rites." More scornful than curious, he passes along a number of malicious and uninformed slanders that were (as Philo and Josephus show) nevertheless standard fare among such anti-Jewish figures as Apion, Chaemeron, and Manetho. He reports that some identify the Jews, *Iudaei*, with the Idaei of Crete:

> Others assert that in the reign of Isis the overflowing population of Egypt, led by Hierosolymus and Judas, discharged itself into the neighboring countries. Many, again, say that they were a race of Ethiopian origin, who in the time of king Cepheus were driven by fear and hatred of their neighbors to seek a new dwelling-place. Others describe them as an Assyrian horde who, not having sufficient territory, took possession of part of Egypt, and founded cities of their own in what is called the Hebrew country, lying on the borders of Syria. Others, again, assign a very distinguished origin to the Jews, alleging that they were the Solymi, a nation celebrated in the poems of Homer, who called the city which they founded Hierosolyma after their own name.
>
> Most writers, however, agree in stating that once a disease, which horribly disfigured the body, broke out over Egypt; that king Bocchoris, seeking a remedy, consulted the oracle of Hammon, and was bidden to cleanse his realm, and to convey into some foreign land this race detested by the gods. The people, who had been collected after diligent search, finding themselves left in a desert, sat for the most part in a stupor of grief, till one of the exiles, Moyses by name, warned them not to look for any relief from God or man, forsaken as they were of both, but to trust to themselves, taking for their heaven-sent leader that man

who should first help them to be quit of their present misery. They agreed, and in utter ignorance began to advance at random.

Nothing, however, distressed them so much as the scarcity of water, and they had sunk ready to perish in all directions over the plain, when a herd of wild asses was seen to retire from their pasture to a rock shaded by trees. Moyses followed them, and, guided by the appearance of a grassy spot, discovered an abundant spring of water. This furnished relief. After a continuous journey for six days, on the seventh they possessed themselves of a country, from which they expelled the inhabitants, and in which they founded a city and a temple.

Describing their temple, Tacitus accuses the Jews of having worshiped the image of a donkey—a common claim that may have depended on a (very) confused reading of Gen 36:24.[22]

Moyses, wishing to secure for the future his authority over the nation, gave them a novel form of worship, opposed to all that is practiced by others. Things sacred with us, with them have no sanctity, while they allow what with us is forbidden. In their holy place they have consecrated an image of the animal by whose guidance they found deliverance from their long and thirsty wanderings. They slay the ram, seemingly in derision of Hammon, and they sacrifice the ox, because the Egyptians worship it as Apis. They abstain from swine's flesh, in consideration of what they suffered when they were infected by the leprosy to which this animal is liable. By their frequent fasts they still bear witness to the long hunger of former days, and the Jewish bread, made without leaven, is retained as a memorial of their hurried seizure of corn.

We are told that the rest of the seventh day was adopted, because this day brought with it a termination of their toils; after a while the charm of indolence beguiled them into giving up the seventh year also to inaction. But others say that it is an observance in honor of Saturn, either from the primitive elements of their faith having been transmitted from the Idaei, who are said to have shared the flight of that God, and to have founded the race, or from the circumstance that of the seven stars which rule the destinies of men Saturn moves in the highest orbit and with the mightiest power, and that many of the heavenly bodies complete their revolutions and courses in multiples of seven.

In what may be a garbled reference to Exod 3:22, Tacitus expresses resentment of the Jewish collection of funds from "the most degraded out of other races"; as we have seen, local magistrates often opposed Jews sending contributions out of their country to Jerusalem. Tacitus also resents the fact that Jews ate apart and avoided marriage with non-Jews. Note in what follows Tacitus's disdain for those who convert to Judaism.

This worship, however introduced, is upheld by its antiquity; all their other customs, which are at once perverse and disgusting, owe their strength to their very badness. The most degraded out of other races, scorning their national beliefs, brought to them their contributions and presents [compare Exod 3:22]. This augmented the wealth of the Jews, as also did the fact, that among themselves they are inflexibly honest and ever ready to show compassion, though

Fig. 4.11. *The empress Poppaea Sabina (30–65 c.e.), Nero's second wife, is described by Roman historians as murderously ambitious; in contrast, Josephus describes her as a "God-fearer" sympathetic to Judaism (Ant. 20.195). Archaeological Museum of Olympia. Photo in the public domain.*

they regard the rest of mankind with all the hatred of enemies. They sit apart at meals, they sleep apart, and though, as a nation, they are singularly prone to lust, they abstain from intercourse with foreign women; among themselves [however] nothing is unlawful.

Circumcision was adopted by them as a mark of difference from other men. Those who come over to their religion adopt the practice, and have this lesson first instilled into them, to despise all gods, to disown their country, and set at naught parents, children, and siblings.

Still they provide for the increase of their numbers. It is a crime among them to kill any newly-born infant. They hold that the souls of all who perish in battle or by the hands of the executioner are immortal. Hence a passion for propagating their race and a contempt for death. They are wont to bury rather than to burn their dead, following in this the Egyptian custom; they bestow the same care on the dead, and they hold the same belief about the lower world. Quite different is their faith about things divine. The Egyptians worship many animals and images of monstrous form; the Jews have purely mental conceptions of Deity, as one in essence. They call those profane who make representations of God in human shape out of perishable materials. They believe that Being to be supreme and eternal, neither capable of representation, nor of decay. They therefore do not allow any images to stand in their cities, much less in their temples. This flattery is not paid to their kings, nor this honor to our Emperors. From the fact, however, that their priests used to chant to the music of flutes and cymbals, and to wear garlands of ivy, and that a golden vine was found in the temple, some have thought that they worshipped father Liber, the conqueror of the East, though their institutions do not by any means harmonize with the theory; for Liber established a festive and cheerful worship, while the Jewish religion is tasteless and mean.

(Tacitus, *History* 5.2-5, trans. Church and Brodribb)

131. The danger of conversion to Judaism (Juvenal)

Juvenal (c. 60–130 c.e.) bemoaned the progression, over generations, from flirtation with Judaism to full-scale commitment, showing the anxiety Romans could feel over rites that seemed to "flout the laws of Rome."

Some who have had a father who reveres the Sabbath worship nothing but the clouds and the divinity of the heavens and see no difference between eating swine's flesh, from which their father has abstained, and that of man; and in time they take to circumcision. Having been wont to flout the laws of Rome, they learn and practice and revere the Jewish law, and all that Moses handed down in his secret tome, forbidding to point out the way to any not worshipping the same rites, and conducting none but the circumcised to the desired fountain. For all which the father was to blame, who gave up every seventh day to idleness, keeping it apart from all the concerns of life.

(Juvenal, *Satires* 14.96-107, trans. Braund, LCL)

132. The offense of Jewish beggars (Juvenal)

Though exaggerated in its rudeness, another of Juvenal's *Satires* may indicate the poor estate of many Jews (and other foreign residents) in Rome in the early second century. Juvenal tells of a poor elderly friend leaving Rome because he no longer feels safe in the city. He and his friend stop at the Porta Capena:

Here Numa held his nightly assignations with his mistress; but now the holy fount and grove and shrine are let out to Jews, who possess a basket and a truss of hay for all their furnishings.

The elderly friend complains of the threat of being bullied by a thug who takes him, in his poverty, for a Jew.

The fellow stands up against me, and bids me halt; obey I must. What else can you do when attacked by a madman stronger than yourself? "Where are you from?" shouts he; "whose vinegar, whose beans have blown you out? With what cobbler have you been munching cut leeks and boiled wether's chaps? What, sir, no answer? Speak out, or take that upon your shins! Say, where is your stand? In what prayer-shop [*proseuchē*] shall I find you?" Whether you venture to say anything, or make off silently, it's all one: he will thrash you just the same, and then, in a rage, take bail from you. Such is the liberty of the poor man: having been pounded and cuffed into a jelly, he begs and prays to be allowed to return home with a few teeth in his head!

(Juvenal, Satires 3.290-301, trans. Ramsay)

Under Nero, War

As we saw in chapter 1, Paul was put to death in Rome under Nero, probably in 64 C.E. The emperor who (as we saw in chapter 3) boasted of having no need for the sword wielded the sword against Paul and, within but a few years, launched a war to put down rebellion in Judea (66–70 C.E.). In his *Jewish War* and *Jewish Antiquities*, which remain our best historical sources for this period, Josephus sought to blame the war on a marginal group of self-interested Jews who put themselves outside the three legitimate "schools" of Judaism—Pharisees, Sadducees, and Essenes. Although he also narrates a dreary tale of Roman oppression and provocation, it is to a "fourth philosophy," which he dates from an abortive uprising just after the death of Herod the Great, that Josephus attributes "the destruction of the congregation of the people."

Fig. 4.12. *A sestersius issued by Emperor Vespasian, earlier the general who had laid siege to Jerusalem, represents conquered Judeans, a male with his hands bound and a mourning woman beneath a palm tree. The caption on the obverse reads "Judea defeated; by order of the Senate." RIC 2:426.*

133. The "fourth philosophy" (Josephus)

Because these events transpired after Paul's death, we will not linger over their interpretation. But because Paul's political views are regularly set in contrast to the so-called Zealot option of the fourth philosophy and because that comparison has been contested as too simplistic, Josephus's account of the fourth philosophy's origin in a revolt against Roman taxation deserves attention.[23]

> Yet was there one Judas, a Gaulonite, of a city whose name was Gamala, who, taking with him Saddok, a Pharisee, became zealous to draw them to a revolt, who both said that this taxation was no better than an introduction to slavery, and exhorted the nation to assert their liberty; as if they could procure them happiness and security for what they possessed, and an assured enjoyment of a still greater good, which was that of the honor and glory they would thereby acquire for magnanimity. They also said that God would not otherwise be assisting to them, than upon their joining with one another in such councils as might be successful, and for their own advantage; and this especially, if they would set about great exploits, and not grow weary in executing the same; so men received what they said with pleasure, and this bold attempt proceeded to a great height.
>
> All sorts of misfortunes also sprang from these men, and the nation was infected with this doctrine to an incredible degree; one violent war came upon us after another, and we lost our friends which used to alleviate our pains; there were also very great robberies and murder of our principal men. This was done in pretense indeed for the public welfare, but in reality for the hopes of gain to themselves; whence arose seditions, and from them murders of men, which sometimes fell on those of their own people (by the madness of these men towards one another, while their desire was that none of the adverse party might be left,) and sometimes on their enemies; a famine also coming upon us, reduced us to the last degree of despair, as did also the taking and demolishing of cities; nay, the sedition at last increased so high, that the very temple of God was burnt down by their enemies' fire. Such were the consequences of this, that the customs of our fathers were altered, and such a change was made, as added a mighty weight toward bringing all to destruction, which these men occasioned by their thus conspiring together; for Judas and Saddok, who excited a fourth philosophic sect among us, and had a great many followers therein, filled our civil government with tumults at present, and laid the foundations of our future miseries, by this system of philosophy, which we were before unacquainted withal. Concerning it I will discourse a little, and this the rather because the infection which spread thence among the younger sort, who were zealous for it, brought the public to destruction.
>
> The Jews had for a great while had three sects of philosophy peculiar to themselves; the sect of the Essenes, and the sect of the Sadducees, and the third sort of opinions was that of those called Pharisees; of which sects, although I have already spoken in the second book of the *Jewish War*, yet will I a little touch upon them now. . . .

Josephus describes each of the three "appropriate" schools or sects (*haireseis*) of Judaism. Note how he characterizes views that he declares are incompatible with genuine Judaism.

> But of the fourth sect of Jewish philosophy, Judas the Galilean was the author. These men agree in all other things with the Pharisaic notions; but they have an inviolable attachment to liberty, and say that God is to be their only Ruler and Lord. They also do not value dying any kinds of death, nor indeed do they heed the deaths of their relations and friends, nor can any such fear make them call any man lord. And since this immovable resolution of theirs is well known to a great many, I shall speak no further about that matter; nor am I afraid that any thing I have said of them should be disbelieved, but rather fear, that what I have said is beneath the resolution they show when they undergo pain. And it was in Gessius Florus's time that the nation began to grow mad with this distemper, who was our procurator, and who occasioned the Jews to go wild with it by the abuse of his authority, and to make them revolt from the Romans.
>
> (Josephus, *Antiquities* 18.1.1-2, 6 [§§4-11, 23-25], trans. Whiston)

Jewish Attitudes to Roman Rule

Josephus's account of four "schools" or "sects" of Jewish "philosophy" (no. 133 above) is artificial. We should nevertheless recognize a range of attitudes to Roman rule among Jews in the century or more leading up to the war of 66–70, attitudes ranging from enthusiasm for the rise of Augustus to profound resentment of the Romans as a plague upon the earth.

134. Augustus the "guardian of peace" (Philo)

One of the most remarkable expressions of praise of Augustus's virtues is offered by Philo of Alexandria in the course of his *Embassy to Gaius*. The passage is remarkable not because of Philo's appreciation of Augustus's achievements—in that he shared the perception of very many inhabitants of the empire—but because his argument brings him so close to an endorsement of ritual honors for the emperor, which would be tantamount to idolatry. The context is of course all-important: Philo is condemning the actions of Alexandrians who invaded synagogues and set up statues of the emperor Gaius (Caligula) inside them. His argument is that these were viciously anti-Jewish attacks, not gestures of genuine reverence for the emperor; for after all, the Alexandrians had never shown such enthusiasm for Augustus, who was so much more worthy of it.

Note not only the extravagance of Philo's rhetoric ("the whole human race," he declares, "was on the verge of utter destruction" until Augustus appeared) but also his careful avoidance of attributing any responsibility for the civil war to Augustus or Antony themselves. Instead "islands" and "continents" warred against each other until Augustus arose.

Again, consider him who in all the virtues transcended human nature, who on account of the vastness of his imperial sovereignty as well as nobility of character was the first to bear the name of the August or Venerable, a title received not through lineal succession as a portion of its heritage but because he himself became the source of the veneration which was received also by those who followed him; who from the moment that he had charge of the common weal took in hand the troubled and chaotic condition of affairs.

For islands were engaged with continents in fierce rivalry for primacy, and continents with islands, all having for their leaders and champions those of the Romans in great positions who stood foremost in repute. And again the great regions which divide the habitable world, Europe and Asia, were contending with each other for sovereign power with the nations of both brought up from the uttermost parts of the earth waging grievous war all over sea and land, battling on either element, so that the whole human race exhausted by mutual slaughter was on the verge of utter destruction, had it not been for one man and leader Augustus whom men fitly call the averter of evil.

This is the Caesar who calmed the torrential storms on every side, who healed the pestilences common to Greeks and barbarians . . . this is he who not only loosed but broke the chains which had shackled and pressed so hard on the habitable world. This is he who exterminated wars both of the open kind and the covert which are brought about by the raids of brigands. This is he who cleared the sea of pirate ships and filled it with merchant vessels. This is he who reclaimed every state to liberty, who led disorder into order and brought gentle manners and harmony to all unsociable and brutish nations, who enlarged Hellas by many a new Hellas and Hellenized the outside world in its most important regions, the guardian of the peace, who dispensed their dues to each and all, who did not hoard his favors but gave them to be common property, who kept nothing good and excellent hidden throughout his life.

This great benefactor they ignored during the forty-three years in which he was sovereign of Egypt, and set up nothing in our meeting-houses in his honor, neither image, nor bust, nor painting. And yet if it was right to decree new and exceptional honors to anyone, he was the proper person to receive them.

He was what we may call the source and fountain-head of the Augustan stock in general. He was also the first and the greatest and the common benefactor in that he displaced the rule of many and committed the ship of the commonwealth to be steered by a single pilot, that is himself, a marvelous master of the science of government. For there is justice in the saying, "It is not well that many lords should rule," since multiplicity of suffrages produces multiform evils. But besides all these, the whole habitable world voted him no less than celestial honors. These are so well attested by temples, gateways, vestibules, porticoes, that every city which contains magnificent works new and old is surpassed in these by the beauty and magnitude of those appropriated to Caesar, and particularly in our own Alexandria.

(Philo, *Embassy to Gaius* 143-50, trans. Colson, LCL)

135. Mixed opinion regarding Rome (Babylonian Talmud)

"What have the Romans ever done for us?" The question receives humorously mixed answers in *Monty Python's Life of Brian*. Such mixed assessments of Rome's accomplishments were present from the beginning, however. The following anecdote comes from the Babylonian Talmud, compiled in the sixth century c.e.[24]

> R. Judah, R. Jose, and R. Simeon were sitting, and Judah, a son of proselytes, was sitting near them. R. Judah commenced [the discussion] by observing, "How fine are the works of this [Roman] people! They have made streets, they have built bridges, they have erected baths." R. Jose was silent. R. Simeon b. Yohai answered and said, "All that they made they made for themselves; they built market-places to set harlots in them; baths to rejuvenate themselves; bridges to levy tolls for them." Now, Judah the son of proselytes went and related their talk, which reached the government. They decreed: "Judah, who exalted [us], shall be exalted; Jose, who was silent, shall be exiled to Sepphoris; Simeon, who censured, let him be executed."
>
> (*b. Shabbat* 33b, trans. Freedman)

Fig. 4.13. *Relief carved on the Arch of Titus, Rome (erected after 81 c.e.). This depiction shows Roman soldiers carrying the golden lamp stand and other sacred objects looted from the temple and leading captive Jews in a triumphal procession. Ordinarily Rome was careful not to offend conquered peoples and preserved their sacred shrines intact. But because Vespasian and his son Titus (who sacked Jerusalem and succeeded his father as emperor) could not claim the dynastic heritage of the Julio-Claudian house, they played up the thorough destruction of an "impious" nation in their iconography.[25] Photo in the public domain.*

Disguised Defiance

In chapter 3 we saw expressions of open defiance of Rome on the part of the British rebels Boudicca and Calgacus. Unfortunately, the literary sources to which we are most accustomed were far less interested in passing along messages of Judean defiance. Josephus, for example, allowed King Agrippa to acknowledge to the rebels of Jerusalem that "there are many who wax eloquent on the insolence of the procurators and pronounce pompous panegyrics on liberty," but Josephus wrote nothing more about them, devoting his creative energy instead to a long speech in which Agrippa warned his fellow Jews that Roman rule was inevitable, preferable to war, and God-willed (*War* 2.348-404).

When we do hear notes of Judean defiance, they are most often camouflaged. They may be disguised as edifying biblical paraphrase, as when the *Liber antiquitatum biblicarum* (first century c.e.) discovered examples of militant noncooperation in the patriarchal narratives of Genesis,[26] or as the elegant philosophical treatise on reason's superiority to the emotions that we know as 4 Maccabees, which announces at last that for his crimes, "divine justice pursued *and will pursue* the accursed tyrant"—for the knowing reader, we may presume, a *Roman* tyrant (18:22). We sample here other oblique Judean outcries against Rome.

136. Doom to befall the Roman Empire (*Sibylline Oracles*)

The first Sibyl may have been an ecstatic prophet in archaic Greece; by the second century b.c.e., the Roman Senate consulted the dread "Sibylline books" to divine the future at moments of great peril, but these were lost in a fire in 83 b.c.e. The fourteen books of the *Sibylline Oracles* were collected in the fifth century c.e. They have in common a Greek poetic form, but the third book includes unmistakably Jewish oracles pertaining to the age of Cleopatra and Augustus and, later, to the destruction of the Jerusalem temple at the hands of the Romans. This nineteenth-century translation seeks to capture the rhythm of the original.

> But when Rome shall o'er Egypt also rule
>   Governing always, then shall there appear
> The greatest kingdom of the immortal King
>   Over men. And a holy Lord shall come
> To hold the scepter over every land
>   Unto all ages of fast-hastening time.
> And then shall come inexorable wrath
>   On Latin men; three shall by piteous fate
> Endamage Rome. And perish shall all men,
>   With their own houses, when from heaven shall flow
> A fiery cataract. . . .
> Alas for you, O Libya, and alas,
>   Both sea and land! O daughters of the west,
> So shall you come unto a bitter day.
>   And you shall come pursued by grievous strife,
> Dreadful and grievous; there shall be again

> A dreadful judgment, and you all shall come
> By force unto destruction, for you tore
>> In pieces the great house of the Immortal,
> And with iron teeth you chewed it dreadfully.
>> Therefore shall you then look upon thy land
> Full of the dead, some of them fallen by war
>> And by the demon of all violence,
> Famine and plague, and some by barbarous foes.
>> And all your land shall be a wilderness,
> And desolations shall your cities be.
>> > > (*Sibylline Oracles* 3.55-65, 398-410, trans. Terry)

137. POMPEY "THE SINNER" (PSALMS OF SOLOMON)

The *Psalms of Solomon*, composed in the first century B.C.E., refer, but only obliquely, to Pompey's invasion of Judea and desecration of the temple in 63 B.C.E. The second of these *Psalms* has the form of a lament offered to God.

> Arrogantly the sinner broke down the strong walls with a battering ram and you did not interfere.
> Gentile foreigners went up to your place of sacrifice; they arrogantly trampled it with their sandals.
> Because the sons of Jerusalem defiled the sanctuary of the Lord—they were profaning the offerings of God with lawless acts;
> Because of these things (God) said, "Remove them far from me; they are not sweet-smelling."
> The beauty of his glory was despised before God; it was completely disgraced.
> The sons and the daughters [were] in harsh captivity,
>> Their neck in a seal, a spectacle among the gentiles.
> He did [this] to them according to their sins,
>> So that he abandoned them to the hands of those who prevailed.
> For he turned away his face from their mercy,
>> (from) young and old and their children once again,
>> For they sinned once again by not listening.
> And the heavens were weighed down,
>> and the earth despised them,
>> for no one on (the earth) had done what they did.
> And the earth shall know all your righteous judgments, O God.
>> > > (*Psalms of Solomon* 2, trans. Collins)

138. THE ROMANS AS PLUNDERERS OF THE EARTH (1QpHab)

Dated by radiocarbon analysis to between 120 and 5 B.C.E., the so-called *Habakkuk Pesher* from Cave 1 at Qumran (1QpHab) offers important but cryptic clues to the beginning of a community of pious men who followed a "Teacher of Righteousness" in opposition to a "Wicked Priest," presumably a high priest in Jerusalem. The text is of extraordinary importance for the history of the community(ies?) behind the Dead Sea Scrolls and provides a point of comparison for Paul's interpretation of scripture

Fig. 4.14. *The Jew Mordecai triumphs over his people's enemies. Fresco from the synagogue at Dura-Europos, third century C.E. Photo: Erich Lessing/Art Resource, New York.*

as written "for our sake" (Rom 4:23; 1 Cor 9:10; 10:6). Our present interest is in the *Pesher's* view of the Romans, whom we may identify through the text's coded reference to the Kittim's worship of their military standards and siege techniques.

This passage and the next (from *4 Ezra*) may be contrasted with the imperial view of Roman "peace" and "friendship" in chapter 3. Also compare the language, in the eighth paragraph, of the observers of the law "expiating" the guilt of their people through their suffering, with the language of 4 Maccabees (see no. 81 in chapter 2). Geza Vermes translates the Hebrew phrase *y'šhmw kl rš'y 'mw*, as "all the wicked of his people shall expiate their guilt" (reading *y'šhmw* as "they shall expiate"); other translators render the phrase, "all the evildoers of his people will be pronounced guilty for the reproof of those who kept his commandments" (Florentino García Martínez), or, "it is at their rebuke [that of the Gentiles? the chosen?] that all the wicked of His people shall be condemned" (Michael Wise, Martin Abegg, and Edward Cook).[27]

In the extract that follows, quotations from the book of Habakkuk are set in italics. The phrase "interpreted, this concerns . . ." translates the Hebrew *pešer* or *pišro*, literally "the meaning of it [is] . . ."

> "*For behold, I rouse the Chaldeans, that [bitter and hasty] nation*" [Hab 1:6a]. Interpreted, this concerns the Kittim [who are] quick and valiant in war, causing many to perish. [All the world shall fall] under the dominion of the Kittim, and the [wicked . . .] they shall not believe in the laws of [God . . .]
>
> ["*Who march through the breadth of the earth to take possession of dwellings which are not their own,*" Hab 1:6b.] . . . They shall march across the plain,

smiting and plundering the cities of the earth. For it is as He said, *"To take possession of dwellings which are not their own."*

"They are fearsome and terrible; their justice and grandeur proceed from themselves" [Hab 1:7]. Interpreted, this concerns the Kittim who inspire all the nations with fear [and dread]. All their evil plotting is done with intention and they deal with all the nations in cunning and guile.

"Their horses are swifter than leopards and fleeter than evening wolves. Their horses step forward proudly and spread their wings; they fly from afar like an eagle avid to devour. All of them come for violence; the look on their faces is like the east wind" [Hab 1:8-9a]. [Interpreted, this] concerns the Kittim who trample the earth with their horses and beasts. They come "from afar," from the islands of the sea, to devour all the peoples "like an eagle" which cannot be satisfied, and they address [all the peoples] with anger and [wrath and fury] and indignation. For it is as He said, *"The look on their faces is like the east wind."*

"They scoff [at kings,] and princes are their laughing-stock" [Hab 1:10a]. Interpreted, this means that they mock the great and despise the venerable; they ridicule kings and princes and scoff at the mighty host.

"They laugh at every fortress; they pile up earth and take it" [Hab 1:10b]. Interpreted, this concerns the commanders of the Kittim who despise the fortresses of the peoples and laugh at them in derision. To capture them, they encircle them with a mighty host, and out of fear and terror they deliver themselves into their hands. They desroy them because of the sins of their inhabitants.

"The wind then sweeps on and passes; and they make of their strength their god" [Hab 1:11]. Interpreted, [this concerns] the commanders of the Kittim who, on the counsel of [the] House of Guilt, pass one in front of the other; one after another [their] commanders come to lay waste the earth. [*"And they make of their strength their god"*:] interpreted, this concerns [. . . all] the peoples . . .

[*"Art thou not from everlasting, O Lord, my God, my Holy One? We shall not die.]* *Thou hast ordained them,* [O Lord,] *for judgment; Thou hast established them, O Rock, for chastisement. Their eyes are too pure to behold evil; and Thou canst not look on distress"* [Hab 1:12-13a]. Interpreted, this saying means that God will not destroy His people by the hands of the nations; God will execute the judgment of the nations by the hand of His elect. And through their chastisement all the wicked of His people shall expiate their guilt who keep His commandments in their distress. For it is as He said, *"Too pure of eyes to behold evil"*: interpreted, this means that they have not lusted after their eyes during the age of wickedness. . . .

"Thou dealest with men like the fish of the sea, like creeping things, to rule over them. They draw [them all up with a fish-hook], and drag them out with their net, and gather them in [their seine. Therefore they sacrifice] to their net. Therefore they rejoice [and exult and burn incense to their seine; for by them] their portion is fat [and their sustenance rich," Hab 1:14-16.] . . . the Kittim. And they shall gather in their riches, together with all their booty, *"like the fish of the sea."* And as for that which He said, *"Therefore they sacrifice to their net and burn incense to their seine"*: interpreted, this means that they sacrifice to their standards and worship their weapons of war. *"For by them their portion is fat and their sustenance rich"*: interpreted, this means that they divide their yoke and their tribute—"their sustenance"—over all the peoples year by year, ravaging many lands.

"Therefore their sword is ever drawn to massacre nations mercilessly" [Hab 1:17]. Interpreted, this concerns the Kittim who cause many to perish by the sword—youths, grown men, the aged, women, and children—and who even take no pity on the fruit of the womb.

"Of what use is an idol that its maker should shape it, a molten image, a fatling of lies? For the craftsman puts his trust in his own creation when he makes dumb idols" [Hab 2:18]. Interpreted, this saying concerns all the idols of the nations which they make so that they may serve and worship them. But they shall not deliver them on the Day of Judgment.

"Woe [to him who says] to wood, 'Awake,' and to dumb [stone, 'Arise!' Can such a thing give guidance? Behold, it is covered with gold and silver but there is no spirit within it. But the Lord is in His holy Temple]: let all the earth be silent before him!" [Hab 3:19-20]. Interpreted, this concerns all the nations which serve stone and wood. But on the Day of Judgment, God will destroy from the earth all idolatrous and wicked men.

(1QpHab 2.10—5.7; 5.12—6.12; 11.10—13.4, trans. Vermes)

139. A VISION OF THE END OF THE ROMAN EMPIRE (4 EZRA)

Another disguised indictment of the brutality of Roman conquest comes from a later period, several decades after the Roman war on Judea (66–70 c.e.). Here, in a vision given to the prophet Ezra, a great lion (symbolizing Judah) addresses a mighty eagle (symbolizing the Roman Empire).

Listen and I will speak to you. The Most High says to you, "Are you not the one that remains of the four beasts that I had made to reign in my world, so that the end of my times might come through them? You, the fourth that has come, have conquered all the beasts that have gone before; and you have held sway over the world with great terror, and over all the earth with grievous oppression; and for so long you have lived on the earth with deceit. You have judged the earth, but not with truth, for you have oppressed the meek and injured the peaceable; you have hated those who tell the truth, and have loved liars; you have destroyed the homes of those who brought forth fruit, and have laid low the walls of those who did you no harm. Your insolence has come up before the Most High, and your pride to the Mighty One. The Most High has looked at his times; now they have ended, and his ages have reached completion. Therefore you, eagle, will surely disappear, you and your terrifying wings, your most evil little wings, your malicious heads, your most evil talons, and your whole worthless body, so that the whole earth, freed from your violence, may be refreshed and relieved, and may hope for the judgment and mercy of him who made it."

(4 Ezra 11:38-46 NRSV)

140. THE IMPORTANCE OF "CAUTION" (PHILO)

We must take into account more than a simple variety of Jewish attitudes toward Roman rule. In his treatise *On Dreams*, Philo gives a fascinating glimpse into the pressures that inequalities in political power exert on speech. Philo regards Joseph's dream in Genesis 37 (in which other sheaves of grain bow down to his sheaf) as an

Fig. 4.15. *Marble bust of the emperor Vespasian, c. 70 C.E. Museo Capitolino, Rome. Photo: Neil Elliott.*

example of the ambitious and avaricious, those "who are companions of vain opinion" and "place themselves above all things, above all cities, and laws, and national customs"; who move from demagoguery to overturning the common good, seeking their own advantage by "reducing those under their power" (2.78-79).

There are, Philo suggests, two ways of responding to such oppressive power holders. One is the way of impulsive defiance, of "unseemly freedom of speech" that only brings down on the community the wrath of the powerful:

> Do not these men then talk foolishly, are they not mad, who desire to display their inexperience and freedom of speech to kings and tyrants, at times daring to speak and to do things in opposition to their will? Do they not perceive that they have not only put their necks under the yoke like brute beasts, but that they have also surrendered and betrayed their whole bodies and souls likewise, and their wives and their children, and their parents, and all the rest of the numerous kindred and community of their other relations? . . . Therefore, being pricked with goads, and flogged, and mutilated, and suffering all the cruelties which can be inflicted in an inhuman and pitiless manner before death, all together, they are led away to execution and put to death.
>
> These are the rewards of unseemly freedom of speech, not of that which is accounted such by right-thinking judges, but of that license which is full of folly, and insanity of mind, and of incurable distemper.

The alternative is "caution": "what a wall is to a city, that caution is to an individual." The caution of a pilot who refuses to put to sea in the midst of an angry storm, the caution needed to "use incantations" in order to tame wild beasts or poisonous asps, this is the caution needed with "certain men who are more savage and more treacherous than boars, or serpents, or asps." It is the caution Abraham used when he flattered the sons of Cheth (Hittites) (Gen 23:7), not out of respect "but because he fears their present power and their scarcely conquerable strength, and is on his guard not to provoke them."

As if to draw back from the brink of his own "unseemly freedom of speech," Philo retreats for a moment from his comparison of oppressive rulers with wild unthinking beasts. But he also makes clear that he considers there *is* a right time for defying and resisting the powerful.

> What? Do not we also, when we are spending our time in the market-place, frequently wonder at the masters, and also at the beasts of burden? But we wonder at these two classes, with different and not the same feelings. For we look upon the masters with honor, and upon the beasts of burden with fear, lest some injury should be done to us by them. But when an opportunity offers, it is a good thing to attack our enemies and put down their power; yet when we have no such opportunity, it is better to be quiet; and if we wish to find perfect safety as far as they are concerned, it is advantageous to caress them.
>
> (Philo, *On Dreams* 2.83-92, passim, trans. Yonge)[28]

"Plight" and "Solution"

In the following pages, we will sample texts having some bearing on one or another way of understanding Paul's relation to his ancestral religion.

As mentioned above, Paul's opposition of justification by faith to justification by "works of law" has long been understood as contrasting life in Christ with life in Judaism. Some of Paul's other statements make that neat opposition difficult, however. In Galatians, for example, he narrates the rebuke he gave to Cephas in Antioch: "We ourselves are Jews by birth and not Gentile sinners; yet we know that a person is justified not by the works of the law but through faith in Jesus Christ. And we have come to believe in Christ Jesus, so that we might be justified by faith in Christ, and not by doing the works of the law, because no one will be justified by the works of the law" (Gal 2:15-16 NRSV). His language suggests that understanding that justification is possible only through faith was knowledge that he and Cephas shared *as Jews*. Indeed, already in Deuteronomy Moses warned Israel not to imagine that they possessed their own righteousness before God (9:4-6). In writings closer to Paul's time, other Jews declared their faith in language similar to Paul's.

141. Righteousness from God alone (the Dead Sea Scrolls)

The discovery of the first of the Dead Sea Scrolls in 1947 revealed that Jews in Paul's day were aware (as were the authors of the Hebrew Bible) that justification (which here, like "righteousness," translates the Hebrew *ṣedāqâ*) was the prerogative of God alone, not a human achievement.

> For yours, O God of knowledge, are all righteous deeds and the counsel of
>   truth;
> but to the children of humanity is the work of iniquity and deeds of deceit. . . .
> For I know there is hope in your grace and expectation in your great power.
> For no one can be just in your judgment or your trial.
>   (*Thanksgiving Scroll,* 1QH 1.26; 9.14-15; trans., Vermes, adapted)

> As for me,
>   my justification is with God.
> In his hand are the perfection of my way
>   And the uprightness of my heart.
> He will wipe out my transgression
>   Through his righteousness
> . . . for the rock of my steps is the truth of God
>   and his might is the support of my right hand.
> From the source of his righteousness
>   Is my justification . . .
> As for me,
>   I belong to wicked humanity,
>   To the company of ungodly flesh.
> My iniquities, rebellion, and sins,
>   Together with the perversity of my heart,
> Belong to the company of worms
>   And to those who walk in darkness.
> For humanity has no way,
>   And no one is able to justify one's steps
> Since justification is with God
>   And perfection of way is out of his hand.
> . . . As for me,
>   if I stumble, the mercies of God
>   shall be my eternal salvation.
> If I stagger because of the sin of flesh,
>   My justification shall be
>   By the righteousness of God which endures forever.
> . . . He will draw me near by his grace,
>   and by his mercy will he bring my justification.
> He will judge me in the righteousness of his truth
>   And in the greatness of his goodness
>   He will pardon all my sins.
> Through his righteousness he will cleanse me
>   Of human uncleanness
>   And of the sins of human children,
> That I may confess to God his righteousness
>   And his majesty to the most high.
>   (*Community Rule,* 1QS 11:2-15, trans. Vermes, adapted)

Fig. 4.16. *The caves near Qumran, in which the Dead Sea Scrolls were discovered. Photo: Marshall D. Johnson.*

142. A RULE OF LIFE (THE *COMMUNITY RULE*)

As in Paul's own letters (see, for example, Romans 12:17-20), so in the Dead Sea Scrolls we find an emphasis on righteousness being God's prerogative alone side by side with injunctions to a strict code of conduct. Here is part of the commitment made by an initiate to the *yaḥad* (community).

> I will pay to no one the reward of evil.
> I will pursue [my neighbor] with goodness.
> For judgment of all the living is with God, and it is he who will render to each
>   his reward.
> I will not envy in a spirit of wickedness,
>   my soul shall not desire the riches of violence.
> I will not grapple with the people of perdition
>   until the Day of Revenge,
> But my wrath shall not turn from the men of falsehood
>   and I will not rejoice until judgment is made.
>   (*Community Rule*, 1QS 10.17-21, trans. Vermes, modified)

143. "RIGHT-MAKING POWER" (PLATO'S *REPUBLIC*)

Though our focus in this chapter is Paul's relationship to Judaism and his fellow Jews, it is worth noting that the question, what makes for justice? was common enough in the ancient world. We have already seen (no. 92; fig. 3.15) that the language of "works" (Greek *erga*) was intertwined with status and justice in Roman imperial ideology. But already in Plato's *Republic* (c. 380 B.C.E.), Socrates narrated a dialogue he had with his friend Glaucon on the requirements of a good citizen. Note the language about a "power" that makes people just, comparable to New Testament scholar Ernst Käsemann's insistence that Paul's language about *dikaiosynē tou theou* should be translated "God's right-making power."[29]

[SOCRATES] "Now we come to justice: [the good citizen] will be just as and in the way we have said so often."

[GLAUCON] "Absolutely necessary."

"Very well," I said. "I wonder if justice seems perhaps blurred in some way? Do we think it to be anything else in him than what it was shown to be in the city?"

"I think not," said he.

"Well," said I, "we should be able to assure ourselves completely, if any further doubt comes up in our minds, by applying tests from common life."

"What, may I ask?"

"For example, compare that city and the man who is like it in nature and training, and see if we may agree whether such a man, if entrusted with a deposit of gold or silver, would be likely to withhold it for himself? Who do you think would believe that he would be more likely to do that than people who were not as just as he is?"

"No one would believe that," he said.

"Take sacrilege and theft and treachery, either privately towards friends or publicly towards the state—would he be above all that?"

"Yes," he said.

"And further, he would not be false to his oath in any way, or to his other agreements."

"How could he?"

"Adultery, again, and dishonor to parents and neglect of divine service are proper to anyone rather than to him."

"Anyone else," he said.

"What is the cause of this? Surely that each of the parts in him does its own business about ruling and being ruled?"

"That is the cause," he said, "nothing else."

"Then what are you looking for in justice but this power which produces such men and cities?"

"Nothing but that, I declare," said he.

"Then our dream has come perfectly true, and we have made real what we said we imagined, how at the very beginning of our foundation of the city, some good providence has really been bringing us upon a principle and outline of justice."

"Yes, entirely true!"

"Indeed it really was, Glaucon—and that is why it helps us, a kind of image of justice, that the one who is a cobbler by nature ought properly to fix shoes and do nothing else, and the carpenter to carpenter, and so on."

"So it seems."

"But in truth, justice, it appears, was something like this; not, however, in a man's outward practice, but inwardly and truly he must do his own business in himself. He must not have allowed any part of himself to do the business of other parts, nor the parts in his soul to meddle in many businesses with each other; but he must have managed his own well, and must have ruled himself by himself, and set all in order, and become a friend to himself. He must have put all three parts in tune within him,[30] highest and lowest and middle, exactly like the three chief notes of a scale, and any other intervals between that there may be; he must have bound all these together and made himself completely one out of many, temperate and balanced; and then only do whatever he does, getting of wealth, or care of the body, or even matters of state or private contract. In all these he must believe and name as just and beautiful behavior whatever action preserves this condition and works along with it, and he must call wisdom the knowledge that presides over this practice; but as he must call unjust dealing whatever dissolves it, and brute ignorance, again, the opinion that presides over such."

"What you say, Socrates," he said, "is perfectly true."

(Plato, *Republic* 442E-443E, trans. Rouse, adapted)

Frustration with the Law?

One way to read Romans 7 is as Paul's recollection of his own anguish, as a Jew, at the impossibility of keeping the law. Another reads the passage as an expression of Paul's anguish even as a Christian who remains incapable of doing what he knows is right ("I do not understand my own actions. For I do not do what I want, but I do the very thing I hate," 7:15). Much of the tradition of Christian exegesis of this passage has been absorbed with those options. (The question is an old one: in the late fourth century an elderly priest named Simplician wrote to Augustine to ask who the "I" in the passage was.) In the twentieth century, however, scholars wondered whether Paul's supposed anguish was belied by his expression of confidence in Philippians 3 ("as to righteousness under the law, [I was] blameless," 3:6) and elsewhere.[31] Some parts of Romans 7 read as a positive defense of the law, which remains "holy" and its commandment "holy and just and good" (7:12).[32] Paul's speaking in the first person plural ("I") may be his use of *prosopopoiia*, "speech in character," by which he means rhetorically to depict not his own experience but a hypothetical attitude, such as that of a person who lacks self-mastery (even though they possess the law). (Again, the insight was present in the early church: Origen recognized Paul's use here of *prosopopoiia*.)[33]

144. The Irony of intention (Epictetus)

Others in Paul's day spoke of the difference between intention or wish and result.[34] In the following passages Epictetus uses a form of *prosopopoiia* to evoke the phenomenon of one's actions not serving one's intentions. Is Paul using a similar commonplace in Romans 7, or describing a unique interaction between law and sin?[35]

Why is it that though you wish for something, it does not occur and though you don't wish for something, it does occur? For this is a most definite demonstration of bad luck and unhappiness. I wish for something and it doesn't occur; then who is more miserable than I? I don't wish for something and it happens; then who is more miserable than I?

(Arrian, *Discourses of Epictetus* 2.17.17-18)

Every sin involves a struggle. For if the person sinning does not wish to sin, but rather to do right, it is obvious that the person is not doing what he wants. For what does the thief want to do? What is for his own benefit. If stealing is not beneficial for him, he is therefore not doing what he wants. Every rational mind is naturally misled when in a struggle. And for as long as a person does not closely attend to the fact that they are in a struggle, there will be nothing protecting them from doing what their enemy is pressing on them. But once the struggle is recognized, one must withdraw from the struggle and flee, just as harsh necessity forces one to stand up against a lie when one senses that it is a lie. But for as long as this lie is not evident, a person will nod in approval to it as if it is the truth.

(Arrian, *Discourses of Epictetus* 2.26.1-3)

Now I am called to perform something. Now I depart, paying attention to the rules that must be kept, to be modest, dependable, without desire and without turning toward outward things, and finally I attend to people, what they say, how they act, and this not to be mean, nor that I may blame or mock, but I turn toward myself, to check if I also sin in these ways. "How then shall I quit sinning?" Once I also sinned, but now I no longer do, thanks to God.

(Arrian, *Discourses of Epictetus* 4.4.6-7, trans. Reasoner)

This text goes on to describe how one should be consistent in one's behavior, setting one's heart only on what is under one's control, that is, one's own thoughts and feelings.

"Works of the Law" and "Works-Righteousness"?

In the past it was possible for scholars like Markus Barth and Lloyd Gaston to write that Paul's language of "justification from works of law" was peculiar; nothing like it appeared in Jewish literature. They suggested that perhaps Paul was talking not about Judaism but about the distinctive experience of *non-Jews* seeking—mistakenly—to use "works of law" to achieve their own righteousness.[36]

145. "Works of the law . . . reckoned as justice" (4QMMT)

In the 1990s, a number of fragments from the Dead Sea Scrolls were identified as parts of multiple copies of a single letter—obviously of importance to the community that copied and treasured it—addressed by a leader of a sect or party to a person in authority over a different community ("your people"), explaining the differences between them. The document has been named 4QMMT after Cave 4 at Qumran and the Hebrew phrase *miqṣat ma'ase ha-torah,* "some of the works of Torah," used in it. It is also known as the *Halakhic Letter.*

Martin Abegg suggested that Paul's phrase "works of the law" might have some connection to the phrase "some works of law" in 4QMMT. James D. G. Dunn, who has been eager to find continuities between Paul and Judaism, has identified some similarities between the treatment of the Torah in 4QMMT and in Paul's letters.[37] The concern with the offerings of Gentiles and with blessings and curses (compare Galatians 3) and the conviction that the author is living in "the last days" are points for comparison. There are differences, too, however, including the apparent concern in 4QMMT for ritual procedures in the Jerusalem temple, which play no role in Paul's letters. Two fragments of the letter, 4Q396 and 4Q398, are presented below.[38]

(4Q396, Col I) [. . .] they do [no]t slaughter in the temple. [And concerning pregnant animals: we think that one should not sacrifice t]he mother and the fetus on the same day [. . . And concerning the eating: w]e think that one can eat the fetus [. . .] so and that the word is written: "a pregnant animal" *Blank* [And concerning the Ammonite and the Moabite and the bastard and the one with crushed testicles and one whose] penis [has been cut] off, if these enter [the assembly . . . and] t[a]ke [wives to beco]me [one] bone

(Col II) and to be respectful towards the temple. [And also concerning the blind] who cannot see: they should keep themselves from all unclean[ness; and the uncleanness of the sin-offering] they do not see. *Blank* And also the de[af who have not] heard the law and the precept and the purity regulation, and have not heard the prec[epts of] Israel for whoever neither sees nor hears, does not [know] how to behave. But these are approaching the purity of the temple. And also [concerning liquid str]ea[ms, we] say that in these there is no [purity. Neither can liquid streams] separate impure from pu[re, because the liquid of the liquid streams] and their containers is alike, [the same] li[quid. And one should not let] dogs [enter the holy camp,] because they might eat [some of the bones from the temple with the flesh] [on] them. Because Jeru[sa]l[em is the holy camp, it is the place]

(Col III) which he has chosen from among all the tribes of Is[rael, since Jer]usalem is the head [of the cam]ps of Israel. *Blank* And also con[cerning the plan]tation of fruit tree[s] planted in the land of Israel, it is like the first-fruits, it is for the priests. *Blank* And the tithe of the cattle and of the flocks is for the priests. And also concerning lepers: we s[ay that] they should [not] enter . . . (a place) with holy purity, but [in isolation] [they shall stay outside a house. And] also it is written that from the moment he shaves and washes he should stay outside [his tent for seven d]ays. But now, even when they are still unclean [lepers approach (a place) wi]th holy purity, the house. And you know [. . .] and it is taken away from him, must bring {it} [a sin-offering. And concerning him who acts offensively it is wri]tten that he is a slanderer and a blasp[he]mer. [And also: when they have the uncleanness of leprosy] they should not eat any of the ho[l]y things

(Col IV) until the sun sets on the eighth day. And concerning [the uncleanness of the corpse of] a man: we say that every bone, [whether stripped of flesh] or complete, is subject to the law concerning a dead or murde[d person.] And concerning the fornications carried out in the midst of the people: they are me[mbers of . . .] (of) holiness, as it is written: "Holy is Israel." And concerning the [pure] an[imal] it is written that he shall not let two species mate; and concerning clo[thing, that no] materials are to be mixed; and he will not sow his field or [his] vi[neyard with two species] [be]cause they are holy. But the sons of Aaron are the ho[liest of the holy] [and y]ou know that a part of the priests and of the peo[ple mingle] [and they] unite with each other and defile the [holy] seed [and also] their (own) [seed] with fornications, be[cause . . .]

4Q398 Frags. 11-13 [the bles]sing[s . . .] in the days of Solomon the son of David and also the curses [which] came in the days of [Jer]oboam son of Nebat and up to the ex[i]le of Jerusalem and of Zedekiah, king of Juda[h] [that] he should bring them in [. . .]. And we are aware that part of the blessings and curses have occurred that are written in the b[ook of Mos]es. And this is the end of days, when they will return in Israel to the L[aw . . .] and not turn bac[k] and the wicked will act wick[edly] and [. . .] and [. . .] remember the kings of Israe[l] and reflect on their deeds, how whoever of them was respecting [the . . . La]w was freed from afflictions; and those so[u]ght the Law

Frags. 14-17 col I [in our actions disloyalty or deceit or evil, for concerning these things we gi]ve [. . .] we [have written that you must understand the bo]ok of Moses [and the books of the prophets and of David and the annals of each] generation [and in] the book is written [. . .] and the former times . . . [it is writ]ten that you [shall stray from the path and evil will encounter] you. And it is written: and it shall happen when [all] these [things shall befa]ll you at the en[d] of days, the blessing [and the] curse, [then you shall take] it to your he[art] and will turn to him with all your heart [and with al]l [your] soul [at the en]d [of time] and . . .

Col II [forgiv]en (their) sins. Remember David, one of the "pious" [and] he, too, was freed from many afflictions and was forgiven. And also we have written to you some of the works of the Torah which we think are good for you and for your people, for we s[a]w that you have intellect and knowledge of the Law. Reflect on all these matters and seek from him that he may support your counsel and keep far from you the evil scheming{s} and the counsel of Belial, so that at the end of time, you may rejoice in finding that some of our words are true. And it shall be reckoned to you as justice when you do what is upright and good before him, for your good and that of Israel.

(4Q396, 398, trans. García-Martínez)

146. Justification by works? (4 Ezra)

E. P. Sanders found just one witness in Jewish literature to righteousness through works: *4 Ezra*, which he considered anomalous. Written at the end of the first century C.E., the book represents "a religion of individual self-righteousness," in which the understanding of Israel's covenant "has collapsed" and "all that is left is legalistic perfectionism." Looking back on the Roman destruction of the temple and the terrible slaughter of men, women, and children whom Ezra considers innocent, the book presents the repeated and consistent revelation, through the angel Uriel, that none of the doomed were truly innocent according to God's high standard. The angel

Fig. 4.17. *Lions and menorot decorate the bottom of a glass vessel from Dura Europos, second century* C.E. *Photo in the public domain.*

"adamantly insists that only those who obey the law perfectly will be saved and that these will be very few"—and the angel carries the apocalypse's message.[39]

The seer asks why Israel's covenant has not been fulfilled and wicked nations have been allowed to triumph over Israel. The angel responds that the path of righteousness is very narrow, and very few—even in Israel—find it. Note the importance the angel ascribes to Adam's sin—and the absence of any suggestion that the Torah was given as a remedy to sin.

> For I made the world for [Israel's] sake, and when Adam transgressed my statutes, what had been made was judged. And so the entrances of this world were made narrow and sorrowful and toilsome; they are few and evil, full of dangers and involved in great hardships. But the entrances of the greater world are broad and safe, and really yield the fruit of immortality. Therefore unless the living pass through the difficult and vain experiences, they can never receive those things that have been reserved for them.
>
> (4 *Ezra* 7:3-5, trans. Metzger)

Ezra protests that this arrangement restricts those who may be saved to an unreasonably small number. The angel rebukes him:

> He said to me, "You are not a better judge than God, or wiser than the Most High! Let many perish who are now living, rather than that the law of God which is set before them be disregarded! For God strictly commanded those who came into the world, when they came, what they should do to live, and what they should observe to avoid punishment. Nevertheless they were not obedient, and spoke against him.
>
> (7:10-15)

Ezra persists, expressing sympathy and sorrow for those who have been condemned:

> I answered and said, "O sovereign Lord, I said then and I say now: Blessed are those who are alive and keep your commandments! But what of those for whom I prayed? For who among the living is there that has not sinned, or who among men that has not transgressed your covenant? And now I see that the world to come will bring delight to few, but torments to many. For an evil heart has grown up in us, which has alienated us from God, and has brought us into corruption and the ways of death, and has shown us the paths of perdition and removed us far from life—and that not just a few of us but almost all who have been created!"
>
> (7:45-48)

The angel again rebukes him; note the language in the second paragraph of Ezra possessing a "treasure of works" that will stand him in good stead at the last judgment.

> He answered me and said, "Weigh within yourself what you have thought, for he who has what is hard to get rejoices more than he who has what is plentiful. So also will be the judgment which I have promised; for I will rejoice over the few who shall be saved, because it is they who have made my glory to prevail now, and through them my name has now been honored. And I will not grieve over the multitude of those who perish; for it is they who are now like a mist, and are similar to a flame and smoke—they are set on fire and burn hotly, and are extinguished. . . .
>
> "Do not be associated with those who have shown scorn, nor number yourself among those who are tormented. For you have a treasure of works laid up with the Most High; but it will not be shown to you until the last times."
>
> (7:59-61, 76-77)

A final angelic rebuke admonishes Ezra again not to identify himself with those who have perished.

> But you have often compared yourself to the unrighteous. Never do so! But even in this respect you will be praiseworthy before the Most High, because you humble yourself, as is becoming for you, and have not deemed yourself to be among the righteous in order to receive the greatest glory. For many miseries will affect those who inhabit the world in the last times, because they have walked in great pride. But think of your own case, and inquire concerning the glory of those who are like yourself, because it is for you that Paradise is opened. . . . Therefore do not ask any more questions about the multitude of those who perish. For they also received freedom, but they despised the Most High, and were contemptuous of his Law, and forsook his ways. Moreover they have even trampled upon his righteous ones, and said in their hearts that there is no God—though knowing full well that they must die.
>
> (8:47-58)

147. "Works of law" as boundary markers (Jubilees)

James D. G. Dunn has argued that the phrase "works of law" referred not to an attitude of legalistic "works-righteousness" but to a "sense of Israel's privilege," to "the law as marking out this people in its set-apartness to God" and "protecting Israel's privileged status and restricted prerogative." Dunn cites a passage from *Jubilees* to illustrate this sense of privilege; a similar passage comes from *2 Baruch*. The first passage from *Jubilees* explains the eternal meaning of the command to Abraham to circumcise his son. Note that the command is implicitly universal: the uncircumcised are regarded as having rejected God's covenant.

> This law is for all the eternal generations. . . . And anyone who is born whose own flesh is not circumcised on the eighth day is not from the sons of the covenant which the LORD made for Abraham since (he is) from the children of destruction. And there is therefore no sign upon him so that he might belong to the LORD because (he is destined) to be destroyed and annihilated from the earth and to be uprooted from the earth because he has broken the covenant of the LORD our God. Because the nature of all of the angels of the presence and all of the angels of sanctification was thus from the day of their creation. And in the presence of the angels of the presence and the angels of sanctification he sanctified Israel so that they might be with him and with his holy angels. . . .
>
> For the Lord did not draw Ishmael and his sons and his brothers and Esau near to himself, and he did not elect them because they are the sons of Abraham, for he knew them. But he chose Israel that they might be a people for himself. And he sanctified them and gathered them from all of the sons of man because (there are) many nations and many people, and they all belong to him, but over all of them he caused spirits to rule so that they might lead them astray from following him. But over Israel he did not cause any angel or spirit to rule because he alone is their ruler and he will protect them.
>
> (*Jubilees* 15:25-27, 30-32, trans. Wintermute)

In a second passage, Abraham gives a farewell admonition to his grandson Jacob.

> Blessed is my son, Jacob, and all his sons,
> unto the Lord, Most High, forever.
> May the Lord give you righteous seed,
> And may he sanctify some of your sons in the midst of all the earth.
> May the nations serve you,
> And all the nations bow down before your seed . . .
> Separate yourselves from the gentiles,
> And do not eat with them,
> And do not perform deeds like theirs.
> And do not become associates of theirs.
> Because their deeds are defiled,
> And all of their ways are contaminated, and despicable, and abominable.
> They slaughter their sacrifices to the dead,
> And to the demons they bow down. . . .
> But (as for) you, my son, Jacob,
> May God Most High help you,
> And the God of heaven bless you.
> And may he turn you from their defilement,
> And from all their errors.
>
> (*Jubilees* 22:11-12, 16-17, trans. Wintermute)

148. The law as Israel's possession (2 Baruch)

A similar sense of Israel's privilege is evident in a prayer in *2 Baruch*, from the early second century C.E.

> Protect us in your grace,
> And in your mercy help us.
> Look at the small ones who submit to you,
> And save all those who come to you.
> And do not take away the hope of our people,
> And do not make short the times of our help.
> For these are the people whom you have elected,
> And this is the nation of which you found no equal.
> But I shall speak to you now,
> And I shall say as my heart thinks.
> In you we have put our trust because, behold, your law is with us,
> and we know that we do not fall as long as we keep your statutes.
> We shall always be blessed; at least, we did not mingle with the nations.
> For we are a people of the Name;
> we, who received one law from the One.
> And that law that is among us will help us,
> and that excellent wisdom which is in us will support us.
>
> (2 Baruch 48:18-24, trans. Klijn)

When—and Why—Did God Give the Law?

As we have seen, Paul's statements in Romans and Galatians raise a number of inter-twined questions beyond the scope of this book. Some have to do with the purpose of the giving of Torah. When Paul tells the men in the Galatian assemblies that "if you let yourselves be circumcised, Christ will be of no benefit to you" and that "you who want to be justified by the law have cut yourselves off from Christ" (Gal 5:2, 4), he seems to oppose Christ and Torah as alternative means to salvation—but was the Torah understood in that way in Judaism? In seeking to dissuade the Galatian men from accepting circumcision, Paul argues that the law was introduced long after Abraham (Gal 3:15-18); in Rom 4:13-14 he considers how people could be punished for sin before the Torah was given. But various Jewish texts depict the righteous obeying God's commands long before Sinai. And were the nations responsible for keeping God's commandments even if they did not receive the Torah?—Or had they in fact been offered Torah but rejected it? All of these questions have received thorough and complex exploration in different studies that cannot be adequately summarized here. A few samples may nevertheless show the sorts of texts that scholars find relevant to these questions.

149. The commandments given to Adam (Ben Sira)

The Wisdom of Yeshua ben Sira, completed by 180 B.C.E. and accepted by the early churches (in Greek as The Wisdom of Jesus son of Sirach, in Latin as Ecclesiasti-cus), maintains that God gave the commandments to Adam and Eve.[40] The interval

Paul seeks to introduce in Rom 5:13-14 between creation and the giving of the law is absent here.

> It was [God] who created the human being (Adam) from the beginning
>> and he left him in the power of his inclination.
> If you choose, you can keep the commandments,
>> and to act faithfully is a matter of your own choice.
> . . .
> Before each person are life and death,
>> and whichever one chooses will be given.
>
> (Ben Sira 15:14-17, NRSV)[41]

150. A RECITAL OF FAILURES (THE *DAMASCUS DOCUMENT*)

A similar understanding of what scholars would call "salvation history"—that human beings were accountable to God's commandments from the beginning; that a few were righteous but most disobeyed; that the generation of Sinai is remembered primarily for their disobedience, not for their reception of Torah; and that the present readers and hearers are called to be part of a righteous minority in their own generation—is evident in other writings from the second and first centuries B.C.E. Here is the beginning of the so-called *Damascus Document*, fragments of which were found among the Dead Sea Scrolls.

> Listen now, all you who know righteousness, and consider the works of God; for he has a dispute with all flesh and will condemn all those who despise him.
>
> For when they were unfaithful and forsook him, he hid his face from Israel and his sanctuary and delivered them up to the sword. But remembering the covenant of the forefathers, he left a remnant to Israel and did not deliver it up to be destroyed. And in the age of wrath, three hundred and ninety years after he had given them into the hand of King Nebuchadnezzar of Babylon, he visited them, and he caused a plant root to spring from Israel and Aaron to inherit his land and to prosper on the good things of his earth. And they perceived their iniquity and recognized that they were guilty men, yet for twenty years they were like blind men groping for the way. And God observed their deeds, that they sought him with a whole heart, and he raised for them a Teacher of Righteousness to guide them in the way of his heart. And he made known to the latter generations that which God had done to the latter generation, the congregation of traitors, to those who departed from the way. . . .
>
> Hear now, my sons, and I will uncover your eyes that you may see and understand the works of God, that you may choose that which pleases him and reject that which he hates, that you may walk perfectly in all his ways and not follow after thoughts of the guilty inclination *yēṣer 'ašmâ* and after eyes of lust. For through them, great men have gone astray and mighty heroes have stumbled from former times till now. Because they walked in the stubbornness of their heart, the heavenly Watchers fell; they were caught because they did not keep the commandments of God. And their sons also fell who were tall as cedar trees and whose bodies were like mountains. All flesh on dry land perished; they were as though they had never been because they did their own

will and did not keep the commandments of their Maker so that his wrath was kindled against them.

Through it [that is, the guilty inclination], the children of Noah went astray, together with their kin, and were cut off. Abraham did not walk in it, and he was accounted a friend of God because he kept the commandments of God and did not choose his own will. And he handed them down to Isaac and Jacob, who kept them, and were recorded as friends of God and party to the covenant forever.

The children of Jacob strayed through them and were punished in accordance with their error. And their sons in Egypt walked in the stubbornness of their hearts, conspiring against the commandments of God and each of them doing that which seemed right in his own eyes. They ate blood, and he cut off their males in the wilderness. And at Kadesh he said to them, "Go up and possess the land" [Deut 9:23]. But they chose their own will and did not heed the voice of their maker, the commands of their teacher, but murmured in their tents; and the anger of God was kindled against their congregation. Through it their sons perished, and through it their kings were cut off; through it their mighty heroes perished and through it their land was ravaged. Through it the first members of the covenant sinned and were delivered up to the sword because they forsook the covenant of God and chose their own will and walked in the stubbornness of their hearts, each of them doing his own will.

But with the remnant which held fast to the commandments of God he made his covenant with Israel forever, revealing to them the hidden things in which all Israel had gone astray.

(*Damascus Document* 2.14—3.13, trans. Vermes)

151. Abraham studied the Torah (*Jubilees*)

The book of *Jubilees*, written perhaps in the early second century B.C.E., presents Noah as already instructing his children in specific commandments (including the firstfruits offering) that he received from Enoch, Methuselah, and Lamech before him (7:34-39). Although Abraham was often regarded in Jewish literature as the first proselyte—having left the idolatry of Ur and of his father's house behind to follow the Lord—the book of *Jubilees* depicts him instead as descending from a primordial Hebrew stock. When he prays for direction, an angel of the Lord reveals to him the language of his ancestors and, indeed, of creation, then gives him ancient books, written in Hebrew, to study—by implication, written books of the Torah long before the Torah was given to Moses on Mount Sinai. In this narrative, Abraham's father is not a pagan but a Hebrew himself, who sends his son on his way with a blessing. The angel is the narrator.

Behold, the word of the Lord was sent to [Abraham] through me, saying: "Get up from your country, and from your kindred and from the house of your father, and go to a land which I will show you, and I shall make you a great and numerous nation.

"And I will bless you and I will make your name great, and you shall be blessed in the earth, and in you shall all families of the earth be blessed, and I will bless those that bless you, and curse those that curse you.

"And I will be a God to you and your son, and to your son's son, and to all your seed: fear not, from henceforth and unto all generations of the earth I am your God."

And the Lord God said: "Open his mouth and his ears, that he may hear and speak with his mouth, with the language which has been revealed"; for it had ceased from the mouths of all the children of humanity from the day of the overthrow of Babel.

And I opened his mouth, and his ears and his lips, and I began to speak with him in Hebrew in the tongue of the creation.

And he took the books of his fathers, and these were written in Hebrew, and he transcribed them, and he began from henceforth to study them; and I made known to him that which he could not understand, and he studied them during the six rainy months.

And it came to pass in the seventh year of the sixth week that he spoke to his father and informed him, that he would leave Haran to go into the land of Canaan to see it and return to him.

Fig. 4.18. *Abraham. Fresco from the synagogue at Dura-Europos, third century* c.e. *Photo: Erich Lessing/Art Resource, New York.*

And Terah his father said unto him; "Go in peace: May the eternal God make your path straight. And the Lord be with you, and protect thee from all evil, and grant unto you grace, mercy and favor before those who see you, and may none of the children of men have power over you to harm you; go in peace."

(*Jubilees* 12:22-29, trans. Charles, adapted)

152. Abraham obeyed the unwritten law (Philo)

Philo of Alexandria similarly held that Abraham and the other patriarchs kept all of Torah, not, however, because he had been instructed in Hebrew but because he was attempting to live according to nature. (Compare what Paul has to say in Rom 2:12-15 about those who keep the law by living according to what they know by nature.)

Now these are those men who have lived irreproachably and admirably, whose virtues are durably and permanently recorded, as on pillars in the sacred scriptures, not merely with the object of praising the men themselves, but also for the sake of exhorting those who read their history, and of leading them on to imitate their conduct; for these men have been living and rational laws; and the Lawgiver has magnified them for two reasons; first, because he desired to show that the commandments which are given are not inconsistent with nature; and, secondly, that he might prove that it is not very difficult or laborious for those who wish to live according to the laws established in these books, since the earliest men easily and spontaneously obeyed the unwritten principle of legislation before any one of the particular laws were written down at all.

So that a man may very properly say, that the written laws are nothing more than a memorial of the life of the ancients, tracing back in an antiquarian spirit, the actions and thoughts that they adopted; for these first men, without ever having been followers or pupils of any one, and without ever having been taught by instructors what they ought to do or say, but having embraced a line of conduct consistent with nature from attending to their own natural impulses, and from being prompted by an innate virtue, and looking upon nature herself to be, what in fact she is, the most ancient and duly established of laws, actually spent their whole lives making laws, never of deliberate purpose doing anything open to reproach, and for their accidental errors making atonement before God, and appeasing him by prayers and supplications, so as to gain for themselves the enjoyment of an entire life of virtue and prosperity, both in respect of their deliberate actions, and those which proceeded from no deliberate purpose.

(Philo, *Life of Abraham* 4-6, trans. Yonge, adapted)

153. The Nations offered Torah? (Ben Sira)

Lloyd Gaston pointed out that later rabbinic Judaism came up with creative ways to resolve the tension between universal accountability to God's commands and the specificity of the Torah being given to Israel on Mount Sinai, for example, by recounting how the Torah was offered to other nations in turn, who refused it.[42] These texts are too late to be directly relevant but may have been anticipated by earlier writings:

see, for example, the selections from *Jubilees* (above, nos. 147, 151) and the following passage in the Wisdom of Ben Sira (Ecclesiasticus), which suggests that the nations were responsible to God through "rulers" (comparable to angelic powers, or the "mediator" of Gal 3:16?).

> The Lord created man out of earth,
>> And turned him back to it again.
> He gave to them few days, a limited time,
>> But granted them authority over the things of the earth.
> He endowed them with strength like his own,
>> And made them in his own image.
> He filled them with knowledge and understanding,
>> And showed them good and evil.
> He bestowed knowledge upon them,
>> And allotted to them the law of life.
> He established with them an eternal covenant,
>> And showed them his judgments.
> And he said to them, "Beware of all unrighteousness,"
>> And he gave commandments to each of them concerning his neighbor.
> He appointed a ruler for every nation,
> But Israel is the Lord's own portion.
>
> (Ben Sira 17:1-17, NRSV)[43]

We turn in the next chapter to another dimension of Paul's relationship to Torah and Judaism with immediate consequences for his apostolic work: the Jewish perception of impurity among the nations.

QUESTIONS FOR REFLECTION

1. To what extent, and in what ways, was Paul like other Jews of the Roman Diaspora? In what ways was he different? How should we understand Paul's statements about his own background and identity as a "Hebrew born of Hebrews"?

2. How do different Roman attitudes and policies toward Jews cast light on what Paul wrote about "the governing authorities" in Rom 13:1-7? How does that passage compare with different Jewish attitudes toward the Roman Empire?

3. What is at stake in questions about Paul's understanding of Judaism and the Torah?—about Paul's "conversion"?

4. How do Jewish expressions of concern about idols, about foods, and about purity help us understand what Paul said about these things in the *ekklēsiai*?

5. What did Paul mean when he insisted that no one could be set right before God "out of works of law"?

6. In the light of materials in this chapter, how do you understand what was going on in Antioch, in Galatia, in Rome, or in Judea?

FOR FURTHER READING

On Judaism in the Second Temple period:

Collins, John J. *Between Athens and Jerusalem: Jewish Identity in the Hellenistic Diaspora.* New York: Crossroad, 1983.

Feldman, Louis H., and Meyer Reinhold, eds. *Jewish Life and Thought among Greeks and Romans: Primary Readings.* Minneapolis: Fortress Press, 1996.

Kraft, Robert A., and George W. E. Nickelsburg, eds. *Early Judaism and Its Modern Interpreters.* Bible and Its Modern Interpreters 2. Atlanta: Scholars, 1986.

Nickelsburg, George W. E. *Jewish Literature between the Bible and the Mishnah: A Historical and Literary Introduction.* 2nd ed. Minneapolis: Fortress Press, 2005.

Nickelsburg, George W. E., and Michael E. Stone, eds. *Early Judaism: Texts and Documents on Faith and Piety.* Rev. ed. Minneapolis: Fortress Press, 2009.

Sanders, E. P. *Judaism: Practice and Belief 63 BCE–66 CE.* London: SCM; Philadelphia: Trinity Press International, 1992.

Schiffman, Lawrence H., and James C. VanderKam, eds. *Encyclopedia of the Dead Sea Scrolls.* 2 vols. New York: Oxford University Press, 2000.

Schürer, Emil. *The History of the Jewish People in the Age of Jesus Christ (175 B.C.–A.D. 135).* Translated by T. A. Burkill et al. Revised and edited by Geza Vermes, Fergus Millar, Martin Goodman, Matthew Black, and Pamela Vermes. Edinburgh: T&T Clark, 1973–87.

Stone, Michael E., ed. *Jewish Writings of the Second Temple Period.* CRINT, Section 2, Literature of the Jewish People in the Period of the Second Temple and the Talmud 2. Assen: Van Gorcum; Philadelphia: Fortress Press, 1984.

Strack, H. L., and G. Stemberger. *Introduction to the Talmud and Midrash.* Translated by Markus Bockmuehl. Minneapolis: Fortress Press, 1992.

Vermes, Geza. *An Introduction to the Complete Dead Sea Scrolls.* Rev. ed. Minneapolis: Fortress Press, 1999.

On Paul and Judaism and the Jewish law:

The literature here is vast, complex, and controversial. In recent years the long-standing and pervasive dominance of the Christian theological tradition has come increasingly to be questioned by scholars—an increasing number of whom are Jews.

Here we name only a small sample of important, diverse works and bibliographic surveys that may guide the interested reader into the field.

Barclay, John M. G. *Jews in the Mediterranean Diaspora: From Alexander to Trajan (323 BCE–117 CE)*. Edinburgh: T&T Clark, 1996.

Bird, Michael F., and Preston M. Sprinkle. "Jewish Interpretation of Paul in the Last Thirty Years." *Currents in Biblical Research* 6 (2008): 355–76.

Bolton, David, and Emmanuel Nathan. "New Understandings of Paul and His Jewish Heritage." *Studies in Christian-Jewish Relations* 3 (2008): 1–7.

Boyarin, Daniel. *A Radical Jew: Paul and the Politics of Identity*. Contraversions 1. Berkeley and Los Angeles: University of California Press, 1990.

Campbell, William S. *Paul and the Creation of Christian Identity*. Library of New Testament Studies. London: T&T Clark, 2008.

Eisenbaum, Pamela. *Paul Was Not a Christian: The Real Message of a Misunderstood Apostle*. New York: HarperOne, 2009.

Gaston, Lloyd. *Paul and the Torah*. Vancouver: University of British Columbia Press, 1987.

Langton, Daniel R. *The Apostle Paul in the Jewish Imagination: A Study in Modern Jewish-Christian Relations*. Cambridge: Cambridge University Press, 2010.

———. "The Myth of the 'Traditional View of Paul' and the Role of the Apostle in Modern Jewish-Christian Polemics." *JSNT* 28 (2005): 69–104.

Nanos, Mark D., ed. *Paul between Jews and Christians*. Special issue of *Biblical Interpretation* 13 (2005).

The Paul Page. http://www.thepaulpage.com. The Paul Page is "an expanding website dedicated to exploring recent trends in Pauline studies like 'the new perspective on Paul' and 'Paul and Empire,' " founded in 1999 by Mark M. Mattison. Editorial board: Don Garlington, Mark Goodacre, Mark M. Mattison, and Ian Packer.

Sanders, E. P. *Paul and Palestinian Judaism: A Comparison of Patterns of Religion*. Philadelphia: Fortress Press, 1977.

Tomson, Peter J. *Paul and the Jewish Law*. CRINT, Section 3, Jewish Traditions in Early Christian Literature 1. Assen: Van Gorcum; Philadelphia: Fortress Press, 1990.

Westerholm, Stephen. *Perspectives Old and New on Paul: The "Lutheran" Paul and His Critics*. Grand Rapids: Eerdmans, 2004.

Zetterholm, Magnus. *Approaches to Paul: A Student's Guide to Recent Scholarship*. Minneapolis: Fortress Press, 2009. This textbook is an accessible survey of approaches, introducing the issues involved in contemporary discussion.

Fig. 5.1. *Bread and fish (see John 21). Early Christian fresco from the Catacomb of St. Callisto, Rome, second or third century* c.e. *Photo in the public domain.*

5 | The Communities around Paul: The *Ekklēsiai*

I n this chapter we continue some of the exploration begun in chapter 4. The challenge Paul faced in his apostolic work was to create holy communities among "the nations." As Nils A. Dahl observed decades ago, in a number of his letters "Paul states the goal of his intercession and whole endeavor in terms like these: 'so that you . . . may be pure and blameless for the day of Christ' [Phil 1:10-11], or 'guiltless in the day of our Lord Jesus Christ' [1 Cor 1:8]."[1] Paul *repeatedly* addresses his communities as "the holy ones" or "the saints" (Greek *hagioi*). Although interpreters have long focused attention on Paul's understanding of "justification," it is as reasonable to understand sanctification—the "making holy" of the congregation—as his fundamental concern: "for God did not call us to impurity but in holiness" (1 Thess 4:7 NRSV).

Holiness and Impurity

The challenge Paul faced arose precisely from his self-understanding as an apostle *to the nations*, for the nations were perceived by many Jews as the site of terrible impurity. How could the nations be made "holy"? Non-Jews were certainly familiar with the concept of holiness as it demarcated the sacred space of a shrine and governed who might approach the image of the god, and under what circumstances; but the Jewish understanding of holiness and purity was quite distinct.

154. That only the holy may enter temples (inscriptions)

The following laws, inscribed on the walls of temples from the late second and first centuries B.C.E., illustrate how temples in Greek cities required holiness of those who approached them to worship the gods. Note from the third example that different requirements apply to the impurity contracted by sex with one's spouse and sex with another partner.

> They should purify themselves and then they may enter into the temple of the god.[2]
>> Those who are pure may enter.[3]
>> The citizens and all others should purify themselves and then may enter into the temple of the gods; from their own wife and from their own husband on that very day, from [sexual contact with] another woman and another man let them be cleansed after two days [of separation]. Likewise also from mourning and childbearing a woman is cleansed on the second day. From a burial and the carrying of a corpse, after being sprinkled and going through the gate behind which the sanctuary is situated, they shall be clean on the same day.[4]

Gentile Impurity in the Early Assemblies

Relations between Jews and non-Jews in the early Jesus assemblies—both the Judean assemblies that Paul persecuted (Galatians 1) and the assemblies elsewhere that Paul founded and supported—were the occasion for controversy and conflict, but the reasons are not perfectly clear. Several New Testament passages have played central roles in scholarly debate, but the interpretation of those passages remains in dispute as well.

According to Acts 10, after receiving a bewildering vision in which a voice commands him to "rise, kill, and eat" unclean animals, Peter meets the God-fearing Roman centurion Cornelius and his entourage. He declares to them, "You yourselves know that it is unlawful for a Jew to associate with or to visit a Gentile; but God has shown me that I should not call anyone profane or unclean" (Acts 10:28). Interpretive questions abound. Was the voice in Peter's vision God's voice, or a demonic temptation to violate the commandments regarding *kashrut* (kosher foods)?[5] Did Peter's refusal expose a narrow prejudice that he needed to outgrow, or demonstrate his proper loyalty to the Torah? Is the point of the story that the Christian movement must go forward by abandoning the kosher laws, or that embracing faithful non-Jews is perfectly "kosher"? Furthermore, although passages such as those in *Jubilees* reviewed above (see no. 147) urge that Jews "separate . . . from the Gentiles . . . because their deeds are defiled," nothing in the Torah expressly forbids Jews from "associating with or visiting a Gentile."

Paul's own account in Galatians 2 of the fateful scene in Antioch when "certain people . . . from James" led Cephas and other Jews to withdraw from eating with non-Jews (2:11-14) is another important but ambiguous text. If it was unlawful for Jews to socialize with non-Jews, and even more to eat with them, then we might suppose that the assemblies in Judea and Antioch must have been disregarding the law—and Saul the Pharisee must have persecuted them for just that offense. But the Torah is full of commands that assume that Jews engage with non-Jews on a daily basis. Indeed, such encounters would have been inevitable in the Hellenistic and Roman cities where

Jews were the distinct minority. Further, nowhere in his letters does Paul explicitly encourage Jews in the Jesus assemblies to eat nonkosher food (and thus to disobey the Torah). Paul clearly urged *non-Jews* not to accept circumcision or take on other aspects of the Torah, but that was arguably because he saw in these individuals the fulfillment of Isaiah's prophecies about the righteous nations of the end times (Isa 45:22-25; 49:6-8; 60:3).[6]

Nevertheless, there are indications that some Jews in Paul's day considered people from the nations to be inherently impure (see no. 147). The designation "impure" or "unclean" (Hebrew *ṭāmē'*; Greek *akathartos*) is often misunderstood. The distinction of "pure" (Hebrew *ṭohŏrâ*; Greek *katharos*) and impure in Torah is concerned, first, with who may have access to the sacred precincts of the temple, and under what conditions. Various things may cause ritual impurity—bodily emissions (semen, menstrual fluid), skin eruptions, contact with a corpse—making one ineligible to enter the temple until one has performed the required purification; but such concerns were presumably less important the farther one got from the temple. (One theory concerning the Pharisees identifies them with the *ḥabĕrîm* in the rabbinic literature, laypeople who sought to practice in their homes the level of purity required of priests in the temple; but that identification is questioned.)[7]

155. The Pharisees and (permitted) uncleanness (m. Ḥagigah)

If, on another theory, the Pharisees were a class of scribal "retainers" whose services were necessary to the operations of the temple, we might understand such concern with avoiding uncleanness as an occupational necessity. The Torah discusses what the rabbis would later call *midrās* uncleanness (Leviticus 15), caused when persons or objects come into contact with menstrual fluid, semen, and other bodily discharges. In the Mishnah we find this concern extended on the apparent principle that the greater one's involvement with holy things in the temple, the more careful one must be about contact with others who must be presumed to be more liable to *midrās* uncleanness. (We might ask whether this concern would extend beyond the bounds of the land of Israel.)

> For Pharisees the clothes of an *Am-haaretz* [a halakhically nonobservant "person of the land"] count as suffering *midras*-uncleanness; for them that eat Heave-offering the clothes of Pharisees count as suffering *midras*-uncleanness; for them that eat of Hallowed Things, the clothes of them that eat Heave-offering count as suffering *midras*-uncleanness; for them that occupy themselves with the Sin-offering water, the clothes of them that eat of Hallowed Things count as suffering *midras*-uncleanness.
>
> (*m. Ḥagigah* 2.7, trans. Danby)

156. Defilement in the midst of Israel (Dead Sea Scrolls)

But even before Paul, some Jews had come to regard other Jews as having defiled the land through their conduct. So the *Community Rule* among the Dead Sea Scrolls (1QS) describes as metaphorical idolaters Israelites who did not accept the rulings of the sect who produced the *Rule*. Similarly, the *Damascus Document* from Qumran describes the assaults of the evil one against those in Israel:

> During all those years Belial [the evil one] shall be unleashed against Israel, as He [God] spoke by the hand of Isaiah, son of Amoz, saying, "Terror and the pit and the snare are upon you, O inhabitants of the land" [Isa 24:17]. Interpreted, these are the three nets of Belial with which Levi, son of Jacob, said that he catches Israel by setting them up as three kinds of righteousness. The first is fornication, the second is riches, and the third is profanation of the Temple. Whoever escapes the first is caught in the second, and whoever saves himself from the second is caught in the third [Isa 24:18].
>
> (*Damascus Document* 4.13-18, trans. Vermes)

Impurity among the Nations

The Torah is also concerned with what might be called *moral* impurity (or "prohibited impurity"), which threatens the sanctity of the land of Israel and cuts a person off from the people. The writings of Second Temple Judaism regarded the causes of prohibited impurity—murder, incest (and illicit sexual contact broadly), and idolatry—as abhorrent and, to our present concern, as distinctly characteristic of the non-Jewish world. Understanding these three prohibited causes of impurity is essential to understanding much of the conflict within and around the assemblies in which Paul worked.

Purity and impurity are chiefly the concern of the "Priestly" material in the Torah. See David P. Wright, "Unclean and Clean (OT)," *ABD* 6:629–41; Jonathan Klawans, "Concepts of Purity in the Bible," in *The Jewish Study Bible*, ed. Adele Berlin and Marc Zvi Brettler (New York: Oxford University Press, 2004), 2041–48; idem, *Impurity and Sin in Ancient Judaism* (New York: Oxford University Press, 2000).

---

157. The Food of non-Jews (m. 'Avodah Zarah)

In 1 Corinthians Paul writes at length about the question of food offered to idols. Idolatry was the chief concern when Jews contemplated eating with non-Jews, even outside the context of sacrifice to another god (which would have been prohibited for Jews). Had a particular piece of meat come from an animal sacrificed to another god? Had a bottle of wine been ritually offered to another god when it was opened? For these reasons Diaspora literature frequently describes faithful Jews as taking care to maintain their own diets even in non-Jewish surroundings (Dan 1:8-16; Jdt 12:2-4); for these reasons, too, Josephus was concerned to rehearse rights secured by Jewish communities to guarantee their own access to kosher foods (see no. 119 above). The

Mishnah offers lengthy considerations of these questions on the part of rabbis who presumed the foods in question were either offered at table, or sold in the market-place, by potential idolaters. We may ask to what extent the context of the common table in the *ekklēsia* would have occasioned greater trust of non-Jews.

> These things that belong to gentiles are forbidden, and it is forbidden to have any benefit at all from them: wine, or the vinegar of gentiles that at first was wine; Hadrianic earthenware; and hides pierced at the heart. . . . Flesh that is entering in unto an idol [but has not yet been sacrificed] is permitted, but what comes forth [from the sacrifice] is forbidden, for it is as "the sacrifice of the dead" [Ps 106:28]. So R. Akiba. It is forbidden to have business with them that are going on an idolatrous pilgrimage [lest one indirectly support their idolatry], but with them that are returning it is permitted.
>
> The skin-bottles of gentiles or their jars that are filled with the wine of an Israelite are forbidden, and it is forbidden to have any benefit at all from them. So R. Meir. But the Sages say: It is not forbidden to have any benefit at all from them. The grape-stones and grape-skins of the gentiles are forbidden and it is forbidden to have any benefit at all from them. So R. Meir. But the Sages say: When moist they are forbidden, but when dried they are permitted. The fish-brine and Bithynian cheese of the gentiles are forbidden, and it is forbidden to have any benefit at all from them. So R. Meir. But the Sages say: It is not forbidden to have any benefit at all from them.
>
> R. Judah said: While they were on a journey R. Ishmael asked R. Joshua and said to him, "Why have they forbidden the cheese of the gentiles?" He answered, "Because they curdle it with rennet from a carcass." . . .
>
> These things of the gentiles are forbidden, but it is not forbidden to have any benefit at all from them: milk which a gentile milked when no Israelite watched him; their bread and their oil (Rabbi and his court permitted the oil), stewed or pickled vegetables into which it is their custom to put wine or vinegar; minced fish, or brine containing no fish. . . . Lo, these are forbidden, but it is not forbidden to have any benefit at all from them.
>
> (*m. ʿAvodah Zarah* 2.3-5, 6, trans. Danby)

Sexual Immorality among the Nations

Hellenistic Jewish literature also dwelled at length on the impurity of sexual immorality among the nations. There is abundant evidence for what Jews considered the sexual vices of their pagan neighbors. The evidence runs from the mundane, such as the following graffiti and epitaph, which could have been sampled from any number of other cities in the Roman Mediterranean world.

158. Erotic graffiti from Pompeii

> If anyone's looking for tender embraces in this town, he should know that all the girls are available.
>
> (*CIL* IV 1796, trans. Berg)[8]

The following graffito was found beneath the stairs of a house in the same city, probably written by Cornelia Helena; the inscription is noteworthy because a magistrate named Rufus lived next door to the place where the inscription was found:

> Cornelia Helena is loved by Rufus.
>
> (CIL IV 4637, trans. Berg)[9]

Another graffito probably highlights the power of the master of a house to make sexual use of his domestic slaves.

> Take advantage of the cook, when you like, as suits you.
>
> (CIL IV 1863, trans. Berg)[10]

159. A FINAL JOKE (TOMB RELIEF)

The following inscription was found in Aesernia, Italy, on the tombstone of an innkeeper and his wife. Their names, L. Calidius Eroticus and Fannia Voluptata, suggest that their hospitality included more than room and board. The inscription depicts an innkeeper settling the bill with a guest; it accompanies carved reliefs of two figures, one counting on his fingers, and to their right, a mule (see Fig. 5.2).

> "Innkeeper, let us settle the bill!"
> "You had one half-liter of wine, one penny's worth of bread, and two pennies
>   for the pillow."
> "Fine."
> "And eight pennies for the girl."
> "This also is fine."
> "Hay for your mule—two pennies."
> "That mule will do me in!"
>
> (ILS 7478, CIL IX 2689)[11]

The evidence also runs to the more literary, including various epigrams and satires. Note that what we might call sexual morality is less important in these texts than concern for the rank and status of the persons involved. For example, the Romans defined *adultery* as intercourse with someone other than one's spouse of equal rank and status: sex with one's slaves was not considered adulterous. It is reasonable to ask, then, how a slave who was subject to a master's or mistress's sexual demands might have heard the exhortations to obey their masters (Eph 6:5-8; 1 Tim 6:1-2).[12]

160. EASY LOVE (HORACE)

> If your groin is swelling,
> and a housemaid or a slave boy is at hand,
> arousing constant desire,
> do you prefer to burst with tension?
> Not me: I enjoy love that is available and easy.
>
> (Horace, *Sermons* 1.2.116-19, trans. Berg)

Fig. 5.2. *Tombstone of Calidius Eroticus and Fannia Voluptata, probably first century* c.e. *The Louvre, Paris. Photo from the Corpus Inscriptionem Latinerum, under the aegis of the Berlin-Brandenburg Academy of Science, online at http://cil.bbaw.de.*

161. AN UNCHASTE COUPLE (MARTIAL)

Your wife calls you a maid-chaser,
but she herself is a chaser of litter-bearers.

(Martial, Epigrams 2.34.1-2, trans. Berg)

162. COURTESANS CRITICIZE A LASCIVIOUS PHILOSOPHER (LUCIAN)

In the following dialogue by Lucian (second century c.e.), two courtesans, Chelidonion and Drosis, discuss Drosis's recent loss of a young customer named Clinias. The philosopher Aristainetos has forbidden Clinias, his new student, to visit his lover because, the courtesans suspect, he wants to possess Clinias for himself. Note that Lucian's implied judgment is of the philosopher's hypocrisy—also, perhaps, of the boy's parents, who are less concerned that he be subjected to a philosopher's importunities than to the favors of common courtesans.

CHELIDONION: So little Clinias has stopped visiting your house? I haven't seen him for some time.

DROSIS: It is true, Chelidonion. His master has shut him up in their rooms. He stops the boy from coming to see me.

CHELIDONION: Whom are you talking about? You don't mean Diotimos who is teaching at the gymnasium? Diotimos is a good friend of mine.

DROSIS: No; I refer to the most debauched of philosophers, Aristainetos.

CHELIDONION: You mean the long-faced, funeral-faced man with the shaggy whiskers? He takes the little fellows for walks through the Poikile.

DROSIS: Yes, that is the charlatan. I wish he'd die in a hurry! May the executioner drag him to his peace by his whiskers!

CHELIDONION: But how could a character like this false philosopher have seduced Clinias?

DROSIS: I don't know, Chelidonion. The boy hasn't set his foot in my street for the last three days; I am rather worried. It was I, you know, who taught him what a woman is; and he hasn't slept with another woman since his first lesson. Having bad presentiments in regard to my Clinias, I sent Nebris, my slave, to see if he was at the Agora or in the Poikile. Nebris tells me she saw him walking with Aristainetos. She nodded to the boy from a distance, and Clinias blushed and was discomfited but did not look at her again. Then they reentered the city. Nebris followed as far as the Dipylon, but, since they did not come out again, she returned without learning anything more.

You can imagine how worried I have been since then. I don't know what will become of the boy. I have always treated him fairly. At first I was afraid some other woman had got him and his love for me had turned to hate. It also seemed possible that his father had forbidden him to see his Drosis. This evening, however, Dromon, the boy's slave, came to me with this letter. Take it and read, Chelidonion. You can read, can't you?

CHELIDONION: Let us see now. The penmanship is not especially good. You can see this letter was written in a hurry. He writes:

"Oh, how much I love you, my Drosis! The gods, every one of them, will vouch for the degree of my affection. Know, therefore, that it is not by reason of dislike but by necessity that I have come to be separated from you. My father has entrusted me to Aristainetos to study philosophy, and my master has found out everything about the two of us and has scolded me severely, saying it was not meet for the son of Architeles and Erasicleia to carry on with a courtesan. He says that he will convince me that virtue is preferable to voluptuousness—"

DROSIS, (interrupting): May the imbecile suffer an apoplectic fit! Think of teaching such philosophy to a young man!

CHELIDONION (resuming the letter): "—so that I am forced to obey my master. He follows me wherever I go and guards me carefully and lets no woman approach me. He promises me that if I learn his kind of wisdom and do what he requires of me, I shall, after some efforts, become a virtuous and happy man. I write this letter hurriedly. I hope no one is looking.

> Be happy and think sometimes of your,
> Lost forever,
> Clinias"

. . .

DROSIS: I am dying for the little fellow's love. He is like a kitten. Dromon tells me that Aristainetos is reputed to have a weakness for young boys. That is, under the pretext of teaching them rhetoric and philosophy, the whiskered codger lives with the most handsome of his pupils. According to Dromon, Aristainetos has already had an interesting conversation with Clinias on the subject and promises to make the boy like to the gods. He reads to him of the love affairs that the old philosophers had with their disciples, and tells him that the gods don't interest themselves in women, but prefer the company of good philosophers like himself. However, Dromon threatens to complain to the boy's father. . . .

CHELIDONION: . . . Do not worry, Drosis. Everything will turn out fine. In my opinion you ought to leave an inscription on the part of the Keramic wall where Architeles takes his daily walk. He will understand the danger his son is in and will save him from his doom.

DROSIS: But shall we be able to write without being seen?

CHELIDONION: It will be done at night, Drosis, with a piece of charcoal that we shall pick up on the way.

DROSIS: Fine! Stand with me, Chelidonion, in my fight against the pedant. We courtesans must not allow those whiskered philosophers to mislead the young generation.

(Lucian, *Mimes of the Courtesans*, trans. Cullen)

163. THE "EDUCATION OF CORINNA"

In another satire, Lucian depicts a widow, Crobyle, her funds depleted, talking her daughter Corinna into life as a courtesan. In the Greek world, it was not uncommon for a man to hire a courtesan to accompany him to banquets, where he would enjoy her company before having sex with her afterward, or (as Corbyle mentions) for a host to hire courtesans for his guests. Bruce Winter has suggested that this practice explains the connection in 1 Cor 6:12-20 between gluttony and sexual indulgence.[13] Lucian's satire suggests that lower-class women like Crobyle had less of a sense of shame regarding sex; he does not address the sense of shame on the part of a courtesan's clients.

> CROBYLE: Well, Corinna, you see now that it wasn't so terrible to lose your virginity. You have spent your first night with a man. You have earned your first gift, no less than a hundred drachmas. With that I'll buy you a necklace.

Fig. 5.3. *A courtesan holds out a drinking vessel for a guest at a banquet. Fresco from the Casa dei Casti Amanti, Pompeii, 62–79 c.e. Photo in the public domain.*

CORINNA: Yes, dear mother, do buy me a necklace. Let it be a necklace made of fine, shining stones like the one Philainis wears.

CROBYLE: I promise. It will be just like the one Philainis wears. But listen: I want to teach you how you should conduct yourself with men. Take my words to heart, daughter. We have only your favor with men to depend on for a living.

You can't imagine how hard it has been for us to get along since your blessed father's death. We lacked nothing when he was alive.... After his death . . . (and our money ran out—*Ed.*) I found work weaving and turning thread, barely earning enough to buy bread with. I have raised you, however, my precious little daughter. You are the only hope left me.... Now I think you are big enough to support your tired mother. Not only that: you can even earn enough to dress richly, to buy yourself the newest robes of purple, and slaves.

CORINNA: What do you mean, mother? Why do you say that?

CROBYLE: Don't you understand, little fool? Why, you will earn a great deal being attentive to nice young men, drinking in their company and going to bed with them—for money, of course.

CORINNA: (*scandalized*): You mean like Lyra, the daughter of Daphnis? . . . But she is—a courtesan!

CROBYLE: What of it? There is no harm in that. You will become rich. You are sure to have many lovers.
  Corinna cries, saying nothing.

CROBYLE: Why, Corinna! Why do you weep? Don't you see how many courtesans there are, how they are all sought after, and how they all make money? I knew Daphnis when she was in rags—that was before she got sense enough to make use of her body. Look at her now! She struts like a queen, all bespangled with gold, wearing flowery dresses, and no less than four slaves behind her.

CORINNA: And how did she get all that, dear mother?

CROBYLE: Well, in the first place, by dressing elegantly and being amiable and cheery with everybody. She does not giggle at any little thing, as you do; instead, she only smiles, which is much more attractive. She treats shrewdly, but without double-crossing, the men that come to see her or take her to their houses. She never approaches them first. When she is paid to assist at a banquet, she takes care not to get drunk—it is foolish and men can't bear it—and she does not stuff herself with food like an imbecile, so that when she gets into bed she is in condition to serve her lover well. She no more than touches the various dishes served—delicately, with her fingertips, and always in silence. And she never guzzles her wine, but drinks slowly, quietly, in gentle little sips.

CORINNA: But supposing she is thirsty, dear mother?

CROBYLE: Especially when she is thirsty, foolish girl! And she never speaks more than is necessary, and never pokes fun at anybody present, and has eyes only for the man who has paid her. That is why everybody appreciates her. Furthermore, when it is time to get into bed, she never resorts to any obscenity, but does her task with care and loving attention. In bed, she bears one thing in mind—to win the man and make a steady lover of him. That is why everybody speaks highly of her. If you take this lesson to heart and do likewise we, too, shall be rich, for she is far from having your looks and your complexion. But I won't say anything more. Long may you live, little daughter, and prosper!

CORINNA: But tell me, dear mother: Will all those that will pay me be as handsome as Eucritos, the fellow I slept with yesterday?

CROBYLE: Not all. There will be better looking fellows. And some will be very vigorous and energetic—you know what I mean; while others will not be quite as handsome.

CORINNA: And shall I have to give myself to the homely fellows too?

CROBYLE: Especially to them, my child. It is that class that pays best. The beautiful kind only want to give their looks. I repeat: be careful to attach yourself to men who pay best—if you want to have people point you out on the street and say: "Do you see that Corinna, the daughter of Crobyle? Do you notice how rich she became, and what happiness she brings to her old mother? Oh, thrice happy has she rendered her, blessed be the girl!"

(Lucian, *The Education of Corinna*, trans. Cullen)[14]

A Sexual Double Standard

Obviously Greek and Roman cultures exhibit a double standard regarding the sexual morality of a husband and a wife. To be female in the Hellenistic and Roman worlds in which Paul moved meant that one's rights were severely limited. Wives of men holding equestrian and senatorial rank enjoyed somewhat more autonomy, but it is unlikely that many women of this rank were active in Paul's communities.

Fig. 5.4. *Erotic fresco from the Casa dei Casti Amanti (IX 12.6-8), Pompeii, 62–79 c.e. A courtesan supports a young man who has passed out from wine at a banquet; another courtesan brings a fan. Many of the frescos adorning the dining rooms of Pompeii villas are far more explicit in depicting sexual activities at banquets. Photo in the public domain.*

164. THE MODESTY OF A PROPER WIFE IN BED (PLUTARCH)

Plutarch (second century C.E.) illustrates what was expected of a married woman in Roman society.

> The wedded wife ought, especially when the light is out, not to be the same as ordinary women, but when her body is invisible, her virtue, her exclusive devotion to her husband, her constancy and her affection, ought to be most in evidence.
>
> (Plutarch, *Marital Precepts* 144F, trans. Treggiari)

165. "PROTECTING" ONE'S WIFE FROM DEBAUCHERY (PLUTARCH)

Plutarch quite frankly acknowledged and encouraged the double standard as a way of preserving one's wife's respectability.

> The lawful wives of the Persian kings sit beside them at dinner, and eat with them. But when the kings wish to be merry and get drunk, they send their wives away, and send for their music-girls and concubines. In so far they are right in what they do, because they do not concede any share in their licentiousness and debauchery to their wedded wives. If therefore a man in private life, who is incontinent and dissolute in regard to his pleasures, commit some peccadillo with a paramour or a maid-servant, his wedded wife ought not to be indignant or angry, but she should reason that it is respect for her which leads him to share his debauchery, licentiousness, and wantonness with another woman.
>
> (Plutarch, *Marital Precepts* 140B, trans. Babbitt)

These quotations illustrate a double standard in Roman expectations for men's and women's behavior. Roman social historian Susan Treggiari summarizes the ethical inconsistency in this way:

> Implicit in the advice to wives to ignore the philandering of their husbands is the idea that it meant little. We may picture a continuum which runs roughly from brief encounters with a man's own slaves or prostitutes and music-girls through other people's slaves (where negotiation or poaching was involved) to respectable but unmarried women of a lower social class, and then to wives and women of his own class and long-standing affairs. The last was the most serious transgression: an offence against the husband, the mistress's virtue, social ideals, and the man's own wife, especially since marriage with the mistress became a possibility (though one endangered by the Augustan Law). Where the mistress was of lower status, the greatest offence to the wife was caused when the husband kept her or introduced her into the home.[15]

166. THAT A WIFE'S FRIENDS SHOULD BE HER HUSBAND'S (PLUTARCH)

Paul addresses in Corinth a situation in which a woman might be a member of the *ekklēsia* while her husband remained outside, worshiping other gods. Such a situation clearly went against social expectations, as Plutarch's advice to a newlywed couple illustrates. (As we shall see in chapter 5, deviation from the household religion on the part of women or slaves was considered dangerous.)

> A wife ought not to make friends of her own, but to enjoy her husband's friends in common with him. The gods are the first and most important friends. Wherefore it is becoming for a wife to worship and to know only the gods that her husband believes in, and to shut the front door tight upon all queer rituals and outlandish superstitions. For with no god do stealthy and secret rites performed by a woman find any favor.
>
> (Plutarch, *Marital Precepts* 140D, trans. Babbitt)

The Censure of Sexual Immorality

Augustus took pride in his own efforts to revise existing marriage law in what one scholar has called an exercise in "social engineering."[16] By enacting rewards and punishments that encouraged members of the Senate and equestrians to marry, to marry within their class, to have children, and not to condone adultery, Augustus apparently sought to create a distinct senatorial "class" of exemplary virtue (and, not incidentally, to channel wealth more exclusively through inheritance within that class). Augustus claimed as well to be concerned to increase the birth rate and thus repopulate a nation ravaged by war; but this was not likely his primary motive. Of course, one effect of his legislative intervention was to posture himself as the unique champion of Roman morality.[17]

This bold innovation—for marriage and inheritance had never before been made so clearly a matter of public policy—is relevant for the study of Paul for several reasons. First, the fact that Augustus felt it necessary points to a phenomenon against which the legislation was aimed: men and women were engaging in sexual and romantic relationships across lines of rank and status and therefore sharing and passing on wealth outside of the strict lines of inheritance within equestrian families. Some scholars have concluded that in the first century b.c.e., women had begun to gain more freedom for themselves, counter to the "double standard" just described—for example, the freedom to decide what to do with their own money—and that these more independent women might have played prominent roles in the assemblies around Paul.[18] On the other hand, Augustus's legislation had to do primarily with women of equestrian rank (or women involved with men of that rank), and we should expect few such women to have been represented in those assemblies.

Second, Augustus's program focused as well on the public and conspicuous virtue of the senatorial "class"—including even the imposition of a "dress code" to distinguish proper Roman matrons (chastely married to one husband) from adulterers and prostitutes. The admonitions in a letter such as 1 Timothy regarding women's dress and adornment suggest that its author shared similar concerns, perhaps in an effort to make the assembly appear socially respectable in Roman eyes. Although that letter was probably not written by Paul, we see in 1 Cor 11:2-16 Paul's own apparent concern to regulate the way the assembly's women presented themselves in public.[19]

These texts and others in Paul's letters (for example, 1 Corinthians 7) continue to vex interpreters. Was Paul responding to situations that he considered problematic because he shared upper-class concerns like those expressed in Augustus's legislation? Was he taking part in a longer-lasting Hellenistic philosophical discussion regarding marriage?[20] These questions are beyond the scope of this book, but a few selections may nevertheless be illustrative.

167. Augustus's marriage legislation

Here is Suetonius's summary of the legislation and the reaction to it.

> He revised existing laws and enacted some new ones, for example, on extravagance, on adultery and chastity, on bribery, and on the encouragement of marriage among the various classes of citizens. Having made somewhat more stringent changes in the last of these than in the others, he was unable to carry it out because of an open revolt against its provisions, until he had abolished or

Fig. 5.5. *Marble bust of Augustus's wife Livia, c. 31 B.C.E. Augustus presented his own household as an example of propriety and modesty—even to the point of prosecuting his own daughter for immorality. Museo Palazzo Massimo, Rome. Photo: Neil Elliott.*

mitigated a part of the penalties, besides increasing the rewards and allowing a three years' exemption from the obligation to marry after the death of a husband or wife. When the knights even then persistently called for its repeal at a public show, he sent for the children of Germanicus and exhibited them, some in his own lap and some in their father's, intimating by his gestures and expression that they should not refuse to follow that young man's example. And on finding that the spirit of the law was being evaded by betrothal with immature girls and by frequent changes of wives, he shortened the duration of betrothals and set a limit on divorce.

(Suetonius, *Augustus* 34, trans. Rolfe)

168. A PROTEST AGAINST AUGUSTAN MORALITY (PROPERTIUS)

An earlier attempt at similar legislation (in 28 B.C.E.) apparently failed. The relief expressed by the poet Propertius, at not having to give up his love for a woman of subordinate status, is probably representative of the wider resentment on the part of the equestrians mentioned in the previous selection. These men did not want to be forced into a marriage of rank, which presumably means that they did not want to give up relationships with women of inferior rank.[21]

Cynthia rejoiced when that law was repealed; we had both wept a long time at the thought that it would separate us. Even Jupiter cannot separate two people in love; ah, but Caesar is powerful. Caesar's power is in armies, however—the power of conquest means nothing in love.

(Propertius, *Elegies* 2.7, trans. Elliott)

169. THE FREQUENCY OF DIVORCE AND REMARRIAGE (SENECA)

Augustus's concern was not only with morality or with keeping up moral appearances among the elites (although he clearly wished to present the Roman senatorial class as worthy to rule over their inferiors). Apparently he was troubled by the frequency with which some elite men and women were moving from marriage to marriage, producing children in different lineages whose inheritance of wealth would further blur the lines between higher and lower orders.

Writing in a later decade, Seneca complained in an aside that elite women divorced and remarried with a casualness that he found scandalous. The motives of such women may have been not just self-amusement, as Seneca implies, but to secure for themselves a level of financial security. (Seneca did not level a similar indictment against men, who presumably were doing as much of the divorcing and remarrying but who might not have been as motivated by the need for financial security.)

Is there any woman that blushes at divorce now that certain illustrious and noble ladies reckon their years, not by the number of consuls, but by the number of their husbands, and leave home in order to marry, and marry in order to be divorced? They shrank from this scandal as long as it was rare; now, since every gazette has a divorce case, they have learned to do what they used to hear so much about. Is there any shame at all for adultery now that matters have come to such a pass that no woman has any use for a husband except to inflame her paramour? Chastity is simply a proof of ugliness. Where will you find any woman so wretched, so unattractive, as to be content with a couple of paramours—without having each hour assigned to a different one? And the day is not long enough for them all, but she must be carried in her litter to the house of one, and spend the night with another. She is simple and behind the times who is not aware that living with one paramour is called "marriage"! As the shame of these offences has disappeared now that their practice has spread more broadly, so you will make ingrates more numerous and increase their importance if once they begin to count their number.

(Seneca, *On Benefits* 3.16.2-3, trans. Basore, LCL)

170. The Philosophical Censure of Immorality (Musonius Rufus)

Musonius Rufus, a Stoic teacher active in Rome in the year 50 c.e., is an example of moral rigorism on the part of philosophers. Note the concerns that govern the following discussion of sexual pleasures: first, the importance of self-control, of not

Fig. 5.6. *Bust of Vibia Matidia, an aristocratic Roman woman of the early second century c.e. Her elaborate hairstyle would have been a signal to Augustus's contemporaries that she was one of the "new women" against which his legislation was directed. Museo Capitolino, Rome. Photo: G. Dagli Orti; DeA Picture Library/Art Resource, New York.*

being "ruled" by one's desires; next, procreation as the one proper purpose of sex within marriage. Note too that in condemning the "victimless" sexual use of a man's slaves Musonius rejects the double standard we have seen in earlier selections.

Sexual pleasures are not the most trivial part of the life of ease, for those who follow this life seek not only lawful partners but also unlawful ones, not only females but also males, sometimes chasing the former, at other times asking for the latter, and not content with those who are readily at hand, they desire the hard-to-get, seeking shameful connections; all of the preceding are major reproaches of what it means to be a man.

Those not seeking a life of ease and not pursuing evil should regard only those sexual pleasures as righteous that occur within marriage, when completed for the procreation of children, because this is lawful, but to regard them as intended for pleasure alone is unjust and unlawful, even if this view is held within a marriage. But with regard to all other sorts of sexual relations, those pursued adulterously are most lawless, and of these, relations involving males with males are not more tolerable, because such a connection is a shameless act, contrary to nature.

And without even considering adultery, as many connections with women that lack lawful legitimacy are all shameful and are performed with no regard for self-control. The one who consistently practices self-control will not hook up with a courtesan nor with a free woman outside of marriage, nor—by Zeus— with his slave girl. For the unlawful character of these acts of intercourse renders them indecent and matters of shame and great disgrace for those who look for them, so that no one would practice them openly nor allow anyone to do so, even if one seldom gets embarrassed, while those who are not fully ruined might dare to do them in a concealed and secret way.

And even to try to cover over these relations is to agree that they are sin. "By Zeus," [someone will say,] "it is not as in the case of the adulterer wronging the husband of the defiled woman; the one who hooks up with a courtesan, or—by Zeus—with an unmarried woman, wrongs no one, for he didn't ruin anyone's hope for having children." But I still hold out and insist that everyone who sins and commits wrong—even if it is not one of one's neighbors— immediately wrongs himself above all, making himself appear worse and more dishonorable. For the one who sins becomes worse and more dishonorable to the extent of his sin. So even if I should not consider the wrong itself, still the person is shameful who by lack of self-control always must go toward the inferior part of pleasure and rejoices in getting dirty, as pigs do.

Isn't such a man who sleeps with his slave girl at least such a person, though some think him especially above reproach, since every master is considered intrinsically empowered to use his own slave however he wants? This perspective does not hold water for me. For if it does not seem shameful nor unfitting for the master to sleep with his own slave girl, and especially if she happens to be unattached, let him consider how it would appear to him, if the mistress of the house slept with a man-slave. For would this be tolerable, not only if a lawfully married woman approached a slave, but even if an unmarried woman did this?

And further, one will not consider the husbands worse than their wives, inferior to their wives at supervising their desires, the stronger in opinion inferior to the weaker, the rulers inferior to the ruled, will he? For the men should definitely be better, if indeed they are regarded as leaders over the women. But if they appear to be morally out of control, [they will even also be regarded as] evildoers. Is it even necessary to say that it is a deed of moral anarchy and nothing else for the master to lie with his slave girl? This is obvious.

(Musonius Rufus, *Discourse 12: Concerning Sexual Pleasures*, trans. Reasoner)

Jewish Responses

There are abundant references in Second Temple Jewish literature to the sexual incontinence of the non-Jewish world. The Wisdom of Solomon, for example, links all manner of wickedness in the pagan world to the practice of idolatry, its wellspring— in a way that has often been compared with Paul's language in Rom 1:18-32.

Then it was not enough for them to err about the knowledge of God,
But though living in great strife due to ignorance,
They call such great evils peace.
For whether they kill children in their initiations, or celebrate secret mysteries,
Or hold frenzied revels with strange customs,
They no longer keep either their lives or their marriages pure,
But they either treacherously kill one another, or grieve one another by adultery,
And all is a raging riot of blood and murder, theft and deceit, corruption, faithlessness, tumult, perjury,
Confusion over what is good, forgetfulness of favors,
Defiling of souls, sexual perversion,
Disorder in marriages, adultery, and debauchery.
For the worship of idols not to be named
Is the beginning and cause and end of every evil.

(Wisdom of Solomon 14:22-27 NRSV)

Hellenistic Jews such as Philo of Alexandria did more than simply condemn what they considered the sexual vices of their neighbors, however. They sought to demonstrate that the Torah in fact expressed a single, superior standard, its specific commands embodying universally valid principles worthy of universal respect.

Thus, rather than simply ascribe different sexual norms to cultural differences (as Plato did, for example, in comparing the legislation of different cities regarding "intercourse with men and boys," *Laws* 836A), Philo presented Jewish sexual ethics in terms of the Hellenistic values of self-control (*enkrateia*), procreation for the sake of the city, and the promotion of manly courage or virtue (*aretē*)—although the Torah itself does not usually provide rationales for its commandments, beyond occasionally stipulating that certain practices are "abomination" (Hebrew *tôʿēbâ*; Greek *bdelygma*) or "depravity" (Hebrew *zimmâ*; Greek *asebēma*). (Compare the arguments made by Musonius Rufus in the preceding selection.)

171. "Unnatural" behavior among the pagans (Philo)

So, for example, Philo discussed "pederasty" (*to paiderastein*), a word that in English means the sexual use of a boy by an older man. Philo seems instead to be describing men who seek to seduce other men by making themselves up in feminine ways—perhaps for prostitution?—and, toward the end of this passage, taking aim at the roles such "feminized" men are accorded at the head of public ritual processions. He seems thus not to have a single target in view but to be criticizing a range of behaviors he considers "unmanly." Note the deployment of the arguments just mentioned, particularly the importance of procreation. All other sexual behavior is for Philo "unnatural" or, better, "beyond nature" (*para physin*: see Rom 1:26-27). This paragraph comes just after Philo has condemned the practice of intentionally marrying a sterile woman, which is also unproductive and thus "unnatural." (Compare also Philo, *On the Contemplative Life* 59-62.)

> Much graver than the above [intentionally marrying a woman who cannot bear children] is another evil, which has ramped its way into the cities, namely pederasty [*to paiderastein*]. In former days the very mention of it was a great disgrace, but now it is a matter of boasting not only to the active but to the passive partners who habituate themselves to endure the disease of effemination, let both body and soul run to waste, and leave no ember of their male sex-nature to smolder. Mark how conspicuous they braid and adorn the hair of their heads, and how they scrub and paint their faces with cosmetics and pigments and the like, and smother themselves with fragrant unguents. For of all such embellishments, used by all who deck themselves out to wear a comely appearance, fragrance is the most seductive. In fact the transformation of the male nature to the female is practiced by them as an art and does not raise a blush.
>
> These persons are rightly judged worthy of death by those who obey the law, which ordains that the man-woman [*androgynon*] who debases the sterling coin of nature should perish unavenged, suffered not to live for a day or even an hour, as a disgrace to himself, his house, his native land and the whole human race. And the lover of such may be assured that he is subject to the same penalty. He pursues an unnatural pleasure and does his best to render cities desolate and uninhabited by destroying the means of procreation. Furthermore he sees no harm in becoming an instructor in the grievous vices of unmanliness and effeminacy by prolonging the bloom of the young and emasculating the flower of their prime, which should rightly be trained to strength and robustness. Finally, like a bad husbandman he lets the deep-soiled and fruitful fields lie sterile, by taking steps to keep them from bearing, while he spends his labor night and day on soil from which no growth at all can be expected. The reason is, I think, to be found in the prizes awarded in many nations to licentiousness and effeminacy. Certainly you may see these hybrids of man and woman continually strutting about through the thick of the market, heading the processions at the feasts, appointed to serve as unholy ministers of holy things, leading the mysteries and initiations and celebrating the rites of Demeter.
>
> (Philo, *On the Special Laws* 3.37-39, 42, trans. Colson, LCL)

Homosexual practices—especially relationships between older men and boys—were relatively common in the Greek world, less so in Roman culture. Neither culture understood such relationships to express an exclusive homosexual orientation; rather, a figure like Socrates illustrates the expectation that a man would marry a woman to have children, but look elsewhere—to heterosexual and homosexual liaisons alike—for friendship and sexual gratification. Paul's references to women and men committing "degrading" and "shameless" homosexual acts (Rom 1:26-27 NRSV) and to *malakoi* and *arsenokoitai* (1 Cor 6:9-10)—words that have been translated in notoriously different ways over time—remain controversial, not least because homosexual practices in Paul's day were not correlated with homosexual orientation in the way we routinely presume that they do.

See Tikva Frymer-Kensky, "Sex and Sexuality," *ABD* 5:1144–46; Martti Nissinen, *Homoeroticism in the Biblical World: A Historical Perspective,* trans. Kirsi Stjerna (Minneapolis: Fortress Press, 1998); L. William Countryman, *Dirt, Greed, and Sex: Sexual Ethics in the New Testament and Their Implications for Today,* rev. ed. (Minneapolis: Fortress Press, 2007); Dale B. Martin, "Heterosexism and the Interpretation of Romans 1:18-32," in idem, *Sex and the Single Savior: Gender and Sexuality in Biblical Interpretation* (Louisville: Westminster John Knox, 2006). For a different understanding of Rom 1:24-27 see Neil Elliott, *The Arrogance of Nations: Reading Romans in the Shadow of Empire,* Paul in Critical Contexts (Minneapolis: Fortress, 2008), 72-83.

Sexual Immorality in the *Ekklēsiai*

We have dwelt at some length on the perception of sexual immorality because it plays such an important role—even if a stereotyped one—in Paul's exhortation (so, for example, Rom 1:26-27; 1 Cor 6:9-11, 13-20; 7:5, 9, 32-38; 1 Thess 4:3-8; compare Eph 5:25-33; Col 3:18-19). Usually these exhortations are issued as "reminders," but in one place Paul assails a whole assembly for tolerating the actual immorality of a member who is sleeping with his father's wife—immorality of "a kind that is not found even among pagans" (1 Cor 5:1). It is possible that the immorality was tolerated because of the stature of the offender, or perhaps what Paul perceived as immorality was not recognized by at least some of the Corinthians as a case of actual incest: here the role of Roman law may be relevant.[22] Nevertheless, it is clear that in Greek, Roman, and Jewish cultures alike, actual incest was considered a great offense.

172. The horror of incest (Sophocles)

For example, in Sophocles' play *Oedipus the King* (429 B.C.E.), the terrible destiny awaiting Oedipus arises from his father's long-past offense. Laius had violated the hospitality of King Pelops by sexually assaulting the king's youngest son, who had been entrusted to his care as a tutor. Cursed to perish by the hand of his own son, Laius took the terrible precaution of pinning his infant son's heels together and ordering his wife, Jocasta, to kill the child. (Note again that pederasty on the part of a married man was not unusual and did not label Laius a "homosexual.") But Jocasta gave the child to a servant, who abandoned him in a field; he was rescued by a shepherd, who named him Oedipus ("swollen-foot"), and through a series of events came to be raised as the adopted son of King Polybus of Corinth. Seeking later to know his own identity he asked the Delphic Oracle who his true parents were and was told that he would "Mate with your own mother and shed with your own hands the blood of your own father."

Shocked, he fled Corinth to avoid killing his adopted father; but on the road he met Laius, whom he did not recognize, and when Laius refused to give way, Oedipus struck him down—unwittingly killing his own father. He proceeded to Thebes, where he met the widow Jocasta—his own mother—and, again unknowingly, married her. The main action of the play involves Oedipus doggedly pursuing the murderer of the city's king to alleviate the curse that threatens his city—not realizing that the city can be saved only when he himself is "purged" from it (the language used also in 1 Cor 5:7-8 and Deut 19:19). At one point he presses the blind prophet Teiresias to reveal what he knows:

> Teiresias. Let me go home; prevent me not; 'tis best
>   That you should bear your burden and I mine.
> Oedipus. For shame! no true-born Theban patriot
>   Would thus withhold the word of prophecy.

(Thwarted and defied, Oedipus accuses the prophet himself of being a traitor to the city.)

> Oedipus. I am enraged, and will not stint my words,
>   But speak my whole mind. You, I think, are he,
> Who planned the crime, aye, and performed it too,
>   All save the assassination; and if you
>   Had not been blind, I would be sworn to say
> That you alone had done the bloody deed.
> Teiresias. 'Tis so? Then I charge you to abide
>   By your own proclamation; from this day
> Speak not to these or me. You are the man,
>   You the accursed polluter of this land. . . .
> I say you are the murderer of the man
>   Whose murderer you pursue.
> Oedipus. You will rue it
>   Twice to repeat so gross a calumny.

TEIRESIAS. Must I say more to aggravate your rage?
OEDIPUS. Say all you will; it will be but waste of breath.
TEIRESIAS. I say you live now with your nearest kin
  In infamy, unwitting in your shame. . . .
Thus then I answer: since you have not spared
  To twit me with my blindness—you have eyes,
Yet see not in what misery you have fallen,
  Nor where you dwell, nor with whom for a mate.
You know your lineage? Nay, you know it not,
  And all unwitting are a double foe
To your own kin, the living and the dead;
  Aye and the dogging curse of mother and sire
One day shall drive you, like a two-edged sword,
  Beyond our borders, and the eyes that now
See clear shall hence see only endless night.
  Ah, whither shall your bitter cry not reach,
What crag in all Cithaeron but shall then
  Reverberate your wail, when you have found
With what a nuptial song you were borne
  Home, but to no fair haven, on the gale!
Aye, and a flood of ills you cannot guess
  Shall set you and your children in one line.
Flout then both Creon and my words, for none
  Of mortals shall be stricken worse than you.

The prophecy comes true: all is at last revealed by the shepherd who had rescued Oedipus the child. Jocasta hangs herself; discovering her body, Oedipus blinds himself and begs to be exiled from the city.
          (Sophocles, *Oedipus the King* 320-23; 345-53; 362-77; 412-28,
                                        trans. Storr, alt.)

The Roman Concern for Social Order

The immorality addressed in 1 Corinthians 5 was, as best we can tell, unusual in the assemblies Paul knew. More often, other challenges confronted the nascent communities. Some, perhaps, had been accustomed to the standards, the worship, and the teaching of the synagogues, having been sympathetic frequenters of the synagogue as "God-fearers" (*theosebeis* or *seboumenoi*) before entering the *ekklēsia*. But now they were not onlookers but active participants, "saints," "holy ones" themselves. Called to give up the worship of idols, they were also thus expected to withdraw from the fabric of family, social, and civic life to which they had been accustomed. Such withdrawal—and participation in a new and unfamiliar community with ambiguous connections to a foreign religion, Judaism—would have evoked suspicion of an intensity that may be difficult for contemporary readers to imagine.

The Roman cities in which Paul's assemblies sprang up were cities in which expectations regarding social order were clear and powerful. People were to know their place and keep to it—and thus preserve the civic order. As we have seen in chapter 2, the worship of the city's gods was considered key to maintaining civic harmony and peace.

Those in power expressed concern not just regarding enemies at the frontiers but about potential dangers lurking in their cities, even in their own households. That women—or slaves—should steal away to worship gods other than those of their husbands and masters was for them a scandalous and frightening prospect.

173. The danger of women's ecstasy (Euripides)

A keen anxiety surrounded religious rites performed by women, out of sight—or supervision—of the city elders. The anxiety was ancient: it was the premise already in the fifth century B.C.E. when Euripides wrote his play *The Bakchai* (Latin: *Bacchae*, "The Devotees of Bacchus," or Dionysos), in which slaughter at women's hands was actually inspired by the god himself, to the city's undoing.

King Pentheus of Thebes returns to his city alarmed at reports that a mysterious stranger is spreading the worship of Dionysos; even his father-in-law and the priest Teiresias are joining in. What Pentheus does not realize is that the stranger is the god himself, hailed throughout the play by a worshipful chorus.

> PENTHEUS: Scarce had I crossed our borders, when mine ear
> Was caught by this strange rumor, that our own
>   Wives, our own sisters, from their hearths are flown
> To wild and secret rites; and cluster there
>   High on the shadowy hills, with dance and prayer
> To adore this new-made God, this Dionyse,
>   Whate'er he be!—And in their companies
> Deep wine-jars stand, and ever and anon
>   Away into the loneliness now one
> Steals forth, and now a second, maid or dame,
>   Where love lies waiting, not of God! The flame,
> They say, of Bacchios wraps them. Bacchios! Nay,
>   'Tis more to Aphrodite that they pray.

(The charges—that apart from the solemnities of civic cult, the combination of women, wine, and darkness will result in degenerate licentiousness—were common accusations in the Hellenistic and Roman worlds, eventually leveled against early Christianity as well.) Pentheus is duly alarmed and vows to destroy the rite and its founder.

> PENTHEUS: They tell me, too, there is a stranger come,
> A man of charm and spell, from Lydian seas,
>   A head all gold and cloudy fragrancies,
> A wine-red cheek, and eyes that hold the light
>   Of the very Cyprian. Day and livelong night
> He haunts amid the damsels, o'er each lip
>   Dangling his cup of joyance!—Let me grip

Him once, but once, within these walls, right swift
  That wand shall cease its music, and that drift
Of tossing curls lie still—when my rude sword
Falls between neck and trunk!

(This characterization of Dionysos as dangerously effeminate would be taken up centuries later by Octavian in his campaign against Mark Antony, when the latter adopted Dionysos as his champion. Pentheus orders his guard to hunt down the stranger. They find him—rather, Dionysos surrenders himself to them—and they bring him to Pentheus for questioning. The king is haughty and insulting; the god, still mistaken by Pentheus as only a priest of Dionysos, parries the questions until Pentheus touches on his rites.)

PENTHEUS: How is your worship held, by night or day?
DIONYSOS: Most oft by night; 'tis a majestic thing,
  The darkness.
PENTHEUS: —Ha! With women worshipping?
  'Tis craft and rottenness!
DIONYSOS: —By day no less,
  Whoso will seek may find unholiness.
PENTHEUS: Enough! Thy doom is fixed, for false pretense
  Corrupting Thebes.
DIONYSOS: —Not mine; but thine, for dense
  Blindness of heart, and for blaspheming God!

(Pentheus has the stranger, whom he does not yet recognize, imprisoned; but an earthquake releases him and sets fire to the palace. Dionysos encounters his antagonist again and invites him to join in the sacred rites by going into the fields in disguise, dressed as a Maenad and wearing a woman's wig. Consumed with curiosity, Pentheus agrees. It is a mistake. A shepherd, eyewitness to what follows, returns to the palace to give his report. He saw the king take his position high in a pine tree to spy on the revelers—who included his own mother, Agavê.

MESSENGER: But out of Heaven a Voice—oh, what voice else?—
  'Twas he that called! "Behold, O damosels,
I bring you him who turns to despite
  Both you and me, and darkens my great Light.
'Tis yours to avenge!" So spake he . . .
  Then came the Voice again. And when they knew
Their God's clear call, old Cadmus' royal brood,
  Up, like wild pigeons startled in a wood,
On flying feet they came, his mother blind,
  Agavê, and her sisters, and behind
All the wild crowd . . .

(The messenger reports that the Maenads tugged at the pine tree until Pentheus fell to earth.)

MESSENGER: —and there hard by
Was horror visible. 'Twas his mother stood
    O'er him, first priestess of those rites of blood.
He tore the coif, and from his head away
    Flung it, that she might know him, and not slay
To her own misery. He touched the wild
    Cheek, crying: "Mother, it is I, your child,
Your Pentheus, born to you in Echion's hall!
    Have mercy, Mother! Let it not befall
Through sin of mine, that you should slay your son!"
    But she, with lips afoam and eyes that run
Like leaping fire, with thoughts that ne'er should be
    On earth, possessed by Bacchios utterly,
Stays not, nor hears; 'round his left arm she put
    Both hands, set hard against his side her foot,
Drew . . . and the shoulder severed!—not by might
    Of arm, but easily, as the God made light
Her hands' grim work. And at the other side
    Was Ino rending; and the torn flesh cried,
And on Autonoë pressed, and all the crowd
    Of ravening arms. Yea, all the air was loud
With groans that faded into sobbing breath,
    Dim shrieks, and joy, and triumph-cries of death,
And here was borne a severed arm, and there
    A hunter's booted foot; white bones lay bare
With rending; and swift hands now bloodied
    Tossed as in sport the flesh of Pentheus dead.
His body lies afar. The precipice
    Has part, and parts in many an interstice
Lurk of the tangled woodland—no light quest
    To find. And, ah, the head! Of all the rest,
His mother has it, pierced upon a wand,
    As one might pierce a lion's, and through the land,
Leaving her sisters in their dancing place,
    Bears it on high! Yea, to these walls her face
Was set, exulting in her deed of blood,
    Calling upon her Bromios, her God,
Her Comrade, Fellow-Render of the Prey,
    Her All-Victorious, to whom this day
She bears in triumph . . . her own broken heart!
    For me, after that sight, I will depart
Before Agavê comes.—Oh, to fulfill
    God's laws, and have no thought beyond His will,
Is man's best treasure. Aye, and wisdom true,
    I think, for things of dust to cleave unto!

(Agavê, entranced from the rite, returns to her son's palace, bearing his head trium-
phantly, thinking it the head of a lion. Her father meets her at the gate and compels

her at last to recognize what she has done. She accepts banishment from Thebes for her crime; she no longer has a home either in her city nor with the Maenad band. The Chorus draws the terrible lesson of the play.)

> CHORUS: There may be many shapes of mystery,
>   And many things God makes to be,
>   Past hope or fear.
> And the end men did look for came not,
>   And a path is there where no man thought.
>   So has it fallen here.
>
> (Euripides, *The Bacchae*, passim, trans. Murray)

174. THE BACCHIC RITES ARRIVE IN ROME (LIVY)

If Euripides' tragedy ended with a city condemned for its scorn of the god, the first appearance of the Bacchic rites in Italy in 186 B.C.E. was perceived by the Senate more as a straightforward threat to civic peace. Writing a century later, the historian Livy looked back on the episode with the greatest gravity. The murderous activities that in

Fig. 5.7. *King Pentheus is attacked by Maenads. Fresco from a private home in Pompeii, between 62 and 79 C.E. Dionysian themes were very popular in Pompeian frescos. Photo in the public domain.*

Euripides' tragedy were the terrible result of the god's entrancement were, for Livy, the contours of an all-too-real conspiracy—one that threatened the very security of the Roman state.

Note, in Livy's characterization of the Bacchic rites, elements that quickly became stereotypical accusations against foreign religions. The combination of women, wine, and darkness led inevitably to lasciviousness and all manner of wickedness.

> An unknown Greek—with none of the skills which that most learned people brought to us for the development of mind and body—came first into Etruria, offering sacrifices and telling fortunes, not one who practiced a religion of full disclosure . . . but a high priest of secret, nocturnal rites. There were rites of initiation that were first passed on to a few people, then these began to be divulged among men and women.

Fig. 5.8. *Dancing Maenad. Second-century (c.e.) Roman relief, copy of a Greek original, attributed to Callimachus. Museo del Prado. Photo in the public domain.*

The pleasures of wine and banquets were added to those of religion, so that many were drawn in. When souls were lit up with wine and nighttime, and the gathering of women and men, young and old had extinguished every distinction of modesty, all sorts of perversion began to be practiced, since each person had readily available the particular delight to which he or she was more inclined. Nor was there just one kind of crime—freeborn men and women were openly connecting, there were false witnesses, there were false identity markers, wills and depositions all coming out of the same laboratory. From the same place came deaths by poison and slaughter, so that sometimes there were no bodies produced for burial. Much was daringly perpetrated by guile, more by violence. The violence was hidden, for in the face of the din of drumbeats and cymbal clangings no voice of protest among the orgies and murders could be heard.

This blemish of evil penetrated from Etruria into Rome like a disease-carrying infection.

(Livy then relates the specific events that brought the dark facts of the Bacchic rites to light. A young man named Publius Aebutius had been conspired against by his mother and a hostile stepfather, who sought to gain control of his inheritance. They plotted to initiate him into the Bacchic mysteries, but his lover, a notorious prostitute named Hispala Faecenia who had won her freedom after a childhood as a sex slave, objected: not because she could not stand to sleep apart from him for the requisite ten-day preparation, but because she feared for his life.)

The woman . . . became distraught and cried, "The gods know better!" She said it would be better for her and for him to die than for him to [be initiated]. She began to pray down threats and dangers on those who had advised him so. Surprised at her words and such agitation, the young man asked her what was the matter. . . .

While still a slave girl, she said, she had accompanied her mistress and entered into those sacred rites, but as a freedwoman she had never approached the place. She knew it to be a laboratory for all sorts of perversions, and it was common knowledge that for the last two years, no one older than twenty had been initiated. When anyone was put forward for initiation, she said, he or she was handed over as a victim for the priests. They would lead each victim to a place resounding with howling, singing of music, cymbal clanging and drumbeats, so that the voice of protest could not be heard while the victim was being forcibly violated.

She then pleaded and made him promise that he would break off this plan however he could, not to jump into a place where all sorts of abominations would have to be experienced and then actually practiced. She did not allow him to leave until the youth promised that he would keep himself away from those sacred rites.

(The young man sought out his aunt, who heard his story and promptly sent him to the city consul. Alarmed, the consul sought to corroborate the allegations by questioning Hispala.)

Finally pulling herself together . . . she said she was in great fear of the gods, whose secrets she was about to articulate, and much more afraid of the men who, if identified, would physically tear her apart. . . . The consul told her to set her mind at ease, saying that it was his personal concern to make sure she could live safely in Rome.

Then Hispala disclosed the origin of the sacred rites. In the beginning they had been the sacred rites of women; it had been the policy that not a single man be admitted. Three days had been set per year as the time in which they were initiated—during the daytime—into the Bacchic rites. The priestesses had customarily been chosen from the matrons who took turns in the position. But when Paculla Annia from Campania had become priestess, she had changed everything at the prompting of the gods. She for the first time had initiated men, her sons Minius and Herennius Cerrinius; she had moved the sacred rites from daytime to nighttime, and from three days per year to five days per month for initiations.

From then on, when the sacred rites were held indiscriminately—even men mingling with women—and the license provided by nighttime adopted as well, no evil deed, no shameful crime was neglected there. The violations of men among themselves were more common than those among women. If any could not endure to be shamed or were hesitant toward the villainies, they were offered as sacrifices. To hold nothing off-limits was the highest religious virtue among them. Men would prophesy as though deranged, with wild thrusts of the body. Women dressed as Bacchae, with hair askew and carrying burning torches, used to run to the Tiber, dunk their torches in the water, and raise them, flaming brightly because they were composed of active sulphur and calcium.

Men, who were bound to contraptions for torture and carried out of view to concealed caves, were said to have been seized by the gods. These were ones who had refused to take the oath, join in the evil deeds, or experience rape. The number of the Bacchic followers was quite high, almost now a second nation, including some nobles, both men and women. For the last two years a guideline had been in place that no one over twenty years old should be initiated; those of that age were targeted as well suited for corruptions and defilements.

(Alarmed, the consul whisked Hispala and Aebutius to safe custody and went before the Senate. The consul's speech urging the expulsion of the Bacchic rites made clear that the religion not only was foreign but threatened the very safety of the Roman state.)

They were alarmed and fearful when they learned what inroads the Bacchanalia had made in Rome. They instructed the consuls to ensure that neither Aebutius or Hispala Faecenia should experience any harm for the testimony they had offered. They sent deputies to flush out more informers and arrest the priests of this religion, and placed guards at key places in order to shut down its orgies. Once these steps were taken, they called a public assembly to address the Romans about this threat to their national security. . . .

The consul climbed onto the speakers' platform and announced a public assembly. When the consul completed the solemn chant of prayer that officials were accustomed to use in invocation before addressing the nation, he began as follows:

"Never for any gathering, citizens, has this solemn invocation of the gods been not only so fitting but also so necessary. Let this remind you that these are the gods that your ancestors designated for worship, veneration and prayer—not those who would incite our allured minds with evil foreign religions, as by the whips of the Furies, to every impiety and lust. . . .

"I am confident you have grasped that the Bacchanalia have for quite a while been in all Italy and now are even in many places within Rome; this is not only a rumor, but you know it also from the nocturnal rustling and howls that sound through the whole city. But I am also sure that you are ignorant of other aspects of what the matter is. . . .

"So, first: a great number are women, they have been the source of this evil. Then there are males who are similar to women, ravished and ravishing others, crazy, rendered senseless by sleep-deprivation, wine, crashing and howling in the night. The secret society does not have much strength at this point, but on the other hand it has the makings of great strength, for daily its numbers are growing.

"Your ancestors did not want you to gather without cause, unless the flag was set out on the prison and the army led out for an election, or the tribunes had called for a gathering of the commoners, or some official had called for an assembly. And wherever there was a mass of people, there they judged there should be a legally approved leader of the crowd. Now: what sort of meeting do you honestly believe [the Bacchic assembly] to be? Keep in mind first that it meets at night, then that it is one in which women and men are indiscriminately involved. If you realized at what ages the males are initiated, you would not only feel compassion for them, you would feel ashamed.

"O citizens, in your judgment should young men initiated into this sacred mystery be made soldiers? Should weapons be committed to those led out of this obscene rite? Will these who have been ruined by rape, both their own and that of others, decide with the sword for the purity of your wives and children?"

(Livy, *History of Rome* 39.8-15, trans. Reasoner)

175. The danger of women's rites by night (Cicero)

More than a century later, Cicero cited the episode just narrated as a worthy precedent as he proposed his own laws subjecting women's participation—even in the mysteries of Ceres, a traditional Roman god—to civic supervision.

> Well then, let us return to our legal maxims, by which it is most diligently ordained that the clear daylight should be the safeguard of female virtue in the eyes of the multitude; and that they should only be initiated in the mysteries of Ceres, according to the Roman custom.
>
> In reference to this topic, we have an extraordinary instance of the severity of our ancestors in the public indictment and prosecution of the Bacchanals by the senate, supported by the Consular armies. And this severity of the Roman government is not singular, since Diagonas of Thebes, in the middle of Greece, suppressed all nocturnal mysteries by a perpetual prohibition. And

Aristophanes, the most facetious of the old Greek comedians, so satirized the new gods and the nocturnal rites of their worship, that he represents Sabazius and other foreign deities condemned as aliens, and obliged to pack off from the city.

(Cicero, *Laws* 2.35, trans. Barham)

176. The specter of slaves practicing a foreign religion (Tacitus)

The threat of actual slave revolt was real enough, as the example of Spartacus had proved. But the ruling class also expressed anxiety that slaves could undermine the established order by foreign religious practices that they either brought from their homelands or adopted. The strong expectation that slaves would participate in the religion of their masters was not always realized—according to Philo, the thousands of Jews who had been brought to Rome by Pompey as prisoners of war had insisted on maintaining their native customs and had been emancipated (*Embassy* 155).[23]

The prospect of a large part of the population practicing foreign rites could even be regarded as a national security concern. During Nero's reign, a slave murdered his master—the prefect of Rome—and according to a traditional custom, all of the victim's slaves—some four hundred—were to be put to death as a warning to others. A mass demonstration stormed the Senate demanding the slaves be spared. One senator, C. Cassius, rose to plead for the penalty, arguing that the other slaves must have been culpable in the murder; that a failure to act decisively would only embolden other slaves to similar crimes; and that even if innocent slaves suffered, the terror applied would serve a more important social good. The ancient lawgivers had rightly held their slaves in constant suspicion—how much more so should they?

"An ex-consul has been murdered in his house by the treachery of slaves, which not one hindered or divulged, though the Senate's decree, which threatens the entire slave-establishment with execution, has been till now unshaken.

"Vote impunity, in heaven's name, and then who will be protected by his rank, when the prefecture of the capital has been of no avail to its holder? Who will be kept safe by the number of his slaves when four hundred have not protected Pedanius Secundus? Which of us will be rescued by his domestics, who, even with the dread of punishment before them, regard not our dangers?

"Was the murderer, as some do not blush to pretend, avenging his wrongs because he had bargained about money from his father or because a family-slave was taken from him? Let us actually presume that the master was justly slain. Is it your pleasure to search for arguments in a matter [regarding the penalty] already weighed in the deliberations of wiser men than ourselves?

"Even if we had now for the first time to come to a decision, do you believe that a slave took courage to murder his master without letting fall a threatening word or uttering a rash syllable? Let us grant that he concealed his purpose, that he procured his weapon without his fellows' knowledge. Could he pass the night-guard, could he open the doors of the chamber, carry in a light, and accomplish the murder, while all were in ignorance? There are many preliminaries to guilt; if these are divulged by slaves, we may live singly amid numbers, safe among a trembling throng; but at last, if we must perish, let it be with vengeance on the guilty.

"Our ancestors always suspected the temper of their slaves, even when they were born on the same estates, or in the same houses with themselves and thus inherited from their birth an affection for their masters. But now that we have in our households nations with different customs to our own, with a foreign worship or none at all, it is only by terror you can hold in such a motley rabble. But, it will be said, the innocent will perish. Well, even in a beaten army when every tenth man is felled by the club, the lot falls also on the brave. There is some injustice in every great precedent, which, though injurious to individuals, has its compensation in the public advantage."

(Tacitus, *Annals* 14.44, trans. Church and Brodribb)

The suspicions of social subordinates and women just reviewed were part of the context of a number of official actions taken against "foreign" religions in Rome (see the table in fig. 5.9). Neither in the republic nor in the empire did Rome have a formal policy of tolerance (or intolerance) regarding religion. Rather, as Leonard V. Rutgers has argued, in circumstances of political unrest different emperors were willing to follow ancient precedent and take action against a conspicuous minority population that could plausibly be portrayed as a threat to the civic order. "Foreign" religions, especially those that were perceived as especially attracting slaves and women, were obvious targets. From time to time the Jewish community in Rome (as in other cities) was subject to specific actions of suppression or expulsion. This general atmosphere of suspicion toward foreign religion was part of the context of Paul's assemblies. Recall also our discussion of imperial attitudes and actions toward Jewish communities in chapter 4.

Year	Religion	Measure	Source
429 B.C.E.	different sacrificial rites	prohibition of open practice	Livy 4.30.7-11
241 B.C.E.	Fortuna from Praeneste	prohibition of consultation of oracle	Valerius Maximus 1.3.2
213 B.C.E.	different sacrificial rites	prohibition of open practice; confiscation of scriptures	Livy 25.1.6-12
186 B.C.E.	Bacchanalia	comprehensive prohibition; series of prosecutions	*CIL* I 581; Livy 39.8-19; Cicero, *On Laws* 2.15.37
139 B.C.E.	astrology; Judaism	expulsion, removal of altars from open spaces	Valerius Maximus 1.3.3
58 B.C.E.	Isis and Sarapis	removal of altars from open spaces	Varro, *Ant.* frag. 46ab; Servius Aenius 8.698; Cicero, *Att.* 2.17.2
53 B.C.E.	Isis and Sarapis	destruction of sanctuary	Cassius Dio 40.47.3-4
50 B.C.E.	Isis and Sarapis	vandalism of sanctuary	Valerius Maximus 1.3.4
48 B.C.E.	Isis and Sarapis	destruction of wall around sacred area	Cassius Dio 42.26.2
28 B.C.E.	Egyptian religions	prohibition of passage through the Pomerium (the sacred city boundary)	Casslus Dio 53.2.4
21 B.C.E.	Egyptian religions	prohibition of passage into city	Cassius Dio 54.6.6
19 C.E.	Egyptian religions, Judaism	destruction of religious utensils, execution of priests, arrests and banishment among military	Tacitus, *Ann.* 2.85.4; Suetonius, *Tib.* 36; Josephus, *Ant.* 18.65-84; Philo, *Leg.* 160-61
41 C.E.	Judaism	comprehensive prohibition	Cassius Dio 60.6.6
49 C.E.	Judaism	expulsion	Acts 18:2; Suetonius, *Claud.* 25.4; Orosius 7.6.15
64 C.E.	Christianity	executions	Tacitus, *Ann.* 15.44

Fig. 5.9. *Roman actions against "foreign" religions*[24]

The Challenge of Community

Called to give up sexual immorality and idolatry, new members of Paul's assemblies would have confronted hard decisions: should a slave who was a member of the *ekklēsia* refuse his master's sexual demands and risk the consequences? Should a member who was married to a civic official withdraw from his bed? What of the head of the household: how did his relationships change with his wife, his children, his slaves (if he owned any), the business associates with whom he had been accustomed to enjoy banqueting after the theater—was all this now forbidden him? Could members who faced such challenges perhaps for the first time rely on the assembly to offer them a level of support that they no longer enjoyed in their households?

Paul's letters—especially the Corinthian correspondence—show the tensions that these changes generated within the community's life. The apostle's simple request to "greet one another with a holy kiss" (Rom 16:16; 1 Cor 16:20; 2 Cor 13:12; 1 Thess 5:26) would itself have been fraught with concern. Members who might have occupied very different ranks outside the assembly were now expected to share a gesture of intimacy as if they were peers; slaves could expect to receive the gesture of affection—but to be expected to offer no more. Could "sister" and "brother" in Christ embrace each other if they were married to others? The preceding selections suggest that such a practice might quickly invite rumors and scorn from outsiders. Surely it was initially uncomfortable within the assembly as well, at least for some.[25]

Giving up the Past

As we have seen in chapter 2, philosophical schools recognized the difficulty of adopting a new and dramatically different way of life, and teachers adapted their "psychagogy" to support, as well as to challenge, new members. Abraham J. Malherbe has argued that the same distress would have been felt by new members in Paul's assemblies; he cites passages such as the following to illustrate the consequent need for care.[26]

Fig. 5.10. *Christians gather for a common meal (the Lord's Supper?). Fresco from the Catacomb of St. Callistos, Rome, third century. Photo in the public domain.*

177. A proselyte prays for relief (*Joseph and Aseneth*)

In the story of Joseph and Aseneth, a Hellenistic novel that expands significantly on Gen 41:45, Aseneth, the daughter of an Egyptian priest, prays to God after she is drawn by Joseph to embrace Judaism. Her prayer expresses the distress experienced by some converts.[27]

> Preserve me, Lord, for I am desolate, for my father and my mother have renounced me, because I destroyed and crushed their gods, and now I am an orphan and desolate. I have no other hope but in you, Lord, for you are the father of orphans, the protector of the persecuted, and the helper of the distressed. . . . Look upon my orphan state, Lord, for I have fled to you.
>
> (*Joseph and Aseneth* 12:11; 13:1, trans. Malherbe)

178. On showing special consideration for proselytes (Philo)

In his discussion of the virtues promoted by the Torah, Philo emphasizes the special consideration that Moses the lawgiver encouraged for "incomers" (*epēleutai*), that is, proselytes, consideration owed them precisely because of the difficulty of the commitment they have made to a new way of life. He apparently refers to laws governing respect and care for the *gēr*, the "alien" (NRSV), which the LXX occasionally translates *prosēlytos*, "proselyte." From these Philo goes on to distinguish "settlers," *metoikoi*, by which he may mean native Egyptians.

> Having laid down laws for members of the same nation, he [Moses] holds that the incomers too should be accorded every favor and consideration as their due, because abandoning their kinsfolk by blood, their country, their customs and the temples and images of their gods, and the tributes and honors paid to them, they have taken the journey to a better home, from idle fables to the clear vision of truth and the worship of the one and truly existing God. He commands all members of the nation to love the incomers, not only as friends and kinsfolk but as themselves both in body and soul: in bodily matters, by acting as far as may be for their common interest; in mental, by having the same griefs and joys, so that they may seem to be the separate parts of a single living being which is compacted and unified by their fellowship in it. I will not go on to speak of the food and drink and raiment and all the rights concerning daily life and necessary needs, which the law assigns to incomers as due from the native born, for all these follow the statutes, which speak of the friendliness shown by him who loves the incomer even as himself.
>
> (Philo, *On the Virtues* 102-3, trans. Colson, LCL)

Finding a Place on the Civic Landscape

One challenge for the fledgling Christ movement was simply its novelty. Its members may well have been active in other ethnic, professional, and religious associations in the past, many of them respected and even honored on the civic landscape. Such respect could not automatically be expected for a new group, especially one that seemed at odds with important civic values in other ways. Nevertheless, the opinion of outsiders was a continuing concern for Paul (see, for example, Rom 12:13-21; 1 Cor 14:16, 24; 1 Thess 4:10-12).

As noted in chapter 1, some controversy remains concerning the precise nature of the "God-fearers" depicted in Acts, but it seems clear enough now that, while the designation was widely used in the Diaspora, it did not confer any specific halakhic status. There is nevertheless evidence that God-fearers were recognized both by the synagogue and civically, as benefactors not only of the synagogue but also, perhaps, of the wider community.

179. God-fearers in Aphrodisias

A marble pillar from Aphrodisias, for example, is inscribed with the names of more than one hundred and twenty donors who apparently gave to a "soup kitchen" run by the synagogue.[28]

> God our help. Building [?] for the soup kitchen [?]. Below [are] listed the [members] of the decany of the disciples of the law, also known as those who fervently praise God, [who] erected, for the relief of suffering for the community, at their personal expense, [this] memorial [building]:
>
> Jael, president, with son Joshua, magistrate; [*margin* Samuel, elder, from Perge]; Theodotos, employee of the [emperor's] court, with son Ilarianos; Samuel, leader of the decany [?], a proselyte; Joses son of Iesseos; Benjamin, psalm-singer [?]; Judas the good-tempered; Ioses, a proselyte; Sabbatios son of Amachoios; Emmonios, Godfearer; Antoninos, Godfearer; Samuel son of Politianos; Joseph, a proselyte, son of Eusebios; and Judas son of Theodoros; and Antipeos son of Hermes; and Sabathios, the fragrant; and Samuel, old priest.
> (Synagogue inscription from Aphrodisias, trans. Feldman)[29]

We possess no such inscriptions for the Pauline assemblies, but as Elisabeth Schüssler Fiorenza has pointed out, Paul is careful to acknowledge benefactors to his apostolic work in his letters—replicating the forms of patronage seen everywhere else in the Greek and Roman world.[30] Bruce Winter has argued that Paul's letters already show the early Christian community adopting some of the patterns of benefaction known from Jewish communities and Hellenistic cities alike.[31]

180. Suspicion of new associations (Pliny and Trajan)

We have seen (in chapters 2 and 3) some of the voluminous correspondence between the emperor Trajan and his governor in Bithynia, Pliny, in the early second century c.e. One letter from Pliny asks permission to organize a new fire company—obviously an urgent need; but note both Pliny's caution in asking and the emperor's wariness in refusing the request.

(Pliny to Trajan)

> While I was making the rounds of a different area of the province, a wide-ranging conflagration consumed many domestic dwellings and two public structures—the senior citizens' building and the temple to Isis—though a road runs between them. The fire spread out widely, at first by violent wind, then by the apathy of the people who stood idly by, unmoving, standing still as

spectators before such a catastrophe. And also there is no hose in public holdings, no water bucket, nor any other tool for firefighting. These items are now provided as I ordered.

Please reflect, master, on whether you think a company of firemen—numbering only 150—might be set up. I shall take care that no one shall be received into the company who is not a fireman, and that what is granted this group by law will not be used for something else. It won't be hard to keep track of so few.

(*Trajan responds*)

According to the precedent of those in other places, you have thought that it would be possible to set up a company of firemen in Nicomedia. But we need to remember that in this province and especially in its cities, it is groups of this sort that have caused trouble. Whatever we name them and for whatever purpose we grant people to come together, in short order they become political and religious brotherhoods.[32] It therefore would be preferable to make available what is needed for fighting fires, and to call homeowners themselves to do the firefighting, and if circumstances demand, to employ the people who throng to the scene.

(Pliny, *Epistles* 10.33-34, trans. Reasoner)

181. Suspicion of associations for "the weak" (Trajan)

As we also saw in chapter 1, "strength" or "power" and "weakness" were social categories that aligned with prestige and wealth (or their absence). In another letter to Pliny, the emperor Trajan addressed "societies of weaker people" (*collegia tenuiorum*), groups of poor people who pooled what little resources they had to supply such necessities as food or private burials for their members. The letter shows both how poor people were regarded as "weaker" members of society and how unwilling the Romans were (except in a case, like this one, of a preexisting law) to allow social groups among the lower classes to meet.

If the citizens of Amisus, whose petition you send with your letter, are allowed by their own laws, granted them by formal treaty, to form a benefit society, there is no reason why we should interfere: especially if the contributions are not used for riotous and unlawful assemblies, but to relieve poverty among the weaker people. In all other cities which are subject to our own law these institutions must be forbidden.

(Trajan, *Epistles* 10.93, trans. Radice, adapted)

182. The later suppression of Christian associations (Pliny)

We cite these letters to suggest that the sort of wariness shown by the emperor and his governor might have been directed, in the previous century, to Paul's assemblies to the extent that they gained a public profile. We know from other correspondence between the two that in fact their suspicions took in Christians in their day. In a famous exchange, Pliny asks about Christians about whom he claims to have no

Fig. 5.11. *Statue of the emperor Trajan from Dacia, second century.*

prior knowledge. At the emperor's insistence, he had outlawed associations; some Christians had continued to meet in early morning gatherings, however, and this had apparently sufficed to make them vulnerable to accusations from non-Christian neighbors.

(Pliny to Trajan)

It is my practice, my lord, to refer to you all matters concerning which I am in doubt. For who can better give guidance to my hesitation or inform my ignorance? I have never participated in trials of Christians. I therefore do not know what offenses it is the practice to punish or investigate, and to what extent. And I have been not a little hesitant as to whether there should be any distinction on account of age or no difference between the very young and the more mature; whether pardon is to be granted for repentance, or, if a man has once been a Christian, it does him no good to have ceased to be one; whether the name itself, even without offenses, or only the offenses associated with the name are to be punished.

Meanwhile, in the case of those who were denounced to me as Christians, I have observed the following procedure: I interrogated these as to whether they were Christians; those who confessed I interrogated a second and a third time, threatening them with punishment; those who persisted I ordered executed. For I had no doubt that, whatever the nature of their creed, stubbornness and inflexible obstinacy surely deserve to be punished. There were others possessed of the same folly; but because they were Roman citizens, I signed an order for them to be transferred to Rome.

Soon accusations spread, as usually happens, because of the proceedings going on, and several incidents occurred. An anonymous document was published containing the names of many persons. Those who denied that they were or had been Christians, when they invoked the gods in words dictated by me, offered prayer with incense and wine to your image, which I had ordered to be brought for this purpose together with statues of the gods, and moreover cursed Christ—none of which those who are really Christians, it is said, can be forced to do—these I thought should be discharged. Others named by the informer declared that they were Christians, but then denied it, asserting that they had been but had ceased to be, some three years before, others many years, some as much as twenty-five years. They all worshiped your image and the statues of the gods, and cursed Christ.

They asserted, however, that the sum and substance of their fault or error had been that they were accustomed to meet on a fixed day before dawn and sing responsively a hymn to Christ as to a god, and to bind themselves by oath, not to some crime, but not to commit fraud, theft, or adultery, not falsify their trust, nor to refuse to return a trust when called upon to do so. When this was over, it was their custom to depart and to assemble again to partake of food— but ordinary and innocent food. Even this, they affirmed, they had ceased to do after my edict by which, in accordance with your instructions, I had forbidden political associations. Accordingly, I judged it all the more necessary to find out what the truth was by torturing two female slaves who were called deaconesses. But I discovered nothing else but depraved, excessive superstition.

I therefore postponed the investigation and hastened to consult you. For the matter seemed to me to warrant consulting you, especially because of the number involved. For many persons of every age, every rank, and also of both sexes are and will be endangered. For the contagion of this superstition has spread not only to the cities but also to the villages and farms. But it seems possible to check and cure it. It is certainly quite clear that the temples, which had been almost deserted, have begun to be frequented, that the established religious rites, long neglected, are being resumed, and that from everywhere sacrificial animals are coming, for which until now very few purchasers could be found. Hence it is easy to imagine what a multitude of people can be reformed if an opportunity for repentance is afforded.

(Pliny, *Epistles* 10.96, trans. Reasoner)

(Trajan replies)

You observed proper procedure, my dear Pliny, in sifting the cases of those who had been denounced to you as Christians. For it is not possible to lay down any

Fig. 5.12. *The Three Young Men in the fiery furnace (Daniel 3). Fresco in the Catacomb of St. Priscilla, Rome, third century* c.e. *The theme presumably appealed to Christians who felt themselves to be in distress. Photo in the public domain.*

general rule to serve as a kind of fixed standard. They are not to be sought out; if they are denounced and proved guilty, they are to be punished, with this reservation, that whoever denies that he is a Christian and really proves it—that is, by worshiping our gods—even though he was under suspicion in the past, shall obtain pardon through repentance. But anonymously posted accusations ought to have no place in any prosecution. For this is both a dangerous kind of precedent and out of keeping with the spirit of our age.

(Trajan, *Epistles* 10.97, trans. Reasoner)

Tensions at the Table

The assemblies faced challenges not only from without but also from within. Earlier in this chapter, we considered questions of Jews and non-Jews sharing food at common meals, no doubt an issue with which many early Christian communities wrestled (to judge from the variety of answers proposed in Mark 7; Acts 10 and 15; Romans 14–15; and elsewhere). And we have seen that banqueting and sexual gratification were strongly linked in the cultural environment in a way that (on Plutarch's view) would have kept wives well away from the tables at which their husbands sated themselves.

Social rank and status also raised tensions. Paul criticizes the Corinthian assembly for a meal practice in which "each of you goes ahead with your own supper, and one goes hungry and another becomes drunk" (1 Cor 11:21). Disparities between rich and poor would have been felt keenly at meals where patrons and clients were expected to know their respective places, and portions, at table. Similarly, disparities between slave and free would inevitably have been expressed at common tables in a culture in which slaves were expected to serve food, as well as to be sexually available to guests at banquets.

183. The careful observance of rank at meals (Pliny)

Even among the freeborn, public meals and banquets were the occasion for the careful observance of social rank. Slaves at Roman *convivia* were required to stand and to remain silent throughout the meal, yet they could take some pleasure in giving poorer food and drink to guests who ranked below others.[33] A letter from Pliny, governor of Bithynia, to a young protégé illustrates how conscious the Romans were of the social gradations that hosts could enforce at public meals—even as Pliny himself advised moderation as a way of displaying that supreme Roman virtue, self-control.

> It would take too long to recall, nor does it matter, how it happened that I, a man of few friends, should share a meal with someone who thinks he has a high standard of living while also being economical, though it seems to me that his lifestyle is simultaneously greedy and extravagant. For he set some excellent courses before himself and a few others, but cheap morsels to the rest. He had even divided up the wine in small flasks according to three types, not to give people the opportunity to choose, but rather to take away such an opportunity. One kind was for us—for himself and me, another for a few friends—for he maintains certain levels of friendships, and the third was for our freedmen—his and mine.
>
> Someone seated by me noticed and asked whether I thought this was a good idea. I said "No." "So then," he asked, "what habit do you follow?"
>
> "I set before everyone the same items, since I invited them for a meal, not for a grade-report. I put all things on an equal level for those I have equalized at the table and couch of my dining room."
>
> "Does this extend even to your freedmen?"
>
> "Even that far; I consider them comrades then, not freedmen."
>
> And he replied, "That's a lot for you!"
>
> "Hardly," I replied.
>
> "How can you do it?" he asked.
>
> "You need to realize that my freedmen don't drink the same wine I do, but I drink the same wine the freedmen drink." And by God. if you can show restraint in your appetite, it is not too much to use yourself what you share with many guests. Hold that in check, then; regress on the scale of social order, as it were. If you are thrifty in consumption, you will realize that your moderation is a considerably more proper response to them than an unfavorable insult.
>
> So what? Let not the extravagance of some people's dining tables be foisted on you, a young man of excellent character, under cover of stinginess. Since my dear friendship is due you, when something like this arises, be forewarned by my experience—you should avoid it! So keep in mind that nothing should be shunned more than that recent linking of extravagance and greed, which are rather loathsome when distinct and separated, and even more loathsome when joined together. Be well.
>
> (Pliny, *Epistles* 2.6, trans. Reasoner)

184. The status of a slave (the papyri)

However warm the familial rhetoric in one of the *ekklēsiai*, would a master and his slave have sat together at the meal as "brothers"? The disparity in power—including the right of the master to sell or beat an unsatisfactory slave or even, in the extreme case of a fugitive slave (one possible scenario behind the letter to Philemon), the right to authorize the slave's destruction—must have eroded any genuine sense of fraternity. Norman R. Peterson put that question at the heart of his effort to "rediscover Paul," insisting that it is "logically and socially impossible to relate to one and the same person as both one's inferior and as one's equal."[34] How could slave and master have related as "brothers" when one held the power of life and death over the other? As we have seen, some in the ancient Mediterranean world considered slavery completely natural: so, for example, Aristotle (see no. 3 above). And so an official in Roman Egypt authorized a deputy to arrest his runaway slave. *If* Onesimus were a runaway slave, it is possible that his master (and others in the assembly addressed by Paul's letter to Philemon) might have thought along similar lines.

Fig. 5.13. *A bronze slave collar asking the viewer to return the slave to his owner if found away from home, fourth to sixth century* c.e. *Museo Nazionale Romano, Rome. Photo: Scala/Art Resource, New York.*

Flavius Ammonas . . . to Flavius Dorotheus, officialis, greeting. I order and depute you to arrest my slave called Magnus, who ran away and is staying at Hermopolis and has carried off certain articles belonging to me, and to bring him as a prisoner together with the head-man of Sesphtha. This order is valid, and in answer to the formal question I gave my consent. I, Flavius Ammonas, officialis on the staff of the praefect of Egypt, have made this order.

(*P. Oxy.* 1423, trans. Grenfell and Hunt)

185. Impulses toward equality (Aristotle)

There were exceptions to that view, however, already in Aristotle's day (he refers to the Sophists):

Others, however, maintain that for one man to be another man's master is contrary to nature, because it is only convention that makes the one a slave and the other a freeman and there is no difference between them by nature, and that therefore it is unjust, for it is based on force.

(Aristotle, *Politics* 1.2.3, trans. Rackham, LCL)

186. Absence of slaves among the Essenes (Philo)

There were exceptions as well among some Jews in Paul's day (the Essenes). It is not inconceivable that some in the assemblies around Paul might have held similar views.

Not a single slave is to be found among them, but all are free, exchanging services with each other, and they denounce the owners of slaves, not merely for their injustice in outraging the law of equality, but also for their impiety in annulling the statute of Nature, who mother-like has born and reared all men alike, and created them genuine brothers, not in mere name, but in very reality, though this kinship has been put to confusion by the triumph of malignant covetousness, which has wrought estrangement instead of affinity and enmity instead of friendship.

(Philo, *Every Good Man Is Free* 79, trans. Colson, LCL)

187. The sexualization of slaves at banquets (Seneca)

We have seen that meals in the Greek and Roman worlds were known for combining excess in eating and drinking with sexual indulgence.[35] The Roman *convivium* was famous for a different set of sexual attractions from that of the Greek *symposion*, however. While the emperor Tiberius is said to have hosted a banquet in which the food was served by naked women (Suetonius, *Tiberius* 42.2), this was an exception to the Roman pattern, which favored male over female slaves for public meals. The Roman *convivium* featured pourers of wine who were young, beardless, attractive men with long hair and Greek names. While they were not supposed to flirt with the guests, their owners could use them however they chose.[36] Seneca described the expectation as a regrettable duty for the slaves:

The server of the wine has to dress like a woman and to wrestle with his advancing years; he can't get away from his boyhood, but is continually dragged back to it. His body hair is plucked away, and he is kept beardless; he is forced to keep awake all night, dividing his time between the drunkenness and lust of his master.

(Seneca, *Epistle* 47.7, trans. D'Arms)

188. THE SEXUALIZATION OF SLAVES AT BANQUETS (PHILO)

Philo's description was part of a more extensive and more censorious indictment of Roman banqueting as the occasion of gluttony, drunkenness, and sexual licentiousness.

> And perhaps some people may be inclined to approve of the arrangement of such entertainments which at present prevails everywhere, from an admiration of, and a desire of imitating, the luxury and extravagance of the Italians which both Greeks and barbarians emulate. For they make all their preparations with a view to show rather than to real enjoyment; for they use couches called triclinia, and sofas all round the table made of tortoiseshell, and ivory, and other costly materials; . . . and a vast array of drinking cups arrayed according to each separate description; . . . and well-shaped slaves of the most exquisite beauty, ministering, as if they had come not more for the purpose of serving the guests than of delighting the eyes of the spectators by their mere appearance. Of these slaves, some, being still boys, pour out the wine; and others more fully grown pour water, being carefully washed and rubbed down, with their faces anointed and pencilled, and the hair of their heads admirably plaited and curled and wreathed in delicate knots; . . . and being clothed in tunics of the most delicate texture, and of the purest white. . . . Others, again, are young men just beginning to show a beard on their youthful chins, having been, for a short time, the sport of the profligate debauchees, and being prepared with exceeding care and diligence for more painful services; being a kind of exhibition of the excessive opulence of the giver of the feast, or rather, to say the truth, of their thorough ignorance of all propriety, as those who are acquainted with them well know.
>
> (Philo, *Contemplative Life* 48-52, trans. Yonge)

189. THE BANQUET AS AN OCCASION OF ABUSE (PETRONIUS)

A contemporary of Paul, Petronius described in his *Satyricon* a banquet in which the disparities of power along lines of rank, status, and gender overlapped. Petronius offered a contemptuous portrait of Trimalchio, a freedman who had become fabulously wealthy and paraded his success for all to see. Trimalchio showers abuse on his wife by behaving lewdly with his male slave in front of dinner guests. In Petronius's eyes, every ostentatious gesture reveals Trimalchio to be a lout; he represents all that was wrong with a social order that allowed social inferiors to amass wealth beyond their station.

> These dainties being dispatched, Trimalchio turned to the servants, saying, "What! haven't you had your dinners yet? Be off now, and let the relay take your

Fig. 5.14. *A slave carries a tray in preparation for a banquet. Mosaic from Roman Carthage, second century c.e. The Louvre, Paris. Photo: Erich Lessing/Art Resource, New York.*

places." Hereupon a second set of attendants came in, the outgoing slaves crying, "Farewell, Gaius!" and the incoming, "Hail, Gaius!"

At this point our mirth was disturbed for the first time; for a rather good-looking slave boy having entered along with the new lot of domestics, Trimalchio laid hold of him and started kissing him over and over again. At this Fortunata, to assert "her lawful and equitable rights" (as she put it), began abusing her husband, calling him an abomination and a disgrace, that he could not restrain his filthy passions, ending up with the epithet "dog!"

Trimalchio for his part was so enraged at her railing that he hurled a wine-cup in his wife's face. Fortunata screamed out, as if she had lost an eye, and clapped her trembling hands to her countenance. Scintilla was equally alarmed, and sheltered her shuddering friend in her bosom.[37] At the same time an officious attendant applied a pitcher of cold water to her cheek, over which the poor lady drooped and fell a-sighing and a-sobbing.

But Trimalchio went on. "What! what!" he stormed, "has this slut no memory? Didn't I take her from the stand in the slave-market, and make her a free woman among her equals? But there, she puffs herself out, like the frog in the fable; she's too proud to spit in her own bosom, the blockhead. If you are born in a hovel, you shouldn't dream of a palace. As I hope to prosper, I'll see to it this Cassandra of the camp is brought to reason. Why! when I was only worth two cents, I might have married ten millions of money. You know I might. Agatho, perfumer to the lady next door, drew me aside, and 'I'll give you a hint,' said he; 'don't let your race die out.' But I, with my silly good nature, and not wanting to seem fickle-minded, I've driven my ax into my own leg. All right! I'll make you long yet to dig me up again with your fingernails! And to show this minute the harm you've done yourself, I forbid you, Habinnas, to put her statue on my tomb at all, that I may not have any scolding when I'm gone. I'll teach her I can do her mischief; I won't have her so much as kiss my dead body!"

After this thunderclap, Habinnas began to entreat him to forget and forgive. "Nobody," he urged, "but goes wrong sometimes; we're men after all, not gods." Scintilla spoke to the same purpose with tears in her eyes, and begged him in the name of his good spirit and addressing him as Gaius, to be pacified.

Trimalchio could restrain his tears no longer, but cried, "As you hope, Habinnas, to enjoy your little fortune, if I've done anything wrong, spit in my face. I kissed the good, careful lad, not because he's a pretty boy, but because he's so thrifty and clever. I tell you he can recite ten pieces, reads his book at sight, has bought himself a Thracian costume out of his daily rations, besides an armchair and a pair of cups. Does he not deserve to be the apple of my eye? But Fortunata won't have it. That's your pleasure, is it, you tipsy wench? I warn you, make the most of what you've got, you cormorant; and don't make me nasty, sweetheart, else you'll get a taste of my temper. You know me; once I've made up my mind, I'm just as hard as nails!"

(Petronius, *Satyricon* 74-75, trans. Allinson)

It would be reasonable to assume that texts like these reflected social norms and expectations that were effective in the wider environment in which Paul issued his call for holy living, mutual regard, and fraternal love. But we can do more than assume: the letters to Corinth reveal just such tensions.

Pleas for Unity as One Body

Among other rhetorical strategies, Paul called on members of the assemblies to show each other respect and deference as different but interconnected members of a single body (Rom 12:3-8; 1 Cor 12:12-27). Yung-Suk Kim has shown that Paul meant more than just a plea for unity: the body was also a metaphor for organic vitality and growth.[38] Nevertheless, the trope would have been instantly familiar to Paul's contemporaries, among whom the plea to act as a single body was a well-worn argument for political cohesion and cooperation, especially across class lines.[39] One example from later rabbinic literature shows the currency of the trope in Judaism.

Fig. 5.15. *A woman holds a (eucharistic?) chalice at an agapē feast. Fresco from the Catacomb of Saints Peter and Marcellinus, Rome, second or early third century. Photo in the public domain.*

190. Israel as a lamb (Mekilta de Rabbi Ishmael)

What is the nature of the lamb? If it is hurt in one limb, all its limbs feel pain. So also are the people of Israel. One of them commits a sin and all of them suffer from the punishment. But the nations of the world are not so. One of them may be killed and yet the others may rejoice at this downfall.

(*Mekilta de Rabbi Ishmael*, Exodus 29:6, trans. Lauterbach)[40]

191. The Roman people as a body (Livy)

Perhaps the earliest use of the trope still available to us comes from the historian Livy's account of events in the fifth century B.C.E. In 494 the plebeian order (the nonelite order of free citizens) was on the brink of rebellion against the patrician elite because their sons, the majority of the Roman armed forces, had not been paid for their service in Rome's imperial adventures abroad. When their champion, the "dictator" (speaker) Marcus Valerius, introduced into the Senate a bill authorizing their pay, he was rebuffed and his bill defeated. His response was to resign from the Senate with a threatening flourish.

Valerius introduced, as the very first business of the Senate, the treatment of the men who had been marching to victory, and moved a resolution as to what decision they ought to come to with regard to the those who owed money. When his motion was rejected, he said, "I am not acceptable as an advocate of concord. Depend upon it, you will very soon wish that the Roman plebs had champions like me. As far as I am concerned, I will no longer encourage my fellow-citizens in vain hopes nor will I be dictator for no purpose. Internal dissensions and foreign wars have made this office necessary to the commonwealth; peace has now been secured abroad, at home it is made impossible. I would rather be involved in the revolution as a private citizen than as dictator." So saying, he left the Senate chamber and resigned his dictatorship. The reason was quite clear to the plebs; he had resigned office because he was indignant at the way they were treated. The non-fulfillment of his pledge was not due to him; they considered that he had practically kept his word, and on his way home they followed him with approving cheers.

The troops, the vast majority of them from the plebs, withdrew to camp outside of Rome, in effect leaving the city without police protection.

A great panic seized the city; mutual distrust led to a state of universal suspense.[41] Those plebeians who had been left by their comrades in the city feared violence from the patricians; the patricians feared the plebeians who still remained in the city, and could not make up their minds whether they would rather have them go or stay. "How long," it was asked, "would the multitude who had seceded remain quiet? What would happen if a foreign war broke out in the meantime?" They felt that all their hopes rested on concord among the citizens, and that this must be restored at any cost.

Alarmed, the Senate dispatched an intermediary to negotiate with the seceding troops. Note that in his appeal, which relies on the metaphor of the social body, he implicitly identifies the plebs—the lower class of free citizens—with the outer members of the body, less "central" than the patricians.

The Senate decided, therefore, to send as their spokesman Menenius Agrippa, an eloquent man, and acceptable to the plebs as being himself of plebeian origin. He was admitted into the camp, and it is reported that he simply told them the following fable in a primitive and earthy style.

"In the days when all the parts of the human body did not agree together as they do now, but each member took its own course and spoke its own speech, the other members, indignant at seeing that everything acquired by their care and labor and service went to the belly, while it, undisturbed in the middle of them all, did nothing but enjoy the pleasures provided for it, entered into a conspiracy; the hands were not to bring food to the mouth, the mouth was not to accept it when offered, the teeth were not to chew it. But while in their resentment they were anxious to coerce the belly by starving it, the members themselves wasted away, and the whole body was reduced to the last stage of exhaustion. Then it became evident that the belly rendered no idle service, and the nourishment it received was no greater than that which it bestowed by returning to all parts of the body this blood by which we live and are strong, equally distributed into the veins, after being matured by the digestion of the food."

By using this comparison, and showing how the internal disaffection among the parts of the body resembled the animosity of the plebeians against the patricians, he succeeded in winning over his audience.

(Livy, *History of Rome* 2.31-33, trans. Roberts, adapted)[42]

The speech was a success; the plebeian troops negotiated a compromise with the anxious patricians in the Senate. Agrippa Menenius himself was celebrated as a hero of the plebs, and years later, at his death, when it was found that his estate was not adequate to pay for his funeral, "he was buried by the plebeians, each man contributing a bronze coin toward the expense."

To return to the cautionary note sounded at the beginning of this book: Reviewing "parallels" to Paul's language, for example, concerning the social "body," does not demonstrate either that Paul knew a specific text adduced here as a parallel or meant to evoke that text in the ears of his audience. Nor, to the contrary, does it demonstrate that Paul meant to repudiate the parallel as unworthy of his gospel. Our sampling in this chapter of aspects of the social environment is meant only to show some of the challenges that his communities would have faced as they sought to realize the social values of the *ekklēsia,* as they understood those values. What Paul meant to accomplish in the *ekklēsia*—the transformation of society? the presentation of a different way of living together? or only the survival of the small gatherings he called together in cities across the Roman world—and the extent to which his own efforts were aligned with the overriding values of Roman society or agitated against them: these remain lively questions in scholarship today.[43] These questions are part of the continuing appropriation of the apostle's legacy, a theme to which we turn in our final chapter.

To account for the coincidence in Paul's letters of the rhetoric of close affection and solidarity and a lack of clear rejection of social inequalities, Gerd Theissen describes a "**love-patriarchalism**" that "places a high value on the obedience of women, children, and slaves and has little room for the nonfamilial ethical radicalism of the Synoptic tradition." This ethic "allows social inequities to continue but transfuses them with a spirit of concern, of respect, and of personal solicitude." See *The Social Setting of Pauline Christianity: Essays on Corinth*, ed. and trans. John H. Schütz (Philadelphia: Fortress Press, 1982), 37, 139.

QUESTIONS FOR REFLECTION

1. At various places in his letters, Paul refers to women as leaders in congregations and as colleagues in his apostolic work. What challenges would women have faced as they took such roles? With what social expectations would they have contended at group meals, or in public occasions when their husbands or male relatives participated in the civic cult?

2. Given the suspicion voiced by some Romans regarding gatherings to worship foreign gods—and especially gatherings away from the public square or gatherings in which women and slaves were active—what pressures might members of Paul's assemblies have been aware of? How might a Roman official have heard passages like 1 Cor 5:3-5; 14:26-33; Eph 5:18-20; or Col 3:16?

3. "There is no longer Jew or Greek, there is no longer slave or free," Paul wrote (Gal 3:28). "There is no longer male and female; for all of you are one in Christ Jesus." What expectations might have complicated living out that principle in congregations where some members were slaves and others were free—or even (as in Philemon) where some members had remained slaves to other members?

4. "Not many of you were powerful, not many were of noble birth," Paul wrote to the Corinthians (1 Cor 1:26)—but apparently a few were. How important was social status for determining one's place in the assembly and how one related to others? How would a leader like Paul have persuaded others to adopt his standards for behavior; what might have prevented some members of the *ekklēsia* from agreeing with him?

5. In what different ways do you think people from different social statuses might have been attracted to the *ekklēsia*?

FOR FURTHER READING

Friesen, Steven. "Poverty in Pauline Studies: Beyond the So-Called New Consensus." *JSNT* 26 (2004): 323–61.

Georgi, Dieter. *Remembering the Poor: The History of Paul's Collection for Jerusalem.* Nashville: Abingdon, 1982. German original, 1965.

Harland, Philip A. *Associations, Synagogues, and Congregations: Claiming a Place in Ancient Mediterranean Society.* Minneapolis: Fortress Press, 2003.

Meeks, Wayne A. *The First Urban Christians: The Social World of the Apostle Paul.* New Haven: Yale University Press, 1983.

Meggitt, Justin J. *Paul, Poverty, and Survival.* Studies of the New Testament and Its World. Edinburgh: T&T Clark, 1998.

Osiek, Carolyn, and Margaret Y. MacDonald. *A Woman's Place: House Churches in Earliest Christianity.* Minneapolis: Fortress Press, 2006.

Norman R. Peterson, *Rediscovering Paul: Philemon and the Sociology of Paul's Narrative World* (Philadelphia: Fortress Press, 1985).

Still, Todd D., and David G. Horrell, eds. *After the First Urban Christians: The Social-Scientific Study of Pauline Christianity Twenty-Five Years Later.* London: T&T Clark, 2009.

Taussig, Hal. *In the Beginning Was the Meal: Social Experimentation and Early Christian Identity.* Minneapolis: Fortress Press, 2009.

Theissen, Gerd. *The Social Setting of Pauline Christianity: Essays on Corinth.* Trans. John Schütz. Philadelphia: Fortress, 1983.

Winter, Bruce W. *Roman Wives, Roman Widows: The Appearance of New Women and the Pauline Communities.* Grand Rapids: Eerdmans, 2003.

———. *Seek the Welfare of the City: Christians as Benefactors and Citizens*, First-Century Christians in the Graeco-Roman World. Grand Rapids: Eerdmans, 1994.

Wlre, Antolnette Clark. *The Corinthian Women Prophets: A Reconstruction through Paul's Rhetoric.* Minneapolis: Fortress Press, 1990.

Fig. 6.1. *Paul the wonder-worker—miraculously surviving the bite of a poisonous viper on Malta (Acts 28:1-6). Fresco in Canterbury Cathedral, eleventh century. Photo: Art Resource, New York.*

6 | Paul's Legacy

Any truly comprehensive discussion of the apostle Paul's legacy (which is certainly beyond the scope of this chapter!) would necessarily include such momentous historical developments as the Protestant Reformation, when statements in Paul's letters—and perhaps as important, his example in opposing the apostle Peter "to his face" (Gal 2:11)—fueled ecclesiastical, cultural, and political divisions that echo down to the present.

If Romans and Galatians were the central texts in those controversies, Philemon and the Pastoral Letters were the scriptural battlefield on which nineteenth-century abolitionists and advocates of slavery in the United States opposed each other as they sought biblical warrant for each side. Writing in 1845, the abolitionist George Bourne declared that he found "not a particle of evidence" in the letter to Philemon that the recipient was a slaveholder or that Onesimus was a slave; the "too-common pro-slavery assumption that they respectively were such, is therefore a mere begging of the question; and that not only without, but against the evidence furnished by the same epistle."[1] Several years later, John Gregg Fee argued that the letter itself demonstrated that Onesimus was not a slave but "a natural brother to Philemon. . . . Paul calls him 'a brother beloved, especially to me, but how much more unto thee both IN THE FLESH and in the Lord.'"[2]

On the other hand, in 1834 Charles Colcock Jones published *A Catechism for Colored Persons*,[3] in which phrases from the Pauline letters were used to teach slaves

> to count their Masters "worthy of all honour," as those whom God has placed over them in this world; "*with all fear*," they are to be "*subject to them*" and obey them in all *things*, possible and lawful, with good will and endeavor to *please them well*, . . . and let Servants serve their masters as faithfully behind their backs as before their faces. God is present to see, as their masters are not.[4]

301

Jones, a white missionary to slaves in Georgia, described the reaction of a group of slaves to a sermon he preached on Philemon, to similar effect, in 1833:

> I was preaching to a large congregation on the *Epistle to Philemon*: and when I insisted on fidelity and obedience as Christian virtues in servants and upon the authority of Paul, condemned the practice of *running away*, one-half of my audience deliberately rose up and walked off with themselves; and those that remained looked anything but satisfied, either with the preacher or his doctrine. After dismission, there was no small stir among them; some solemnly declared that "there was no such Epistle in the Bible"; others, that they did not care if they ever heard me preach again! . . . There were some too, who had strong objections against me as a Preacher, because I was a master, and said, "his people have to work as well as we."[5]

The use of Paul's letters in this way profoundly affected the perception of the Bible among slaves. Some contemporaries attested that slaves believed that a real Bible from God did exist, "but they frequently say the Bible now used is master's Bible," because they so frequently heard "Servants, obey your masters" when the Bible was quoted.[6] Paul's legacy remains profoundly intertwined with the dynamics of racism in U.S. culture today.[7]

In the late twentieth century, formal statements by theologians in war-ravaged Central America, apartheid South Africa, and the global South repeatedly identified as one of the principal apparatuses of an oppressive "State Theology" the regular appeal to Paul's exhortation in Romans 13 to "be subject to the governing authorities."[8] It is all the more remarkable, therefore, that theologians of liberation have also found in Paul's writings the earliest Christian impulses of the "preferential option for the poor."[9] Before his death at the hands of a Salvadoran death squad, Ignacio Ellacuría, S.J., repudiated a spiritualized interpretation of Paul's mysticism when he wrote: "Dying with Jesus and being resurrected with him in baptism, according to Paul, are not primarily mystical but primarily historical; they are the most faithful reenactment and continuation of the life of Jesus, and they bring consequences like those that Jesus suffered, as long as the world remains like the world in which Jesus lived."[10]

In these ways—and many more (we could discuss controversies over Paul's legacy as it is deployed in patriarchy, misogyny, and violence against women; heterosexism and violence against homosexual men and women; the long history of Christian anti-Judaism; and on, and on)—the interpretation of Paul remains a vital and urgent concern.[11]

The point of this chapter is not to attempt to explore those contemporary questions adequately, however, but to show that similar questions were alive from the beginning among those who sought to remember or to appeal to Paul's memory. The following documents provide only a sample of the disparate interpretations and appropriations of Paul in the first centuries of Christianity.

Paul the Writer of (Even More) Letters

One of the ways in which Paul influenced subsequent generations of Christians was through his letters. Not only did men and women take up his letters, collect them, and, on occasion, treasure them, but they also *imitated* them, as they wrote pseudonymous letters in Paul's name—some of which very probably ended up in our New Testament (see chapter 2).

Whether a particular letter in the New Testament—say, Ephesians—is or is not genuine remains a matter of considerable debate among interpreters. Sometimes that debate is posed, especially in popular Christianity, in terms of the authority of the Bible; but scholars know that the contents of the New Testament have varied over time, with some early churches including in it writings that everyone today agrees are pseudepigraphic.[12] (On occasion, some Christian readers who want to hold to a high view of biblical authority imagine—in the face of historical data to the contrary— that the Holy Spirit "must have" protected the transmission of the "true" New Testament down to our own time. This is a curiously narcissistic argument, implying that later readers are more the objects of the Holy Spirit's solicitude than readers in the early centuries of the church, who were "allowed" to hold very different views of what was or was not genuine!)

Most scholars prefer to examine external evidence (early attestation for a writing) and internal evidence (paleography, style, vocabulary, and historical situation represented in a text) as impartially as possible. Even on these terms, however, there can be honest disagreements. How different does the vocabulary of a particular text need to be from acknowledged genuine letters to be judged pseudepigraphic? —Could not very *similar* vocabulary show that a pseudepigrapher was deliberately imitating one or more genuine letters? And where is the burden of proof: must a scholar demonstrate that a text *could not possibly* have come from Paul's hand, or is it enough to show that it is *unlikely* that Paul wrote it?

Scholars often use an additional criterion to determine whether a text might betray the purpose of a pseudepigrapher. Are there telltale signs that a text might have been written to be effective for a *later* audience or in a situation *after* the death of its purported author? For example, in 1 Timothy, "Paul" (the purported author) writes, after a series of instructions regarding church officers and conduct becoming women, "I hope to come to you soon, but I am writing these instructions to you so that, *if I am delayed*, you may know how one ought to behave in the household of God" (3:14-15). The letter thus guarantees its own value for a later generation. Similarly, the author of "Ephesians" (so-called, even though the earliest manuscripts do not include the phrase "in Ephesus" in 1:1) writes to his readers, "Surely *you have already heard* of the commission of God's grace that was given me for you" (3:2). The letter then effectively summarizes Paul's relevance for readers who have never met him—although it is ostensibly addressed to a congregation where he spent a year and a half, according to Acts! Similarly, furthermore, the author of Colossians claims that Paul strives for the believers in Colossae, in Laodicea, and "for all who have not seen my face" (2:1). Such gestures "over the heads" of the addressed readers, so to speak, give the impression that Paul himself already had a later generation in mind—perhaps the generation of a later pseudepigrapher?

Our purpose here is not to settle, or even to introduce, these questions in any adequate way. Rather, it is to pose a question regarding all of the following texts that purport to be written by Paul: what purpose was that fiction intended to serve?

192. The Letter to the Laodiceans

Near the end of Colossians, the author declares that he has also sent a letter to the Laodiceans and that he wants the Colossians and Laodiceans to exchange and read the letter the others received from him (Col 4:16). It is an understandable request, since Colossae and Laodicea were neighboring cities in Asia Minor. As if to complete the picture, someone later wrote the *Letter to the Laodiceans* by compiling sayings from Paul's actual letters. (Although the Muratorian fragment alleges that this writing was forged to support Valentinian Gnosticism, no particular Gnostic traits are evident in it.) This exercise in pseudonymity shows that the effort to provide a summary or "center" of Paul's theology did not first occur in the modern period![13]

> Paul, an apostle not of mortals nor by mortals, but by Jesus Christ, to the brothers and sisters who are at Laodicea, Grace be unto you and peace from God the Father and the Lord Jesus Christ.
>
> I give thanks unto Christ in all my prayers, that you continue in him and persevere in his works, looking for the promise at the day of judgment. Neither let the vain talk of some upset you, the talk of those who sneak in to turn you away from the truth of the gospel that was preached by me. And now God shall cause that those who are following me shall continue ministering so that the truth of the gospel keeps spreading, accomplishing goodness and the work of salvation, which is eternal life. And now my prison chains, in which I suffer in Christ and in which I am glad and rejoice, are visible to all. And this is eternal salvation for me, which is also brought about by your prayers, and the ministry of the Holy Spirit, either by life or by death. For truly for me to live is Christ, and to die is joy. And he shall also work his mercy in you, that you may have the same love, and be of the same mind. So, dearly beloved, as you have heard in my presence, so hold fast and work in the fear of God, and it shall be for you life eternal. For it is God who works in you. And act without thinking twice in whatever you do. And for the rest, dearly beloved, rejoice in Christ, and beware of those that are polluted by money. Let all your petitions be made openly before God, and be steadfast in the mind of Christ. And do whatever is sound and true and sober and just and worthy of love. And keep firm in your heart what you have heard and received. And peace shall be to you.
>
> The saints greet you. The grace of the Lord Jesus be with your spirit. And make sure that this is read by the church members of Colossae and that the one sent to Colossae is read to you.
>
> (*Letter to the Laodiceans*, trans. James, modified)

Third Corinthians in the *Acts of Paul*

We may discern more of an agenda in other pseudepigraphic correspondence, conventionally called 3 *Corinthians*. The text probably circulated independently before it was incorporated into a larger work called *The Acts of Paul*. We have included several components of the *Acts of Paul* in different places in this chapter; a brief discussion of the whole at this point is appropriate.

One of the most elaborate and informative sources for early Christian traditions about Paul, the *Acts of Paul* is also the most complex. The document comes to us literally in pieces, in a bewildering variety of manuscripts—none of which includes the whole *Acts of Paul*—from different times and provenances. According to Wilhelm Schneemelcher, the *Acts of Paul* was probably first combined with the apocryphal *Acts of Andrew*, the *Acts of John*, the *Acts of Peter*, and the *Acts of Thomas* (and probably the *Acts of Philip* as well) into a single collection, the apocryphal *Acts of the Apostles*, within Manicheism. That collection was subsequently transmitted through the ninth-century Christian authority Photius.[14] The *Acts of Paul* itself is no longer available in any of the extant manuscripts but must be reconstructed from a number of partial witnesses. The writing was nevertheless attested quite early. Tertullian (c. 200) knew it and repudiated it because it was being used to endorse the ordination of women (see below, no. 203), but his contemporary Hippolytus and, somewhat later, Origen both knew and respected it.[15]

The narrative breathes the distinctive air of the second- and third-century Christian novels. The heroic apostle tries to protect his beleaguered community from the emperor's suspicion and wrath; miracles and prodigies abound; the community of believers—and willing martyrs—grows steadily. As Schneemelcher observes, the narrative is meant to edify; it corresponds "to church ideas in the second half of the second century, but not to the reality of the apostle's own lifetime." Questions of Judaism and the law do not arise (as they did for Paul himself); neither is there interest in qualifications for church offices (as for the early post-Pauline letters). Rather, the central contest is between the empire's power and the lordship of Christ and his apostle.[16]

Richard I. Pervo finds in the *Acts of Paul* "the most radical . . . form of Paulinism yet witnessed," apart from Marcionism. It "brooks no compromise with the world"; it champions "moral rigorism, vigorous eschatology, embrace of ecstatic prophecy, and acceptance of women prophets." He concludes that the *Acts* comes from "a similar environment" to that of the "New Prophecy" of Montanus, Priscilla, and Maximilla, in late-second- and early-third-century Asia Minor, even if it is not a direct representative of it.[17]

The various manuscript witnesses for the *Acts of Paul* allow for the reconstruction of the original as follows:

1. a very fragmentary beginning, apparently narrating Paul's vision on the road to Damascus and subsequent travel to Jerusalem
2. a (now fragmentary) narration of Paul in Antioch

3. the *Acts of Paul and Thekla,* an enormously popular narrative that circulated independently in more than forty Greek manuscripts, in which Paul's convert Thekla becomes not only his partner in mission but the central figure in this part of the narrative (see below, no. 202)

4. episodes with Paul in Myra, Sidon, and Tyre (after which the narrative breaks off)

5. episodes with Paul in Ephesus, Philippi, and Corinth: in one manuscript tradition, a third letter to Corinth (3 *Corinthians*) is included here, though it is clearly earlier and independent of the *Acts of Paul* narrative

6. travel to Italy

7. the *Martyrdom of the Holy Apostle Paul,* which also circulated independently early on, in a number of texts, as a reading for the feast of Paul's martyrdom (see below, no. 221)

Just as some of these components originally circulated independently, so we present some of them in different parts of this chapter, without regard to their possible place in the original sequence of the *Acts of Paul.*

193. THIRD CORINTHIANS

Paul's reference in 1 Cor 5:9 to a previous letter to the Corinthians—otherwise unknown to us—provided the opportunity for some Christian writer, probably of the second century c.e., to compose a brief narrative, including an exchange of correspondence between the Corinthians and Paul, to fill the gap. The author of the *Acts of Paul* subsequently included this correspondence in his narrative. Because the correspondence was probably composed so late, no scholar gives it any weight when seeking to reconstruct the actual history of Paul's correspondence with the Corinthians.

As mentioned above, there is a more definite theological agenda to this correspondence. Paul is asked to refute proponents of the teachings that "there is no resurrection of the flesh," that the world and the human body are not God's creations, and that Jesus Christ only *appeared* to be crucified. (The insistence that "we must not use the prophets" may reflect the influence of Marcion, who rejected Jewish scripture.) To refute these teachings, "Paul" goes beyond what Paul himself wrote in his unquestioned letters, affirming, for example, the birth of Jesus from Mary—something Paul himself never mentions. (Note that 3 *Corinthians* is concerned to affirm not the miraculous birth to a virgin but Jesus' normal human birth to the lineage of David!) Note too that 3 *Corinthians* also adds scriptural proof-texts for the resurrection that do not appear in Paul's own letters.

Docetically minded Christians might reasonably enough have taken some of the statements in Paul's letters—that "flesh and blood cannot inherit the kingdom of God" (1 Cor 15:50), for example, or that Christ was raised in a "spiritual" rather than a "physical" body (15:42-49)—as evidence that Paul was on their side. *Third Corinthians* "improves" on Paul's own letters, then, by supplying the apostle's explicit condemnation of such views.

"**Docetism**"—from the Greek verb *dokein,* meaning "to appear" or "to seem"—is a general term for an assortment of beliefs held in early Christianity, according to which the spirit Christ was incompatible with human flesh. Thus, contrary to the depictions in the Gospels in our New Testament, Christ only "appeared" to die. These views were eventually condemned by catholic Christianity as heretical. (We use the word *catholic* in the sense used by early Christian writers to mean "universal," *kath' holou.*) See J. N. D. Kelly, *Early Christian Doctrines,* 5th ed. (New York: Harper & Row, 1976), 141–45.

When he was departed from [. . .] and would go to Philippi. Now when Paul was come to Philippi [. . .] he entered into the house of [. . .] and there was great joy among the brothers and sisters and for everyone [. . .] prayed that a messenger be sent to Philippi. For the Corinthians were in great trouble concerning Paul, that he would depart out of the world, before it was time. For there were certain men come to Corinth, Simon and Cleobius, saying that there is no resurrection of the flesh, but that of the spirit only, and the human body is not the creation of God, and also concerning the world, that God did not create it, and that God does not know the world, and that Jesus Christ was not actually crucified, but was only apparently crucified, and that he was not born of Mary, nor of the seed of David. And in short, there were many things that they had taught in Corinth, deceiving many others and deceiving also themselves.

When therefore the Corinthians heard that Paul was at Philippi, they sent a letter to Paul in Macedonia by Threptus and Eutychus the deacons. And the letter went as follows:

(*The Corinthians' Letter to Paul*)

"Stephanus and the elders that are with him, even Daphnus and Eubulus and Theophilus and Zenon, to Paul their brother, eternal greeting in the Lord.

"There have come unto Corinth two men, Simon and Cleobius, who are overthrowing the faith of many with corrupt words which do thou prove and examine. For we have never heard such words from you nor from the other apostles but all that we have received from you or from them, that we hold fast. Since therefore the Lord hath had mercy on us, that while you are still in the flesh we may hear these things again from you, if it be possible, either come to us or write to us. For we believe, according as it has been revealed to Theonoë, that the Lord has delivered you out of the hand of the lawless one.

"Now the things that these men say and teach are these: They say that we must not use the prophets, and that God is not almighty, and that there shall be no resurrection of the flesh, and that man was not made by God, and that Christ came not down in the flesh, neither was born of Mary, and that the world is not made by God, but by the angels. So, brother, we pray you to use all diligence and come to us, that the church of the Corinthians may remain without offense, and the madness of these men may be made plain.

"Farewell, always in the Lord."

The deacons Threptus and Eutyches brought the letter to Philippi, so that Paul received it, being in bonds because of Stratonice the wife of Apollophanes, and he forgot his bonds, and was greatly agitated, and cried out, saying, "It would be better for me to die and be with the Lord than to continue in the flesh and hear such things and the calamities of false doctrine, so that trouble comes on trouble. And over and above this so great affliction, I am in bonds and behold these evils by which the schemes of Satan are accomplished." While Paul was in great affliction, therefore, he wrote a letter with the following response.

(*Paul's Letter to the Corinthians*)

"Paul, a prisoner of Jesus Christ, to the brothers and sisters in Corinth, greeting.

"While in the middle of many tribulations, I am not surprised that the teachings of the evil one run freely. For my Lord Jesus Christ will hasten his coming, and will set at naught those who falsify his words. For I delivered to you in the beginning the things that I received from the holy apostles who were before me, who were at all times with Jesus Christ, namely, that our Lord Jesus Christ was born of Mary who is of the seed of David according to the flesh, the Holy Spirit being sent out from heaven from the Father to her by the angel Gabriel that he might come down into this world and redeem all flesh by his flesh, and raise us up from the dead in the flesh, like as he showed to us himself by his example. And because he took on human form he was formed by his Father; therefore was he sought when he was lost, that he might be quickened by adoption.

"For to this end did God Almighty who made heaven and earth first send the prophets to the Jews, that they might be drawn away from their sins. For he designed to save the house of Israel, therefore he conferred a portion of the spirit of Christ on the prophets and sent them to the Jews first and they proclaimed the true worship of God for a long length of time. But the prince of iniquity, desiring to be God, laid hands on them and slew them and bound all flesh by evil lusts and the end of the world by judgment drew near.

"But God Almighty, who is righteous, would not cast away his own creation, but had compassion on them from heaven and sent his Spirit into Mary in Galilee, who believed with all her heart and received the Holy Spirit in her womb, that Jesus might come into the world, that by that flesh whereby that wicked one had brought in death (had triumphed), by the same he should be shown to be overcome.

"For by his own body Jesus Christ saved all flesh and restored it to life, that he might show forth the temple of righteousness in his body. In whom (or whereby) we are saved, in whom if we believe we are set free.

"Know therefore that those who agree with such people are not children of righteousness but children of wrath who reject the wisdom of God, saying that the heaven and the earth and all that are in them are not the work of God. They therefore are children of wrath, for cursed are they, following the teaching

Fig. 6.2. *A mother and child—almost certainly Mary and the infant Jesus. Early Christian fresco in the Catacomb of St. Priscilla, Rome, late second century* C.E. *Although Paul himself never mentions the birth of Jesus to Mary, the virgin birth quickly became a popular motif in Christian art and devotion. Photo in the public domain.*

of the serpent, whom you should drive out from among you and flee from their doctrine. For you are not children of disobedience, but of the well-beloved church. Therefore is the time of the resurrection proclaimed to all.

"And as for that which they say, that there is no resurrection of the flesh, they indeed shall have no resurrection into life, but into judgment, because they believe not in him that is risen from the dead, not believing nor understanding, for they know not, Corinthians, the seeds of wheat or of other seeds, how they are cast bare into the earth and are corrupted and rise again by the will of God with bodies, and clothed. And not only that body that is cast in rises again, but blesses many more itself, fertile and prospering.

"And if we must not take an example from seeds only, but from more noble bodies, you know how Jonah the son of Amittai, when he would not preach to the people of Nineveh, fled and was swallowed by the sea monster; and after three days and three nights God heard the prayer of Jonah out of the lowest hell, and no part of him was consumed, not even a hair or eyelash. How much more, you of little faith, shall he raise up you that have believed in Christ Jesus, like as he himself arose.

"Likewise also a dead man was cast on the bones of the prophet Elisha by the children of Israel, and he arose, both body and soul and bones and spirit [2 Kgs 13:20-21], how much more shall you who have been cast on the body and bones and spirit of the Lord arise again in that day, having your flesh whole, even as he arose? Likewise also concerning the prophet Elijah, he raised up the widows' son from death [1 Kgs 17:17-24], how much more shall the Lord Jesus raise you up from death at the sound of the trumpet, in the blinking of an eye? For he has showed us an example in his own body.

"If, then, you receive any other teaching, God shall be witness against you. And let no one trouble me, for I bear these bonds that I may win Christ, and I therefore bear his marks in my body that I may attain to the resurrection of the dead. And whoever abides in the rule that has been received from the blessed prophets and the holy gospel shall receive a reward from the Lord, and after rising from the dead this person shall obtain eternal life. But whoever transgresses in these things, with this person is the fire, and with them that walk in a similar manner who are a generation of vipers, whom you should reject by the power of the Lord. And peace, grace, and love shall be with you."

(3 Corinthians, trans. James, adapted)

194. Paul's correspondence with Seneca

The book of Acts describes Paul's unsuccessful presentation of his gospel to Stoic and Epicurean philosophers in Athens (Acts 17:16-34). That scene, along with Paul's repudiation of "words of wisdom" (1 Cor 2:1-5) and the warning in Colossians to avoid being captured by "philosophy and empty deceit" (Col 2:8), might give a strong impression of the apostle's antagonism to philosophy and philosophers. As we saw in chapter 1, on the other hand, Paul's self-presentation might in some ways have *resembled* that of popular philosophers in Roman culture.

The latter impression lingered, kept alive in part by Luke's narrative (after all, Paul was winning a respectful hearing on the Areopagus up until he mentioned the resurrection of the dead, Acts 17:30-33) and in part by the ostensibly incidental request in 2 Tim 4:13 that Timothy bring Paul's cloak, books, "and above all the parchments" (the signal possessions of a Roman philosopher). The pattern was repeated, as other writings were composed depicting Paul as able to hold his own among the philosophers of his day.

The foremost example is the apocryphal correspondence between Paul and Seneca, the Roman Stoic philosopher and advisor to Nero. Although we have no evidence that the two men were aware of each other, the correspondence depends for its plausibility on the slight premise that Seneca was Paul's contemporary. (Seneca lived from about 4 b.c.e. until 65 c.e., when Nero forced him to commit suicide.) Neither would the correspondence have seemed impossible or even unlikely to early readers familiar with Paul's letters or the book of Acts. Paul himself declared in Philippians that his imprisonment for the sake of Christ had come to be known "through the

Fig. 6.3. *A modern photograph of the Areopagus (or Hill of Mars), taken from the Acropolis, shows the scale of the outcropping on which Paul addressed an audience of philosophers in Acts 17. The figure of Dionysos, who decided to follow Paul (17:34), also became the object of pseudonymity in the sixth century as the purported author of the* Mystical Theology *and other works. Photo: Ken Russell Salvador.*

whole Praetorian Guard" (1:13). Further, he sent greetings to the Philippians from some "in the emperor's household" (4:22). Luke described Paul as a Roman citizen (22:22-29), able to defend himself with some eloquence before Roman governors (Felix, then Festus, Acts 24–25) and client kings (Agrippa, 25:13-32) and to claim the right to appeal to Caesar himself (25:11-12). These elements of Luke's portrayal were picked up in later literature, for example, in the *Martyrdom of the Holy Apostle Paul* (see below, no. 221).

The letters are spurious and not terribly profound, giving little indication of the thought of either Paul or Seneca as we know them. They were well known in the Latin church, however, where they were regarded as genuine for centuries. Both Jerome and Augustine make mention of them. Like most letters in Paul's world, they are very short. The correspondence was probably written in the fourth century, probably to advance the Christian cause in the Latin West[18] by magnifying Paul's prestige through association with the eminent Seneca. As Richard I. Pervo sums up the message of the correspondence, "Do not despise Christianity because its primary texts lacked literary elegance. If it was good enough for Seneca . . ."[19] The letters might also have addressed curiosity regarding Paul's ability to move among the upper circles of Roman political power; so they allow us a glimpse into how some Christians imagined Paul's compatibility with philosophy and his relationship to the highest echelons of

Roman society. Note that the correspondence includes fourteen letters—the number of "Pauline" letters in the New Testament, if one includes Hebrews as a letter of Paul (as did many early Christians).[20]

(1) Seneca Greets Paul

I believe, Paul, that you have been informed of the talk I had yesterday with my Lucilius about the secret mysteries and other things, for some sharers in your teaching were with me. For we had retired to the gardens of Sallust, where, because of us, those whom I speak of, going in another direction, saw and joined us. Certainly we wished for your presence, and I would have you know it. We were much refreshed by the reading of your book, by which I mean some of the many letters that you have addressed to some city or capital of a province, and which inculcate the moral life with admirable precepts. These thoughts, I take it, are not uttered by you but through you, but surely sometimes both by you and through you: for such is the greatness of them and they are warm with such nobility that I think whole generations of people could apply and perfect them. Best wishes for your good health, brother.

(2) Paul Greets Seneca

I received your letter yesterday with delight, and should have been able to answer it immediately, if I had the young man available whom I intended to send to you. For you know when, and by whom, and at what moment, and to whom things ought to be given and entrusted.[21] I beg, therefore, that you will not think yourself neglected, when I am respecting the dignity of your person.

Now in that you somewhere write that you are pleased with my letter, I think myself happy in the good opinion of such a man. For you would not say it, you, a critic, a sophist, the teacher of a great prince, and indeed of all—unless you spoke truth.

I trust you may long be in health.

(3) Seneca Greets Paul

I have arranged some writings in a volume, and given them their proper divisions. I am also resolved to read them to Caesar, if only fortune be kind, that he may bring a new ear to the hearing. Perhaps you, too, will be there. If not, I will at another time fix you a day, that we may look over the work together. Indeed, I could not produce this writing for him, without first conferring with you—if only that could be done without risk—that you may know that you are not being neglected.

Farewell, dearest Paul.

(4) Paul Greets Annaeus Seneca

Whenever I hear your letters read, I think of you as present, and imagine nothing else but that you are always with us. As soon, then, as you begin to come, we shall see each other at close quarters.

I wish you good health.

(5) Seneca Greets Paul

We are much pained by your retirement. What is it? What causes keep you away? If it be the anger of the lady, because you have left the old rite and sect, and have converted others, there will be a possibility of pleading with her, that she may consider it as done on due reflection and not lightly.[22]

(6) Paul Greets Seneca and Lucilius

Of the subject on which you have written I must not speak with pen and ink, of which the former marks out and draws somewhat, and the latter shows it clearly, especially as I know that among you—that is, in your homes and in you—there are those who understand me. Honor is to be paid to all [Rom 13:7], and so much the more because men catch at opportunities of being offended. If we are patient with them, we shall certainly overcome them at every point, provided they be people who can be sorry for their actions.
    Farewell.

(7) Annaeus Seneca Greets Paul and Theophilus

I profess myself well content with the reading of your letters that you sent to the Galatians, Corinthians, and Achaeans; and may we so live together as you show yourself to be inspired with the divine fear. For it is the Holy Spirit that is in you and high above you that expresses these exalted and adorable thoughts. I would therefore have you careful of other points, that the polish of the style may not be wanting to the majesty of the thought. And, brother, not to conceal anything from you, and have it on my conscience, I confess to you that the Augustus was moved by your views. When I read to him the exordium about virtue, he said that he wondered how a man who had not received a standard education could reason in this way. I replied that the gods often speak by the mouths of the simple, not through those who try deceitfully to show what they can do by their learning. And when I cited him the example of Vatienus the rustic, to whom two men appeared in the territory of Reate, who afterwards were recognized as Castor and Pollux, he appeared fully convinced.
    Farewell.

(8) Paul Greets Seneca

Though I am aware that Caesar, even if he sometimes lapses, is a lover of our wonders, you will suffer yourself to be, not wounded but admonished. For I think that you took a very serious step in bringing to his notice a matter alien to his religion and training. For since he is a worshipper of the gods of the nations, I do not see why you thought you would wish him to know this matter, unless I am to think that you did it out of excessive attachment to me. I beg you not to do so in the future. For you must be careful not to offend the empress in your love for me. Yet her anger will not hurt us if it lasts, nor do good if it does not. As a queen, she will not be angry. As a woman, she will be offended.
    Farewell.

(9) Seneca Greets Paul

I know that you are not so much disturbed on your own account by my letter to you on the showing of your letters to Caesar, as by the nature of things, which so calls away the minds of men from all right learning and conduct—so that I am not surprised, for I have learned this for certain by many examples. Let us then act differently, and if in the past anything has been done carelessly, you will pardon it. I have sent you a book on elegance of expression.

Farewell, dearest Paul.

(10) To Seneca, Greetings from Paul

Whenever I write to you and do not place my name after yours I do a serious thing and one unbefitting my school. For I ought, as I have often declared, to be all things to all men, and to observe in your person that which the Roman law has granted to the honor of the Senate, and choose the last place in writing a letter, not striving to do as I please in a confused and disgraceful way.[23] Farewell, most devoted of masters. Given on the fifth of the calends of July, when Nero was consul for the fourth time, with Messala as the other consul.[24]

(11) Seneca Greets Paul

Hail, my dearest Paul. If you, so great a man, so beloved in all ways, be—I say not joined—but intimately associated with me and my name, it will indeed be well with your Seneca. Since, then, you are the summit and topmost peak of all people, would you not have me glad that I am so near you as to be counted a second self of yours? Do not, then, think that you are unworthy to be named first on the heading of letters, lest you make me think you are testing me rather than playing with me—especially as you know yourself to be a Roman citizen. For the rank that is mine, I would it were yours, and yours I would were mine.

Farewell, dearest Paul.

Given on the 10th of the kalends of April; when Apronianus and Capito were consuls.[25]

(12) Seneca Greets Paul

Hail, my dearest Paul, Think you that I am not in sadness and grief, that you innocent ones are so often condemned to suffer? And next, that the whole people thinks you so callous and so prone to crime, that you are supposed to be the authors of every misfortune in the city? Yet let us bear it patiently and content ourselves with what fortune brings, until supreme happiness puts an end to our troubles. Former ages had to bear the Macedonian, Philip's son, and, after Darius, Dionysius, and our own times endured Gaius Caesar, for all of whom their will was law. The source of the many fires that Rome suffers is plain. But if humble men could speak out what the reason is, and if it were possible to speak without risk in this dark time, all would be plain to all. Christians and Jews are commonly executed as contrivers of the fire. Whoever the criminal is, whose pleasure is that of a butcher, and who veils himself with a lie, he is reserved for his due season, and as the best of men is sacrificed, the one for the many, so he, vowed to death for all, will be burned with fire. A hundred and thirty-two houses and four blocks have been burned in six days; the seventh day brought a pause in the fire.

I pray that you may be well, brother.

Given the fifth of the calends of April, while Frugi and Bassus were consuls.[26]

(13) Seneca Greets Paul

Much in every part of your works is enclosed in allegory and enigma, and therefore the great force that is given you of matter and talent should be beautified, I do not say with elegance of words, but with a certain care. Nor should you fear what I remember you have often said, that many who affect such things vitiate the thought and emasculate the strength of the matter. But I wish you would yield to me and humor the genius of Latin, and give beauty to your noble words, that the great gift that has been granted you may be worthily treated by you.

Farewell.

Given on the day before the nones of June, while Leo and Sabinus were consuls.[27]

(14) Paul Greets Seneca

To your meditations have been revealed those things that the Godhead has granted to few. With confidence, therefore, I sow in a field already fertile a most prolific seed, not such matter as is liable to corruption, but the abiding word, an emanation from God who grows and abides for ever. This your wisdom has attained and you will see that it is unfailing—so as to judge that the laws of heathens and Israelites are to be shunned. You may become a new author, by showing forth with the graces of rhetoric the irreproachable wisdom of Jesus Christ, which you, having nearly reached, will instill into the temporal monarch, his servants, and his intimate friends. Yet the persuading of them will be a rough and difficult task, for many of them will hardly incline to your admonitions. Yet the word of God, if it be instilled into them, will be a vital gain, producing a new man, incorrupt, and an everlasting soul that shall hasten from her to God.

Farewell, Seneca, most dear to me.

Given on the calends of August, while Leo and Sabinus were consuls.

(*Letters of Paul and Seneca*, trans. James, adapted)

Paul the Philosopher and Theologian

If imitation is the sincerest form of flattery, we might regard those pseudepigraphers who tried to imitate Paul's letters as offering their own kind of flattery. Apart from pseudepigraphy, early attestations of Paul's letters show that he was considered a teacher and his letters were read as a repository of authoritative truth. For example, Paul's influence on Ignatius, bishop of Antioch in the first decades of the second century, was "prominent and explicit." Ignatius clearly knew Paul's letters and language well; he looked back on Peter and Paul with reverence (*Romans* 4.3); his concern for unity in community life and his view of martyrdom as an imitation of Christ were both probably learned from Paul's letters.[28]

Paul the Gnostic

Elsewhere, some of the most enthusiastic interest shown early on in Paul's teaching was that of Gnostic Christians, who considered Paul a kindred spirit and an articulate guide to spiritual truth. Paul was claimed by Gnostic Christians in the second century. Marcion included in his scriptures only a single Gospel and the letters of Paul. On the testimony of the Muratorian fragment, the *Letter to the Laodiceans* (see above, no. 192) and another to the Alexandrians (which is not extant) were written "to suit the heresy of Marcion." Valentinus claimed to have been taught by Paul's own disciple Theodas (Clement of Alexandria, *Strom.* 7.17, 106). As Elaine Pagels has shown, the language in key passages in Paul's letters could readily be interpreted along a Gnostic line.[29]

The term **Gnosticism** itself has a sort of Pauline pedigree. 1 Timothy 6:20-21 calls readers to reject "what is falsely called knowledge" (Greek *gnōsis*); later, Irenaeus used the phrase when he wrote his *Against Heresies*, formally titled *Refutation and Overthrow of Falsely Called Knowledge* (c. 185), apparently because the Christians whom he meant to criticize called themselves "knowing ones" (*gnōstikoi*). Birger Pearson writes that "Gnostic" teaching consists in "an innovative reinterpretation of biblical and Jewish traditions" in which "Platonist philosophy was a decisive factor." Saving knowledge "comes by revelation from a transcendent realm, mediated by a revealer who has come from that realm in order to awaken people to a knowledge of God and a knowledge of the true nature of the human self."

So much is clear. But whether the Gnostic play on Jewish traditions indicates that Gnosticism "arose out of a Jewish milieu" or rather represents a hostile construal of Jewish writings on the part of hellenized non-Jewish Christians is open to debate. See Birger A. Pearson, *Ancient Gnosticism: Traditions and Literature* (Minneapolis: Fortress Press, 2007), esp. 11–15 (quoted here); Bentley Layton, "Prolegomena to the Study of Ancient Gnosticism," *The Social World of the First Christians: Essays in Honor of Wayne A. Meeks*, ed. L. Michael White and O. Larry Yarbrough (Minneapolis: Fortress Press, 1995), 334–50; Karen L. King, *What Is Gnosticism?* (Cambridge, Mass.: Belknap Press of Harvard University Press, 2005).

195. The Prayer of the Apostle Paul

We would be at a disadvantage if we relied for our picture of Gnosticism only on the criticisms made by their opponents. The Nag Hammadi codices, leather-bound books buried, apparently by an Egyptian Christian, outside a Pachomian monastery in the late fourth century and rediscovered in 1947, provide invaluable primary information about the myths that opponents attributed to Gnostics.

Paul appears in Gnostic writings as a champion of a distinctly Gnostic faith. The *Prayer of the Apostle Paul* appears in the books from Nag Hammadi. It includes language characteristic of the earlier Pauline tradition—"fullness," for example (Greek *plērōma*: Eph 3:19; Col 1:19; 2:9-10)—as well as language unknown from Paul, for example, the "psychic God."

> . . . [your] light, give me your [mercy! My] Redeemer, redeem me, for [I am] yours; the one who has come forth from you. You are [my] mind; bring me forth! You are my treasure house; open for me! You [are] my fullness; take me to you! You are (my) repose; give me [the] perfect thing that cannot be grasped!
>
> I invoke you, the one who is and who pre-existed in the name [which is] exalted above every name, through Jesus Christ, [the Lord] of Lords, the King of the ages; give me your gifts, of which you do not repent, through the Son of Man, the Spirit, the Paraclete of [truth]. Give me authority [when I] ask you; give healing for my body when I ask you through the Evangelist, [and] redeem my eternal light soul and my spirit. And the First-born of the Pleroma of grace—reveal him to my mind!
>
> Grant what no angel eye has [seen] and no archon ear (has) heard and what has not entered into the human heart which came to be angelic and (modeled) after the image of the psychic God when it was formed in the beginning, since I have faith and hope. And place upon me your beloved, elect, and blessed greatness, the First-born, the First-begotten, and the [wonderful] mystery of your house; [for] yours is the power [and] the glory and the praise and greatness for ever and ever. [Amen.]
>
> Prayer of Paul (the) Apostle.
>
> In Peace.
>
> Christ is holy.
>
> (*Prayer of the Apostle Paul*, trans. Mueller)

196. The (Gnostic) Apocalypse of Paul

Two different documents go by the name *Apocalypse of Paul*. What follows is the text that appears in the Nag Hammadi library.[30] It offers a brief account of the revelation given to Paul on the way to Damascus, but identifies this vision with a heavenly ascent like the one Paul relates in 2 Corinthians 12. Note that visions of Christ as a child are not unusual in second- and third-century Christian literature; here it is the Spirit who appears as a child. Phrases in brackets indicate conjectures where the text is fragmentary.

> . . . the road. And [he spoke to him], saying, "[By which] road [shall I go] up to [Jerusalem]?" The little child [replied, saying], "Say your name, so that [I may show] you the road." [The little child] knew [who Paul was]. He wished to make conversation with him through his words [in order that] he might find an excuse for speaking with him.

Fig. 6.4. *Codex IV from Nag Hammadi, open to the* Apocryphon (Secret Book) of John. *Photo in the public domain.*

The little child spoke, saying, "I know who you are, Paul. You are he who was blessed from his mother's womb. For I have [come] to you that you may [go up to Jerusalem] to your fellow [apostles. And] for this reason [you were called. And] I am the [Spirit who accompanies] you. Let [your mind awaken, Paul], with [. . .]. For [. . .] whole which [. . .] among the [principalities and] these authorities [and] archangels and powers and the whole race of demons, [. . .] the one that reveals bodies to a soul-seed."

And after he brought that speech to an end, he spoke, saying to me, "Let your mind awaken, Paul, and see that this mountain upon which you are standing is the mountain of Jericho, so that you may know the hidden things in those that are visible. Now it is to the twelve apostles that you shall go, for they are elect spirits, and they will greet you." He raised his eyes and saw them greeting him.

Then the Holy [Spirit] who was speaking with [him] caught him up on high to the third heaven, and he passed beyond to the fourth [heaven]. The [Holy] Spirit spoke to him, saying, "Look and see your [likeness] upon the earth." And he [looked] down and saw those [who were upon] the earth. He stared [and saw] those who were upon the [. . . Then he] gazed [down and] saw the [twelve] apostles [at] his right [and] at his left in the creation; and the Spirit was going before them.

(In the fourth heaven Paul watches as a soul is brought forward "out of the land of the dead" for judgment. Convicted of sins upon earth, the soul is cast down into "a body that had been prepared for it," apparently indicating reincarnation.)

> [Then I gazed] upward and [saw the] Spirit saying [to me], "Paul, come! [Proceed toward] me!" Then as I [went], the gate opened, [and] I went up to the fifth [heaven]. And I saw my fellow apostles [going with me] while the Spirit accompanied us.

(Paul and his fellow apostles continue their journey to higher and higher heavens. In the seventh heaven Paul encounters "an old man" who may represent the Gnostic understanding of the God of the Hebrew Bible and, thus, of catholic Christianity.)

> [Then we went] up to the seventh [heaven and I saw] an old man [. . .] light [and whose garment] was white. [His throne], which is in the seventh heaven, [was] brighter than the sun by [seven] times. The old man spoke, saying to [me], "Where are you going, Paul, O blessed one and the one who was set apart from his mother's womb?" But I looked at the Spirit, and he was nodding his head, saying to me, "Speak with him!" And I replied, saying to the old man, "I am going to the place from which I came." And the old man responded to me, "Where are you from?" But I replied, saying, "I am going down to the world of the dead in order to lead captive the captivity that was led captive in the captivity of Babylon." The old man replied to me, saying, "How will you be able to get away from me? Look and see the principalities and authorities." [The] Spirit spoke, saying, "Give him [the] sign that you have, and [he will] open for you." And then I gave [him] the sign. He turned his face downwards to his creation and to those who are his own authorities.
>
> And then the <seventh> heaven opened and we went up to [the] Ogdoad (the Eighth). And I saw the twelve apostles. They greeted me, and we went up to the ninth heaven. I greeted all those who were in the ninth heaven, and we went up to the tenth heaven. And I greeted my fellow spirits.
>
> (*Apocalypse of Paul*, trans. MacRae and Murdock)

197. Gnostic distinctions among people (*Tripartite Tractate*)

Another work found in the Nag Hammadi codices, the *Tripartite Tractate*, distinguishes groups of people using terminology reminiscent of Paul's language in 1 Corinthians. There Paul distinguishes the "mature" (*teleioi*, 2:6) and "spiritual" (*pneumatikoi*, 2:13) from "unspiritual" (NRSV) or "natural" (KJV) persons (*psychikoi*, literally, "related to the soul or life") and describes the Corinthians as having initially been "people of the flesh" (*sarkikoi*, 3:1, 3). The later Coptic text uses Greek loanwords for those who are "spiritual" (*pneumatikoi*), oriented to the (merely) human mind (*psychikoi*), and "material" (*hylikoi*).

> Mankind came to be in three essential types, the spiritual, the psychic, and the material, conforming the triple disposition of the Logos, from which were brought forth the material ones and the psychic ones and the spiritual ones. Each one of the three essential types is known by its fruit. And they were not

known at first but only as the coming of the Savior who shone upon the saints and revealed what each was.

The spiritual race, being like light from light and like spirit from spirit, when its head appeared, it ran toward him immediately. It immediately became a body of its head. It suddenly received knowledge in the revelation. The psychic race is like light from a fire, since it hesitated to accept knowledge of him who appeared to it. (It hesitated) even more to run toward him in faith. Rather, through a voice it was instructed and this was sufficient, since it is not far from the hope according to the promise, since it received, so to speak as a pledge, the assurance of the things which were to be. The material race, however, is alien in every way; since it is dark, it shuns the shining of the light because its appearance destroys it. And since it has not received its unity, it is something excessive and hateful toward the Lord at his revelation.

The spiritual race will receive complete salvation in every way. The material will receive destruction in every way, just as one who resists him. The psychic race, since it is in the middle when it is brought forth and also when it is created, is double according to its determination for both good and evil.

(*Tripartite Tractate*, NHC I.5, trans. Attridge and Mueller)

198. ECHOES OF PAUL IN GNOSTIC TEACHING (IRENAEUS)

Paul's distinction of *pneumatikoi*, *psychikoi*, and *sarkikoi* people in 1 Corinthians 2–3, or his discussion of "knowledge" (*gnōsis*) in relation to eating meat that had been offered to idols in 1 Corinthians 8, or his declaration in 1 Cor 15:50 that "flesh and blood cannot inherit the kingdom of God," might have seemed compatible with Gnostic teachings and practices as we know them from the following passage from Irenaeus in his *Refutation and Overthrow of Falsely Called Knowledge* (*Against Heresies*). Irenaeus goes on to add accusations that the Gnostics have committed sexual sins and idolatry because they believe the actions of their material bodies inconsequential for their true spiritual selves.

> [The Gnostics] further hold that the consummation of all things will take place when all that is spiritual has been formed and perfected by Gnosis; and by this they mean spiritual people who have attained to the perfect knowledge of God, and been initiated into these mysteries by Achamoth. And they represent themselves to be these persons.
>
> Animal people, again, are instructed in animal things; such people, namely, as are established by their works, and by a mere faith, while they have not perfect knowledge. We of the church, they say, are these persons. Wherefore also they maintain that good works are necessary to us, for that otherwise it is impossible to be saved. But as to themselves, they hold that they shall be entirely and undoubtedly saved, not by means of conduct, but because they are spiritual by nature. For, just as it is impossible that material substance should partake of salvation (since, indeed, they maintain that it is incapable of receiving it), so again it is impossible that spiritual substance (by which they mean themselves) should ever come under the power of corruption, whatever the sort of actions in which they indulged. . . .

Wherefore also it comes to pass that the "most perfect" among them addict themselves without fear to all those kinds of forbidden deeds of which the Scriptures assure us that "they who do such things shall not inherit the kingdom of God" [Gal 5:21]. For instance, they make no scruple about eating meats offered in sacrifice to idols, imagining that they can in this way contract no defilement. Then again, at every heathen festival celebrated in honor of the idols, these are the first to assemble; and to such a pitch do they go, that some of them do not even keep away from that bloody spectacle hateful both to God and mortals, in which gladiators either fight with wild beasts or singly encounter one another.

(Irenaeus, *Against Heresies* 1.6.2-4, trans. Roberts and Rambaut modified)

199. AGAINST THE GNOSTIC CLASSIFICATION OF SOULS (ORIGEN)

Origen of Alexandria was similarly interested in using Paul to thwart Gnostic interpretation. Commenting on the image of the body in Romans 12, Origen opposes the three-part division of human beings taught by Gnostics.

But as for the one who longs to contemplate the works of the wisdom of God in his ways of governing, let him listen to Paul discussing these matters in another passage where he is aware of the divine mysteries. He says, "but in a large house there are vessels not only of gold and silver but also of wood and clay and some indeed for honor, but some for reproach" [2 Tim 2:20]. If, therefore, anyone should cleanse himself from these things, he will be a vessel for honor, sanctified and useful to the Lord, prepared for every good work.

Do you hear Paul in these things in which he had no impudent opponent, how he has explained that there are various kinds of vessels? For there, where there was no worthy hearer but there was an opponent, he mentions only clay vessels; but here he says that there are [vessels] of gold, silver, wood, and clay, some indeed are for honor, but others for reproach, just as he mentioned there. But although there he was silent about the grounds for there being "some for honor, but some for reproach," here he has explained this openly. He says, "For if anyone should cleanse himself from these things"—doubtless, from the defilements of sin—"he will be," he says, "a vessel for honor, sanctified and useful to the Lord, prepared for every good work."

Now in this body, whether, for instance, someone is an eye, which is more highly illustrious within the whole body, or a hand, which can be reckoned in the next position, or an ear or tongue or one of the other members that are viewed to be more honorable; or on the other hand, that someone should be some other member, of those that seem less honorable; I think that it is beyond our comprehension [to ascertain] whether he himself offers some cause, or whether it is by the will of God, without regard to any causes whatsoever, that this one or that one should be constituted this or that member [see 1 Cor 12:14-24].

But lest those who assert that there are different natures of souls and that they have been constituted by different creators seem to find an opportunity for reinforcing their doctrines, let what we have discussed above about the vessels of honor and the vessels of dishonor suffice even for the present passage. For it should never be conceded that either in the present or in the past or even in the future ages divine providence does not dispense each one in such a way that each one's merit, which is acquired through the freedom of will, furnishes material to the one who dispenses. For God is just and there is no injustice with him.

(Origen, *Commentary on Romans* according to Rufinus, 7.18.6; 9.2.16, trans. Scheck)

200. PAUL AS THEOLOGIAN OF A REDEEMED CREATION (IRENAEUS)

Gnostic dualism opposed the irredeemable material world, the creation of a lower, limited deity, to the good, spiritual realm of Christ and the true God. Against such dualism Irenaeus enlisted—we might presume, to the surprise of the Gnostics—Paul himself. Although Paul did not elaborate a "theology of creation," Irenaeus drew from his letters (and from other scriptures) a theology of "recapitulation" (Greek *anakephalaiōsis*) in which creation, though terribly distorted, is redeemed. That is, God made a good world; when human beings distorted it through sin, God remedied their distortion by "recapitulating" or replaying the drama of their failure and reversing it to achieve a different ending. By posing the obedient Christ as antitype against a disobedient Adam as type—a scheme drawn from Romans 5—Irenaeus affirmed a single narrative of "salvation history" and shaped the orthodox theologian tradition after him. To the Adam–Christ typology Irenaeus added an Eve–Mary typology, suggesting that humanity, male and female alike, had sinned in Eden; their experience, male and female alike, had been "summed up" again and their disobedience undone in the persons and acts of an obedient male and female.

> Whence, then, is the substance of the first-formed man? From the Will and the Wisdom of God, and from the virgin earth. "For God had not sent rain," the Scripture says, upon the earth, before man was made; "and there was no man to till the earth" [Gen 2:5]. From this, then, while it was still virgin, God took dust of the earth and formed the man, the beginning of humankind. So then the Lord, summing up afresh this man, took the same dispensation of entry into flesh, being born from the Virgin by the Will and the Wisdom of God; that he also should show forth the likeness of Adam's entry into flesh, and there should be that which was written in the beginning, "the human after the image and likeness" of God [Gen 1:26].
>
> And just as through a disobedient virgin man was stricken down and fell into death, so through the Virgin who was obedient to the Word of God, man was reanimated and received life. For the Lord came to seek again the sheep that was lost; and the human being it was that was lost: and for this cause there was not made some other formation, but in that same which had its descent from Adam he preserved the likeness of the first formation. For it was necessary that Adam should be summed up in Christ, that mortality might be swallowed up and overwhelmed by immortality; and Eve summed up in Mary, that a virgin should be a virgin's intercessor, and by a virgin's obedience undo and put away the disobedience of a virgin.
>
> And the trespass which came by the tree was undone by the tree of obedience, when, hearkening unto God, the Son of man was nailed to the tree;

thereby putting away the knowledge of evil and bringing in and establishing the knowledge of good. Now evil it is to disobey God, even as hearkening unto God is good. And for this cause the Word spake by Isaiah the prophet, announcing beforehand that which was to come—for therefore are they prophets, because they proclaim what is to come: by him then spake the Word thus: "I refuse not, nor gainsay: I gave my back to scourging, and my cheeks to smiting; and my face I turned not away from the shame of spitting." So then by the obedience wherewith he obeyed "even unto death" [Phil 2:8], hanging on the tree, he put away the old disobedience which was wrought in the tree.

(Irenaeus, *Apostolic Preaching* 34, trans. Robinson, modified)

201. PAUL AS A THEOLOGIAN OF THE INCARNATION (AUGUSTINE)

For the orthodox or catholic tradition of Christian theology as well as for Gnostic Christianity, Paul proved an invaluable resource. The theologian and bishop Augustine of Hippo (354–430)—educated in Greek philosophy and Roman rhetoric—wrote in his *Confessions* that he had encountered wisdom in "the Platonic books" but that he had not found in them the deeper truth of the incarnation as described in the prologue to John's Gospel and in Paul's hymn in Philippians 2. Augustine clearly regarded Paul as revealing truths that, although they were intelligible to philosophy, had not been discovered through philosophy. Augustine directs his speech throughout the *Confessions* to God.

First you wanted to show me how you "resist the proud and give grace to the humble" [1 Pet 5:5], and with what mercy you have shown humanity the way of humility in that your "Word was made flesh and dwelt among" men [John 1:14]. Through a man puffed up with monstrous pride, you brought under my eye some books of the Platonists, translated from Greek into Latin. There I read, not of course in these words, but with entirely the same sense and supported by numerous and varied reasons, "In the beginning was the Word and the Word was with God and the Word was God." . . . In reading the Platonic books I found expressed in different words, and in a variety of ways, that the Son, "being in the form of the Father, did not think it theft to be equal with God" [Phil 2:6], because by nature he is that very thing. But that "he took on himself the form of a servant and emptied himself, was made in the likeness of men and found to behave as a man, and humbled himself being made obedient to death, even the death of the Cross so that God exalted him" from the dead "and gave him a name which is above every name, that at the name of Jesus every knee should bow, of celestial, terrestrial, and infernal beings, and every tongue should confess that Jesus is Lord in the glory of God the Father" [Phil 2:6-11]—that these books do not have.

(Augustine, *Confessions* 7.13-14, trans. Chadwick)

Paul the Ascetic

Even for Augustine, the chief value of Paul's letters was not in their ideas alone. Practically from the beginning, Paul was taken as an example of the spiritually disciplined life, of *askēsis* ("training" or "discipline"). Paul's own asceticism (see 1 Cor 9:27) and his admonitions such as those in 1 Corinthians that "it is good for a man not to touch a woman" (7:1) and that he wished all people were like he himself, celibate (7:7-8), were powerful examples in the early assemblies. Antoinette Clark Wire has argued that spiritual women in Corinth had already embraced the sort of sexual continence that Paul had initially advocated and that in 1 Corinthians, Paul, suddenly alarmed, was backtracking, seeking to qualify his own earlier stance![31] The author of 1 Timothy went even further than Paul, warning against the hypocrisy of "liars," deceived by demons, who "forbid marriage and demand abstinence from foods" (4:3-5) and going so far as to question the value of "physical training" (*sōmatikē gymnasia*, 4:7-8).

In the Roman world, far more than for many contemporary readers, the question of marriage or sexual continence was tied up with power relations between the genders. To advocate or to practice sexual continence was to renounce marriage, and that meant an implicit challenge to the patriarchal social order itself. We find statements in Paul's letters that seem to assume a clear gender hierarchy (for example, the notoriously convoluted argument in 1 Cor 11:2-16) alongside his declaration that "in Christ there is no longer . . . male and female" (Gal 3:28). In 1 Corinthians we read Paul's insistence that women "be silent in the churches" (14:34-35, if these lines are genuine), but in the same letter he refers to a woman praying and prophesying in the assembly (11:5), and he refers repeatedly and with respect to women who are his apostolic colleagues or are leaders in the assemblies (Phil 4:2-3; Rom 16:1-3, 6-7, 12-13). Our purpose here is not to resolve these interpretive issues but to sample some of the ways Paul's legacy was remembered and reshaped in later generations.

202. The *Acts of Paul and Thekla*

Paul's ascetic teaching and practice were matters of controversy and dispute in early Christianity. The "profane myths and old wives' tales" against which 1 Timothy warned (4:7) might have been the popular stories about Thekla, a woman of Iconium who became the apostle's convert and colleague, that have come down to us in various manuscripts and versions of the *Acts of Paul*.[32] As noted above, the *Acts of Paul* is a collection of materials, some of which may have circulated independently before being gathered together. The account of Paul and Thekla that appears as the third chapter in the *Acts of Paul* may itself have come from two independent sources and was widely disseminated before inclusion in the *Acts*.[33]

The opening of this part of the *Acts of Paul* gives us the earliest physical description of the apostle. A believer named Onesiphorus waits with his wife and children for the apostle to enter Iconium; they rely on the description that Titus has given them.[34]

> [Onesiphorus] saw among those approaching someone who looked like the profile Titus had given him. He saw Paul coming, a short man, bald headed, bowlegged, healthy, eyebrows together, with nose a little long, full of grace—for at times he looked like a man, while at other times he had an angel's face.

(Paul's traveling companions, Demas and Hermoghenes, are untrustworthy. Onesiphorus nonetheless invites them all into his house and offers them food. Paul begins to preach "regarding self-control and the resurrection.")

"Blessed are the pure in heart, for they shall see God. Blessed are those who keep the physical body pure, for they shall become the temple of God. Blessed are those with self-control, for God shall speak to them. Blessed are those who turned away from this world, for they shall find favor with God. Blessed are those who live with their wives as though they do not have wives, for they shall inherit God. Blessed are those who have the fear of God, for they shall become God's angels. . . .

"Blessed are those who for the love of God have left the form of the world, for they shall judge angels and be blessed at the right hand of the Father. Blessed are the merciful, for they shall be shown mercy and shall not experience the bitter day of judgment. Blessed are the virgins' bodies, for they shall find favor with God and they shall not lose the reward of their purity, for the Father's word will become the work of salvation for them on the day of his Son, and they shall have rest for ever."

And while Paul was saying these things in the middle of the church that met in Onesiphorus's house, a virgin named Thekla, whose mother was named Theokleia, and who was engaged to a man named Thamyris, was sitting by a nearby window of the house, hearing night and day talk about purity being spoken by Paul. And she did not budge from the window, but instead grew strong in faith, rejoicing. And when she saw many women and virgins

Fig. 6.5. *Thekla in her tower listens to Paul's teaching. Ivory relief, eleventh century. British Museum, London. Photo: Erich Lessing/Art Resource, New York.*

approaching Paul, she longed to stand herself in Paul's presence and hear the word of Christ. For as yet she had not seen Paul's form, but had only heard his word.

When she did not move from the window, her mother sent for Thamyris. He came joyfully, as if he were already taking Thekla as his wife. So Thamyris said to Theokleia, "Where is my Thekla?" And Theokleia replied, "I have news to tell you about, Thamyris. For three days and three nights, Thekla has not got up from the window, neither to eat nor to drink, but remains cheerfully attentive, with the result that she is devoted to a strange man who teaches a variety of deceitful matters, so that I wonder how such self-respect as the virgin had is now disturbed so heavy-handedly.

"Thamyris, this man shakes up the city, even including your Thekla! For all the women and all the young men approach him, being taught by him that 'It is necessary,' as he says, 'to fear God alone and live purely.' Now even my daughter is bound by his words, as a spider on the window, held by this new desire and strange passion. For the virgin pays attention to his words, and is captured. But you go and speak to her, for she is engaged to you."

When Thamyris approached—simultaneously loving her and fearing for her disturbed state of mind—he exclaimed, "Thekla, you are betrothed to me, why do you sit here like this? What sort of passion keeps you disturbed? Shame on you—turn to your Thamyris!"

Then her mother said the same things: "Child why do you sit looking down, paralyzed and answering nothing?" And they were crying loudly, Thamyris losing his wife, Theokleia her child, and the servant girls their mistress; so there was a great outcry of mourning in the house. And while things were going on like this, Thekla did not move, but continued paying attention to Paul's word.

(Thekla hears and embraces Paul's "word of virgin life." By renouncing her engagement to Thamyris she provokes his anger. He recruits Paul's companions Demas and Hermagoras to betray the apostle; they secretly oppose Paul's teaching of virginity and hold to a docetic understanding of the resurrection like that opposed in 3 Corinthians, above. Thamyris hauls Paul before the magistrate, who has him jailed. Thekla visits Paul by night but they are discovered and, though innocent, suspected of adultery. They are arraigned together before the governor.)

After consultation, [the governor] called Thekla, saying, "Why do you not marry Thamyris according to the law of the Iconians?" But she stood looking intently at Paul. When she didn't answer, her mother Theokleia cried out saying, "Burn the lawless one, burn her who would not be a bride in the middle of the theater, so that all the women taught by this one may fear."[35]

And the governor was deeply disturbed, and after beating Paul, expelled him from the city, while he sentenced Thekla to be burned. And immediately the governor got up and went to the theater. And the whole crowd as if from necessity went to the fateful event. But as a lamb in the desert looks for her shepherd, so Thekla sought Paul. And after scanning the crowd she saw the Lord—in Paul's form—sitting there, and she said, "Since I cannot bear this on my own, Paul came back to watch me." And she clung to him with her gaze until he went up to the heavens.

Then the young men and virgins brought wood and straw in order to burn Thekla. When she was led in naked, the governor wept and wondered at her inner strength. They arranged the wood and the executioners ordered her to climb up on the pyre. And after making the sign of the cross, she ascended on the wood, and they ignited it. But though a large fire burned, the fire did not touch her; for God had compassion and caused a sound deep underground, and a cloud above, filled with water and hail, overshadowed them, and the whole pitcher, as it were, was poured out so that many were even in danger of drowning; so the fire was put out, saving Thekla.

(Meanwhile Paul hides, with Onesiphorus and his wife and children, in an open grave along the road out of Iconium. Paul gives one of the children his cloak, with which to buy bread; the child meets Thekla in the marketplace and leads her back to Paul. Their reunion is an emotional scene common to Hellenistic novels.)

And there was much love inside the tomb, with Paul rejoicing along with Onesiphorus and everyone else. They had five loaves and vegetables and water and salt, and they were ecstatic about the holy deeds of Christ. And Thekla said to Paul, "I will cut my hair and follow you wherever you go." But he said, "The time is not right; you are beautiful. Do not let another temptation worse than the first seize you, so that you cannot withstand it but weaken and yield." And Thekla said, "Only give me the seal in Christ and no temptation will touch me." And Paul said, "Be patient and you will receive the water."[36]

(The story shifts to Antioch, where variations on the preceding events take place. Again, Thekla's resistance to marriage becomes a civic issue; now, however, she has some of the women of the city—and female animals as well!—on her side.)

Paul sent Onesiphorus and all his household back to Iconium, so that he could take Thekla and enter Antioch. As soon as they entered, a ruler of Syria named Alexander seized Thekla after seeing her, and began trying to bribe Paul with cash and presents. But Paul said, "I do not know who the woman is whom you are describing, nor is she mine." But (Alexander), being very strong, grasped (Thekla) on the street. She did not yield, but looked about for Paul, and cried out bitterly, "Do not violate a foreign woman, do not violate the Lord's slave-girl! I am first an Iconian, and I have been thrown out of the city because I did not want to marry Thamyris." And grabbing Alexander, she tore his robe and pulled the wreath from his head; thus she made him a spectacle.

While simultaneously desiring her and feeling ashamed at what had happened to him, he led her before the governor, who sentenced her to the wild animals after she confessed that she had done these things. But the women there were outraged and began crying at the bench, "Evil verdict! Foul verdict!" But Thekla asked the governor that she might remain pure until the time she fought with the wild animals. And a certain wealthy noblewoman named Tryphaina, whose daughter had died, took her into her safekeeping and had her for a comfort.

Now when they made the grand entrance with the wild animals, they bound her to a fierce lioness, and the noblewoman Tryphaina followed her.

But when Thekla was placed on top of her in order to provoke her, the lioness merely licked her feet, and the crowd was astonished. The official charge on her placard was "Sacrilege." But the women with their children were crying out above her, "O God, a foul verdict has come in this city!"

(On the next day, as Thekla prepares to face wild animals, the rest of the city's women are divided for and against her.)

Then there was a great roar and the din of wild animals and the cry of the people and the women who were sitting together, crying out, "Bring in the sacrilegious one!" But others were saying, "Let the city and its lawlessness be destroyed! Arrest all of us, proconsul! A bitter spectacle! An evil verdict!"

But Thekla, after being taken from Tryphaina's hand, was disrobed, then she received a belt and was thrown into the stadium. And lions and bears were thrown onto her. And a fierce lioness came running toward her but curled up at her feet, while the crowd of women cried loudly. And a bear began rushing toward her, but the lioness ran, intercepted the bear and tore into it. And again, a lion who belonged to Alexander himself and had been trained to go against people, rushed her; but the lioness fought with the lion and died along with him. The women mourned more loudly, since her helper the lioness died.

Fig. 6.6. Gladiators with spears fight a tiger in the arena. Mosaic from Constantinople, fifth century. Great Palace Museum, Istanbul. Photo in the public domain.

(Having withstood repeated lethal assaults in the amphitheater, Thekla has proven her resolve; she is ready to be baptized.)

> Then they threw in many wild animals, while she stood, praying with folded hands. When she finished her prayer, she turned and saw a large pool filled with water and said, "Now is the time for me to be washed." And she pulled herself toward it, saying "In the name of Jesus Christ, I will be baptized on the last day!" And the women watching her and all the crowd cried out, saying, "Don't throw yourself into the water!" with the result that even the governor wept, because such a beautiful woman was about to be devoured by seals. But she threw herself into the water in the name of Jesus Christ. But there came a bolt of lightning and the seals floated up to the surface, dead. And there was a great cloud of fire around her so that the wild animals could not touch her, nor could her nakedness be seen.
>
> Now when some other, more fearsome wild animals were thrown in, the women began screaming, and some of them were throwing branches, some nard, some cassia, some balsam, so that the water was filled with perfume. And because all these were thrown down, the wild animals—now subdued in slumber—did not touch her. So then Alexander said to the governor, "I have more frightening bulls, let us tie the beast-fighter to them!" But after grimacing, the governor turned, saying "Do what you want." And they tied her by her feet to the middle of the bulls, and placed hot branding irons under their stomachs to rile up the animals so that they would kill her. So then they lurched—but the fire burning around her consumed the ropes, and she became unbound.

(To this point the ordeal has been a series of sadistic attacks on Thekla, all thwarted miraculously. What happens next is more mundane—but raises the terrible prospect that the emperor will have reason to seek reprisal against the city. The noblewoman Tryphaina is a relative of the emperor; when she faints, her servant-girls begin to cry out that she has died. Alarmed that the emperor might bring reprisal against the city for the excesses that appear to have cost Tryphaina her life, the governor ends Thekla's ordeal. She proclaims the power of God and the governor releases her to the unanimous acclaim of the city's women—who now include Tryphaina, revived.)

> And after Tryphaina was informed of the good news, she joined with the crowd. She embraced Thekla and said, "Now I believe that the dead are raised. Now I believe that my child lives. Come inside and I will deed over all I have to you." So then Thekla entered with her and rested in her house for eight days, teaching her the word of God, so that she and most of her handmaids believed, and their joy was great in that house.
>
> But Thekla longed for Paul and continued to seek him, sending inquiries regarding him everywhere. At last she was informed that he was in Myra. And after taking young men and a handmaid, making preparations, and sewing her scarf in the style of a man's cloak, she went to Myra, found Paul speaking the word of God, and approached him. But when he saw her and the crowd with her, he was alarmed, thinking, "Has some other temptation beset her?" But realizing his concern, she said to him, "I have received the bath, Paul, for the

one who works alongside you in the gospel, worked also with me so that I was washed."

And Paul, taking her hand, led her into the house of Hermes and heard everything from her, so that he was greatly amazed, and the ones who heard were strengthened and they prayed on Tryphaina's behalf. Then Thekla got up and said to Paul, "I am returning to Iconium," And Paul said, "Go and teach the word of God." And since Tryphaina had sent many pieces of clothing and gold with Thekla, she left these with Paul for the ministry to the poor.[37]

(Returning to Iconium, Thekla discovers that her erstwhile fiancé Thamyris has died. She wins her mother to the faith so that they are reconciled at last.)

And after bearing witness regarding these things, she went to Seleucia, enlightened many with God's word, then fell asleep with a good sleep.

(*Acts of Paul* 3, trans. Reasoner)

We should not exaggerate Thekla's independence; after all, throughout the narrative, even when absent, "Paul is the master, the shepherd, Thecla the lamb and pupil."[38] She is nevertheless the central figure in this part of the *Acts of Paul*, and the narrative of her message and example are meant to be revolutionary. As Richard I. Pervo observes, her story represents "a nearly diametrically opposite view to those of the Pastoral Epistles on such matters as authority, church and society, and ethics. . . . Rejection of marriage sets the mission against the fundamental institution of Greco-Roman society—the household. Although married couples can be found . . . there is no suggestion that they procreate, and Paul, like the heroes of other Acts, certainly disrupts marriage" and thus threatens the social order.[39]

203. Rejection of the *Acts of Thekla* (Tertullian)

As we noted above, the Pastoral Letters oppose those who teach the renunciation of marriage. Whether or not the author of 1 Timothy had in mind the sorts of traditions about women's independence from marriage that were represented in the *Acts of Paul*, Tertullian of Carthage (c. 160–220 C.E.) certainly did. He sought to discredit the *Acts* as a recent composition written "under Paul's name," although the *Acts of Paul* clearly does not purport to have been written *by* Paul himself. Clearly Tertullian's heated opposition to the text arose from its being read as favoring women's active leadership in the church. Note, however, that Tertullian did not accuse the author of fabricating a narrative to serve that agenda. Note too that he relies on 1 Timothy—a letter that (as we have seen) might have been written precisely to counteract more egalitarian tendencies in some Pauline assemblies—and on 1 Cor 14:34-35, a text suspected by some contemporary scholars of being an interpolation.[40]

But if certain Acts of Paul, which are falsely so named, claim the example of Thecla for allowing women to teach and to baptize, let men know that in Asia the presbyter who compiled that document, thinking to add of his own to Paul's reputation, was found out, and though he professed he had done it for love of Paul, was deposed from his position. How could we believe that Paul should

Fig. 6.7. *Ayathekla, a pilgrimage site in southern Turkey. Photo: Klaus-Peter Simon.*

give a female power to teach and to baptize, when he did not allow a woman even to learn by her own right? "Let them keep silence, he says, and ask their husbands at home" [1 Cor 14:34-35].

(Tertullian, *On Baptism* 17, trans. Evans)

204. Against the emancipation of slaves (Ignatius)

Just as Tertullian and Irenaeus relied on the letters of Paul to reject the elevation of women to leadership roles in the church, so some early Christian writers rejected the practice (or advocacy) of emancipating slaves. The admonition in 1 Tim 6:1-2 may already have been motivated by that practice in some assemblies, possibly in memory of Paul. The apostle's own attitude toward slavery remains a matter of controversy among scholars. The rhetorical ambiguity of Philemon is notorious, and Paul's terse comments in 1 Cor 7:17-24 are no clearer. (Note the alternative translations of 7:21 offered in the text and footnote of the RSV and NRSV.)[41] We know, however, from a number of early Christian writers that some Christians *did* advocate the emancipation of slaves. The practice was encouraged by Hermas in *The Shepherd* (*Mand.* 8.10, *Sim.* 12.8; compare *1 Clem.* 55.2), but it dismayed Ignatius, whose letters to various churches are steeped in Pauline exhortation.

> Let not the widows be neglected. Be yourself their protector after the Lord. Let nothing be done without your approval, and do nothing yourself without God, as indeed you do nothing; stand fast. Let the meetings be more numerous. Seek all by their name. Do not be haughty to slaves, either men or women; yet

do not let them be puffed up, but let them rather endure slavery to the glory of God, that they may obtain a better freedom from God. Let them not desire to be set free at the church's expense, that they be not found the slaves of desire [*epithymia*].

(Ignatius, *To Polycarp* 4, trans. Lake, modified)

205. Against "emancipatory" readings of Paul (John Chrysostom)

In the course of his exegesis of Philemon, John Chrysostom (347–407 c.e.) sought to counteract accusations from outside the church that Christians advocated the emancipation of slaves. He relies on 1 Timothy—not the last time that the probably pseudonymous Pastoral Letters would determine the interpretation of that letter or of Paul's view of slavery more generally. Chrysostom's protests may be read as evidence that *some* Christians *were* advocating the release of slaves as a matter of Christian confession.

> But what is more important than all, that the word of God be not blasphemed, as [Paul] himself says in one of his Epistles. "Let as many servants as are under the yoke count their own masters worthy of all honor, that the name of God and his doctrine be not blasphemed" [1 Tim 6:1]. For the Gentiles also will say that even one who is a slave can be well pleasing to God. But now many are reduced to the necessity of blasphemy, and of saying Christianity has been introduced into life for the subversion of everything, masters having their servants taken from them, and it is a matter of violence.
>
> (Chrysostom, *Homily on Philemon*, Argument, trans. Schaff)

206. Paul's moral example (Augustine)

One of the most celebrated readers of Paul's letters was Augustine. We have already seen (no. 200 above) that Augustine found in Paul an intellectual satisfaction he had not encountered among the writings of Neoplatonists. But Augustine's account of the dramatic turning point in his own life (subsequently termed his "conversion") centers not on one or another theological idea but on the firm resolve expressed in Paul's exhortation in Romans 13 and 14.

By Augusine's day, the sexual continence of which Paul spoke had been regularized within Christianity in clerical and monastic life. Augustine himself had been anguished as he and his friends wrestled with career decisions: to pursue philosophy or ecclesiastical office would mean dramatic renunciations of future marriages and of the leisured life they had enjoyed. Confronted by a visitor's account of the spiritual austerities of Saint Anthony, Augustine accused himself of a failure of will.[42]

> Thus I was sick and tormented, reproaching myself more bitterly than ever, rolling and writhing in my chain till it should be utterly broken. By now I was held but slightly, but still was held. And you, O Lord, pressed upon me in my inmost heart with a severe mercy, redoubling the lashes of fear and shame; lest I should again give way and that same slender remaining tie not be broken off, but recover strength and enchain me yet more securely.

I kept saying to myself, "See, let it be done now; let it be done now." And as I said this I all but came to a firm decision. I all but did it—yet I did not quite. Still I did not fall back to my old condition, but stood aside for a moment and drew breath. And I tried again, and lacked only a very little of reaching the resolve—and then somewhat less, and then all but touched and grasped it. Yet I still did not quite reach or touch or grasp the goal, because I hesitated to die to death and to live to life.

(Augustine has a vision of a company of chaste young men and women but feels incapable of joining them as an act of his own will.)

This struggle raging in my heart was nothing but the contest of self against self. And Alypius kept close beside me, and awaited in silence the outcome of my extraordinary agitation.

Now when deep reflection had drawn up out of the secret depths of my soul all my misery and had heaped it up before the sight of my heart, there arose a mighty storm, accompanied by a mighty rain of tears. That I might give way fully to my tears and lamentations, I stole away from Alypius. . . . I flung myself down under a fig tree—how I know not—and gave free course to my tears. The streams of my eyes gushed out an acceptable sacrifice to you. And, not indeed in these words, but to this effect, I cried to you: "And you, O Lord, how long? How long, O Lord? Will you be angry forever? Oh, remember not against us our former iniquities." For I felt that I was still enthralled by them. I sent up these sorrowful cries: "How long, how long? Tomorrow and tomorrow? Why not now? Why not this very hour make an end to my uncleanness?"

I was saying these things and weeping in the most bitter contrition of my heart, when suddenly I heard the voice of a boy or a girl—I know not which—coming from the neighboring house, chanting over and over again, "Pick it up, read it; pick it up, read it." Immediately I ceased weeping and began most earnestly to think whether it was usual for children in some kind of game to sing such a song, but I could not remember ever having heard the like. So, damming the torrent of my tears, I got to my feet, for I could not but think that this was a divine command to open the Bible and read the first passage I should light upon. For I had heard how Anthony, accidentally coming into church while the gospel was being read, received the admonition as if what was read had been addressed to him: "Go and sell what you have and give it to the poor, and you shall have treasure in heaven; and come and follow me." By such an oracle he was forthwith converted to you.

So I quickly returned to the bench where Alypius was sitting, for there I had put down the apostle's book when I had left there. I snatched it up, opened it, and in silence read the paragraph on which my eyes first fell: "Not in rioting and drunkenness, not in chambering and wantonness, not in strife and envying, but put on the Lord Jesus Christ, and make no provision for the flesh to fulfill the lusts thereof" [Rom 13:13].

I wanted to read no further, nor did I need to. For instantly, as the sentence ended, there was infused in my heart something like the light of full certainty and all the gloom of doubt vanished away. Closing the book, then, and putting my finger or something else for a mark I began—now with a tranquil

Fig. 6.8. *Augustine takes up the letters of Paul. Fresco by Benozzo Gozzoli, 1464–65, in the Capella Sant'Agostino, San Gimignano. Photo in the public domain.*

countenance—to tell it all to Alypius. And he in turn disclosed to me what had been going on in himself, of which I knew nothing. He asked to see what I had read. I showed him, and he looked on even further than I had read. I had not known what followed. But indeed it was this, "Him that is weak in the faith, receive" [Rom 14:1]. This he applied to himself, and told me so. By these words of warning he was strengthened, and by exercising his good resolution and purpose—all very much in keeping with his character, in which, in these respects, he was always far different from and better than I—he joined me in full commitment without any restless hesitation.

Then we went in to my mother, and told her what happened, to her great joy. We explained to her how it had occurred—and she leaped for joy triumphant; and she blessed you, who are "able to do exceedingly abundantly above all that we ask or think." For she saw that you had granted her far more than she had ever asked for in all her pitiful and doleful lamentations. For you so converted me to you that I sought neither a wife nor any other of this world's hopes, but set my feet on that rule of faith which so many years before you had showed her in her dream about me. And so you turned her grief into gladness more plentiful than she had ventured to desire, and dearer and purer than the desire she used to cherish of having grandchildren of my flesh.

(Augustine, *Confessions* 8.11.25–12.30, trans. Outler, modified)

207. The virtues of the ascetic life (Jerome)

In the year 403, Jerome wrote a letter to a Laeta, a woman in Rome, to instruct her in how to raise her newborn daughter, Paula. Besides some very ascetic demands in the letter, Jerome also asks Laeta to send her daughter to the convent in Bethlehem that her grandmother and aunt were directing. Laeta accepted this request; the girl Paula was sent to the convent and, years later, became its mother superior. Note how Jerome uses the apostle Paul's words in the excerpts quoted here to offer an ascetic model for Paula's life.

Let her learn even now not to drink "wine wherein is excess" [Eph 5:18]. Until they have reached their full strength, however, strict abstinence is dangerous for young children: so till then, if needs must, let her visit the baths, and "take a little wine for the stomach's sake" [1 Tim 5:23] and have the support of a meat diet, lest her feet fail before the race begins. "I say this by way of indulgence and not by way of command" [1 Cor 7:6], fearing weakness, not wantonness. Moreover, what the Jewish superstition does in part, solemnly rejecting certain animals and certain products as food, what the Brahmans in India and the Gymnosophists in Egypt observe on their diet of only porridge, rice, and fruit, why should not Christ's virgin do altogether? If a glass bead is worth so much, surely a pearl must have a higher value. The child of promise must live as those lived before her who were born under the same vow. Let an equal favor bring with it also an equal labor. Paula must be deaf to all musical instruments, and never even know why the flute, the lyre, and the harp came into existence.[43]

. . . Let her not converse with worldlings, nor associate with virgins who neglect their vows. Let her not be present at slaves' weddings, nor take part in noisy household games. I know that some people have laid down the rule that a Christian virgin should not bathe along with eunuchs or with married women, inasmuch as eunuchs are men at heart, and women big with child are a revolting sight. For myself I disapprove altogether of baths in the case of a full-grown virgin. She ought to blush at herself and be unable to look at her own nakedness. If she mortifies and enslaves her body by vigils and fasting, if she desires to quench the flame of lust and to check the hot desires of youth by a cold chastity, if she hastens to spoil her natural beauty by a deliberate squalor, why should she rouse a sleeping fire by the incentive of baths?

You will answer: "How shall I, a woman of the world living in crowded Rome, be able to keep all these injunctions?" Do not then take up a burden which you cannot bear. When you have weaned Paula as Isaac was weaned, and when you have clothed her as Samuel was clothed, send her to her grandmother and her aunt. Set this most precious jewel in Mary's chamber, and place her on the cradle where Jesus cried. Let her be reared in a monastery amid bands of virgins, where she will learn never to take an oath, and to regard a lie as sacrilege. Let her know nothing of the world, but live like the angels; let her be in the flesh and without the flesh, thinking all mankind to be like herself. . . .

O happy virgin! O happy Paula, daughter of Toxotius! By the virtues of her grandmother and her aunt she is nobler in sanctity even than in lineage. Oh, if you could only see your mother-in-law and your sister, and know the mighty souls that dwell within their feeble bodies! Then I doubt not that you would obey your innate love of chastity and come to them even before your daughter, exchanging God's first decree for the Gospel's second dispensation. You would surely count as nothing your desire for other children and would rather offer yourself to God. But inasmuch as "there is a time to embrace and a time to refrain from embracing" [Eccl 3:5] and "the wife hath not power over her own body" [1 Cor 7:4] and "every man should abide in the same calling wherein he was called" [1 Cor 7:20] in the Lord, and because he who is under the yoke ought so to run as not to leave his companion in the mire, pay back in your children all that you defer paying in your own person.

(Jerome, Letter 107.8, 11, 13 to Laeta, NPNF)

Paul the Compelling Preacher and Wonder-Worker

The Acts of the Apostles leaves the reader at the end with the picture of Paul preaching unhindered in Rome. This portrait is perhaps the most enduring aspect of Paul's legacy. He is remembered as having freely proclaimed God's word around the northern arc of the Mediterranean (see Rom 15:18-20, 22-24).

Was Paul a good preacher? In his letters he declared that he was not—perhaps using irony to defend himself against charges on the part of some in Corinth that his style was not up to their standards (see 1 Cor 2:1-5; 2 Cor 10:10; 11:6). In Paul's view these negative descriptions served to highlight his divine calling and empowerment to preach, as was the case for certain prophets in Jewish scripture who delivered powerful messages, though they were not naturally gifted as orators (Exod 4:10-17; 7:1-2; Jer 1:6-10; 1 Cor 2:3-4; 2 Cor 10:10). Paul also wrote that in his apostolic travels he had performed "signs and wonders and mighty works" (Rom 15:18-19; 2 Cor 12:12), though he never narrated any of these—other than to point out to the Corinthians that he spoke in tongues more than any of them, a gift he would gladly give up for the good of the community (1 Cor 14:18-19). Nevertheless, already in the Acts of the Apostles we see Paul portrayed as a powerful speaker, addressing magistrates with eloquence, and as a miracle worker. These motifs become even more prominent in later apocryphal Acts.

208. THE *ACTS OF TITUS*

In one more apocryphal text, the *Acts of Titus* (which may have depended on the *Acts of Paul*), we see both Paul and his disciple Titus portrayed as powerful preachers and miracle workers. As in many second- and third-century apocryphal *Acts*, the chief contest between the apostles and their environment is a contest of power with the idols of pagan gods. In comparison with Paul's own ambivalence concerning idols (is an idol "nothing," 1 Cor 8:4; 10:19-20, or are offerings to idols being made to "demons," 1 Cor 10:20-21?), note that idols are, so to speak, animated, but by inferior beings who must yield to the power of Christ revealed through the apostles. The *Acts* give Titus a lineage from Minos, king of Crete.

> At age twenty, when he was quite devoted to the poems and dramas of Homer and the other philosophers, he heard a voice saying, "Titus, you must depart from here and save your soul, for this learning will be of no benefit to you" [cf. 2 Tim 3:16]. He wanted to hear the same voice once more, for he was familiar with the deceptions issued vocally from statues. After remaining resistant for nine years, he was instructed in a vision to read the book of the Hebrews. Taking up the book of Isaiah, he came upon the following passage: "Dedicate yourselves to me, you many islands. Israel is saved by the Lord with everlasting salvation." . . .[44]
>
> Now when the proconsul of Crete, who was the uncle of the holy Titus, heard of the salutary birth and baptism of Christ the Master and of the marvelous deeds he performed in Jerusalem and elsewhere, he took counsel with the leading people of Crete and then dispatched Titus with some others to Jerusalem so that he would be able to hear the message and speak and teach those things that he was going to see. Titus arrived, saw, and worshipped Christ the Master. He observed all of his marvelous deeds and also witnessed the Master's salutary sufferings, his burial, resurrection, and divine ascension, as well as the arrival of the all-holy Spirit upon the divine apostles. He became a believer.

(The *Acts* go on to number Titus among the 120 disciples of Acts 1:15 and the 3,000 who came to believe in Christ in Acts 2, citing the reference in the Pentecost account to "Cretans and Arabs." The narrative then follows the canonical Acts for a few paragraphs, summarizing at last that Paul and Titus "enlightened the hearts of unbelievers by working signs and wonders just as [these] all are reported in the Acts of the Apostles."[45] Titus returns to the fore after Paul is freed from the prison in Philippi.)

> At that time Rustillus, who was married to Titus's sister,[46] had completed a second period in the governorship of Crete. Paul and Titus arrived there. When the ruler saw the divinely inspired Titus weighed down with tears, he attempted to compel him to live with him, but the holy Titus did not obey him. Rustillus advised him not to speak against the pagan gods.[47] But the holy Titus expounded the gospel of Christ to him, claiming "If you believe my message, you will be exalted on earth and in the city of Rome." Shortly thereafter his son died. He brought him to Paul at night. Following prayer, Paul raised him.[48] After they had spent three months[49] there, Rustillus sent them on with ample rewards. He went to Rome and was designated consul. Thereafter, because

Rustillus was a relative of Titus, those of the circumcision only engaged in verbal combat, not daring to do anything else to the proclaimers of God's word.

Leaving Crete, they went to Asia. In the course of Paul's teaching at Ephesus, twelve thousand persons came to believe. There the apostle also fought with beasts, being cast to a lion.[50] Titus, Timothy, and Erastus delivered the second epistle to the Corinthians.[51]

Titus, Timothy, and Luke remained with the apostle until his consummation under Nero [*Acts of Paul* 11]. They thereupon returned to Greece and got Luke established there.[52] Titus and Timothy then moved on to Colossae.[53] Timothy subsequently returned to Ephesus while Titus proceeded to Crete.[54]

The Cretans greeted his arrival joyfully, like that of a relative, and decreed a holiday. They adorned the temples of their idols, took in hand the sacred swords, and, clad in their purple-trimmed ephebic tunics they went before him. St Titus addressed them graciously and urged them to be responsive to what he said. He began by singing, in Hebrew,[55] "May God be merciful to us and bless us." . . .[56] They responded that they did not know what he was saying. Only the Hebrews present understood. Presently, as they drew near to the idol of Artemis, it cast itself down, breaking forth with a cry: "You are acting insolently in ignorance!"[57] The holy Titus said to them, "Since you are publicly carrying swords, condemnation therefore falls upon you." They thereupon threw down the swords and remained without food until early morning, reciting the psalm in expectation that they would hear something from the idol. Then, after numerous marvels, they began to exclaim: "There is one god, the one manifested to us this day!"[58] Five hundred came to believe in Christ.

The diet of the apostle consisted of garden vegetables. He dined in goat's hair and sheepskin.[59]

Titus ordained bishops in Cnossus, Hierapytna, Cydonia, Chersonesus, Eleutherna, Lappa, Cisamus, and Cantanus, so that there would be nine bishops with Gortyna as Metropolitan See. He taught them for four years.

Now at that time the Roman emperor Vespasian fell upon Jerusalem and took the Jews there and in every place captive.[60] Yet because of blessed Titus's relatives there was no persecution of the Jews in Crete.

Now a certain Secundus,[61] who had received funds from the emperor Trajan to rebuild a temple of idols, did indeed begin the project. The holy Titus happened by, glimpsed the enormous undertaking, uttered a deep groan, and moved on. The next morning it transpired that the entire foundation had collapsed and that the building-blocks were scattered about.[62] Just as Secundus was on the verge of doing away with himself [cf. Acts 16:27], someone advised him to hasten to Titus. Once there, he knelt down and besought Titus to protect him from liability. The saint replied, "If you should come to believe in my Christ, the building will be erected." In response Secundus asked indulgence for himself and promised to give him a child he loved. The saint said, "Get to work on your task and, as you work, repeat together with the laborers, 'There is but one god, the god in heaven!'" Thereafter this cry was repeated in the course of the work. When the temple was completed, the holy Titus said to the people, "Know well, brothers and sisters, that that place will become a proving-ground for holy relics."

Fig. 6.9. *Marble statue of the goddess Minerva (the Greek Artemis); first century c.e., restored. Museo Palazzo Massimo, Rome. Photo: Neil Elliott.*

When Euphemia, the virgin sister of blessed Titus died, he laid her remains in a place that he had built. There he would often offer hymns and praise to God.

Subsequently, he wrote letters to Dionysius the Areopagite and to others.

Then, after he had wrought many marvelous deeds, he saw the holy angels sent to take him. Fragrant smoke and a cloud glowing more brightly than the sun filled the house. Titus, with transfigured face, let forth a great glad laugh. Raising his hands toward heaven, he cried out, "Lord, I have kept your faith true and have preserved the people intact. Into your hands I commend my spirit.[63] Of your own self strengthen your people." After adding the "amen" he gave up his spirit joyfully and lives for ever.

They then anointed his remains with oils and aromatic spices, clothed them in a white garment, and carried them off for burial. At that moment the temples of the idols collapsed, but the people within them came out unharmed and saw the remains of the saint.

His precious tomb is in fact an altar, at which are the chains used to bind those afflicted by unclean spirits.[64] In this place all who are deemed worthy to embrace the resting place of the saint experience healing.[65]

Now the holy apostle and hierarch of Christ was twenty years of age when he came to Jerusalem.[66] One year passed until the ascension of the Lord. He spent ten years before being ordained apostle and archbishop by the chief disciples of the Lord. Titus contended for eighteen years in the proclamation of the gospel[67] and spent six years in Crete and the other islands. For thirty-nine years he dwelt in his native city, so that the total years of his earthly life were ninety four.

May we all receive mercy from his intercessions, we who give thanks to and believe in our Lord Jesus Christ, to whom belong all glory, honor, and reverence, with the Father and the Holy Spirit, now and always, to the end of the ages. Amen.

(*Acts of Titus*, trans. Pervo)[68]

Paul the Opponent of the True Faith

The author of 2 Peter already warned that in Paul's letters there were "some things in them hard to understand, which the ignorant and unstable twist to their own destruction" (2 Pet 3:15-16). We know from Paul's letters that he was repeatedly in conflict with others in the nascent Christian movement—Peter himself and James not least among them (see Gal 2:11-14). Although the Acts of the Apostles made Paul into a champion of the early Christian mission among non-Jews, Paul remained a controversial figure in some circles for generations. We know from Irenaeus, for example, that he was opposed by a Jewish-Christian group called the Ebionites.

209. The Ebionite repudiation of Paul (Irenaeus)

Those who are called Ebionites agree that the world was made by God; but their opinions in regard to the Lord are similar to those of Cerinthus and Carpocrates. They use the Gospel according to Matthew only, and repudiate the apostle Paul, maintaining that he was an apostate from the law. As to the prophetical writings, they endeavor to expound them in a somewhat singular manner; they practice circumcision, persevere in the observance of those customs which are enjoyed by the law, and in their Judaic style of life, they even adore Jerusalem as if it were the house of God.

(Irenaeus, *Against Heresies* 1.26.2, trans. Roberts and Rambaut, modified)

210. An unnamed "enemy" of the church (Clementine *Recognitions*)

The so-called Clementine literature consists of components of a third-century Christian novel. The novel's protagonist, Clement, grew into manhood alone after his mother took his older brothers and left, under the false shadow of a scandal, and his father left home to find her. Mother and brothers were separated in a shipwreck. By different paths Clement and his brothers become followers of the apostle Peter and, through a series of miraculous events, are restored to their father and mother, the power of the reunion convincing the father to accept Christianity. At length Clement is made Peter's successor as bishop of Rome.[69]

The anti-Pauline components of the novel include the *Homilies*, a collection of Peter's sermons; the *Epistle of Peter to James*; and the *Recognitions*, which narrates the novel's denouement, in which family members long lost to one another are reunited. The historical value of this literature is that it preserves an assessment of Paul very different from that of champion of an eventually triumphant Gentile Christianity[70]—though it hardly gives us a reliable picture of the character of second-century Roman Christianity.

The excerpt below from the *Recognitions* probably derived ultimately from a Jewish Christian, perhaps living in Judea or Jerusalem.[71] The narrator associates himself with James of Jerusalem and describes the assaults of an unnamed "enemy" of the church; his description matches the Paul of Acts 8–9—except that this "enemy" is never rehabilitated. The *Recognitions* in effect blames Paul for the ultimate failure of James to convert his fellow Jews.[72] We pick up the story just after James has persuaded a number of Jews to be baptized and join him in following Jesus (1.66-69).

> Then a certain man who was the enemy entered the temple near the altar with a few others. He cried out and said, "What are you doing, O men, the children of Israel? How have you been carried off so quickly by wretched men who have strayed after a magician?" He said things such as these, and he listened to counterarguments, and, when he was overcome by James the bishop, he began to create a great commotion so that the matters that were rightly being said in calmness would neither be put to the test nor be understood and believed. For this purpose, he let forth an outcry over the foolishness and feebleness of the priests and reproached them. He said, "Why are you delaying? Why are you not immediately seizing all those who are with him?"
>
> When he had said these things, he rose first, seized a firebrand from the altar, and began to smite with it. Then, also the rest of the priests, when they saw him, followed his example. Then, in the great flight that ensued, some fell upon others and others were smitten. There were not a few who died so that much blood poured forth from those who had been killed. Now the enemy threw James from the top of the stairs. Since he fell and was as if dead, he did not smite him a second time.
>
> But when they saw that this had happened to James, they approached and seized him. Now they were more numerous than the others, but out of fear of God, they endured to be killed rather than to kill. While they were much stronger than the others, they seemed to be less, owing to the fear of God.
>
> When evening arrived, the priests closed the temple, and came to James's house and prayed there. Before dawn, we went down to Jericho. We numbered about five thousand men.
>
> After three days, one of the brothers came and told us what had happened since the time that we were in the temple. For the priests were asking him [James] to be with them as a priest in all their reckonings. They did not know that he was a member of our faith. Then, he told us how the enemy, before the priests, promised Caiaphas the high priest that he would massacre all those who believe in Jesus. He departed for Damascus to go as one carrying letters from them so that when he went there, the nonbelievers might help him and might

destroy those who believe. He wanted to go there first because he thought that Peter had gone there.

Now after thirty days he came upon us there in Jericho. We buried two brothers in that place at night. Each year their graves are suddenly white. They quenched the fury of many because they knew that they are members of our faith and that they were worthy of divine remembrance.

(Recognitions, 1.70-71, trans. Jones)

211. THE (CLEMENTINE) *LETTER OF PETER TO JAMES*

This document served as the "cover letter" for the *Homilies* or "preachings" (*Kērygmata*) of Peter. Clearly pseudepigraphic, it expresses the wishful thinking of a later generation of Jewish Christianity. For its author, the representation of Paul as in agreement with the Jerusalem apostles—as in the Acts of the Apostles, for example—was false. The false teaching of "an enemy" of Peter—presumably Paul—and the false representation of that teaching as congruent with Peter's own—are responsible for the terrible multiplication of "opinions" in Christianity. If only James had been able to find worthy candidates for ordination, the letter suggests, these "secret" writings would have had a wider dissemination; the terrible blight of Pauline Christianity might have been stopped at its inception; and worldwide Christianity would have remained united under the episcopal authority of the bishop of Jerusalem.

Fig. 6.10. *This first-century ossuary (a box for retaining the bones of the dead) bears the inscription "Ya'akov [James], son of Yosef, brother of Yeshua [Jesus]." It was on display at the Royal Ontario Museum from November 15, 2002, to January 5, 2003. The authenticity of the inscription has been disputed by the Israel Antiquities Authority but defended by the* Biblical Archaeological Review *and others.*

Peter to James, the lord and bishop of the holy church: Peace be with you always from the father of all through Jesus Christ.

Knowing well that you, my brother, eagerly take pains about what is for the mutual benefit of us all, I earnestly beseech you not to pass on to anyone of the Gentiles the books of my preachings which I (here) forward to you, nor to any one of our own tribe before probation. But if some one of them has been examined and found to be worthy, then you may hand them over to him in the same way as Moses handed over his office of a teacher to the seventy. Wherefore also the fruit of his caution is to be seen up to this day. For those who belong to his people preserve everywhere the same rule in their belief in the one God and in their line of conduct, the Scriptures with their many senses being unable to incline them to assume another attitude. Rather they attempt, on the basis of the rule that has been handed down to them, to harmonize the contradictions of the Scriptures, if haply some one who does not know the traditions is perplexed by the ambiguous utterances of the prophets. On this account they permit no one to teach unless he first learn how the Scriptures should be used. Wherefore there obtain amongst them one God, one law, and one hope.

In order now that the same may also take place among us, hand over the books of my preachings in the same mysterious way to our seventy brothers that they may prepare those who are candidates for positions as teachers. For if we do not proceed in this way, our word of truth will be split into many opinions. This I do not know as a prophet, but I have already the beginning of the evil before me. For some from among the Gentiles have rejected my lawful preaching and have preferred a lawless and absurd doctrine of the man who is my enemy. And indeed some have attempted, while I am still alive, to distort my words by interpretations of many sorts, as if I taught the dissolution of the law and, although I was of this opinion, did not express it openly. But that may God forbid!

For to do such a thing means to act contrary to the law of God which was made known by Moses and was confirmed by our Lord in its everlasting continuance. For he said: "The heaven and the earth will pass away, but one jot or one tittle shall not pass away from the law." This he said "that everything might come to pass." But those persons who, I know not how, allege that they are at home in my thoughts wish to expound the words which they have heard of me better than I myself who spoke them. To those whom they instruct they say that this is my opinion, to which indeed I never gave a thought. But if they falsely assert such a thing while I am still alive, how much more after my death will those who come later venture to do so?

(*Letter of Peter to James*, trans. R. McL. Wilson)

212. The fraudulent nature of visions (Clementine *Homilies*)

The Clementine *Homilies* promote a Jewish version of belief in Jesus that is remarkably un-Pauline (though, as Richard Pervo observes, Clementine Christianity was far more hostile to the Jerusalem temple than anything in Paul or the Acts of the Apostles).[73] Although Paul is never mentioned by name (perhaps because the Clementine literature represented a clearly minority position in a sea of Christianity that embraced Paul as its champion), it frequently attacks Peter's archnemesis, Simon the

Magician, in terms reminiscent of Paul. Toward the end of the seventeenth *Homily*, Peter attacks Simon for basing his authority on visions ("apparitions") instead of personal acquaintance with Jesus. Note phrases reminiscent of Paul's description of his own confrontation with Peter in Galatians 2.

If, then, our Jesus appeared to you in a vision, made himself known to you, and spoke to you, it was as one who is enraged with an adversary; and this is the reason why it was through visions and dreams, or through revelations that were from without, that he spoke to you. But can any one be rendered fit for instruction through apparitions? And if you will say "It is possible," then I ask, "Why did our teacher abide and discourse a whole year to those who were awake?" And how are we to believe your word, when you tell us that he appeared to you? And how did he appear to you, when you entertain opinions contrary to his teaching? But if you were seen and taught by him, and became his apostle for a single hour: proclaim his utterances, interpret his sayings, love his apostles, and do not contend with me who kept company with him.

For you now stand in direct opposition to me, who am a firm rock, the foundation of the Church. If you were not opposed to me, you would not accuse me, and revile the truth proclaimed by me, in order that I may not be believed when I state what I myself have heard with my own ears from the Lord, as if I were evidently a person that was condemned and in bad repute. But if you say that I am condemned, you bring an accusation against God, who revealed Christ to me, and you inveigh against him who pronounced me blessed on account of the revelation. But if, indeed, you really wish to work in the cause of truth, learn first of all from us what we have learned from him, and, becoming a disciple of the truth, become a fellow-worker with us.

(*Homilies* 17.19, trans. Donaldson)

We have used the phrases "Jewish Christian" and "**Jewish Christianity**" to describe the Ebionites, the Clementine literature, and the *Ascents of James* (see no. 213 below) but recognize that both are very problematic categories. Scholars argue over whether Paul should be described as a "Christian" and over the extent to which his declaration of agreement with the Jerusalem apostles (Gal 2:1-10) reflected reality. Was Paul a "Jewish Christian"? Was James? Did groups such as the Ebionites and Nazarenes, described by later Christian authors as following Jesus but (in contrast to other Christian groups) observing Torah, have a genealogical relationship with the Jerusalem congregation led by James? These are lively and important questions deserving more attention than they can receive here. For recent discussions of the various issues involved see Matt Jackson-McCabe, ed., *Jewish Christianity Reconsidered: Rethinking Ancient Groups and Texts* (Minneapolis: Fortress Press, 2007).

213. Paul the lovelorn charlatan (The *Ascents of James*)

Yet another denunciation of Paul as an enemy of the original gospel comes down to us indirectly, through the refutation offered by the fourth-century heresy fighter Epiphanius of Salamis. The text was called the *Ascents of James*, referring to the scene in the *Recognitions* (see above) where James was accosted by an enemy as he climbed the temple steps. The narrative constituted an ad hominem attack on Paul, presumably from a group of Jewish Christians similar to the sources behind the Clementine literature.

> They call other acts "of the apostles." In these there is much that is full of impiety. There they armed themselves against the truth in no minor way. Now they set out certain steps and guides in the *Steps of James* as if he expounds against the Temple and sacrifices and against the fire on the altar and many other things full of babble. Hence, they are not ashamed of denouncing even Paul here through certain contrived falsehoods of their pseudo-apostles' villainy and deceit. They say, on the one hand, that he was a Tarsian, as he himself declares and does not deny. On the other hand, they assert that he was from the Greeks by taking a pretext in the passage spoken by him through love of the truth, "I am a Tarsian, a citizen of no ignoble city" [Acts 21:39]. Then they say that he was a Greek, the child of both a Greek mother and a Greek father; that he went to Jerusalem and remained there a while, that he desired to marry a priest's daughter; that for this reason he became a proselyte and was circumcised; that when he still did not receive such a girl he became angry and wrote against circumcision and against the Sabbath and the law.
>
> (Epiphanius, *The Panarion* 16.6-9, trans. Jones)

Paul the Martyr

As we saw in chapter 1, Nero put a number of Christians to death in 64 in a gruesome punishment for—or perhaps, as a spectacular distraction from—the Great Fire of Rome. Later Christian tradition dated Paul's death to this period and revered it as a martyrdom. That reverence could take different forms for different purposes.

214. Paul's witness before rulers (Clement of Rome)

Writing from Rome to censure dissenters in the church at Corinth, Clement cited Peter and Paul as heroic examples of those who had withstood partisan jealousy, Paul by "bearing witness"—the Greek verb gives us our word *martyr*—before rulers.

> But, to stop giving ancient examples, let us come to those who became athletic contenders in quite recent times. We should consider the noble examples of our own generation. Because of jealousy and envy, the greatest and most upright pillars were persecuted, and they struggled in the contest even to death. We should set before our eyes the good apostles. Because of jealousy and strife Paul pointed the way to the prizes for endurance. Seven times he bore chains; he was sent into exile and stoned; he served as a herald in both the East and the West; and he received the noble reputation for his faith. He taught righteousness

to the whole world, and came to the limits of the west, bearing his witness [*martyrēsas*] before the rulers [*hēgoumenōn*]. And so he was set free from this world and transported up to the holy place, having become the greatest example of endurance.

(1 Clement 5.1-7, trans. Pervo)

215. The "trophies of the apostles" (Eusebius)

The bishop and church historian Eusebius (263–339 c.e.) was concerned to document the monuments of Christian faith. In recording the available traditions regarding the deaths of Peter and Paul (and the persecution under Nero) he cites an otherwise unknown Roman Christian writer named Gaius, who cited the monuments of the martyrs to enhance the prestige and authority of the Roman church against rival Christians, and Dionysios of Corinth, who cited their martyrdoms in the course of strengthening bonds between the Corinthian and Roman churches.

> Thus, then, was Nero the first to be heralded as above all an antagonist of God and stirred up to murder the apostles. It is related that in his day Paul was beheaded at Rome itself, and that Peter likewise was crucified, and this story is accredited by the attachment, which prevails to this day, of the names Peter and Paul in the cemeteries there; and in no less degree also by a churchman, named Gaius, who lived in the time of Zephyrinus, bishop of the Romans.
>
> Gaius, in a written discussion with Proclus, a champion of the heresy of the Phrygians, speaks thus of the places where the sacred tabernacles of the said apostles have been laid: "But I can point out the trophies of the apostles. For if you would go to the Vatican, or to the Ostian Way, you will find the trophies of those who founded this church."
>
> And that they were martyred both on the same occasion, Dionysios, bishop of the Corinthians, writing to the Romans, affirms as follows: "In these ways you also, by such an admonition, have united the planting that came from Peter and Paul of both the Romans and the Corinthians. For indeed both planted also in our Corinth, and likewise taught us; and likewise they taught together also in Italy and were martyred on the same occasion."
>
> (Eusebius, *Church History* 2.25.5-8, trans. Lawler and Oulton)

216. The manner of Paul's and Peter's deaths (Sulpicius Severus)

Sometime after 404 c.e. the Christian historian Sulpicius Severus wrote his *Chronicle* of history from the creation to his own day. He described Nero's persecution as the pattern for all subsequent persecutions of Christians—an argument disputed by scholars today[74]—and connects Paul's and Peter's deaths to that time.

> In the meantime, the number of the Christians being now very large, it happened that Rome was destroyed by fire, while Nero was stationed at Antium. But the opinion of all cast the odium of causing the fire upon the emperor, and he was believed in this way to have sought for the glory of building a new city. And in fact Nero could not, by any means he tried, escape from the charge that the fire had been caused by his orders. He therefore turned the accusation

against the Christians, and the most cruel tortures were accordingly inflicted upon the innocent. Nay, even new kinds of deaths were invented, so that, being covered in the skins of wild beasts, they perished by being devoured by dogs, while many were crucified or slain by fire, and not a few were set apart for this purpose, that, when the day came to a close, they should be consumed to serve for light during the night. In this way, cruelty first began to be manifested against the Christians. Afterwards, too, their religion was prohibited by laws which were enacted; and by edicts openly set forth it was proclaimed unlawful to be a Christian. At that time Paul and Peter were condemned to death, the former being beheaded with a sword, while Peter suffered crucifixion.

(Sulpicius Severus, *Chronicle* 2.29, NPNF)

217. Paul the martyr as sacrifice (Ignatius)

For some early Christians Paul provided an example of martyrdom. Ignatius, journeying under armed guard to Rome in 117 to face execution in the arena, described his path in the metaphorical language of the sacred procession—"among the most important events on the religious calendars of Greco-Roman cities"—a metaphor developed already by Paul (2 Cor 2:14-17).[75] Ignatius wrote to various churches to urge them not to impede his witness; his motive was not (as is sometimes alleged) a sort of spiritual masochism, but to make a clear and unhindered testimony before the authorities.

> Forasmuch as I have gained my prayer to God to see your godly faces, so that I have obtained more than I asked,—for in bondage in Christ Jesus I hope to greet you if it be his will that I be found worthy to the end. For the beginning has been well ordered, if I may obtain grace to come unhindered to my lot. For I am afraid of your love, lest even that do me wrong. For it is easy for you to do what you will, but it is difficult for me to attain to God, if you do not spare me.
>
> For I would not have you "men-pleasers" but "God-pleasers" [see 1 Thess 2:4] even as you do indeed please him. For neither shall I ever have such an opportunity of attaining to God, nor can you, if you be but silent, have any better deed ascribed to you. For if you are silent concerning me, I am a word of God; but if you love my flesh, I shall again be only a cry. Grant me nothing more than that I be poured out to God, while an altar is still ready, that forming yourselves into a chorus of love you may sing to the Father in Christ Jesus, that God has vouchsafed that the bishop of Syria shall be found at the setting of the sun, having fetched him from the sun's rising. It is good to set to the world toward God, that I may rise to know him.
>
> (Ignatius, *To the Romans* 1-2, trans. Lake, LCL)

218. The *Martyrdom of Polycarp*

In the following decades, official persecutions of the churches gave rise to a Christian adaptation of the Jewish genre of martyrological literature (for example, 4 Maccabees). In that literature Paul is not only an example but also a teacher. In the back-and-forth in which accused Christians defiantly refuse the demands of Roman magistrates, a key element of their profession of innocence is the protest that they have always honored the emperor to the extent allowed by their faith. That is, as Luise Schottroff has observed, "the requirement and/or the declaration of loyalty belongs together with persecution." Schottroff goes on to suggest that Rom 13:1-7 was routinely read in the second-century church as instruction for facing martyrdom: quoting H.-M. Schelkle, she declares that it became "'a requisite for the martyr apology.' The forensic situation of the persecuted Christians becomes the hour of trial for the commandment to love one's enemy, for the renunciation of vengeance, and for loyalty to the state."[76] Indeed, Paul himself anticipated such persecution, Schottroff argues; in Rom 13:1-7 "he is describing and recommending behavior that has its home in the typical recurring situation which is fundamentally a part of being Christian."[77]

Early in the twentieth century, New Testament scholars introduced the method of form criticism to correlate stereotyped forms in biblical texts with routinized *Sitze im Leben,* or "situations in life." Schottroff's appeal to a "typically recurring situation" in early Christianity appeals to this form-critical concept.

Whether or not that argument explains the purpose of Rom 13:1-7, it may bear on documents such as the *Martyrdom of Polycarp*, which has as one of its purposes holding up the conduct of Polycarp, bishop of Smyrna, as exemplary. The text observes that Polycarp at first left his residence to evade the authorities and moved from house to house—unlike the hasty impetuosity of others who turned themselves in to the authorities as Christians, then later recanted out of fear of torture. The police closed in, however, and seized a slave in a house Polycarp had just left and, through torture, learned the bishop's next destination.

> Taking the slave, then, police and cavalry went out on Friday about supper-time, with their usual arms, as if they were advancing against a robber. And late in the evening they came up together against him and found him lying in an upper room. And he might have departed to another place, but would not, saying, "the will of God be done."
>
> So when he heard that they had arrived he went down and talked with them, while those who were present wondered at his age and courage, and whether there was so much haste for the arrest of an old man of such a kind. Therefore he ordered food and drink to be set before them at that hour, whatever they should wish, and he asked them to give him an hour to pray without hindrance. To this they assented, and he stood and prayed—thus filled with the grace of God—so that for two hours he could not be silent, and those who listened were astounded, and many repented that they had come against such a venerable old man.
>
> Now when he had at last finished his prayer, after remembering all who had ever even come his way, both small and great, high and low, and the whole

Catholic Church throughout the world, the hour came for departure, and they set him on an ass, and led him into the city, on a "great Sabbath day." And the police captain Herod and his father Niketas met him and removed him into their carriage, and sat by his side, trying to persuade him and saying, "But what harm is it to say, 'Lord Caesar,' and to offer sacrifice, and so forth, and to be saved?"

But he at first did not answer them, but when they continued he said, "I am not going to do what you counsel me." And they gave up the attempt to persuade him, and began to speak fiercely to him, and turned him out in such a hurry that in getting down from the carriage he scraped his shin; and without turning round, as though he had suffered nothing, he walked on promptly and quickly, and was taken to the arena, while the uproar in the arena was so great that no one could even be heard.

Now when Polycarp entered into the arena there came a voice from heaven: "Be strong, Polycarp, and play the man." And no one saw the speaker, but our friends who were there heard the voice. And next he was brought forward, and there was a great uproar of those who heard that Polycarp had been arrested. Therefore when he was brought forward the proconsul asked him if he were Polycarp, and when he admitted it he tried to persuade him to deny, saying, "Respect your age," and so forth, as they are accustomed to say: "Swear by the genius of Caesar, repent, say: 'Away with the Atheists'"; but Polycarp, with a stern countenance, looked on all the crowd of lawless heathen in the arena, and waving his hand at them, he groaned and looked up to heaven and said: "Away with the Atheists."

But when the proconsul pressed him and said, "Take the oath and I let you go, revile Christ," Polycarp said: "For eighty and six years have I been his servant, and he has done me no wrong, and how can I blaspheme my King who saved me?"

But when he persisted again, and said: "Swear by the genius of Caesar," he answered him: "If you vainly suppose that I will swear by the genius of Caesar, as you say, and pretend that you are ignorant who I am, listen plainly: I am a Christian. And if you wish to learn the doctrine of Christianity fix a day and listen."

The proconsul said: "Persuade the people." And Polycarp said: "You I should have held worthy of discussion, for we have been taught to render honor, as is meet, if it hurt us not, to princes and authorities appointed by God. But as for those, I do not count them worthy that a defense should be made to them."

And the proconsul said: "I have wild beasts. I will deliver you to them, unless you repent." And he said: "Call for them, for repentance from better to worse is not allowed us; but it is good to change from evil to righteousness." And he said again to him: "I will cause you to be consumed by fire, if you despise the beasts, unless you repent." But Polycarp said: "You threaten with the fire that burns for a time, and is quickly quenched, for you do not know the fire which awaits the wicked in the judgment to come and in everlasting punishment. But why are you waiting? Come, do what you will."

Thereafter the crowd is worked up to such a frenzy that the proconsul orders Polycarp burned alive; his death is described as a victory over the coercion of the magistrate.

(*Martyrdom of Polycarp* 7-11, trans. Lake, LCL)

219. THE TRIAL OF THE SCILLITAN MARTYRS

In the year 180 C.E. a group of Christians in Numidia were brought before the proconsul in Carthage in what Tertullian described as the first persecution of Christians in Africa. For our purposes, the report of their trial is interesting both because they cherish the writings of Paul (perhaps bound into a single codex, like Papyrus 46 from this same period: see Fig. 2.5) and because they address the proconsul in language reminiscent of Paul's language in Romans 13, professing to "heed the emperor" and pay taxes. "Honor to Caesar, but fear to God" might be an interesting interpretation of Rom 13:7: "fear to whom fear is due, honor to whom honor (is due)."

> When Praesens, for the second time, and Claudianus were the consuls, on the seventeenth day of July, at Carthage, there were brought to the judgment hall Speratus, Nartzalus, Cittinus, Donata, Secunda, and Vestia.
>
> SATURNINUS THE PROCONSUL: You can win the indulgence of our lord the Emperor if you return to a sound mind.
>
> SPERATUS: We have never done ill, we have not lent ourselves to wrong, we have never spoken ill, but when ill treated we have given thanks; because we give honor to our emperor.
>
> SATURNINUS: We too are religious, and our religion is simple, and we swear by the genius of our lord the Emperor, and pray for his welfare, as you also ought to do.
>
> SPERATUS: If you will peaceably lend me your ears, I can tell you the mystery of simplicity.
>
> SATURNINUS: I will not lend my ears to you when you begin to speak evil things of our sacred rites. Instead, swear by the genius of our lord the Emperor.
>
> SPERATUS: The empire of this world I do not know; rather I serve that God, whom no one has seen nor with human eyes can see. I have committed no theft; but if I have bought anything I pay the tax; because I know my lord, the king of kings and emperor of all nations.
>
> SATURNINUS (*to the rest*): Cease to be of this persuasion.
>
> SPERATUS: It is an ill persuasion to do murder, to speak false witness.
>
> SATURNINUS: Do not be partakers of this folly.
>
> CITTINUS: We have none to fear other than our Lord God, who is in heaven.
>
> DONATA: Honor to Caesar as Caesar: but fear to God.
>
> VESTIA: I am a Christian.
>
> SECUNDA: What I am, that I wish to be.
>
> SATURNINUS (*to Speratus*): Do you persist in being a Christian?

SPERATUS: I am a Christian. (*The others agree with him.*)

SATURNINUS: Will you take some time to reconsider?

SPERATUS: In a matter so straightforward there is no reconsidering.

SATURNINUS: What are those things you hold to your chest?

SPERATUS: Books and epistles of Paul, a just man.

SATURNINUS: Take a delay of thirty days and think again.

SPERATUS, *a second time:* I am a Christian. (*The others agree with him.*)

SATURNINUS, *reading the decree from a tablet:* Speratus, Nartzalus, Cittinus, Donata, Vestia, Secunda, and the rest having confessed that they live according to the Christian rite, and having obstinately persisted even after opportunity was offered them to return to the custom of the Romans, it is determined that they be put to the sword.

SPERATUS: We give thanks to God.

NARTZALUS: Today we are martyrs in heaven; thanks be to God.

Saturninus ordered it declared by the herald: Speratus, Nartzalus, Cittinus, Veturius, Felix, Aquilinus, Laetantius, Januaria, Generosa, Vestia, Donata, and Secunda I have ordered to be executed.

ALL TOGETHER: Thanks be to God.

And so they all together were crowned with martyrdom (*another text reads* were beheaded); and they reign with the Father and the Son and the Holy Spirit, for ever and ever. Amen.

(*Acts of the Scillitan Martyrs*, trans. Robinson, adapted)

220. DEDICATORY INSCRIPTION OF POPE DAMASUS

The martyrdom of Paul has continued to function as an authentication for his status as apostle to the nations and true preacher of the gospel. It also has served as an authentication for Rome as the center of the church, as the following inscription shows. Damasus, bishop of Rome from 366 to 384, ordered the inscription made in the Basilica Apostolorum, which was built in the fourth century on the site of a shrine at the third milestone of the Via Appia. This inscription seems to indicate that people believed the remains of both the apostles Peter and Paul had once been held there.

> Whoever you may be that seek the name of Peter and Paul should know that here the saints once dwelt. The East sent the disciples—that we readily admit. But on account of the merit of their blood (they have followed Christ through the stars and attained to the ethereal bosom and the realms of the holy ones) Rome has gained a superior right to claim them as her citizens.
> Damasus would thus tell of your praises, you new stars.
> (Memoriam in the Basilica Apostolorum in Rome, trans. Chadwick)[78]

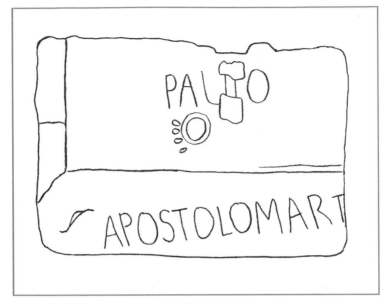

Fig. 6.11. *"To Paul, apostle, martyr." Drawing of the marble cover that covered the tomb of the apostle Paul; from the Basilica di San Paolo fuora di muore, Rome. Holes cut into the slab allowed pilgrims to pour oblations of wine into the tomb.*

221. THE MARTYRDOM OF THE HOLY APOSTLE PAUL (ACTS OF PAUL)

The *Martyrdom of the Holy Apostle Paul* may have been written as much as a century later than the preceding texts; it comes to us as the conclusion of the *Acts of Paul*. It may rely on earlier oral tradition, however, and evidently draws on elements in the canonical writings: Paul's relative freedom to teach in Rome (Acts 28:30-31), his contact with members of the emperor's household (Phil 1:13; 4:22), the auditor who falls out of a window and is miraculously brought back to life (Acts 20:7-12). The first part of the narrative is an elaborate explanation of how Paul came to the emperor's attention.

> Luke from Gaul and Titus from Dalmatia were waiting for Paul in Rome. When Paul saw them he was happy. He rented a barn outside Rome where he taught the word of truth with the brothers. And word got out, so that many souls were added to the Lord, so that the report reached all Rome and a great crowd came to him from Caesar's household who believed, resulting in great joy.
>
> Now Patroclus, a certain wine-taster of Caesar, came one night to the barn; and unable to enter where Paul was because of the crowd, he, sitting at a high window, heard him teaching the word of the God. But because the evil devil is jealous of the love of the brothers, Patroclus fell from the window and died, and this was reported immediately to Nero. But Paul, sensing this in his spirit, said, "Men, brothers, the evil one has occupied a place where he may tempt you. Go

out and find the servant who has fallen from a height, already about to die. Lift him up and bring him here to me."

So they went out and carried him back in. When the crowds saw, they were disturbed. But Paul said to them, "Now brothers, let your faith be evident! Everyone come, let us cry to our Lord Jesus Christ, in order that this servant may live and we may keep living in peace." And as all were mournfully praying, the servant received back his spirit and they set him on a mount and sent him back alive, alone with others who were from Caesar's household.

But Nero was very saddened when he heard of Patroclus's death, and when he entered from the bathhouse he commanded another to stand by his wine. His servants announced to him, saying, "Caesar, Patroclus lives and stands at table!" And when Caesar heard that Patroclus lived, he was frightened and didn't want to enter. But after he entered and saw Patroclus, he became excited and said, "Patroclus, are you alive?" And he replied, "I live, Caesar." Then he asked, "Who brought you to life?" But the servant, with the mind of faith, said, "Christ Jesus, the king of the ages."

At this Caesar was troubled and said, "So is he ready to rule the ages and destroy all kingdoms?" Patroclus replied to him, "Yes, he destroys all kingdoms under heaven, and it will be he alone forever, and there will be no kingdom that will manage to escape him."

After striking his face, (Nero) said, "Patroclus, are you a soldier to that king?" And he replied, "Yes, Lord Caesar, for he even raised me when I had died." And Barsabas Justus the wide-footed and Urion the Cappadocian and Festus the Galatian, those of Nero's inner circle, said, "We are all soldiering for him, for the king of the ages." But he locked them up immediately, tormenting the ones whom he greatly loved, and he commanded that the soldiers of the great king be sought out and he enacted such an order that all Christians and "soldiers of Christ" who were found should be executed.

As emperor and apostle come face-to-face, the contest between their two kingdoms escalates. The prevalence of military metaphors may suggest something about the intended audience of the *Martyrdom*.

And after Paul was bound, he was led in among many other prisoners. Those prisoners, also bound, all were paying attention to him, so that Caesar realized that he was the leader of the prison camp. And he said to him, "O man of the great king, bound as my prisoner, were you thinking you could sneak into the ruling class of the Romans and conscript soldiers from my rule?"

But Paul, filled with the Holy Spirit, said before all, "Caesar, We are conscripting soldiers not only from your rule, but also from the whole world. For our orders are that no one who wants to enlist in the service of my king should be turned away. So that even if you were to be enlisted, becoming a friend to him, not the wealth or the extravagant life you now enjoy will save you, but if you subject yourself and petition him, you shall be saved. For in one day he is about to wage war on the cosmos with fire."

After hearing these words, Caesar ordered all who were bound to be burned with fire, but Paul to be beheaded according to the law for Roman

Fig. 6.12. *The apostle Paul under arrest. Marble relief on a Christian sarcophagus, fourth century* c.e. *Museo Palazzo Massimo, Rome. Photo: Neil Elliott.*

citizens. But Paul did not stay silent about the sentence, but shared it with the prefect Longus and the centurion Cestus.

Thus Nero continued in Rome, unjustly slaying many Christians by the power of the evil one, so that Romans were standing outside his palace crying, "Enough, Caesar! For the men are ours! You are destroying the power of the Romans!" Then he ceased, being persuaded by them, and ordered that no one be touched on the basis of being a Christian, until he should investigate their cases.

Then after that order, Paul was brought to him, and he continued to say that he should be beheaded. But Paul said, "Caesar, it's not for a little while that I live for my king. If you cut off my head, I shall do this: after rising I shall make plain to you that I did not die, but rather that I live for my Lord Jesus Christ, who comes to judge the world."

But Longus and Cestus were saying to Paul, "Where do you have this king, that you believe in him, not wanting to repent in the face of death?"

After sharing with them the word, Paul said, "Men in ignorance and in this error, repent and be saved from the fire that is coming on the whole world. For we are not soldiering for an earthly king as you assume, but rather one from heaven, the living God, who because of the lawless deeds done in this cosmos comes as its judge. And blessed is that person who will believe in him and go on living forever, when he comes, burning the world pure."

They then asked him, "We beg you, help us, and we shall release you." But answering, he said, "I'm not absent without leave from Christ; I'm rather a soldier—in good standing—of the living God! If I had known that I would die, I would have done nothing different, Longus and Cestus. Since I live for God and love myself, I go to the Lord, in order that I may come with him in the glory of his father." They said to him, "How then shall we live, if you are beheaded?"

While they were discussing this, Nero sent a certain Parthenius and Pheres to check if Paul were already beheaded. And they found him still alive. But (Paul), summoning them, said, "Believe in the living God, who will raise me from the dead and all who believe in him." But they said, "We go now to Nero. When you have died and risen, then we shall believe in your God."

But since Longus and Cestus were asking further about salvation, he said to them, "Go quickly to my tomb tomorrow morning where you shall find two men praying, Titus and Luke. They will give you the seal in the Lord."[79] Then after standing toward the east, Paul raised his hands to heaven and prayed for a long time, during the prayer even taking counsel in Hebrew with the fathers.

Then he extended his neck, no longer speaking. When the executioner cut off his head, milk spurted onto the tunic of the soldier. And the soldier and all who were standing around, seeing this, marveled and glorified God who gave Paul such a glorious sign, and they departed to tell Caesar what had happened.

The prodigious death is followed—on the model of the risen Christ's appearances—by appearances of the risen Paul, and conversions.

After hearing about him and wondering and being at a loss for a long time, Paul came around the ninth hour, where many philosophers and the centurion were standing with the Caesar, and he stood before all and said, "Caesar, behold Paul, soldier of God. I did not die, but I live in my God. For you there will be many evils and great retribution quite soon, miserable one, for you have unjustly shed the blood of righteous ones." And after saying these words, Paul departed from him. And after hearing and being greatly troubled, Nero commanded that the prisoners be released, Patroclus also, and those with Barsabas.

And as Paul had directed, Longus and the centurion Cestus came with fear in the morning, approaching Paul's tomb. When they arrived they saw two men praying, and Paul in the middle, so that they—seeing the incredible sight—were really amazed. Titus and Luke, however—gripped with mortal fear when they saw Longus and Cestus coming toward then—turned to flee, but those pursuing said to them, "O men blessed of God, we are not pursuing you to death, as you suppose, but in order that you might give us life, as Paul promised us, whom we just saw standing between you, praying." Then Titus and Luke, hearing these words from them, gave to them the seal in the Lord with great rejoicing, glorifying God, even the father of our Lord Jesus Christ, to whom be glory for ever and ever. Amen.

(*Martyrdom of the Holy Apostle Paul*, trans. Reasoner)

Figs. 6.13–15. *Neoclassical statues present the apostle Paul as an old man with long beard and great sword. The first two images are from the Basilica di San Paolo fuori le muore, Rome. Photos: Neil Elliott. The last photograph is of a statue in St. Peter's Square, the Vatican, courtesy of Michael J. Towle.*

The Sword as the Apostle's Emblem

One of the ironies of Paul's legacy is that the sword—the instrument of Paul's execution at the hands of an emperor who claimed to have no need of recourse to the sword (see above, chapter 3)—came to serve as the identifying symbol for the apostle in Christian iconography (see figs. 6.13–15). The basis for the identification is the language about the word of God as sword in Eph 6:17 and Heb 4:12—both regarded early on as letters of Paul.

QUESTIONS FOR REFLECTION

1. What value should we place on letters written in Paul's name by others, perhaps after his death? Does it matter what their motives were—if we can discern these? Does it make a difference whether a possible pseudepigraphic writing was finally included in the New Testament (for example, 1 Timothy) or not (for example, the *Acts of Paul*)? If we could describe the author of 1 Timothy as trying to extend Paul's message for a later generation, should we judge the person who wrote the *Acts of Paul* "out of love" for the apostle differently?

2. What are some of the contemporary issues in which Paul and his letters are cited? How are his letters being used: is the historical and cultural distance between Paul's situation and the contemporary situation given sufficient respect? Under what circumstances should Paul's letters be given authority in contemporary discussions?

3. How should we go about distinguishing a "faithful" or "responsible" tradition of Paul's interpreters (or "disciples" or a Pauline "school") from wrong or tendentious interpretation? How should we evaluate and use the various historical sources available to us?

4. If Paul could be understood in so many different ways by people living in the first generations after him, how should we understand Paul himself and his own representation of his relationships with others (especially the Jerusalem apostles)?

FOR FURTHER READING

Beker, J. Christiaan Beker. *Heirs of Paul: Paul's Legacy in the New Testament and in the Church Today.* Minneapolis: Fortress Press, 1991.

Hooker, M. D., and S. G. Wilson, eds. *Paul and Paulinism: Essays in Honour of C. K. Barrett.* London: SPCK, 1982.

Meeks, Wayne A., and John T. Fitzgerald, eds. *The Writings of St. Paul: Annotated Texts, Reception and Criticism.* 2nd ed. New York: W. W. Norton, 2007.

Pervo, Richard I. *The Making of Paul: Constructions of the Apostle in Early Christianity.* Minneapolis: Fortress Press, 2010.

Schneemelcher, Wilhelm, ed. *New Testament Apocrypha.* 2 vols. Rev. ed. of the collection initiated by Edgar Hennecke. English translation edited by R. McL. Wilson. Louisville: Westminster John Knox, 1992.

On Gnosticism:

King, Karen L. *What Is Gnosticism?* Cambridge, Mass.: Belknap Press of Harvard University Press, 2005.

Layton, Bentley. *The Gnostic Scriptures: A New Translation with Annotations and Introductions.* Garden City, N.Y.: Doubleday, 1987.

————. "Prolegomena to the Study of Ancient Gnosticism." In *The Social World of the First Christians: Essays in Honor of Wayne A. Meeks,* ed. L. Michael White and O. Larry Yarbrough, 334–50. Minneapolis: Fortress Press, 1995.

Pagels, Elaine. *The Gnostic Paul: Gnostic Exegesis of the Pauline Letters.* Philadelphia: Trinity Press International, 1975.

Pearson, Birger A. *Ancient Gnosticism: Traditions and Literature.* Minneapolis: Fortress Press, 2007.

On Jewish Christianity:

McCabe, Matt Jackson, ed. *Jewish Christianity Reconsidered: Rethinking Ancient Groups and Texts.* Minneapolis: Fortress Press, 2007.

ABBREVIATIONS

4QMMT	Halakhic Letter "Some Works of the Law" found in Qumran Cave 4
1QpHab	Pesher (commentary) to Habakkuk found in Qumran Cave 1
ANRW	*Aufstieg und Niedergang der Römischen Welt*
Augustine, *Conf.*	*Confessions*
BAR	*Biblical Archaeology Review*
b. B. Bat.	Babylonian Talmud, tractate *Baba Bathra*
B.C.E.	before the Common Era
BDAG	Bauer, W., F. W. Danker, W. F. Arndt, and F. W. Gingrich, *Greek-English Lexicon of the New Testament and Other Early Christian Literature,* 3rd ed.
BJRL	*Bulletin of the John Rylands Library*
b. Sanh.	Babylonian Talmud, tractate *Sanhedrin*
BZNW	Beihefte zur Zeitschrift für die neutestamentliche Wissenschaft
CBQ	*Catholic Biblical Quarterly*
C.E.	Common Era
Cicero, *Att.*	*Letters to Atticus*
Of.	*De officiis*
CIL	*Corpus Inscriptionum Latinarum*
Clement of Alexandria	
Strom.	*Stromateis*
col.	column
CRINT	Compendia Rerum iudaicarum ad Novum Testamentum
Eusebius, *PE*	*Praeparatio Evangelica*
FOTC	Fathers of the Church

Hermes, *Mand.*	*Mandates*
Sim.	*Similitudes*
Homer, *Il.*	*Iliad*
Od.	*Odyssey*
IG	*Inscriptiones Graecae*
ILS	*Inscriptiones Latinae Selectae*, ed. Hermann Dessau
JBL	*Journal of Biblical Literature*
JFSR	*Journal for the Feminist Study of Religion*
Josephus, *Ag. Ap.*	*Against Apion*
Ant.	*Antiquities of the Jews*
War	*The Jewish War*
JRS	*Journal of Roman Studies*
JSJSup	Journal for the Study of Judaism Supplement Series
JSNT	*Journal for the Study of the New Testament*
JSNTSup	Journal for the Study of the New Testament Supplement Series
JTS	*Journal for Theological Studies*
LCL	Loeb Classical Library
LSAM	F. Sokolowski, ed., *Lois Sacrées de l'Asie Mineure* (Paris: E. de Boccard, 1955).
LSCG Suppl	F. Sokolowski, ed., *Lois Sacrées des Cités Grecques: Supplément* (Paris: E. de Boccard, 1962).
m. 'Abot	Mishnah tractate *'Abot*
m. Qidd.	Mishnah tractate *Quiddusim*
Mart.	*Martyrdom of the Holy Apostle Paul*
MQR	*Michigan Quarterly Review*
NA	Neutestamentliche Abhandlungen
NHC	Nag Hammadi Codex
NovT	*Novum Testamentum*
NPNF	A Select Library of the Nicene and Post-Nicene Fathers of the Christian Church
NRSV	New Revised Standard Version
NTIC	The New Testament in Context
NTS	*New Testament Studies*
OTP	James H. Charlesworth, ed., *The Old Testament Pseudepigrapha*, 2 vols.
PHerc.	*Papyrus Herculaneum*
Philo, *Leg.*	*Legatio ad Gaium* (*Embassy to Gaius Caligula*)
Spec. Laws	*On the Special Laws*
Plutarch	
Quaest. Conv.	*Quaestiones conviviales*
PMAAR	Papers and Monographs of the American Academy in Rome
P. Herc.	*Papyrus Herculaneum*

P. Mich.	*Papyrus Michigan*
P. Oxy.	*Papyrus Oxyrhynchus*
P. Ryl.	*Papyrus Rylands*
PS	Pseudepigrapha Series
Quintilian, *Decl.*	*Declamationes*
RIC	Harold Mattingly et al., eds., *The Roman Imperial Coinage* 10 vols. (London: Spink, 1923–81)
SBLDS	Society of Biblical Literature Dissertation Series
SBLTT	Society of Biblical Literature Texts and Translations
SEG	*Supplementum Epigraphicum Graecum*
Sextus Empiricus, *Math.*	*Adversus Mathematicos*
SNTSMS	Society for New Testament Studies Monograph Series
Suetonius, *Claud.*	*Claudius*
Tib.	*Tiberius*
SuppNovT	Supplements to *Novum Testamentum*
Tacitus, *Ann.*	*Annals*
TDNT	G. Kittel, ed., *Theological Dictionary of the New Testament*, 10 vols.
Varro, *Ant.*	*Antiquitates rerum humanarum et divinarum (Antiquities of Human and Divine Matters)*
Virgil, *Georg.*	*Georgics*
WA	*Weimar Ausgabe* (standard critical edition of Martin Luther's works)
WBC	Word Biblical Commentary
WUNT	Wissenschaftliche Untersuchungen zum Neuen Testament
Xenophon, *Anab.*	*Anabasis*
Mem.	*Memorabilia*
ZNW	*Zeitschrift für die neutestamentlichen Wissenschaft*

NOTES

Introduction

1. The metaphor is illustrated with absurd consequences in Helen Marion Palmer, *A Fish out of Water* (New York: Random House, 1961).

2. Samuel Sandmel, "Parallelomania," *JBL* 81 (1962): 1. This article is the text of Sandmel's presidential address on December 27, 1961, to what was then known as the Society of Biblical Literature and Exegesis.

3. Johann Jakob Wettstein, *Novum Testamentum graecum: editiones receptae cum lectionibus variantibus codicum mss., editionum aliarum, versionum et patrum nec non commentario pleniore ex scriptoribus veteribus hebraeis, graecis et latinis historiam et vim verborem illustrante opera et studio* (Amsterdam: Dommeriana, 1751–52; repr., Graz, Austria: Akademische Druck- und Verlaganstalt, 1962); *Neuer Wettstein: Texte zum Neuen Testament aus Griechentum und Hellenismus* (Berlin/New York: Walter de Gruyter, 1996–).

4. Gustav Adolf Deissmann, *Licht vom Osten: Das Neue Testament und die neuentdeckten Texte der hellenistisch-römischen Welt* (Tübingen: J. C. B. Mohr, 1908); idem, *Light from the Ancient East: The New Testament Illustrated by Recently Discovered Texts of the Graeco-Roman World*, trans. Lionel R. M. Strachan (London: Hodder & Stoughton, 1927).

5. Paul Fiebig, *Die Umwelt des Neuen Testamentes: Religionsgeschichtliche und geschichtliche Texte, in deutscher Übersetzung und mit Anmerkungen versehen, zum Verständnis des Neuen Testamentes dargeboten* (Göttingen: Vandenhoeck & Ruprecht, 1926).

6. C. K. Barrett, *The New Testament Background: Selected Documents* (London: SPCK, 1956); new edition, *The New Testament Background: Writings from Ancient Greece and the Roman Empire That Illuminate Christian Origins* (San Franscisco: HarperSanFrancisco, 1995).

7. Craig A. Evans and Stanley E. Porter, eds., *New Testament Backgrounds: A Sheffield Reader*, Biblical Seminar 43 (Sheffield: Sheffield Academic Press, 1997).

8. Abraham J. Malherbe, *Moral Exhortation: A Greco-Roman Sourcebook*, Library of Early Christianity 4 (Philadelphia: Westminster, 1986); Stanley K. Stowers, *Letter Writing in Greco-Roman Antiquity*, Library of Early Christianity 5 (Philadelphia: Westminster, 1986); David E. Aune, *The New Testament in Its Literary Environment*, Library of Early Christianity 8 (Philadelphia: Westminster, 1987); M. Eugene Boring, Klaus Berger, and Carsten Colpe, eds., *Hellenistic Commentary to the New Testament* (Nashville: Abingdon, 1995); Hans-Josef Klauck, *The Religious Context of Early Christianity: A Guide to Graeco-Roman Religions*, trans. Brian McNeil (Minneapolis: Fortress Press, 2003).

364 | Notes to Introduction

9. Mary R. Lefkowitz and Maureen B. Fant, *Women's Life in Greece and Rome: A Sourcebook in Translation* (Baltimore: Johns Hopkins University Press, 1982); Ross S. Kraemer, ed., *Maenads, Martyrs, Matrons, Monastics: A Sourcebook on Women's Religions in the Greco-Roman World* (Philadelphia: Fortress Press, 1988).

10. Gustav Adolf Deissmann, *Paulus: eine kultur- und religionsgeschichtliche Skizze* (Tübingen: J. C. B. Mohr [P. Siebeck], 1911); ET, *Paul: A Study in Social and Religious History*, trans. William E. Wilson (New York: G. H. Doran, 1926).

11. John Wordsworth, Henry J. White, et al., *Novum Testamentum domini nostri Jesu Christi: Latine secundum editionem sancti Hieronymi* (Oxford: Clarendon, 1889–1904), 2:12–16.

12. Fred O. Francis and J. Paul Sampley, *Pauline Parallels* (Philadelphia: Fortress Press; Missoula, Mont.: Scholars, 1975; rev. ed. Foundations and Facets: New Testament; Fortress Press, 1984).

13. Walter T. Wilson, *Pauline Parallels: A Comprehensive Guide* (Louisville: Westminster John Knox, 2009).

14. The classic treatment is Richard B. Hays, *Echoes of Scripture in the Letters of Paul* (New Haven: Yale University Press, 1989). See more recently idem, *The Conversion of the Imagination: Paul as Interpreter of Israel's Scripture* (Grand Rapids: Eerdmans, 2005); Christopher D. Stanley, *Arguing with Scripture: The Rhetoric of Quotations in the Letters of Paul* (New York and London: T&T Clark, 2004); and papers from the SBL Seminar on Paul's Use of Scripture, Stanley E. Porter and Christopher D. Stanley, eds., *As It Is Written: Studying Paul's Use of Scripture*, Symposium 50 (Atlanta: Society of Biblical Literature, 2008).

15. Hermann Strack and Paul Billerbeck, *Kommentar zum Neuen Testament aus Talmud und Midrasch*, 6 vols. (Munich: Beck, 1924–28).

16. The Hebrew term *shoah* ("catastrophe") is preferred by some to the more widely used *Holocaust* because the latter implies offensive notions of sacrifice.

17. Rosemary Radford Ruether, *Faith and Fratricide: The Theological Roots of Anti-Semitism* (New York: Seabury, 1974); Krister Stendahl, *Paul among Jews and Gentiles, and Other Essays* (Philadelphia: Fortress Press, 1976); E. P. Sanders, *Paul and Palestinian Judaism: A Comparison of Patterns of Religion* (Philadelphia: Fortress Press, 1977); and idem, *Paul, the Law, and the Jewish People* (Philadelphia: Fortress Press, 1983).

18. Günther Bornkamm, *Paul*, trans. D. M. G. Stalker (New York: Harper & Row, 1971), 11–12.

19. James D. G. Dunn, "The New Perspective on Paul," *BJRL* 65 (1983): 95–122. The scholarly literature devoted to dimensions of the "New Perspective" is now immense and seems to grow exponentially: in the two months August and September 2009, for example, it was the focus of discussion by the Pauline Epistles group at the Catholic Biblical Association, the Convocation of Teaching Theologians in the ELCA (Evangelical Lutheran Church in America), an academic seminar at the Katholieke Universitet Leuven, and a gathering of New Testament scholars in the Twin Cities. A helpful current resource is the Web site maintained by Mark M. Mattison at http://www.thepaulpage.com.

20. Daniel Marguerat, introduction to *Paul, une théologie en construction*, ed. Andreas Dettwiler, Jean-Daniel Kaestli, and Daniel Marguerat, Monde de la Bible 51 [Geneva: Labor et Fides, 2004), 9. Neil Elliott's translation.

21. Magnus Zetterholm, *Approaches to Paul: A Student's Guide to Recent Scholarship* (Minneapolis: Fortress Press, 2009).

22. David Balch, Everett Ferguson, and Wayne A. Meeks, eds., *Greeks, Romans, and Christians: Essays in Honor of Abraham J. Malherbe* (Minneapolis: Fortress Press, 1990); Troels Engberg-Pedersen, *Paul in His Hellenistic Context* (Minneapolis: Fortress Press, 1995); Helmut Koester, *Paul and His World: Interpreting the New Testament in Its Context* (Minneapolis: Fortress Press, 2007).

23. J. Paul Sampley, ed., *Paul in the Greco-Roman World: A Handbook* (Harrisburg, Pa.: Trinity Press International, 2003).

24. John Dominic Crossan and Jonathan L. Reed, *In Search of Paul: How Jesus's Apostle Opposed Rome's Empire with God's Kingdom; A New Vision of Paul's Words and World* (San Francisco: HarperSanFrancisco, 2004).

25. See Dieter Georgi, *Theocracy in Paul's Praxis and Theology* (Philadelphia: Fortress Press, 1990; with a new foreword by Helmut Koester, Minneapolis: Fortress Press, 2009); Richard A. Horsley, ed., *Paul and Empire: Religion and Power in Roman Imperial Society* (Philadelphia: Trinity Press International, 1997); idem, ed., *Paul and Politics: Ekklesia, Israel, Imperium, Interpretation; Essays in Honor of Krister Stendahl* (Harrisburg, Pa.: Trinity Press International, 2000); idem, ed., *Paul and the Roman Imperial Order* (Harrisburg, Pa.: Trinity Press International, 2004). The Paul in Critical Contexts series from Fortress Press is an expression of this increased interest in Paul's political context.

26. Mark Reasoner's previous books have included a study of Paul's letter to the Romans in the context of Roman values of honor and shame and a survey of very different readings of that letter in the history of Christian interpretation: see Mark Reasoner, *The Strong and the Weak: Romans 14.1–15.13 in Context*, SNTSMS 103 (Cambridge: Cambridge University Press, 1999); idem, *Romans in Full Circle: A History of Interpretation* (Louisville: Westminster John Knox, 2005). Neil Elliott's works include a rhetorical-critical study of Romans and books seeking to locate Paul more clearly in the context of political and ideological currents in the Roman Empire: see Neil Elliott, *The Rhetoric of Romans: Argumentative Constraint and Strategy and Paul's Dialogue with Judaism*, JSNTSup 45 (Sheffield: JSOT Press, 1990); idem, *Liberating Paul: The Justice of God and the Politics of the Apostle* (Maryknoll, N.Y.: Orbis, 1994; Fortress Press edition with a new preface, 2006); idem, *The Arrogance of Nations: Reading Romans in the Shadow of Empire*, Paul in Critical Contexts (Minneapolis: Fortress Press, 2008).

Chapter One

1. See Paul Achtemeier, "*Omne verbum sonat*: The New Testament and the Oral Environment of Late Western Antiquity," *JBL* 109 (1990): 16–19, and the essays in *Semeia* 65 (1994).

2. See Christopher D. Stanley, "'Neither Jew nor Greek': Ethnic Conflict in Graeco-Roman Society," *JSNT* 64 (1996): 101–24; James LaGrand, "Proliferation of the 'Gentile' in the NRSV," *Biblical Research* 41 (1996): 77–87.

3. For example, Augustine, *Conf.* 7.27; 8.14; Thomas Aquinas, *Lectures on Romans* 1.22.

4. It is found in the first verse of Romans, 1 Corinthians, 2 Corinthians, Galatians, Ephesians, Colossians, 1 Timothy, 2 Timothy, and Titus.

5. For a fuller discussion see Karl Heinrich Rengstorff, "ἀπόστολος," *TDNT* 1:398–447.

6. In the first verses of Galatians, Ephesians, Colossians, 1 Timothy, 2 Timothy, and Titus, Paul makes it clear that he is sent by Christ Jesus. See also 1 Cor 2:1-2; 3:11; 4:10; Phil 1:18; Col 1:24-28.

7. See Rom 1:11-16, 15:22-32; 1 Cor 4:17-21; 5:3-5; 2 Cor 13:1-10; Robert W. Funk, "The Apostolic Parousia: Form and Significance," in *Christian History and Interpretation: Studies Presented to John Knox*, ed. W. R. Farmer, C. F. D. Moule, and R. R. Niebuhr (Cambridge: Cambridge University Press, 1967), 249–68.

8. Orlando Patterson, *Slavery and Social Death: A Comparative Study* (Cambridge, Mass.: Harvard University Press, 1982).

9. J. Albert Harrill, *Slaves in the New Testament: Literary, Social, and Moral Dimensions* (Minneapolis: Fortress Press, 2006); Jennifer A. Glancy, *Slavery in Early Christianity* (Minneapolis: Fortress Press, 2006).

10. Dale B. Martin, *Slavery as Salvation: The Metaphor of Slavery in Pauline Christianity* (New Haven: Yale University Press, 1990), 137.

11. Jerome, *Commentary on Philemon* on vv. 23-24; *De viris illustribus* 5. For discussion of these (inconsistent) reports and the questions of Paul's citizenship and name, see Jerome Murphy-O'Connor, *Paul: A Critical Life* (Oxford: Clarendon, 1996), 36–43.

12. See Stanley K. Stowers, *The Diatribe and Paul's Letter to the Romans*, SBLDS 57 (Chico, Calif.: Scholars, 1981); Abraham J. Malherbe, *Paul and the Thessalonians: The Philosophic Tradition of Pastoral Care* (Philadelphia: Fortress Press, 1987), ch. 1; idem, *Paul and the Popular Philosophers* (Minneapolis: Fortress Press, 1989).

13. Stanley K. Stowers, *A Rereading of Romans: Justice, Jews, and Gentiles* (New Haven: Yale University Press, 1994), 44–52.

14. Ibid., 51, 57.

15. S. Douglas Olson also mentions Eup. Fragment *190 (Olson, trans. *Athenaeus: The Learned Banqueters*, 7 vols., LCL [Cambridge, Mass.: Harvard University Press, 2007–10]), 1:544 n. 146.

16. For discussion of the text and translation, see Bruce W. Winter, *Philo and Paul among the Sophists: Alexandrian and Corinthian Responses to a Julio-Claudian Movement*, 2nd ed. (Grand Rapids: Eerdmans, 2002), 256–60.

17. Malherbe, *Paul and the Thessalonians*, 19–20.

18. See the entry for σκηνοποιός in *BDAG*, 928–29.

19. The older consensus can be dated to Adolf Deissmann, *Paul: A Study in Social and Religious History* (1926; New York: Harper & Brothers, 1957). In the last quarter of the twentieth century it was made popular by Wayne A. Meeks (*The First Urban Christians: The Social World of the Apostle Paul* [New Haven: Yale University Press, 1983]), Abraham J. Malherbe (*Social Aspects of Early Christianity*, 2nd ed. [Philadelphia: Fortress Press, 1983]), and Gerd Theissen (*The Social Setting of Pauline Christianity: Essays on Corinth*, trans. John Schütz [Philadelphia: Fortress Press, 1982]); see the retrospective essays in Todd D. Still and David G. Horrell, eds., *After the First Urban Christians: The Social-Scientific Study of Pauline Christianity Twenty-Five Years Later* (London: T&T Clark, 2009). It has been challenged by Justin J. Meggitt (*Paul, Poverty, and Survival*, Studies of the New Testament and Its World [Edinburgh: T&T Clark, 1998]) and Steven J. Friesen ("Poverty in Pauline Studies: Beyond the So-called New Consensus," *JSNT* 26 [2004]: 323–61; and see Peter Oakes, *Reading Romans in Pompeii: Paul's Letter at Ground Level* (Minneapolis: Fortress Press, 2009).

20. See Malherbe's discussion in *Paul and the Thessalonians*, ch. 4.

21. The words *influence* and *influential* are clearly "power" words in Latin: . . . amicitiae eorum, qui apud aliquem potentem potentes sunt . . .

22. The Centumviral Court was the primary place where civil lawsuits were conducted in the Roman Republic and Empire. By the time of Pliny, the total membership in this court was set at 180 men. Pliny is describing how nervous he was as a young lawyer to argue before this intimidating court.

23. Translation in the public domain, text at http://www.authorama.com/book/works-of-horace.html.

24. See Victor Ehrenberg and A. H. M. Jones, eds., *Documents Illustrating the Reigns of Augustus and Tiberius*, 2nd ed. (Oxford: Clarendon, 1976), no. 98, with comparison.

25. Ehrenberg and Jones reconstruct "gospels" in this line. There is a gap in the inscription at this point.

26. Ehrenberg and Jones have reconstructed the phrase "because of him the birthday of God began good news for the world" from the unpublished copy of this decree found in Apamea (*Documents* 81-82).

27. Anthony Saldarini, "Pharisees," *ABD* 5:289.

28. Paula Fredriksen, *From Jesus to Christ: The Origins of the New Testament Images of Jesus*, 2nd ed. (New Haven: Yale University Press, 2000), 146; ch. 6.

29. Ibid., 147-48.

30. Ibid., 149-53.

31. Ibid., 153-56. Fredriksen argues that a message of coming redemption—traditionally couched in the language of eschatological battle—spearheaded by a figure recently crucified by Rome would invariably have alarmed pagan neighbors.

32. Ibid., 142–56; C. G. Kruse, "Afflictions . . . ," *Dictionary of Paul and His Letters*, 18–20.

33. Danby provides references in the Torah for all the quoted commandments.

34. See Carol A. Newsom, "Mysticism," in *Enclopedia of the Dead Sea Scrolls*, ed. Lawrence H. Schiffman and James C. VanderKam (New York: Oxford University Press, 2000), 2:591–94. On Paul and the Jewish mystical tradition, see J. W. Bowker, "'Merkabah' Visions and the Visions of Paul," *Journal of Semitic Studies* 16 (1971): 157–73; Peter Schäfer, "New Testament and Hekhalot Literature: The Journey into Heaven in Paul and in Merkavah Mysticism," *Journal of Jewish Studies* 35 (1984): 119–35; James D. Tabor, *Things Unutterable: Paul's Ascent to Paradise in Its Greco-Roman, Judaic, and Early Christian Contexts*, Studies in Judaism (Lanham, Md.: University Press of America, 1986); Alan F. Segal, *Paul the Convert: The Apostolate and Apostasy of Saul the Pharisee* (New Haven: Yale University Press, 1990), ch. 2 ("Paul's Ecstasy," depending on his earlier work, *Two Powers in Heaven: Rabbinic Reports about Christianity and Gnosticism*, Studies in Judaism in Late Antiquity 25 [Leiden: Brill, 1977]; and "Heavenly Ascent in Hellenistic Judaism, Early Christianity, and Their Environments," *ANRW* 2.23.2 [Berlin: de Gruyter, 1980], 1332–94). See also Neil Elliott, *Liberating Paul: The Justice of God and the Politics of the Apostle* (Maryknoll, N.Y.: Orbis, 1994; Fortress Press ed., 2006), ch. 5. Paula R. Gooder's study of 2 Corinthians as a "failed ascent" deserves close attention: *Only the Third Heaven? 2 Corinthians 12.1-10 and Heavenly Ascent*, Library of Biblical Studies 313 (Edinburgh: T&T Clark, 2006).

35. Segal, *Paul the Convert*, 37. Tabor regards it as "impossible" that Paul is here describing his first vision of the risen Christ (*Things Unutterable*, 114–15).

36. F. I. Andersen dates the apocalypse to the late first century c.e. but recognizes that the available manuscripts in Slavonic translation come from much later, after the fourteenth century ("2 (Slavonic Apocalypse of) Enoch," *OTP* 1:114–18).

37. Bowker, "'Merkavah' Visions"; Segal, *Paul the Convert*, ch. 2.

38. On the theme of divine necessity impelling the plot of Acts, including Paul's appearance before "Gentiles and kings" (Acts 9:15), see Mark Reasoner, "The Theme of Acts: Institutional History or Divine Necessity in History?" *JBL* 118 (1999): 635–59.

Chapter Two

1. Paul uses "the gospel" frequently; "the gospel of God" (Rom 1:1; 15:16), "my gospel" (Rom 2:16; 16:25), "a different gospel" (2 Cor 11:4; Gal 1:6-9).

2. J. Christiaan Beker, *Paul the Apostle: The Triumph of God in Life and Thought* (Philadelphia: Fortress Press, 1980); see Neil Elliott, *The Arrogance of Nations: Reading Romans in the Shadow of Empire*, Paul in Critical Contexts (Minneapolis: Fortress Press, 2008), 44.

3. For the issues involving circumstances that might have constrained the shape of Romans, see Karl P. Donfried, ed., *The Romans Debate*, rev. and exp. ed. (Peabody, Mass.: Hendrickson, 1991). Romans is still treated as an adequate expression of Paul's gospel by, among others, James D. G. Dunn, *The Theology of Paul the Apostle* (Grand Rapids: Eerdmans, 1998), esp. xvi. For the issues in identifying "the gospel" in Paul, see L. Ann Jervis and Peter Richardson, eds., *Gospel in Paul: Studies on Corinthians, Galatians, and Romans for Richard N. Longenecker*, JSNTSup 108 (Sheffield: Sheffield Academic Press, 1994).

4. Jouette Bassler, ed., *Pauline Theology*, vol. 1, *Thessalonians, Philippians, Galatians, Philemon* (Minneapolis: Fortress Press, 1991); David M. Hay, *Pauline Theology*, vol. 2, *1 and 2 Corinthians* (Minneapolis: Fortress Press, 1993); David M. Hay and E. Elizabeth Johnson, eds., *Pauline Theology*, vol. 3, *Romans* (Minneapolis: Fortress Press, 1995); E. Elizabeth Johnson and David M. Hay, *Pauline Theology*, vol. 4, *Looking Back, Pressing On*, SBL Symposium Series (Atlanta: Scholars, 1997).

5. Richard I. Pervo, *The Making of Paul: Constructions of the Apostle in Early Christianity* (Minneapolis: Fortress Press, 2010), 150.

6. Ibid., ch. 1–3.

7. For a helpful introduction, see Hans-Josef Klauck, *Ancient Letters and the New Testament: A Guide to Context and Exegesis*, trans. Daniel Bailey (Waco: Baylor University Press, 1998).

8. See Robert W. Funk, "The Apostolic Parousia: Form and Significance," in *Christian History and Interpretation: Studies Presented to John Knox*, ed. W. R. Farmer, C. F. D. Moule, and R. R. Niebuhr (Cambridge: Cambridge University Press, 1967), 249–68.

9. This and the next three selections are taken from Abraham J. Malherbe, *Ancient Epistolary Theorists* (Chico, Calif.: Scholars, 1988).

10. Clarence E. Glad, *Paul and Philodemus: Adaptability in Epicurean and Early Christian Psychagogy*, SuppNovT 81 (Leiden: Brill, 1995), 1.

11. Ibid., 10.

12. See Aristotle, *On Rhetoric: A Theory of Discourse*, newly translated with introduction and notes by George A. Kennedy (Oxford: Oxford University Press, 1991); George A. Kennedy, *Classical Rhetoric and Its Christian and Secular Tradition from Ancient to Modern Times* (Chapel Hill: University of North Carolina Press, 1980); idem, *New Testament Interpretation through Rhetorical Criticism*, Studies in Religion (Chapel Hill: University of North Carolina Press, 1984). For the terminology, in Greek (primarily from Aristotle) and Latin (from Cicero and Quintilian), see Richard A. Lanham, *A Handlist of Rhetorical Terms*, 2nd ed. (Berkeley and Los Angeles: University of California Press, 1991). The move away from a focus on nomenclature to a deeper understanding of the dynamics of persuasion was led by Chaim Perelman and L. Olbrechts-Tyteca, *The New Rhetoric: A Treatise on Argumentation*, trans. John Wilkinson and Purcell Weaver (Notre Dame: University of Notre Dame Press, 1969). For the rhetorical-critical study of Paul, see Duane F. Watson, ed., *Persuasive Artistry: Studies in New Testament Rhetoric in Honor of George A. Kennedy*, JSNTSup 50 (Sheffield: JSOT Press, 1991); idem, "Rhetorical Criticism of the Pauline Epistles since 1975," *Currents in Research* 3 (1995): 219–48.

13. Stanley K. Stowers, *Letter Writing in Greco-Roman Antiquity*, Library of Early Christianity 5 (Philadelphia: Westminster, 1986), 91.

14. Ibid., 107.

15. Ibid., 92.

16. Ibid., 91–92.

17. Abraham J. Malherbe, *Paul and the Thessalonians: The Philosophic Tradition of Pastoral Care* (Minneapolis: Fortress Press, 1987), 36–38. The following three extracts are among the texts Malherbe discusses.

18. See Luther Stirewalt, "The Form and Function of the Greek Letter-Essay," in Donfried, *Romans Debate*, 147–71.

19. Stowers, *Letter Writing*, 93.

20. Chan-Hie Kim, *Form and Structure of the Familiar Letter of Recommendation*, SBLDS 4 (Missoula, Mont.: Society of Biblical Literature, 1972), 7.

21. Ibid., 78.

22. The letter is dated to c. 25 C.E.

23. The letter is dated to 16 C.E. The location is another designation for Oxyrhynchus, based on combining it with its neighboring town Cynopolis. The ellipsis in the second sentence indicates that one or more words are missing from the letter.

24. The text is dated to the first century C.E.

25. The text is dated to 6 C.E.; perhaps the Egyptian scribe reckoned the beginning of Augustus's reign from his victory at Actium.

26. S. K. Stowers's translation of the letter in *Sammelbuch griechischer Urkunden aus Ägypten*, vol. 3, ed. F. Preisigke (Wiesbaden: Harrosowitz, repr. 1974), no. 6263, lines 18-31.

27. John L. White, *The Form and Structure of the Official Petition: A Study in Greek Epistolography*, SBLDS 5 (Missoula, Mont.: Society of Biblical Literature, 1972), 63.

28. *Papyrus Graux* 2 is dated to 55–59 C.E.

29. See Robert Jewett, *Romans: A Commentary*, Hermeneia (Minneapolis: Fortress Press, 2008), 44–46.

30. Robert W. Wall, "The Acts of the Apostles: Introduction, Commentary and Reflections," in *The New Interpreter's Bible* (Nashville: Abingdon, 1994–2004), 10:247.

31. For the dating of Aristobulus, We follow *Fragments from Hellenistic Jewish Authors*, vol. 3, *Aristobulus*, trans. and ed. Carl R. Holladay, SBLTT 39, Pseudepigrapha Series 13 (Atlanta: Scholars, 1995), 45–49.

32. So Patrick Gerard Walsh in his introduction to Cicero, *The Nature of the Gods* (New York: Oxford University Press, 1997), xxiv.

33. See S. K. Stowers, "Diatribe," *ABD* 2:190–93; D. F. Watson, "Diatribe," *Dictionary of Paul and His Letters*, ed. Gerald F. Hawthorne et al. (Downers Grove, Ill.: InterVarsity, 1993), 213–14.

34. In classical Greek theology these deities are responsible for grain.

35. Dindymus and Ida are mountains in Phrygia (central Asia Minor or modern Turkey). Cybele is the mountain goddess of Phrygia. At some point before this Phrygian religion was brought to Rome, Cybele became identified with another goddess known as the Great Mother. Ilium is another word for Troy.

36. "Ausonian leaders" is a poetic equivalent for the Roman princes sent to bring the Great Mother to Rome.

37. Aeneas ("the devout Phrygian") had used these pines to build his ships.

38. Women who remained virgins into their adulthood, including the Vestal Virgins, a group of priestesses in Rome who kept the fire of the goddess Vesta always burning.

39. Clausus was an indigenous tribesman who assisted Aeneas in his battle for Latium.

40. This story was probably reenacted in a play during the Megalensia celebration for the Great Mother, according to James G. Frazer (*Ovid*, vol. 5, *Fasti*, trans. James G. Frazer, rev. G. P. Goold, LCL [Cambridge, Mass.: Harvard University Press, 1931], 212 note a).

41. See no. 92, *Res Gestae* in the section, "Deeds Accomplished by the Divine Augustus" in ch. 3 below. The temple of the Great Mother on the Palatine was destroyed by fire in 3 c.e., so Augustus rebuilt it after that.

42. Paula Fredriksen offers a compelling reconstruction of the rise of these scriptural "proofs" in *From Jesus to Christ: The Origins of the New Testament Image of Jesus*, 2nd ed. (New Haven: Yale University Press, 2000), 133–42.

43. For what follows, see the summary of Richard A. Horsley, *Jesus and the Powers* (Minneapolis: Fortress Press, 2010); Martin Hengel, *Crucifixion in the Ancient World*, 2nd ed. by John Cook (Minneapolis: Fortress Press, forthcoming).

44. Fredriksen refutes a common interpretation, based on Gal 3:10-14, that Jesus' death would have been offensive to Jews for biblical or "halakhic" reasons: *From Jesus to Christ* (2nd ed.), 145–48. For a judicious explication of Paul's theology of the cross, see David A. Brondos, *Paul on the Cross: Reconstructing the Apostle's Story of Redemption* (Minneapolis: Fortress Press, 2006).

45. James D. G. Dunn, *The Theology of Paul the Apostle* (Grand Rapids: Eerdmans, 1998), 174–77.

46. Ibid., 176.

47. Stanley K. Stowers, *A Rereading of Romans: Justice, Jews, and Gentiles* (New Haven: Yale University Press, 1994), 85–92, 122–24.

48. Karl Galinsky, *Augustan Culture: An Interpretive Introduction* (Princeton: Princeton University Press, 1996), 93.

49. R. J. Tarrant, "Poetry and Power: Virgil's Poetry in Contemporary Context," in *The Cambridge Companion to Virgil*, ed. Charles Martindale (Cambridge: Cambridge University Press, 1997), 173–74. H. R. Fairclough considers the *Eclogue* an obvious celebration of Antony and Cleopatra's marriage (*Virgil*, vol. 1, *Eclogues. Georgics. Aeneid: Books 1–6*, trans. H. Rushton

Fairclougy, rev. G. P. Goold, LCL [Cambridge, Mass.: Harvard University Press, 1916], 2); but Galinsky prefers the metaphorical interpretation (*Augustan Culture*, 91–93).

50. "Cumaean" refers to the Sibyl (or prophetess) of Cumae; "the Virgin" is Astraea, goddess of justice; the goddess Lucina presided over childbirth.

51. Galinsky, *Augustan Culture*, 95.

52. Ibid., 105.

53. Veterans of Rome's ancient wars were superior to the current generation.

54. Anchises and Venus were the (human and divine) parents of Aeneas, legendary ancestor of Julius Caesar and, by adoption, Augustus.

Chapter Three

1. Ronald Syme, *The Roman Revolution* (1939; repr., New York: Oxford University Press, 1967). On Augustus's *auctoritas*, see Karl Galinsky, *Augustan Culture: An Interpretive Introduction* (Princeton: Princeton University Press, 1996).

2. On the ideology of the *Pax Augustana*, see Stefan Weinstock, "Pax and the 'Ara Pacis,'" *JRS* 50 (1960): 51, citing Tacitus, *Ann.* 13.41.5; 15.18.1.

3. J. Rufus Fears, "The Theology of Victory at Rome: Approaches and Problems," *ANRW* 2.17.2, 804–7, 813; and idem, "The Cult of Virtues and Roman Imperial Ideology," *ANRW* 2.17.2, 884–85.

4. Text in Victor Ehrenberg and A. H. M. Jones, eds., *Documents Illustrating the Reigns of Augustus and Tiberius*, 2nd ed. (Oxford: Clarendon, 1976), no. 98.

5. The sense of the last lines is apparently that Concordia is being addressed again; "your mother" apparently refers to Livia, the wife of the emperor Augustus, who according to Ovid (6.637-38) dedicated a temple to Concordia. That goddess was considered the consort of Jupiter. Ovid relates also (6.640-48) that this temple was built on the site of a lavish building that had been given to the emperor Augustus but which he considered an extravagant display of wealth; he ordered it destroyed and Livia then dedicated the temple built on that site to Concordia.

6. Mark Antony and his followers.

7. "Those who killed my father" refers to the assassins of Julius Caesar, who had adopted Octavian—later known as Augustus. The two battles he describes here probably refer to the two battles in 42 B.C.E. that Octavian and Mark Antony won against the forces of Julius Caesar's assassins in Philippi. After these battles, the assassins Brutus and Cassius committed suicide.

8. A *curule* triumph was one indicating high distinction, so named from the word for a chair of authority used by consuls and other high officials. *Imperator* is the Roman term for "commander in chief" or "emperor."

9. A council of priests who together supervised the state cult were known as the *pontifices*, literally "bridge-makers" (hence the English word *pontiff*); Augustus was given authority to lead this council.

10. The lack of detail here shows that this victory remains Augustus's most memorable—his victory over Mark Antony at Actium in 31 B.C.E. See Dio Cassius, *History of Rome* 51.17 for description of Mark Antony's temple spoils. All Mediterranean peoples considered it wrong to rob temples (cf. Rom 2:22).

11. See Suetonius, *Augustus* 52; Dio Cassius, *History of Rome* 52.35.3-5; 53.22.3; 54.35.2.

12. Note Paul's alternative quest to bring peoples under the obedience of faith (Rom 1:5; 15:18; 16:26).

13. See also Rom 15:19, where Paul perhaps attempts to trump Augustus here regarding the borders of the divine kingdom.

14. With this reference to India, Augustus here seeks to portray himself as another Alexander the Great.

15. Augustus is emphasizing his generosity and fair dealing. When Parthia and Medea experienced vacancies, princes, kept as noble hostages in Rome, were requested to be sent home to become kings, and Augustus granted their requests. Both vacancies were filled in 9 C.E. (see

Suetonius, *Augustus* 21.3; Tacitus, *Ann.* 2, I. 2. 12, 14; Josephus, *Ant.* 18.46–48. Agrippa, before whom Paul appears in Acts 25:23—26:32, was held in Rome as a noble hostage while a teenager.

16. Here the balance that Augustus is seeking to strike throughout the *Res Gestae* is evident: he wants to portray himself as the most powerful person in the world while at the same time he maintains that he never usurped power or stepped beyond what Roman law and precedents allowed.

17. Inscription published in Allen Brown West, *Latin Inscriptions 1896–1926*, Corinth: Results of Excavations Conducted by the American School of Classical Studies at Athens 8, pt. 2 (Cambridge, Mass.: Harvard University Press, 1931), no. 68; cited from John K. Chow, *Patronage and Power: A Study of Social Networks in Corinth*, JSNTSup 75 (Sheffield: JSOT Press, 1992), 38.

18. Permission to use this image and the next from Stack's LLC (http://www.stacks.com/) is gratefully acknowledged.

19. Suetonius, *Julius Caesar* 76; *Res Gestae* 6.

20. For the relevance of this text and its dating, see J. Rufus Fears, *Princeps a Diis Electus: The Divine Election of the Emperor as a Political Concept at Rome*, PMAAR 27 (Rome: American Academy in Rome, 1977), 122 n. 1.

21. Miriam T. Griffin, *Nero: The End of a Dynasty* (London: Routledge, 1984), 95–97.

22. See Suetonius, *Nero* 44-46; Tacitus, *Ann.* 12.69; Dio Cassius, *History of Rome* 60.35; 59.11. Edward Champlin observes that these three historians depended on three earlier sources now lost to us, all of which agreed "without a doubt . . . that Agrippina was behind the murder of her husband," even though variations in detail reveal that in fact "no one *really* knew that happened, who did it, where it was done, or how it was done" (*Nero* [Cambridge, Mass.: Belknap Press of Harvard University Press, 2003], 446).

23. The youth is Nero; he had earlier given a speech on behalf of the citizens of Troy (Suetonius, *Nero* 7).

24. In October of 42 b.c.e., two battles were fought in Philippi as the forces of Mark Antony and Octavian avenged the death of Julius Caesar on his assassins' armies. "Philippis" is thus the poet's term for two tragic battles in which Rome was fighting itself.

25. Suetonius (*Claudius* 29) says that Claudius executed thirty-five senators and three hundred equestrians and makes it clear that Claudius could not keep track of those whom he had ordered to be killed. This piece of propaganda for Nero is claiming that Nero will not repeat any of the abuses of power found in his predecessor Claudius.

26. Nero is likened to the mythical Numa, second king of Rome, since the propagandist here is dissociating Nero from the abuses of the Roman peace practiced by the Julio-Claudian rulers of the late Republic and early Empire.

27. The *fascēs* were a bundle of rods with an ax in the middle that certain Roman officials carried as a sign of their authority to rule. "Empty *fascēs*" is an expression here to criticize past abuses of the system, in which people were given the *fascēs* though they had no right to exercise the power the *fascēs* symbolized. Under the true peace that Nero's reign is bringing, according to the propaganda here, these past abuses will no longer be a problem.

28. Thus, Robert Jewett, for example, characterizes the early years of Nero's rule as exhibiting "an exemplary form of government and law enforcement, despite the profligate personal habits of Nero himself" (*Romans: A Commentary*, Hermeneia [Minneapolis: Fortress Press, 2008], 47–48). Jewett cites Griffin, *Nero*, 111, but Griffin's fuller argument (83–99) is to the opposite effect.

29. Griffin, *Nero*, 84, 86 (her emphasis).

30. "Roman numerals"—like ancient Greek and Hebrew numerals—were letters used as numbers; in Greek, the letters of Nero's full name equaled the sum of the phrase "murdered his own mother."

31. That is, for all his vaunted musical talent Nero is no more "Apollo" than the Parthian—who is actually far more effective with *his* stringed instrument, the bow.

32. A particularly wicked joke. The emperor Gaius had committed incest with his sister Drusilla, then murdered her; a Senator was then bribed to swear that he had seen her assumed bodily into heaven (Dio Cassius, *History of Rome* 69.11). Seneca's implicit joke is that the supposed assumptions of Augustus and Tiberius were just as real.

33. This last phrase is from Virgil, *Georgics* 4.90. The brunt of the joke is Claudius's chronic poor health.

34. Marcus Valerius Messala Corvinus, after recommending that Augustus be given the title "Father of the Fatherland," was appointed prefect of the city in 25 b.c.e., but resigned after six days in office and is famous for the phrase quoted here by Augustus.

35. As Seneca emphasizes in the following paragraphs, Claudius was rather cruel as an emperor, executing many without even the semblance of a trial (Suetonius, *Claudius* 29).

36. Claudius was known for his devotion to ancient customs (Suetonius, *Claudius* 22).

37. Homer, *Il.* 1.591.

38. The challenge is focused on Claudius's slowness and stammer, though we are not sure what specific phrase of three words' length was in view.

39. Catullus 3.12.

40. Saturnalia was the festival in mid-December dedicated to the god Saturn, in which everyone—including masters and slaves—was to switch roles. The valid judges, who could reemerge now that Claudius had died, are describing the thirteen years of his reign as one long Saturnalian upheaval.

41. A reference to King Minos, who ruled all of Crete justly and then became one of the three judges of the underworld.

42. Horace, *Odes* 2.13.35.

43. "Talthybius," herald, is used here for Mercury.

44. Tiberius Claudius Narcissus was famous as one of Claudius's favorite freedman who served as his loyal secretary (Suetonius, *Claudius* 28, 37). He was executed at the instigation of Agrippina (Claudius's widow and mother of the next emperor, Nero) within weeks of Claudius's assassination. Since he was very wealthy, his household may have continued for some years and perhaps the house church mentioned by Paul in Rom 16:11 was composed of slaves and freedmen/women of his household (Jewett, *Romans*, 967–68).

45. This is a play on a common chant in the worship of Osiris.

46. Suetonius mentions how the paranoid Claudius usually required all those visiting him to be frisked, rooms he was entering to be searched, and a bodyguard to accompany him everywhere (*Claudius* 35). The point here is that since he always wanted to be guarded, he ordered some of his subjects to be executed so that they could attend him in hell.

47. Homer, *Il.* 9.385.

48. Aeacus was one of the three judges in Hades. The law mentioned is most probably the *Lex Cornelia de sicariis et veneficiis* (Cornelian law concerning assassins and poisoners), passed in the first century b.c.e., while Rome was still a Republic.

49. A common proverb.

50. Claudius loved to gamble and throw dice (Suetonius, *Claudius* 5, 33).

51. That is, the witnesses report that they had seen Claudius mistreat Gaius, his nephew, in his youth.

52. On irony, see T. L. Carter, "The Irony of Romans 13," *NovT* 46 (2004): 209–28. For a veiled critique of Nero's propaganda, see Neil Elliott, "Romans 13:1-7 in the Context of Imperial Propaganda," in *Paul and Empire: Religion and Power in Roman Imperial Society*, ed. Richard A. Horsley (Harrisburg, Pa.: Trinity Press International, 1997), 184–204.

53. Worshipers of Pan.

54. The reference is to a period of martial law in Rome in 88–82 b.c.e. Sulla marched his Roman army against the city itself; weapons were handed out to slaves; general terror ruled until Sulla reoccupied the city.

55. Lucina was a goddess of fertility. The "Apollo" who is now king is Nero himself.

56. The editor of the LCL translation of the Einsiedeln *Eclogues* suggests that the author may have meant that actual cattle were making a judgment regarding the golden age; more likely he was simply participating in the abusive language common to his circle.

57. See Ramsay MacMullen, *Roman Social Relations, 50 B.C. to A.D. 284* (New Haven: Yale University Press, 1974), 106, 122, and Appendix B; Mark Reasoner, *The Strong and the Weak: Romans 14.1–15.13 in Context*, SNTSMS 103 (Cambridge: Cambridge University Press, 1999), ch. 3.

58. Essential reading here are the essays by Peter Brunt ("*Laus imperii*") and V. Nutton ("The Beneficial Ideology") in P. D. A. Garnsey and C. R. Whittaker, eds., *Imperialism in the Ancient World: The Cambridge University Research Seminar in Ancient History*, Cambridge Classical Studies (Cambridge: Cambridge University Press, 1978).

59. MacMullen, *Roman Social Relations*, 36.

60. Clifford Ando, *Imperial Ideology and Provincial Loyalty in the Roman Empire*, Classics and Contemporary Thought 6 (Berkeley and Los Angeles: University of California Press, 2000), 67.

61. S. R. F. Price, *Rituals and Power: The Roman Imperial Cult in Asia Minor* (Cambridge: Cambridge University Press, 1984), 52. Similarly, see Richard Gordon, "From Republic to Principate: Priesthood, Religion, and Ideology," in *Pagan Priests: Religion and Power in the Ancient World*, ed. Mary Beard and John North (Ithaca, N.Y.: Cornell University Press, 1990), 192; for Greece, see Susan E. Alcock, *Graecia Capta: The Landscapes of Roman Greece* (Cambridge: Cambridge University Press, 1993).

62. G. E. M. de Ste. Croix points out that "provincial governors . . . profited greatly," beyond what the Roman state itself received (*The Class Struggle in the Ancient Greek World: From the Archaic Age to the Arab Conquests* [Ithaca, N.Y.: Cornell University Press, 1980], 346–47).

63. MacMullen, *Roman Social Relations* 34, 37.

64. David L. Balch suggests that the Jewish slaves may have proven so "intractable" as to be useless as slaves and that this may have been "the first case in which slaves did not assume the religion of their masters" in Rome (*Let Wives Be Submissive: The Domestic Code in 1 Peter*, SBLMS 26 [Chico, Calif.: Scholars, 1981], 69). Balch's discussion in part 2 of the book is important for the context of Paul's assemblies.

65. Editor's translation of the chart from Stefan Krauter, *Bürgerrecht und Kultteilnahme: Politische und kultische Rechte und Pflichten in griechischen Poleis, Rom und antikem Judentum*, BZNW 127 (Berlin: Walter de Gruyter, 2004), 291. Persecution in 64 C.E. added by editor.

Chapter Four

1. Alan F. Segal manages to speak of both: *Paul the Convert: The Apostolate and Apostasy of Saul the Pharisee* (New Haven: Yale University Press, 1990).

2. This is one of a number of game-changing arguments raised by Krister Stendahl in *Paul among Jews and Gentiles, and Other Essays* (Philadelphia: Fortress Press, 1976).

3. E. P. Sanders, *Paul and Palestinian Judaism: A Comparison of Patterns of Religion* (Philadelphia: Fortress Press, 1977).

4. Ibid., 552.

5. Ibid., 551.

6. Heikki Räisänen, *Paul and the Law* (Philadelphia: Fortress Press, 1986), 258, 201. Similarly, Segal wrote that Paul's reflections "on his postconversion experience in the gentile community and his career in converting gentiles . . . form the basis of his theology" (*Paul the Convert*, 143).

7. See Pamela Eisenbaum, "Paul, Polemics, and the Problem of Essentialism," *Paul between Jews and Christians*, ed. Mark D. Nanos, special issue of *Biblical Interpretation* 13, no. 3 (2005): 224–38.

8. Classic expositions of the alternatives are Francis Watson, *Paul, Judaism, and the Gentiles: A Sociological Approach*, SNTSMS 56 (Cambridge: Cambridge University Press, 1986), and Mark D. Nanos, *The Mystery of Romans: The Jewish Context of Paul's Letter* (Minneapolis: Fortress Press, 1996); see also William S. Campbell, *Paul and the Creation of Christian Identity*, Library of New Testament Studies (London: T&T Clark, 2008).

9. Theodor Mommsen, *Römische Geschichte*, vol. 5 (Berlin, 1904), ch. 5. See Peter Schäfer, *Judeophobia: Attitudes toward the Jews in the Ancient World* (Cambridge, Mass.: Harvard University Press, 1997), 1.

10. Technically correct: Homer uses *themistes*, not Josephus's *nomos* (so H. St. J. Thackeray, *Josephus*, vol. 1, *The Life. Against Apion*, LCL [Cambridge, Mass.: Harvard University Press, 1926], 355 note a). Thackeray also observes that Apion would have granted Josephus no earlier a date for Moses' lawgiving than the eighth century B.C.E.

11. Though some scholars have assumed that Paul had no use for the temple and its sacrifices, Paula Fredriksen has argued that his reference to *latreia* can mean nothing else; so most recently "Judaizing the Nations: The Ritual Demands of Paul's Gospel," NTS 56 (2010): 232–52.

12. Leonard V. Rutgers, "Roman Policy towards the Jews: Expulsions from the City of Rome during the First Century C.E.," *Classical Antiquity* 13 (1994): 57.

13. See Anders Nygren, *Commentary on Romans*, rev. ed., trans. Carl C. Rasmussen (Philadelphia: Fortress Press, 1949).

14. Philip F. Esler relies on identity theory to explain tensions between Jews and Gentiles in the Roman world (*Conflict and Identity in Romans: The Social Setting of Paul's Letter* [Minneapolis: Fortress Press, 2003]). See also Schäfer, *Judeophobia*; and John G. Gager, *The Origins of Anti-Semitism: Attitudes toward Judaism in Pagan and Christian Antiquity* (New York: Oxford University Press, 1983).

15. Rutgers, "Roman Policy," 59, 66.

16. Ibid., 67, 69, 74.

17. See Suetonius, *Tiberius* 36; Josephus, *Ant.* 18.63; Philo, *Embassy* 159–61. Rutgers expresses doubts about Dio Cassius's reference, 57.18.5 ("Roman Policy," 62–63).

18. Philo, *Flacc.*, esp. 102, 116–24, 146. See Neil Elliott, *The Arrogance of Nations: Reading Romans in the Shadow of Empire*, Paul in Critical Contexts (Minneapolis: Fortress Press, 2008), 72–85.

19. E. Mary Smallwood, *The Jews under Roman Rule: From Pompey to Diocletian*, Studies in Judaism in Late Antiquity 20 (Leiden: Brill, 1976), 240; Schäfer, *Judeophobia*, 140.

20. For discussion of the issues, see Peter Lampe, *From Paul to Valentinus: Christians at Rome in the First Two Centuries*, trans. Michael Steinhauser, ed. Marshall D. Johnson (Minneapolis: Fortress Press, 2003), 11–16.

21. H. Dixon Slingerland, *Claudian Policymaking and the Early Imperial Repression of Judaism at Rome*, South Florida Studies in the History of Judaism 160 (Atlanta: Scholars, 1997).

22. See Josephus, *Ag. Ap.* 2.7, 9 (Diodorus, Mnaseas); Plutarch, *Quaest. conv.* 4.5. Kauffmann Kohler and Samuel Kraus discuss possible origins of the slander including Egyptian worship of Typhon and later Gnostic exegesis: "Ass-Worship," *Jewish Encyclopedia*, online at http://www.jewishencyclopedia.com/view.jsp?artid=2027&letter=A.

23. Paul is contrasted with the Zealots by Marcus Borg, "A New Context for Romans 13," NTS 19 (1972–73): 205–18; with "competitive zeal," in both Roman and Jewish Zealot forms, by Robert Jewett, *Romans: A Commentary*, Hermeneia (Minneapolis: Fortress Press, 2007, passim). Richard A. Horsley argued against Josephus's artificial fusion of the early uprising by Judas and Saddok with the later Zealot movement: *Jesus and the Spiral of Violence: Popular Jewish Resistance in Roman Palestine* (New York: Harper & Row, 1987).

24. On the problems of dating rabbinic materials and even of identifying the rabbis quoted, see H. L. Strack and G. Stemberger, *Introduction to the Talmud and Midrash*, trans. Markus Bockmuehl (Minneapolis: Fortress Press, 1992), ch. 6.

25. See J. Andrew Overman, "The First Jewish Revolt and Flavian Policy," in *The First Jewish Revolt: Archaeology, History, and Ideology*, ed. Andrea M. Berlin and J. Andrew Overman (New York: Routledge, 2002), 213–20.

26. See Saul M. Olyan, "The Israelites Debate Their Options at the Sea of Reeds: *LAB* 10:3, Its Parallels, and Pseudo-Philo's Ideology and Background," *JBL* 110 (1991): 75–91; Doron Mendels, "Pseudo-Philo's *Biblical Antiquities*, the 'Fourth Philosophy,' and the Political Messianism of the First Century C.E.," in *The Messiah: Developments in Earliest Judaism and Christianity*, ed. J. H. Charlesworth et al. (Minneapolis: Fortress Press, 1992), 261–75; Neil Elliott, *Liberating Paul: The Justice of God and the Politics of the Apostle* (Maryknoll, N.Y.: Orbis, 1994), 156–59.

27. Florentino García Martínez, *The Dead Sea Scrolls Translated: The Qumran Texts in English*, 2nd ed. (Leiden: Brill; Grand Rapids: Eerdmans, 1992), 199; Michael Wise, Martin G. Abegg Jr., and Edward M. Cook, *The Dead Sea Scrolls: A New Translation*, rev. and updated ed. (New York: HarperSanFrancisco, 2005).

28. See Neil Elliott, "The 'Patience of the Jews': Strategies of Resistance and Accommodation to Imperial Cultures," in *Pauline Conversations in Context: Essays in Honor of Calvin J. Roetzel*, ed. Janice Capel Anderson, Philip Sellew, and Claudia Setzer, JSNTSup 221 (Sheffield: Sheffield Academic Press, 2002), 32–41; idem, *Arrogance of Nations*, 36–37.

29. Ernst Käsemann, "The 'Righteousness of God' in Paul," in idem, *New Testament Questions of Today*, trans. W. J. Montague (Philadelphia: Fortress Press, 1969), 168–82.

30. A reference to reason, will, and the appetites.

31. Werner Georg Kümmel, *Römer 7 und die Bekehrung des Paulus*, Untersuchungen zum Neuen Testament 17 (Leipzig: Hinrichs, 1929).

32. Nils A. Dahl, "Missionary Theology in Romans," in idem, *Studies in Paul: Theology for the Early Christian Mission* (Minneapolis: Augsburg, 1977), 70–94.

33. See Stanley K. Stowers, *A Rereading of Romans: Justice, Jews, and Gentiles* (New Haven: Yale University Press, 1994), 264–84.

34. Besides the works cited below, see Hermann Lichtenberger, *Das Ich Adams und das Ich der Menschheit: Studien zum Menschenbild in Römer 7*, WUNT 164 (Tübingen: Mohr Siebeck, 2004).

35. Niko Huttenen argues that, although they use similar terminology, Paul and Epictetus actually diagnose the problem besetting humans differently. "Paul's 'I' groans about contradiction between the right will and the distorted world. Epictetus' 'I' bemoans the contradiction between the distorted will and the right world, where there is nothing really bad, no rule of sin, but rule of God." The resolution to the inner struggle is also different: "Epictetus advises us to adjust our will to accept everything in the world, even death (e.g. *Diatr.* 2.6.11-19; 4.1.103-106). For Paul, this advice is as bad as possible. We should never adjust to this evil world, which is ruled by sin and death (Rom 5:12-15; 7:5, 13, 14)." For Paul, further, the resolution to the struggle comes from being baptized into Christ, which brings forgiveness of sins and the defeat of the power of sin through the resurrection life of Christ (Rom 6:3-11). See Niko Huttenen, "The Human Contradiction: Epictetus and Romans 7," in *Lux Humana, Lux Aeterna: Essays on Biblical and Related Themes in Honour of Lars Aejmelaeus*, ed. Antti Mustakallio, Heikki Leppä, and Heikki Räisänen, Publications of the Finnish Exegetical Society 89 (Helsinki: Finnish Exegetical Society; Göttingen: Vandenhoeck & Ruprecht, 2005), 326, 327.

36. Markus Barth, *Ephesians: Introduction, Translation, and Commentary*, 2 vols., Anchor Bible 34, 34A (Garden City, N.Y.: Doubleday, 1974), 2244–48; Lloyd Gaston, *Paul and the Torah* (Vancouver: University of British Columbia Press, 1987), 25 and passim.

37. Paul uses the phrase "works of the Law" in Gal 2:16; 3:2, 5, 10; Rom 3:20, 28. See Martin Abegg, "Paul, 'Works of the Law' and MMT," *BAR* 20, no. 6 (1994): 52–55; J. D. G. Dunn, "4QMMT and Galatians," in idem, *The New Perspective on Paul*, rev. ed. (Grand Rapids: Eerdmans, 2008), 339–46.

38. Brackets [ ] indicate letters and words that have been worn off the scroll, reconstructed from other copies of the document and from the context. Parentheses ( ) indicate words supplied to provide the sense of the text. Blank indicates a space on the scroll that the scribe appears to have intentionally left empty. Braces {} indicate letters present on the scroll that should be deleted for understanding.

39. Sanders, *Paul and Palestinian Judaism*, 409–12; see also Bruce W. Longenecker, *Eschatology and the Covenant: A Comparison of 4 Ezra and Romans 1–11* (Sheffield: JSOT Press, 1992).

40. The discussion of texts here follows John J. Collins, "Before the Fall: The Earliest Interpretations of Adam and Eve," in *The Idea of Biblical Interpretation: Essays in Honor of James L. Kugel*, ed. Hindy Najman and Judith H. Newman, JSJSup 83 (Leiden: Brill, 2004), 296–301. Ben Sira's description of Adam as originally created mortal is found also in James L. Kugel, *Traditions of the Bible: A Guide to the Bible as It Was at the Start of the Common Era* (Cambridge, Mass.: Harvard University Press, 1998), 127.

41. Collins considers the last verse an allusion to Deut 30:1 ("Before the Fall," 299). It is because of this allusion that he can claim that Sirach views the human as possessing the Torah at creation.

42. Gaston, *Paul and the Torah*, ch. 2, citing *Mekilta Bahodesh* 5; *Lamentations Rabbah* 3:1; *b. Šabbat* 88b; *Exodus Rabbah* 5:9; *Tosefta Soṭah* 8:6; *b. Soṭah* 35b.

43. See Gaston, *Paul and the Torah*, 38–39.

Chapter Five

1. Nils A. Dahl, "Missionary Theology in Romans," in *Studies in Paul: Theology for the Early Christian Mission* (Minneapolis: Augsburg, 1977), 73.

2. *LSAM* 12.3, quoted in Martin Vahrenhorst, *Kultische Sprache in den Paulusbriefen*, WUNT 1.230 (Tübingen: Mohr Siebeck, 2008), 88, and dated to 133 b.c.e.

3. *LSCG Suppl* 54.1, quoted in Vahrenhorst, *Kultische Sprache*, 88, and dated to the first century b.c.e.

4. *LSAM* 12, quoted in Vahrenhorst, *Kultische Sprache*, 90, and located in Pergamon around 133 b.c.e.

5. A passage from the Babylonian Talmud (*b. B.Meṣi'a* 59b) is often adduced in this connection. In a rabbinic dispute R. Eliezer "brought forward every imaginable argument," but without convincing his colleagues. He began to invoke nature around him—"If the *halachah* agrees with me, let this carob-tree prove it!" —"Let this stream of water prove it!" —"Let the walls of this schoolhouse prove it!" Astounding prodigies follow, but these fail to convince. At last R. Eliezer cried out, "'If the *halachah* agrees with me, let it be proved from Heaven!" Whereupon a heavenly voice cried out: 'Why do ye dispute with R. Eliezer, seeing that in all matters the *halachah* agrees with him!' But R. Joshua arose and exclaimed: 'It is not in heaven.' What did he mean by this? Said R. Jeremiah: 'That the Torah had already been given at Mount Sinai; we pay no attention to a heavenly voice, because Thou hast long since written in the Torah at Mount Sinai, 'After the majority must one incline.'"

6. So Paula Fredriksen, *From Jesus to Christ: The Origins of the New Testament Images of Jesus*, 2nd ed. (New Haven: Yale University Press, 2000), 142–56.

7. Jacob Neusner, *From Politics to Piety: The Emergence of Pharisaic Judaism*, 2nd ed. (New York: Ktav, 1979).

8. *CIL* IV 1796, translation from Antonio Varone, *Erotica Pompeiana: Love Inscriptions on the Walls of Pompeii*, trans. Ria P. Berg, Studia archaeological 116 (Rome: "L'erma" di Bretschneider, 2002), 20.

9. *CIL* IV 4637, translation from Varone, *Erotica Pompeiana*, 44.

10. *CIL* IV 1863, translation from Varone, *Erotica Pompeiana*, 155.

11. *CIL* ix.2689; *ILS* 7478.

12. The question has received sustained attention from Peter Oakes, *Reading Romans in Pompeii: Paul's Letter at Ground Level* (Minneapolis: Fortress Press, 2009).

13. Bruce W. Winter, *After Paul Left Corinth: The Influence of Secular Ethics and Social Change* (Grand Rapids: Eerdmans, 2001), 82–93.

14. The name of this dialogue is sometimes given as *Dialogii Meretricii, Courtesan's Dialogues,* or *Prostitute's Conversations.*

15. Susan T. Treggiari, *Roman Marriage: Iusti coniuges from the Time of Cicero to the Time of Ulpian* (Oxford: Clarendon, 1991), 315.

16. Bruce W. Winter, *Roman Wives, Roman Widows: The Appearance of New Women and the Pauline Communities* (Grand Rapids: Eerdmans, 2003), 40.

17. Karl Galinsky comments that the "traditional explanation," that Augustus sought to increase the Roman birthrate "has rightly come to be considered as extraneous and been largely discounted" (*Augustan Culture: An Interpretive Introduction* [Princeton: Princeton University Press, 1996], 128). Galinsky emphasizes the innovative aspect of the legislation—"Greek and Roman writers were quite specific that in a true Golden Age good moral conduct happened of its own accord and needed no legislative remedy" (129)—as evidence that the legislation was, at last, about Augustus himself.

18. Antoinette Clark Wire, *The Corinthian Women Prophets: A Reconstruction through Paul's Rhetoric* (Minneapolis: Fortress Press, 1990).

19. Winter regards the Augustan legislation as the primary context for these texts in Paul's letters (*Roman Wives, Roman Widows*), 47–49.

20. Will Deming, *Paul on Marriage and Celibacy: The Hellenistic Background of 1 Corinthians 7,* 2nd ed. (Grand Rapids: Eerdmans, 2004).

21. See Winter, *Roman Wives, Roman Widows,* 47–49.

22. Winter, *After Paul Left Corinth,* 44–57.

23. David L. Balch suggests that the Jewish slaves may have proven so "intractable" as to be useless as slaves and that this may have been "the first case in which slaves did not assume the religion of their masters" in Rome (*Let Wives Be Submissive: The Domestic Code in 1 Peter,* SBLMS 26 [Chico, Calif.: Scholars, 1981], 69). Balch's discussion in part 2 of the book is important for the context of Paul's assemblies.

24. Reasoner's translation of the chart from Stefan Krauter, *Bürgerrecht und Kultteilnahme: Politische und kultische Rechte und Pflichten in griechischen Poleis, Rom und antikem Judentum,* BZNW 127 (Berlin: Walter de Gruyter, 2004), 291. Persecution in 64 c.e. added by editor.

25. Robert Jewett has noticed that the command to offer a holy kiss occurs in letters where the congregation has been divided (*Romans: A Commentary,* Hermeneia [Minneapolis: Fortress Press, 2008], 973–74). Paul's command serves as a countercultural challenge for people who would normally not touch one another to live out their identity as equal members in the family of God. It is most probable that the kiss was from mouth to mouth, and performed not only man to man and woman to woman, which would be culturally acceptable, but also man to woman. Paul's qualification of the kiss as "holy" seems to be his way of guarding against the abuse of this kiss toward unholy intimacy. A text such as 1 Thess 4:3-12 shows how Paul can warn against fornication while simultaneously arguing for love among the members of the believing community.

26. Abraham J. Malherbe, *Paul and the Thessalonians: The Philosophic Tradition of Pastoral Care* (Philadelphia: Fortress Press, 1987).

27. On the text and the difficulties of assigning it to a particular provenance or date, see George W. E. Nickelsburg, *Jewish Literature between the Bible and the Mishnah: A Historical and Literary Introduction,* 2nd ed. (Minneapolis: Fortress Press, 2005), 332–38.

28. So Louis H. Feldman and Meyer Reinhold understand the reference to *patella*[?]. *Patella,* "dish," might refer to "a dish used for the daily collection of cooked food for the poor" (*Jewish Life and Thought among Greeks and Romans: Primary Readings* [Minneapolis: Fortress Press, 1996], 142 n. 9). Angelos Chaniotis notes that *patellas* designates fast-food sellers; the

inscription might refer to a professional association of cooks (who might also have organized relief efforts): see "Godfearers in the City of Love," *BAR* 36, no. 3 (2010): 39–40.

29. See also Joyce Reynolds and Robert Tannenbaum, *Jews and God-Fearers at Aphrodisias: Greek Inscriptions with Commentary* (Cambridge: Cambridge Philological Society, 1987), 5–7. The inscription continues on another side; both sides together present more than fifty-five Jews (as well as several men with Hebrew names who are identified as "proselytes," perhaps indicating they had adopted Hebrew names upon conversion), and fifty-four God-fearers (*theosebeis*).

30. Elisabeth Schüssler Fiorenza, "Rhetorical Situation and Historical Reconstruction in 1 Corinthians," *NTS* 33 (1987): 386–403.

31. Bruce W. Winter, *Seek the Welfare of the City: Christians as Benefactors and Citizens*, First-century Christians in the Graeco-Roman World (Grand Rapids: Eerdmans, 1994).

32. Trajan's word *hetaeria* can mean either a political or religious group.

33. John H. D'Arms, "Slaves at Roman *Convivia*," in *Dining in a Classical Context*, ed. William J. Slater (Ann Arbor: University of Michigan Press, 1991), 174–75, 177.

34. Norman R. Peterson, *Rediscovering Paul: Philemon and the Sociology of Paul's Narrative World* (Philadelphia: Fortress Press, 1985), 135; see also Neil Elliott, *Liberating Paul: The Justice of God and the Politics of the Apostle* (Maryknoll, N.Y.: Orbis, 1994), 40–52.

35. Alan Booth, "The Age for Reclining and Its Attendant Perils," in *Dining in a Classical Context*, 105.

36. D'Arms, "Slaves at Roman Convivia," 173, 176.

37. Scintilla is the wife of Trimalchio's friend Habinnas. Fortunata and Scintilla had been cuddling and kissing on a couch earlier at the meal (*Satyricon* 67).

38. Yung-Suk Kim, *Christ's Body in Corinth: The Politics of a Metaphor*, Paul in Critical Contexts (Minneapolis: Fortress Press, 2009).

39. Margaret M. Mitchell, *Paul and the Rhetoric of Reconciliation: An Exegetical Investigation of the Language and Composition of 1 Corinthians* (Louisville: Westminster John Knox, 1993).

40. Quoted in C. F. D. Moule, *The Origin of Christology* (Cambridge: Cambridge University Press, 1977), 85.

41. When the plebeian fighting force withdrew from Rome in protest, with no weapons, leaving the city vulnerable to attack, the city was dangerously divided between the noble patricians and the lower ranking plebeians.

42. J. D. G. Dunn (*Romans 9–16*, WBC 38B [Dallas: Word, 1988], 722) makes the connection to the section from Livy. The story of the human body's revolt against the belly may also be found in Xenophon, *Mem.* 2.3.18 and in Cicero, *Of.* 3.5.22.

43. See Gordon Zerbe's taxonomy of approaches to "Paul's politics" in "The Politics of Paul: His Supposed Social Conservatism and the Impact of Postcolonial Readings," *Conrad Grebel Review* 21 (2003): 82–103, reprinted in *The Colonized Apostle: Paul in Postcolonial Perspectives*, ed. Christopher D. Stanley, Paul in Critical Contexts (Minneapolis: Fortress Press, 2011).

Chapter Six

1. George Bourne, *A Condensed Anti-Slavery Bible Argument* (New York: S. W. Benedict, 1845), 82, as quoted in Allen Dwight Callahan, *Embassy of Onesimus: The Letter of Paul to Philemon*, NTIC (Valley Forge, Pa.: Trinity Press International 1997), 11.

2. John Gregg Fee, *An Anti-Slavery Manual* (Mayville, Ky., 1848; repr., New York: Arno, 1969), 112, as quoted in Callahan, *Embassy of Onesimus*, 11.

3. Albert J. Raboteau, *Slave Religion: The "Invisible Institution" in the Antebellum South* (New York: Oxford University Press, 1978), 162.

4. This quotation was taken from Raboteau, *Slave Religion*, 162–63, quoting Mason Crum, *Gullah: Negro Life in the Carolina Sea Islands* (Durham, N.C.: Duke University Press, 1940), 204–5, quoting Charles Colcock Jones, *A Catechism for Colored Persons* (1834; italics original).

5. Tenth Annual Report, Liberty County Association (1845), 24–25, as quoted in Raboteau, *Slave Religion*, 294 (italics original).

6. Raboteau, *Slave Religion*, 295, citing Lewis and Milton Clarke, *Narratives of Lewis and Milton Clarke* (Boston, 1846), 105.

7. See, among other studies, Amos Jones, *Paul's Message of Freedom: What Does It Mean to the Black Church?* (Valley Forge, Pa.: Judson, 1984); and the following articles in *Slavery in Text and Interpretation*, Semeia 83/84 (1998): Richard A. Horsley, "Paul and Slavery: A Critical Alternative to Recent Readings," 153–200; Clarice J. Martin, "'Somebody Done Hoodoo'd the Hoodoo Man': Language, Power, Resistance, and the Effective History of Pauline Texts in American Slavery," 203–33; Allen Dwight Callahan, "'Brother Saul': An Ambivalent Witness to Freedom," 235–50; Abraham Smith, "Putting Paul Back Together Again: William Wells Brown's *Clotel* and Black Abolitionist Approaches to Paul," 251–62.

8. See the "Kairos" statements collected in Robert McAfee Brown, ed., *Kairos: Three Prophetic Challenges to the Church* (Grand Rapids: Eerdmans, 1990), and the discussion in Neil Elliott, *Liberating Paul: The Justice of God and the Politics of the Apostle* (Maryknoll, N.Y.: Orbis, 1994), ch. 1.

9. Among other works, see Elsa Tamez, *The Amnesty of Grace: Justification by Faith from a Latin American Perspective*, trans. Sharon H. Ringe (Nashville: Abingdon, 1993); Jon Sobrino, *No Salvation Outside the Poor: Prophetic-Utopian Essays* (Maryknoll, N.Y.: Orbis, 2008).

10. Ignacio Ellacuría, "The Church of the Poor, Historical Sacrament of Liberation," in *Mysterium Liberationis: Fundamental Concepts of Liberation Theology*, ed. Ignacio Ellacuría and Jon Sobrino (Maryknoll, N.Y.: Orbis, 1993), 547.

11. There is space here only to name a few of many important works: Daniel Boyarin, *A Radical Jew: Paul and the Politics of Identity*, Contraversions 1 (Berkeley and Los Angeles: University of California Press, 1994); Amy-Jill Levine, ed., *A Feminist Companion to Paul* (Cleveland: Pilgrim, 2004); Kwok Pui-lan, *Postcolonial Imagination and Feminist Theology* (Louisville: Westminster John Knox, 2005); Elisabeth Schüssler Fiorenza, *The Power of the Word: Scripture and the Rhetoric of Empire* (Minneapolis: Fortress Press, 2007); and Joseph A. Marchal, *The Politics of Heaven: Women, Gender, and Empire in the Study of Paul*, Paul in Critical Contexts (Minneapolis: Fortress Press, 2008).

12. See, for example, David L. Dungan, *Constantine's Bible: Politics and the Making of the New Testament* (Minneapolis: Fortress Press, 2006); Bruce M. Metzger, *The Canon of the New Testament: Its Origin, Development, and Significance* (New York: Oxford University Press, 1997).

13. M. R. James says that the oldest copy of this letter is from a manuscript written in 546 (*The Apocryphal New Testament* [1924; repr., Oxford: Clarendon, 1955], 478). Richard I. Pervo suggests that the letter has not received the respect it deserves; it "is neither jejune nor disorganized. The author selected elements of what is arguably Paul's most beautiful epistle"— Philippians—"to present a brief guide to the apostle's message" (*The Making of Paul: Constructions of the Apostle in Early Christianity* [Minneapolis: Fortress Press, 2010], 109).

14. Wilhelm Schneemelcher, "Second and Third Century Apocryphal Acts of Apostles: Introduction," in *New Testament Apocrypha*, by Edgar Hennecke, ed. Wilhelm Schneemelcher, English trans. ed. R. McL. Wilson, rev. ed. (Louisville: Westminster John Knox, 1991, 1992), 2:76–77. See also Pervo, *Making of Paul*, 156–64.

15. Wilhelm Schneemelcher, "Acts of Paul," in Schneemelcher, *New Testament Apocrypha*, 2:214–15.

16. Ibid., 231–35.

17. Pervo, *Making of Paul*, 163–64. The early opponents of the "New Prophecy" scorned it as "Montanism," suggesting that Priscilla and Maximilla were not prophets in their own right but devotees of Montanus.

18. See A. Kurfess, "The Apocryphal Correspondence between Seneca and Paul," in *New Testament Apocrypha* (Philadelphia: Westminster, 1965), 2:133–41. In the revised edition of the same work Cornelia Römer recognizes the more modest suggestion that the letters may have begun as a writing exercise: "The Correspondence between Seneca and Paul" (Louisville: Westminster John Knox, 2003), 46–53.

19. Pervo, *Making of Paul*, 115.

20. Ibid., 113.

21. Perhaps an allusion to Seneca's book *De Beneficiis*.

22. The observant Jew Poppaea Sabina was a wife of Nero. See also letter 8 below.

23. Note that the heading for this letter, though from Paul, has placed Paul's name after Seneca's. See 1 Cor 9:20-22; Rom 13:7.

24. M. R. James dates this to 58 c.e. (*Apocryphal New Testament*, 483).

25. M. R. James dates this to 59 c.e. (*Apocryphal New Testament*, 483).

26. M. R. James dates this to 64 c.e. (*Apocryphal New Testament*, 484), and the reference to the fire in Rome also confirms this. See Tacitus, *Ann.* 15.44.

27. According to James, these names are not attested in the list of consuls.

28. Pervo, *Making of Paul*, 134–39.

29. Elaine Pagels, *The Gnostic Paul: Gnostic Exegesis of the Pauline Letters* (Philadelphia: Fortress Press, 1975).

30. For the other *Apocalypse of Paul*, see Schneemelcher, *New Testament Apocrypha*, rev. ed., 2:712–47.

31. Antoinette Clark Wire, *The Corinthian Women Prophets: A Reconstruction through Paul's Rhetoric* (Minneapolis: Fortress Press, 1990).

32. This is the argument of Dennis R. MacDonald, *The Legend and the Apostle: The Battle for Paul in Story and Canon* (Philadelphia: Westminster, 1983). On the *Acts of Paul (and Thekla)*, see Schneemelcher, *New Testament Apocrypha*, rev. ed., 2:220–22; Pervo, *Making of Paul*, 156–64; Shelly Matthews, "Thinking of Thecla: Issues in Feminist Historiography," *JFSR* 17 (2002): 39–65.

33. For a description of how the Antioch material differs from the Iconium material in the *Acts of Thekla* and hence points to different authors, see Elisabeth Esch-Wermeling, *Thekla—Paulusschülerin wider Willen? Strategien der Leserlenkung in den Theklaakten*, Neutestamentliche Abhandlungen 53 (Münster: Aschendorff, 2008).

34. According to the *Acts of Titus*, Paul sent Titus ahead to let people know in each city Paul would visit that he was coming. See Richard I. Pervo, "The 'Acts of Titus': A Preliminary Translation with an Introduction, Notes and Appendices," in *Society of Biblical Literature: Seminar Papers 1996*, Number 35 (Atlanta: Scholars, 1996), 455–82.

35. The mother's reaction may seem harsh to contemporary readers; it shows the importance in Roman society of a family's honor, which in this case Thekla has violated by her unseemly conduct with Paul.

36. Note a novelistic representation of what we know from later Christianity as a church "order" of virgins; Paul holds Thekla back from taking so drastic a vow until it is "time."

37. See Gal 2:10; Rom 15:25-26.

38. Pervo, *Making of Paul*, 161.

39. Ibid., 163.

40. On the textual question in 1 Cor 14:34-35, see Antoinette Clark Wire, *Corinthian Women Prophets*, 229–32; and more recently Philip B. Payne, "Fuldensis, Sigla for Variants in Vaticanus, and 1 Cor. 14:34-35," *NTS* 41 (1995): 240–62.

41. On the ambiguity of 1 Cor 7:21 and the questionable, though ubiquitous, translation of *klēsis* as "station in life," see S. Scott Bartchy, *Mallon Chrēsai: First-Century Slavery and the Interpretation of 1 Corinthians 7:21*, SBLDS 11 (Missoula, Mont.: Scholars, 1973).

42. See Peter Brown, *Augustine of Hippo: A Biography* (Berkeley and Los Angeles: University of California Press, 1967), chapter 10.

43. In both Greek and Roman contexts, these instruments were sometimes played by women to prepare people in their audience for lovemaking. An expected time for the women who played these instruments to appear would be near the end of the meal at a dinner party or banquet.

44. This appears to be a frame enclosing Isa 41:1—45:17. Not only was Isaiah 40–55 popular, but doubtless also the reference to "islands" makes this text appropriate. For the reading of Isaiah in religious quests, see Acts 8:26-39.

45. Acts 2:11 was for the author of the *Acts of Tuti* a godsend, in several senses of that word: "Cretans and Arabs."

46. Another sister, Euphemia, appears in chapter 10. She died a virgin.

47. This recommendation of prudent conduct might possibly be inspired by the *Acts of Paul*, where the governor of Ephesus does not reject Paul's critique of idols but finds it irrelevant.

48. This summary episode appears to imitate incidents common in *Acts of Paul* and other apocryphal *Acts*. The nocturnal setting is motivated by a desire for secrecy rather than by circumstances like those of Acts 20:7-12.

49. Three months: cf. Acts 19:8 (Ephesus) and 20:3 (Greece).

50. The lion could be derived from 1 Cor 15:32 or *Acts of Paul* 7.

51. The author derived the mission of Timothy and Erastus from Acts 19:22, where they are sent to Macedonia. 2 Timothy 4:20 deposits Erastus at Corinth. 2 Corinthians 2:13; 7:6, and chapter 8 relate Titus to Macedonia. Association of journeys mentioned in Acts with the delivery of Pauline correspondence cannot readily be dismissed as crude harmonization, since it is a conjectural procedure that continues to enjoy scholarly favor.

52. The ministry of Luke in Achaea is based upon traditions independent of *Acts of Paul*. One example of this tradition is the "old Gospel Prologue" that states Luke died in Boeotia at age 84. This may be read in K. Aland, ed., *Synopsis Quattuor Evangeliorum* (Stuttgart: Württembergische Bibelanstalt, 1964), 533, and in many introductions to Luke and Acts. The Monarchian Prologue assigns the place of his death to Bithynia (ibid., 547), with almost identical surrounding words (in Latin).

53. New Testament scholars might be tempted to see here a suggestion of the postmortem delivery of Colossians (Col 1:1). In any case Titus, Timothy, and Luke continue the work of the martyred apostle.

54. These data could be derived from the Pastoral Epistles: Ephesus for Timothy in 1 Tim 1:3, and Crete as Titus's base in Titus 1:5.

55. Paul is depicted as conversing with the patriarchs in Hebrew in *Acts of Paul* (*Mart.* 5).

56. Psalm 67 [LXX 66], appropriate because of its references to Gentiles as offering praise to God.

57. This chapter has some affinities with *Acts of John* 42.

58. This text has evidently abbreviated a lengthy account of the humiliation of Artemis. Another version represents a considerable improvement, with substantial dialogue at the climax of which the idol is pulverized at Titus's invocation of Christ's name. It is possible that this edition is closer to the original. In any case experienced readers of hagiography can easily fill in the blanks, as the author of the saint's life expected them to do.

59. This abrupt reference to Titus's lifestyle constitutes another indicator of abbreviation.

60. The Roman general Titus assumed command from his father Vespasian, who had departed in a successful quest for the principate. Thus Titus is the general credited with the capture of Jerusalem.

61. This part of the *Acts* is a legend explaining how the site of a former pagan temple became a healing shrine of St. Titus. The relative fullness of this account indicates that this incident expresses a leading concern of the text.

62. This may be a transformation of the legends surrounding Julian's efforts to rebuild the Temple at Jerusalem.

63. The departing Titus echoes the words of his master, Paul (2 Tim 4:7), the latter's charge (Acts 20:28), and the words of his savior (Luke 23:46).

64. The text presumably means that healed demoniacs have left their former chains as ex-voto offerings and attestations.

65. The relics of Titus were removed to St. Mark's, Venice, following the Arab capture of Crete in 823 and not returned to the island until 1968, according to G. Dragas ("Titus," *The Encyclopedia of Early Christianity*, ed. E. Ferguson et al. [New York: Garland, 1990], 903–5, esp. 904). That same page contains a photograph of the remains of a possibly sixth-century Church of St. Titus at Gortyna. For a more detailed description of this building, see M. Falla Castelfranchi, "Crete," *Encyclopedia of the Early Church*, ed. A. Di Beradino, trans. A. Walford (New York: Oxford University Press, 1992), 1:209.

66. In this pious, chronological summing up it seems to have been appropriate to omit his delay of nine years between initial call and actual departure. It is difficult to reconcile the data in this chapter with the chronology given in chapter 2, which, if cumulative, yields twelve years before the death of Stephen, or seven, if counted from a single starting point. Seven may be correct if one presumes that Paul labored for three years before Titus was ordained to be his assistant. The fourteen (plus three?) years of Gal 2:1 could scarcely be the basis of these calculations.

67. This clause apparently refers to Titus's labor as a companion of Paul.

68. The explanatory notes and internal textual references in this excerpt are the editors' selection of the extensive notes provided by Pervo, with slight alterations.

69. For a plot summary, see J. B. Lightfoot, *The Apostolic Fathers*, part 1, *Clement*, vol. 1 (1890; repr., Grand Rapids: Baker, 1981), 14–16; reprinted in Pervo, *Making of Paul*, 177–84. Sometimes this literature is called "Pseudo-Clementine" but, as Pervo points out, it is not pseudepigraphic—no Christian Clement is being impostured. "Clementine" and "Pseudo-Clementine" refer to the same pieces of literature—the *Recognitions* and *Homilies*.

70. For a survey of the various reconstructions of how the Clementine literature is related to Jewish Christianity, see F. Stanley Jones, *An Ancient Jewish Christian Source on the History of Christianity: Pseudo-Clementine Recognitions 1.27-71*, SBLTT 37, Christian Apocrypha Series 2 (Atlanta: Scholars, 1995), 1–38.

71. Ibid., 166.

72. Pervo, *Making of Paul*, 180.

73. Ibid., 182–83.

74. On the unique circumstances of Nero's persecution, see W. H. C. Frend, *Martyrdom and Persecution in the Early Church* (Oxford: Blackwell, 1965), 165–71; on the mythic and dramatic aspects of Nero's "performance" of the persecution, see Brigitte Kahl, *Galatians Re-Imagined: Reading with the Eyes of the Vanquished*, Paul in Critical Contexts (Minneapolis: Fortress Press, 2010), epilogue.

75. Pervo, *Making of Paul*, 138–39; Paul Duff, "Metaphor, Motif, and Meaning: The Rhetorical Strategy Behind the Image 'Led in Triumph' in 2 Cor 2:14," *CBQ* 53 (1991): 79–92.

76. Luise Schottroff, "'Give to Caesar What Belongs to Caesar and to God What Belongs to God': A Theological response of the Early Christian Church to Its Social and Political Environment," in *The Love of Enemy and Nonretaliation in the New Testament*, ed. Willard M. Swartley (Louisville: Westminster John Knox, 1992), 226, citing K. H. Schelkle, "Staat und Kirche in der patristischen Auslegung von Röm 13,1-7," *ZNW* 44 (1952–53): 223–26.

77. Schottroff, "Give to Caesar," 227.

78. Henry Chadwick ("St. Peter and St. Paul in Rome: The Problem of the *Memoria Apostolorum ad Catacumbas*," *JTS* n.s. 8 [1957]: 34) writes that "a belief that the shrine on the Via Appia had in time past possessed the actual remains of the apostles is presupposed by the only really probable interpretation of the famous metrical inscription of Pope Damasus in the Basilica Apostolorum."

79. Baptism.

LIST OF TRANSLATIONS

In places where no other translation information is specified, the editors have provided their own translation.

Acts of Paul

No. 193: *3 Corinthians.* M. R. James, ed. and trans., *The Apocryphal New Testament* (Oxford: Clarendon, 1955), 480–84.

No. 202: *Acts of Paul and Thekla.* Translation by Mark Reasoner.

No. 208: *Acts of Titus.* Richard I. Pervo, "The 'Acts of Titus': A Preliminary Translation with Introduction, Notes and Appendices," in *SBL Seminar Papers 1996* (Atlanta: Scholars, 1996), 455–82. The translation and notes are gratefully used with the permission of Richard I. Pervo and the Society of Biblical Literature.

No. 221: *Martyrdom of the Holy Apostle Paul.* Translation by Mark Reasoner of the Greek text "Martyrdom of the Holy Apostle Paul," as found in R. A. Lipsius, ed., *Acta Apostolorum Apocrypha I* (New York: Georg Olms, 1972), 104–17.

Acts of the Scillitan Martyrs

No. 219: Translation by J. A. Robinson, online at http://www.earlychristian writings.com/text/scillitan.html.

Apocalypse of Paul. *See under* **Nag Hammadi Documents**

Apuleius

No. 71: Apuleius, *Metamorphoses* 11.4. *Apuleius, Metamorphoses (The Golden Ass)*, vol. 2, *Books 7–11*, ed. and trans. J. Arthur Hanson, LCL (Cambridge, Mass.: Harvard University Press, 1989).

Aristobulus. *See* **Eusebius**

Aristotle

No. 3: *Eudemian Ethics* 1241b12-24. *Aristotle*, vol. 20, *The Athenian Constitution, The Eudemian Ethics, On Virtues and Vices*, trans. H. Rackham, LCL (Cambridge, Mass.: Harvard University Press, 1952).

No. 185: *Politics* 1.2.3. *Aristotle*, vol. 21, *Politics*, trans. H. Rackham, LCL (London: William Heinemann, 1932).

Arrian. *See* Epictetus

Ascents of James. See Epiphanius

Athenaeus

No. 6: *Learned Banqueters* 3.97c, 200b. *Athenaeus: The Learned Banqueters*, trans. S. Douglas Olson, 7 vols., LCL (Cambridge, Mass.: Harvard University Press, 2006–10).

Augustine

No. 201: *Confessions* 7.13-14. *Saint Augustine: Confessions*, trans. Henry Chadwick, World's Classics (Oxford: Oxford University Press, 1991), 121–22.

No. 206: *Confessions* 8.11.25–12.30. Augustine, *Confessions and Enchiridion*, trans. A. C. Outler, Library of Christian Classics 7 (Philadelphia: Westminster, 1955).

Babylonian Talmud

No. 135: b. Šabbat 33b. *Shabbath*, trans. H. Freedman, ed. I. Epstein (London: Soncino, 1962).

2 Baruch (Syriac Apocalypse)

No. 148: *2 Baruch* 48:18-24. A. F. Klijn, "2 (Syriac Apocalypse of) Baruch," in *The Old Testament Pseudepigrapha*, ed. James H. Charlesworth, 2 vols. (Garden City, N.Y.: Doubleday, 1983, 1985), 1:636.

Calpurnius Siculus

No. 99: *Eclogue 1*, 37-88. Reprinted by permission of the publishers and Trustees of the Loeb Classical Library from Vol. 284, *Minor Latin Poets*, vol. 1, trans. J. Wight Duff and Arnold M. Duff (Cambridge, Mass.: Harvard University Press, 1934). Copyright © 1934 by the President and Fellows of Harvard College. Loeb Classical Library® is a registered trademark of the President and Fellows of Harvard College.

Celsus. *See* Origen

Cicero

No. 16: *On Duties* 1.150-51. Cicero, vol. 21, *De officiis*, trans. Walter Miller, LCL (London: William Heinemann, 1913). Text in the public domain.

No. 40: *De republica* 6.1-9. Cicero, *The Republic*, trans. Andrew P. Peabody (Boston: Little, Brown, & Co., 1887).

No. 47: *Letter to Atticus* 9.10.1; **No. 48:** *Letter to Atticus* 12.53. Abraham J. Malherbe, *Ancient Epistolary Theorists* (Chico, Calif.: Scholars, 1988).

No. 70: *On Divination* 2.149. Cicero, vol. 20, *On Old Age, On Friendship, On Divination*, trans. W. A. Falconer, LCL (London: William Heinemann, 1923). Text and translation in the public domain; accessed online at http://penelope.uchicago .edu/Thayer/E/Roman/Texts/Cicero/de_Divinatione/home.html.

No. 74: *On the Nature of the Gods* 1.16–17; **No. 75:** *On the Nature of the Gods* 3.2.5. Cicero, vol. 19, *On the Nature of the Gods. Academics*, trans. H. Rackham, rev. ed., LCL (Cambridge, Mass.: Harvard University Press, 1951).

No. 79: *Ad Verrem* 2.5.61, 64. C. D. Yonge, ed., *The Orations of M. Tullius Cicero*, 4 vols. (London: George Bell & Sons, 1894–1903).

No. 175: *Laws* 2.35. *The Political Works of Marcus Tullius Cicero: Comprising His Treatise on the Commonwealth; and His Treatise on the Laws*, trans. Francis Barham, 2 vols. (London: Edmund Spettigue, 1841–42).

Cleanthes

No. 70: *Hymn to Zeus.* Translated by M. A. C. Ellery (1976). Retrieved from Tom Sienkewicz's website at http://www.utexas.edu/courses/citylife/readings/clean thes_hymn.html.

Clement of Rome

No. 214: *1 Clement* 5.1-7. Translation by Richard I. Pervo, *The Making of Paul: Constructions of the Apostle in Early Christianity* (Minneapolis: Fortress, 2010), 130-31.

Clementine writings

No. 210: *Recognitions* 1.70-71. F. Stanley Jones, *An Ancient Jewish Christian Source on the History of Christianity: Pseudo-Clementine Recognitions 1.27-71*, SBLTT 37, Christian Apocrypha Series 2 (Atlanta: Scholars, 1995), 106–9. Translation by F. Stanley Jones of the Syriac version of *Recog.* 1.70-71 used by permission of the Society of Biblical Literature.

No. 211: *Letter of Peter to James.* Georg Strecker, "Introductory Writings: Letter of Peter to James (*Epistula Petri*)," in *New Testament Apocrypha*, by Edgar Hennecke, ed. Wilhelm Schneemelcher, English trans. R. McL. Wilson, rev. ed. (Louisville: Westminster John Knox, 1991, 1992), 2:493–94.

No. 212: *Homilies* 17.19. Translation by James Donaldson, in *The Ante-Nicene Fathers*, vol. 8, ed. Alexander Roberts and James Donaldson (Grand Rapids: Eerdmans, 1951), 323–24.

Crates

No. 53: *Letter* 35. Ronald F. Hock, in Abraham J. Malherbe, ed., *The Cynic Epistles: A Study Edition*, SBLSBS (Missoula, Mont.: Scholars Press for the Society of Biblical Literature, 1977), 89.

Dead Sea Scrolls

No. 31: *Songs of the Sabbath Sacrifice*, 4Q400 frg. 1.1; 4Q405 frg. 20, col. 2; frgs. 21–22; **No. 138:** *Habakkuk Pesher*, 1QpHab 2.10—5.7; 5.12—6.12; 11.10—13.4; **No. 144:** *Thanksgiving Scroll*, 1QH 1.26; 9.14-15; **No. 141:** *Community Rule*, 1QS 11.2-15; **No. 150:** 1QS 10.17-21; **No. 142:** *Damascus Document* 2.14—3.13; **No. 156:** *Damascus Document* 4.13-18, Geza Vermes, *The Complete Dead Sea Scrolls in English*, rev. ed. (New York: Penguin, 2004).

No. 145: 4Q396, 398. Florentino García Martínez and Eibert J. C. Tigchelaar, *The Dead Sea Scrolls Study Edition*, 2 vols. (Leiden: Brill, 1997–1998), 2:795–99.

Dio Chrysostom

No. 4: *Discourses* 32.11. Reprinted by permission of the publishers and Trustees of the Loeb Classical Library from Vol. 358, *Dio Chrysostom*, vol. 3, *Discourses 31-36*, trans. J. W. Cohoon and H. Lamar Crosby (Cambridge, Mass.: Harvard University Press, 1940). Copyright © 1940 by the President and Fellows of Harvard College. Loeb Classical Library® is a registered trademark of the President and Fellows of Harvard College.

No. 14: *Discourses* 80.1; **No. 50:** *Discourses* 77/78.38. Clarence E. Glad, *Paul and Philodemus: Adaptability in Epicurean and Early Christian Psychagogy*, SuppNovT 81 (Leiden: Brill, 1995), 72.

Einsiedeln *Eclogues*

No. 104: *Eclogue* 2, 18–35. *Minor Latin Poets*, vol. 1, trans. J. Wight Duff and Arnold M. Duff, LCL (Cambridge, Mass.: Harvard University Press, 1934).

Enoch

No. 33: *1 Enoch* 70–71. George W. E. Nickelsburg and James C. VanderKam, *1 Enoch: A New Translation; Based on the Hermeneia Commentary* (Minneapolis: Fortress Press, 2004).

No. 34: *2 Enoch* 8–9. F. I. Andersen, "2 (Slavonic Apocalypse of) Enoch," *The Old Testament Pseudepigrapha*, ed. James H. Charlesworth (Garden City, N.Y.: Doubleday, 1983, 1985), 1:91-221.

Epictetus

No. 49: Arrian, *Discourses of Epictetus* 3.23, passim. *Epictetus*, vol. 2, *Discourses, Books 3–4, Fragments, The Encheiridion*, trans. W. A. Oldfather, LCL (London: William Heinemann, 1928). Text in the public domain.

Nos. 54, 55: Arrian, *Discourses of Epictetus* 1.6.38, 41-42; **No. 55:** Arrian, *Discourses of Epictetus* 2.17.36-38; **No. 76:** 2.20.21-27; **No. 77:** 2.20.32-35. *Epictetus*, vol. 1, *Discourses, Books 1–2*, trans. W. A. Oldfather, LCL (London: William Heinemann, 1925).

No. 144: *Discourses* 2.17.17-18; 2.26.1-3; 4.4.6-7. Translation by Mark Reasoner of the text provided in *Epictetus*, vol. 1, *Discourses, Books 1–2*, trans. W. A. Oldfather, LCL (London: William Heinemann, 1925).

Epiphanius

No. 213: *The Panarion* 16.6-9. F. S. Jones, "A Jewish Christian Reads Luke's Acts of the Apostles," in *SBL Seminar Papers 1995* (Atlanta: Scholars, 1995), 617–18 n. 2.

Euripides

No. 173: *Bacchae*, lines 250–61, 367–77, 405–10, 577–86, 1327–30, 1337–42, 1359–1403, 1674–91. Euripides, *The Bacchae*, trans. Gilbert Murray, Harvard Classics (New York: P.F. Collier & Son, 1909–14).

Eusebius

No. 215: *Church History* 2.25.5-8. H. J. Lawler and J. E. L. Oulton, *Eusebius* (London: SPCK, 1928), 60.

No. 69: *Praeparatio Evangelica* 13.12, 666a-667a. *Fragments from Hellenistic Jewish Authors*, vol. 3, *Aristobulus*, trans. Carl R. Holladay, SBLTT 39, PS 13 (Atlanta: Scholars, 1995), 45–49.

4 Ezra

No. 146: *4 Ezra* 7:3-5, 10-15, 45-48, 59-61, 76-77; 8:47-58. B. M. Metzger, "The Fourth Book of Ezra," in *The Old Testament Pseudepigrapha*, ed. James H. Charlesworth (Garden City, N.Y.: Doubleday, 1983–1985), 1:536-37.

Gallio inscription. *See under* Inscriptions

Hippocrates

No. 39: *Letter* 15. Translation by M. Eugene Boring, in *Hellenistic Commentary to the New Testament*, ed. M. Eugene Boring, Klaus Berger, and Carsten Colpe (Nashville: Abingdon, 1995), 319.

Horace

No. 22: *Satire* 1.9.68-72. Translation in the public domain, text at http://www.authorama.com/book/works-of-horace.html.

No. 84: *Odes* 3.6. John Conington, trans., *The Odes of Horace in English Translation* (1863), online at http://www.archive.org/details/odesandcarmensa00horagoog.

No. 88: *Odes* 4.15. *Horace: The Odes and Epodes*, trans. C. E. Bennett, LCL (New York: Macmillan, 1914).

Nos. 94 and 95: *Odes* 1.12.5-6 and 4.2.33-52. Horace, *The Odes and Epodes*, trans. C. E. Bennett, rev. ed., LCL (Cambridge, Mass.: Harvard University Press, 1927).

No. 160: *Sermons* 1.2.116-19. Translations in Antonio Varone, *Erotica Pompeiana: Love Inscriptions on the Walls of Pompeii*, trans. Ria P. Berg, Studia archaeologica 116 (Rome: "L'erma" di Bretschneider, 2002), 158.

Ignatius

No. 204: *To Polycarp* 4; **No. 217:** *To the Romans* 1-2. *The Apostolic Fathers*, vol. 1, trans. Kirsopp Lake, LCL (Cambridge, Mass.: Harvard University Press, 1912).

Inscriptions

No. 42. Gallio inscription. F. J. Foakes-Jackson and Kirsopp Lake, *The Beginnings of Christianity* (New York: MacMillan, 1920–33), 5:296.

No. 92: *Res Gestae Divi Augusti*. Translation by Mark Reasoner from the Greek and Latin text in *Compendium of Roman History. Res Gestae Divi Augusti*, trans. Frederick W. Shipley, LCL (London: William Heinemann, 1924).

No. 97: *IG* 5.1.1450.

No. 158: *CIL* IV 1796, 4637, 1863. Translations in Antonio Varone, *Erotica Pompeiana: Love Inscriptions on the Walls of Pompeii*, trans. Ria P. Berg, Studia archaeologica 116 (Rome: "L'erma" di Bretschneider, 2002), 20, 44, 155.

No. 178: Synagogue inscription from Aphrodisias, trans. Louis H. Feldman in Louis H. Feldman and Meyer Reinhold, *Jewish Life and Thought among Greeks and Romans: Primary Readings* (Minneapolis: Fortress Press, 1996), 142–43.

No. 219: Memoriam in the Basilica Apostolorum, Rome. Henry Chadwick, "St. Peter and St. Paul in Rome: The Problem of the *Memoria Apostolorum ad Catacumbas*," *Journal of Theological Studies* n.s. 8 (1957): 35.

Irenaeus

No. 198: *Against Heresies* 1.6.2-4; **No. 209:** 1.26.2. *The Writings of Irenaeus*, vol. 1, trans. Alexander Roberts and W. H. Rambaut, Ante-Nicene Christian Library 5 (Edinburgh: T&T Clark, 1868).

No. 200: *Apostolic Preaching* 34. Irenaeus, *The Demonstration of the Apostolic Preaching*, ed. and trans. J. Armitage Robinson (New York: Macmillan, 1920).

Jerome

No. 207: *Letter* 107.8, 11, 13 *to Laeta*. *The Letters of St. Jerome*, trans. W. H. Fremantle, G. Lewis, and W. G. Martley, NPNF, 2nd Series, vol. 6, ed. Philip Schaff and Henry Wace (Buffalo: Christian Literature Publishing Co., 1893).

John Chrysostom

No. 205: *Homily on Philemon*, Argument. *Saint Chrysostom: Homilies on Galatians, Ephesians, Philippians, Colossians, Thessalonians, Timothy, Titus, and Philemon*, NPNF, 1st series, vol. 13, ed. and trans. Philip Schaff (Edinburgh: T&T Clark, 1889). Tanslation accessed online at http://www.ccel.org/ccel/schaff/npnf113.v.vi.i.html.

Joseph and Aseneth

No. 177: *Joseph and Aseneth* 12:11; 13:1. Abraham J. Malherbe, *Paul and the Thessalonians: The Philosophic Tradition of Pastoral Care* (Philadelphia: Fortress, 1987), 44.

Josephus

No. 28: *Jewish War* 2.162-65. *Josephus*, vol. 2, *The Jewish War, Volume I, Books 1–2*, trans. H. St. J. Thackeray, LCL (London: William Heinemann, 1927).

No. 115: *Against Apion* 2.151-56; **No. 117:** *Against Apion* 2.175-81; **No. 128:** *Against Apion* 2.237. *Josephus*, vol. 1, *The Life. Against Apion*, trans. H. St. J. Thackeray, LCL (London: William Heinemann, 1926).

No. 124: *Antiquities* 4.207. *Josephus*, vol. 6, *Jewish Antiquities, Volume II, Books 4–6*, trans. H. St. J. Thackeray and Ralph Marcus, LCL (London: William Heinemann, 1930).

No. 106: *Antiquities* 18.172-75. *Josephus*, vol. 12, *Jewish Antiquities, Volume VIII, Books 18–19*, trans. Louis H. Feldman, LCL (Cambridge, Mass.: Harvard University Press, 1965).

No. 119: *Antiquities* 14.10.1 (§§186–89), 14.10.3 (§§196–98), 14.10.8 (§§213–16), 14.10.12 (§§225–27), 14.10.21 (§§244–46), 14.10.26 (§§265–67); **No. 126:** *Antiquities* 18.3.4 (§§65–80); **No. 128:** *Antiquities* 19.5.2-3 (§§278–91); **No. 133:** 18.1.1-2, 6 (§§4-11, 23–25), trans. William Whiston (1737), online at http://www.gutenberg.org/ files/2848/2848-h/2848-h.htm.

Jubilees

No. 32: *Jubilees* 4:19, 21-26; **No. 147:** *Jubilees* 15:25-27, 30-32; 22:11-12, 16-17. O. S. Wintermute, "Jubilees," in *The Old Testament Pseudepigraphs*, ed. James H. Charlesworth (Garden City, N.Y.: Doubleday, 1983–1985), 2:87, 97-98.

No. 151: *Jubilees* 12:22-29. R. H. Charles, ed., *The Apocrypha and Pseudepigrapha of the Old Testament*, 2 vols. (Oxford: Clarendon, 1913).

Juvenal

No. 131: *Satires* 14.96-107. *Juvenal and Persius*, ed. and trans. Susanna Morton Braund, LCL (Cambridge, Mass.: Harvard University Press, 2004).

No. 132: *Satires* 3.290-301. Juvenal, *Satires*, trans. G. G. Ramsay, LCL (Cambridge, Mass.: Harvard University Press, 1918).

Letter to the Laodiceans

No. 192: *Letter to the Laodiceans.* M. R. James, ed., *The Apocryphal New Testament* (1924; repr., Oxford: Clarendon, 1955), 479.

Letters of Paul and Seneca

No. 194: *Letters of Paul and Seneca.* M. R. James, ed., *The Apocryphal New Testament* (1924; repr., Oxford: Clarendon, 1955), 480–84.

Pseudo-Libanius

No. 48: *Epistolary Styles* 5. Abraham J. Malherbe, *Ancient Epistolary Theorists* (Chico, Calif.: Scholars, 1988).

Livy

No. 174: *History of Rome* 39.8-15. Translation by Mark Reasoner of selections from the Latin text supplied by Evan T. Sage in *Livy, History of Rome, Volume XI, Books 38–39*, LCL (Cambridge, Mass.: Harvard University Press, 1936).

No. 191: *History of Rome* 2.31-33. Titius Livius, *The History of Rome*, vol. 1, trans. William Masfen Roberts (London: J. M. Dent; New York: E. P. Dutton, 1912).

Lucian of Samosata

No. 8: *Double Indictment* 6. Abraham J. Malherbe, *Ancient Epistolary Theorists* (Chico, Calif.: Scholars, 1988).

No. 12: *Runaways* 12–17. *The Works of Lucian of Samosata*, trans. H. W. Fowler and F. G. Fowler, 4 vols. (Oxford: Clarendon, 1905). Public domain.

No. 23: *Passing of Peregrinus* 11–14. *Lucian*, vol. 5, trans. A. M. Harmon, LCL (Cambridge, Mass.: Harvard University Press, 1936).

No. 162: *Mimes of the Courtesans*; **No. 163:** *The Education of Corinna*. Translation by Charles Cullen, online at http://www.sacred-texts.com/cla/luc/motc/index.htm (accessed February 23, 2009).

Martial

No. 100: *Epigram* 7.34. Henry Bohn, *The Epigrams of Martial* (London: George Bell & Sons, 1897). Text online at www.ccel.org.

No. 161: *Epigrams* 2.34.1-2. Translation in Antonio Varone, *Erotica Pompeiana: Love Inscriptions on the Walls of Pompeii*, trans. Ria P. Berg, Studia archaeologica 116 (Rome: "L'erma" di Bretschneider, 2002), 156.

Martyrdon of Polycarp

No. 218: *Martyrdom of Polycarp* 7–11. *The Apostolic Fathers*, vol. 1, trans. Kirsopp Lake, LCL (London: William Heinemann, 1912). Text in the public domain.

Mekilta de Rabbi Ishmael

No. 190: *Mekilta de Rabbi Ishmael*, Exodus 29:6. J. Z. Lauterbach, trans., *Mekilta de-Rabbi Ishmael: A Critical Edition on the Basis of the Manuscripts and Early Editions*, Schiff Library of Jewish Classics (Philadelphia: Jewish Publication Society, 1933–35), 2:205–6.

Mishnah

No. 11: *m. 'Abot* 2.2; No. 29: *m. Yadayim* 4.6-7; No. 30: *m. Makkot* 3.1-3, 10-12; No. 37: *Ḥagigah* 2.1; No. 38: *m. Megillah* 4.10; No. 116: *m. 'Abot* 1.1-18; No. 155: *Ḥagigah* 2.7; No. 157: *'Avodah Zarah* 2.3-5, 6. Herbert Danby, *The Mishnah: Translated from the Hebrew with Introduction and Brief Explanatory Notes* (New York: Oxford University Press, 1933).

Musonius Rufus

No. 5: Fragment 8, *That Kings Also Should Study Philosophy*; No. 10: Fragment 11. Cora E. Lutz, *Musonius Rufus: "The Roman Socrates,"* Yale Classical Studies 10 (New Haven: Yale University Press, 1947).

No. 170: *Discourse 12: Concerning Sexual Pleasures*. Mark Reasoner's translation of C. *Musonii Rufi: Reliquiae*, ed. Otto Hense (Leipzig: B. G. Teubner, 1905), 63–67.

Nag Hammadi Documents

No. 195: *Prayer of the Apostle Paul*. Translation by Dieter Mueller, in *The Nag Hammadi Library in English*, ed. James M. Robinson, 4th rev. ed. (Leiden: Brill, 1996), 27–28.

No. 196: *Apocalypse of Paul*. Translation by George W. MacRae and W. R. Murdock, in *The Nag Hammadi Library in English*, ed. James M. Robinson, 4th rev. ed. (Leiden: Brill, 1996), 257–59.

No. 197: *Tripartite Tractate* (NHC I, 5). Translation by Harold W. Attridge and Dieter Mueller, in *The Nag Hammadi Library*, ed. James M. Robinson, rev. ed. (San Francisco: HarperSanFrancisco, 1990), 94–95.

Origen

No. 13: *Against Celsus* 3.55. Abraham J. Malherbe, *Paul and the Thessalonians: The Philosophic Tradition of Pastoral Care* (Philadelphia: Fortress Press, 1987), 19.

No. 199: *Commentary on Romans* 7.18.6; 9.2.16. *Origen: Commentary on the Epistle to the Romans, Books 6–10*, trans. Thomas P. Scheck, FOTC (Washington, D.C.: Catholic University of America Press, 2002), 120, 203–4.

Ovid

No. 78: *Fasti* 4. Translation of the Latin by Mark Reasoner; *Ovid*, vol. 5, *Fasti*, trans. James G. Frazer and rev. G. P. Goold, LCL (London: William Heinemann, 1931).
No. 89: *Fasti* 1.709-22; **No. 91:** *Fasti* 1.639-50.

Papyri

Graux

No. 64: *P.Graux* 2. Translation by John L. White, in idem, *The Form and Structure of the Official Petition: A Study in Greek Epistolography*, SBLDS 5 (Missoula, Mont.: Society of Biblical Literature, 1972), 153.

Herculaneum

No. 51: *PHerc.* 1082, col. 2.1-14; **No. 52:** Fragment 83.7-10. Clarence E. Glad, *Paul and Philodemus: Adaptability in Epicurean and Early Christian Psychagogy*, SuppNovT 81 (Leiden: Brill, 1995), 109, 143.

Hermopolis

No. 59: *P.Herm.* 1. Translation by Mark Reasoner from text in Chan-Hie Kim, *Form and Structure of the Familiar Letter of Recommendation*, SBLDS 4 (Missoula, Mont.: Society of Biblical Literature, 1972), 204.

Merton

No. 60: *P.Merton* 62. Translation by Mark Reasoner from text in Chan-Hie Kim, *Form and Structure of the Familiar Letter of Recommendation*, SBLDS 4 (Missoula, Mont.: Society of Biblical Literature, 1972), 199.

Michigan

No. 107: *P.Mich.* 422, 424. Ramsay MacMullen, *Roman Social Relations, 50 B.C. to A.D. 284* (New Haven: Yale University Press, 1974), 10.

Oxyrhynchus

No. 9: *P.Oxy.* 2190. Bruce W. Winter, *Philo and Paul among the Sophists: Alexandrian and Corinthian Responses to a Julio-Claudian Movement*, 2nd ed. (Grand Rapids: Eerdmans, 2002).
No. 57: *P.Oxy.* 292; **No. 58:** *P.Oxy.* 746. Translation by Mark Reasoner from text in Chan-Hie Kim, *Form and Structure of the Familiar Letter of Recommendation*, SBLDS 4 (Missoula, Mont.: Society of Biblical Literature, 1972), 202, 200.
No. 184: *P.Oxy.* 1423. B. P. Grenfell and A. S. Hunt, eds., *The Oxyrhynchus Papyri*, Part xiv (London: Egyptian Exploration Society, 192).

PRG

No. 65: *PRG* [*P.Ross.Georg.*] 3.8. Translation by Ramsay MacMullen, in idem, *Roman Social Relations, 50 B.C. to A.D. 284* (New Haven: Yale University Press, 1974), 44–45.

Rylands

No. 63: *P.Ryl.* 152. Translation by John L. White, in idem, *The Form and Structure of the Official Petition: A Study in Greek Epistolography*, SBLDS 5 (Missoula, Mont.: Society of Biblical Literature, 1972), 149.

No. 61: Letter. Friedrich Preisigke, ed., *Sammelbuch griechischer Urkunden aus Ägypten*, 5 vols. (Strassburg: K. J. Trübner, 1915–55), vol. 3, no. 6263; trans. Stanley K. Stowers, in idem, *Letter Writing in Greco-Roman Antiquity*, Library of Early Christianity 5 (Philadelphia: Westminster, 1986), 129.

Petronius

No. 189: *Satyricon* 74–75. Mark Reasoner's adaptation of the translation by Alfred R. Allinson (New York: Panurge, 1930), online at http://www.sacred-texts .com/cla/peto/satyr/ (accessed May 11, 2009).

Philo

No. 25: *Embassy to Gaius* 93–94; **No. 134:** *Embassy to Gaius* 143–50. Reprinted by permission of the publishers and Trustees of the Loeb Classical Library from Vol. 379, *Philo*, vol. 10, *On the Embassy to Gaius, General Indexes*, trans. F. H. Colson, LCL (Cambridge, Mass.: Harvard University Press, 1962). Copyright © 1962 by the President and Fellows of Harvard College. Loeb Classical Library® is a registered trademark of the President and Fellows of Harvard College.

No. 35: *Life of Moses* 155–59; **No. 41:** *Life of Moses* 1.46-48; **No. 123:** *Life of Moses* 2.205-6. *Philo*, vol. 6, *On Abraham, On Joseph, On Moses*, trans. F. H. Colson, LCL (Cambridge, Mass.: Harvard University Press, 1935).

No. 36: *On the Sacrifices of Abel and Cain* 8–9; **No. 67:** *Embassy to Gaius* 276–79, 285–88, 323–29; **No. 114:** *Embassy to Gaius* 279–84; **No. 118:** *Embassy to Gaius* 311–16; **No. 127:** *Embassy to Gaius* 347–73; **No. 140:** *On Dreams* 2.83-92; **No. 152:** *Life of Abraham* 4–6; **No. 188:** *Contemplative Life* 48–52. *The Works of Philo Judaeus, the Contemporary of Josephus*, trans. C. D. Yonge, 4 vols. (London: H. G. Bohn, 1854–90). Quotations from this translation: **Nos. 36, 67.** Public domain.

No. 108: *On the Special Laws* 2.92-95; **No. 109:** 3.159-63; **No. 121:** 1.21-22; **No. 122:** 1.51-53; **No. 171:** 3.37-39, 42. *Philo*, vol. 7, *On the Decalogue, On the Special Laws, Books 1–3*, trans. F. H. Colson, LCL (Cambridge, Mass.: Harvard University Press, 1937).

No. 178: *On the Virtues* 102–3. *Philo*, vol. 8, *On the Special Laws, Book 4, On the Virtues, On Rewards and Punishments*, trans. F. H. Colson, LCL (Cambridge, Mass: Harvard University Press, 1939).

No. 186: *Every Good Man Is Free* 79. *Philo*, vol. 9, trans. F. H. Colson, LCL (Cambridge, Mass.: Harvard University Press, 1941).

Philodemus

No. 15: *On Household Management* 23. Abraham J. Malherbe, *Ancient Epistolary Theorists* (Chico, Calif.: Scholars, 1988).

Plato

No. 7: *Apology of Socrates* 1. *Plato*, vol. 1, *Euthyphro, Apology, Crito, Phaedo, Phaedrus*, trans. Harold North Fowler, LCL (London: William Heinemann, 1914). Translation in the public domain.

No. 143: *Republic* 442E–443E. W. H. D. Rouse, *Great Dialogues of Plato* (New York: Mentor, 1956), 243–44. "Book VI of the Republic" from *The Great Dialogues of Plato* by Plato, translated by W.H.D. Rouse, © 1956, renewed © 1984 by J.C.G. Rouse. Used by permission of Dutton Signet, a division of Penguin Group (USA) Inc.

Pliny

No. 20: *Epistles* 1.18.3; **No. 21:** *Epistle* 3.9.9. *Pliny: Letters*, vol. 1, *Books 1–7*, trans. Betty Radice, LCL (Cambridge, Mass.: Harvard University Press, 1969).

No. 68: *Epistle* 9.21, *To Sabinianus*. Pliny the Younger, *Letters*, trans. W. Melmoth, Harvard Classics (New York: P. F. Collier, 1909–14).

No. 180: *Epistles* 10.33-34; **No. 181:** 10.96. Translation by Mark Reasoner from the text in *Pliny, Letters*, vol. 2, *Books 8–10. Panegyricus*, trans. Betty Radice, LCL (Cambridge, Mass.: Harvard University Press, 1969).

No. 183: *Epistles* 2.6. Translation by Mark Reasoner of the letter found in *Pliny, Letters*, vol. 1, trans. William Melmoth and rev. W. M. L. Hutchinson, LCL (London: William Heinemann, 1915).

Plutarch

No. 164: *Marital Precepts (Conjugalia praecepta)* 144F. Susan Treggiari, *Roman Marriage: Iusti Coniuges from the Time of Cicero to the Time of Ulpian* (Oxford: Clarendon, 1991), 314.

No. 165: *Marital Precepts (Conjugalia praecepta)* 140B; **No. 166:** 140D. Frank Cole Babbitt, trans., *Plutarch, Moralia*, vol. 2, LCL (London: William Heinemann, 1928).

Polybius

No. 72: *Histories* 6.56. *Polybius, The Histories*, vol. 3, *Books 5–8*, trans. W. R. Paton, LCL (London: William Heinemann, 1923).

Prayer of the Apostle Paul. See under **Nag Hammadi Documents**

Propertius

No. 168: Propertius, *The Elegies*, trans. A. S. Kline (2002), available online at http://www.poetryintranslation.com/PITBR/Latin/Prophome.htm.

Psalms of Solomon

No. 137: *Psalms of Solomon* 2. John J. Collins, "Psalms of Solomon," in *The Old Testament Pseudepigrapha*, ed. James H. Charlesworth (Garden City, N.Y.: Doubleday, 1983–1985), 2:651-52.

Pseudo-Demetrius

No. 56: *Epistolary Types*, passim. Abraham J. Malherbe, ed. and trans., *Ancient Epistolary Theorists*, SBLSBS 19 (Atlanta: Scholars, 1988).

Pseudo-Libanius

No. 48: *Epistolary Styles* 5. Abraham J. Malherbe, *Ancient Epistolary Theorists*, SBLSBS 19 (Atlanta: Scholars, 1988).

Res Gestae Divi Augusti. See under **Inscriptions**

Seneca

No. 17: *Epistle* 88, *On Liberal and Vocational Studies. Seneca*, vol. 5, *Ad Lucillum Epistulae Morales II: Letters 66–92*, trans. Richard M. Gummere, LCL (London: William Heinemann, 1920). Translation in the public domain.

No. 18: *Epistle* 14.3-4; No. 45: *Epistle* 40.1; No. 46: *Epistle* 75.1-2; *Seneca*, vol. 4, *Epistles, Volume I, Epistles 1–65*, trans. Richard M. Gummere, LCL (London: William Heinemann, 1917).

No. 19: *Epistle* 105.5; No. 62: *Epistle* 99; No. 80: *Epistle* 101; No. 68: *Epistle* 103; *On the Futility of Planning Ahead. Seneca*, vol. 6, *Epistles, Volume III, Epistles 93–124*, trans. Richard M. Gummere, LCL (London: William Heinemann, 1925). Public domain.

No. 98: *On Mercy* 1.11.3. Translated by Mark Reasoner.

No. 102: *The Apocolocyntosis. Seneca, The Apocolocyntosis*, trans. W. H. D. Rouse, LCL (Cambridge, Mass.: Harvard University Press, 1920).

No. 104: *On Mercy* 1.1-4, 7-9. *Seneca*, vol. 1, *Moral Essays, Volume I, De Providentia. De Constantia. De Ira. De Clementia*, trans. John W. Basore, LCL (London: William Heinemann, 1928).

No. 169: *On Benefits* 3.16.2-3. *Seneca*, vol. 3, *Moral Essays, Volume III, De Beneficiis*, trans. John W. Basore, LCL (Cambridge, Mass.: Harvard University Press, 1935).

No. 187: *Epistle* 47.7. Mark Reasoner's adaptation of translation of John H. D'Arms, "Slaves at Roman *Convivia*," in *Dining in a Classical Context*, ed. William J. Slater (Ann Arbor: University of Michigan Press, 1991).

Sibylline Oracles

No. 136: *Sibylline Oracles* 3.55-65, 398-410. *The Sibylline Oracles translated into English Blank Verse*, trans. Milton Terry (New York: Eaton & Mains, 1899). Accessed online at http://www.sacred-texts.com/cla/sib/sib00.htm.

Socrates. *See* Plato

Socrates (pseudepigraphic)

No. 66: *Epistle* 6. Stanley K. Stowers, in idem, *Letter Writing in Greco-Roman Antiquity*, Library of Early Christianity 5 (Philadelphia: Westminster, 1986), 168–69.

Sophocles

No. 172: *Oedipus the King*, 320–23; 345–53; 362–77; 412–28, trans. F. Storr, LCL (Cambridge, Mass.: Harvard University Press, 1912); online at http://classics.mit.edu/Sophocles/oedipus.html.

Strabo

No. 27: *Geographica* 14.5.13.

Suetonius

No. 44: *Nero* 16; **No. 129:** *Claudius* 25.4; **No. 167:** *Augustus* 34, Suetonius, *Lives of the Caesars*, vol. 2, *Claudius, Nero . . . Domitian. Lives of Illustrious Men: Grammarians and Rhetoricians. Poets . . . . Lives of Pliny the Elder and Passionus Crispus*, ed. and trans. J. C. Rolfe, LCL (London: William Heinemann, 1914). Public domain.

No. 101: *Nero* 28, 39, 45–46, 57. Suetonius, *The Twelve Caesars*, trans. Robert Graves, rev. with an introduction by Michael Grant (New York: Penguin, 1957).

Sulpicius Severus

No. 216: *Chronicle* 2.29. *Sulpitius Severus, Vincent of Lerins, John Cassian*, NPNF, 2nd series, vol. 11, ed. Philip Schaff (Edinburgh: T&T Clark, 1889).

Tacitus

No. 43: *Annals* 15.38-39, 42-44; **No. 105:** *Annals* 1.2.2; **No. 110:** *Annals* 6.12; **No. 111:** *Annals* 13.48; **No. 112:** *Annals* 14.35; **No. 176:** *Annals* 14.44; **No. 125:** *Annals* 2.85; **No. 130:** *History* 5.2-5. Alfred John Church and William Jackson Brodribb, trans., *The Complete Works of Tacitus* (New York: Modern Library, 1942). Public domain.

No. 113: *Agricola* 30–32. Trans. Edward Brooks, LCL (Cambridge, Mass.: Harvard University Press, 1937).

Tertullian

No. 203: *On Baptism* 17. Ernest Evans, *Tertullian's Homily on Baptism* (London: SPCK, 1964). Translation available online at http://www.tertullian.org/articles/evans_bapt/evans_bapt_index.htm.

Trajan

No. 181: *Epistle to Pliny* 10.93; **No. 182:** *Epistle to Pliny* 10.97. *Pliny, Letters,* vol. 2, *Books 8-10. Panegyricus,* trans. Betty Radice, LCL (Cambridge, Mass.: Harvard University Press, 1969).

Tripartite Tractate. See under **Nag Hammadi Documents.**

Virgil

No. 26: *Aeneid* 8.715-31. *Virgil,* vol. 2, *Aeneid: Books 7–12, Appendix Veriliana,* trans. H. Rushton Fairclough and rev. G. Goold, LCL (London: William Heinemann, 1918).

No. 82: *Fourth Eclogue*; **No. 86:** *Aeneid* 1.255-97; **No. 87:** *Aeneid* 6.788-807, 847, 852-53). *Virgil,* vol. 1, *Eclogues, Georgics, Aeneid: Books 1–6,* trans. H. Rushton Fairclough and rev. G. P. Goold, LCL (London: William Heinemann, 1916).

No. 83: *Georgics* 1.121-40. Translation from Karl Galinsky, *Augustan Culture: An Interpretive Introduction* (Princeton: Princeton University Press, 1996), 93–94.

Vitruvius

No. 96: Preface to *On Architecture. Vitruvius, On Architecture,* vol. 1, *Books 1–5,* trans. Frank Granger, LCL (London: William Heinemann, 1931).

ILLUSTRATIONS

The following photographs, released to the public domain or published (by the photographer indicated in the caption) under a Creative Commons or GNU Free Documentation License, are drawn from Wikimedia Commons (www.commons. wikimedia.org): 1.2, 1.3, 1.4, 1.6, 1.11, 1.13, 2.2, 2.3, 2.4, 2.5, 2.7, 2.10, 2.11, 2.13, 2.14, 2.15, 2.18, 2.19, 3.1, 3.4, 3.5, 3.9, 3.12, 3.13, 3.14, 3.16, 3.19, 3.20, 3.22, 3.23, 3.29, 3.30, 3.31, 3.33, 3.34, 4.1, 4.3, 4.4, 4.6, 4.8, 4.9, 4.10, 4.11, 4.12, 4.13, 4.14, 4.17, 4.18, 5.1, 5.3, 5.4, 5.7, 5.8, 5.12, 6.2, 6.3, 6.4, 6.6, 6.7, 6.8, 6.10, 6.14.

INDEX OF SUBJECTS

INDEX OF MODERN AUTHORS

INDEX OF BIBLICAL AND
APOCRYPHAL WRITINGS

INDEX OF OTHER ANCIENT

LITERATURE